T0215046

Sex Work, Health, and Human Rights

Shira M. Goldenberg
Ruth Morgan Thomas • Anna Forbes
Stefan Baral
Editors

Sex Work, Health, and Human Rights

Global Inequities, Challenges, and Opportunities for Action

 Springer

Editors
Shira M. Goldenberg
Faculty of Health Sciences, Simon Fraser
University, Burnaby, BC, Canada

Centre for Gender and Sexual Health Equity
Vancouver, BC, Canada

Anna Forbes
Independent Consultant
Kensington, MD, USA

Ruth Morgan Thomas
The Matrix
Global Network of Sex Work Projects
Edinburgh, UK

Stefan Baral
Center for Public Health and Human Rights
Department of Epidemiology
Johns Hopkins University
Baltimore, MD, USA

This book is an open access publication.
ISBN 978-3-030-64173-3   ISBN 978-3-030-64171-9   (eBook)
https://doi.org/10.1007/978-3-030-64171-9

This book is dedicated to the global sex workers' rights movement which has and continues to demonstrate incredible resilience in their tireless advocacy for sex workers' human rights, dignity, well-being, and safety.

Preface

Sex workers comprise a diverse population which includes women, men, transgender, and gender-diverse individuals; people living with HIV, people who use drugs, people who have experienced incarceration, documented and undocumented migrants, and indigenous people and others. Sex work takes place across a wide range of different work environments (e.g. brothels, entertainment venues, indoor and outdoor public and private spaces, and online). Sex work happens across many different socio-cultural, legal, policy, and human rights contexts. Globally, sex workers continue to face unacceptable health and human rights inequities, including an elevated burden of violence, HIV and sexually transmitted infections, unmet sexual and reproductive health needs, and gaps in appropriate primary and mental health care. In stark contrast to popular misconceptions, sex workers also exert agency in their work and labour mobilisation efforts—including through powerful community empowerment initiatives advocating for decriminalisation of sex work, improved working conditions, and protection from violence and discrimination.

Whereas the vast majority of research on sex workers' health needs has focused on biomedical and behavioural approaches to HIV and STI prevention and treatment, the broader health and labour needs of sex workers remain much less well understood. Research clearly shows the need to move beyond individualistic approaches to sex workers' health to address the crucial influence of structural factors. These include punitive and criminalised legal and policy environments; stigma and discrimination; migration and mobility patterns; disproportionate experiences of violence; and unsafe labour conditions. For example, criminalisation of sex work in various forms remains widespread across most global settings and is linked to negative outcomes including HIV and STI transmission, and increased rates of violence and mortality among sex workers. Public discourse and policy in many countries tend to lean toward outcomes that punish sex workers and their clients further. This response drives sex workers underground, where unmet health needs and unsafe working conditions are worsened rather than improved. This edited volume documents an important body of research across diverse global contexts affirming the salience of these structural factors in shaping sex workers' health and labour outcomes, indicating that interventions with a corresponding emphasis on ameliorating these structural inequities are needed to produce meaningful and sustainable improvements.

To inform effective actions to advance the health and rights of sex workers, this edited volume aims to provide a comprehensive overview of health and social inequities faced by sex workers globally; articulate structural determinants of sex workers' health and occupational outcomes (e.g. legislation, migration, healthcare delivery settings); and describe evidence-based interventions and 'best practices', including the roles of the full decriminalisation of sex work, community empowerment models, and multi-level and integrated intervention approaches. This book documents the importance of supporting sex workers and their organisations in promoting, defining, and demanding fulfilment their own health and occupational needs. To overcome barriers posed by stigma, criminalisation, and other structural factors, sex workers in numerous countries are adopting 'community empowerment' approaches to advocate for their human rights, including their right to non-judgmental health care and security of the person. Designed by and for sex workers over the last three decades, community empowerment is a framework to guide sex workers in diverse settings to move toward collective advocacy for their rights, including rights-based health care and recognition of their human and labour rights. This book reviews the progress, challenges, and the diverse issues raised by implementing this approach.

Evidence Gaps and Opportunities Addressed by this Edited Volume

This edited volume draws upon both academic and community perspectives to synthesise research evidence as well as lessons learned from regional and local-level experiences across different global settings. A rich body of information has documented the needs of sex workers and 'best practices' for reducing them, from both academic and community perspectives over the past few decades, including structural, behavioural, and biomedical interventions. This edited volume strives to bring together these understandings to catalyse action and inform future research, policy, and programming.

Now, perhaps more than ever, is a time where we need to step up to close the gap in sex workers' health and human rights. The current COVID-19 pandemic has exacerbated these longstanding inequities, magnifying the already-precarious conditions in which sex workers work and live. Since the pandemic began, sex workers across diverse regions of the world have been facing severe hardship and injustice, including a loss of income; increased crackdowns by the state, including raids, displacement, and other forms of police harassment and brutality; and increased stigma and discrimination [1, 2]. Sex workers are often unable to access government benefits and supports afforded to other types of workers, such as emergency and ongoing financial employment-related support, particularly in settings where sex work is criminalised. These barriers are further amplified for migrant workers, who also face barriers to social protections due to gaps in eligibility for foreigners as well as fear that disclosure of engagement in sex work could result in negative consequences when it comes to immigration. For example, in an April 2020 survey conducted by the Butterfly sex work project in Toronto, Canada, 40% of migrant sex workers said they were either not eligible to apply for emergency employment benefits during COVID-19 because of undocumented work status or were afraid to apply because of criminalised or undocumented work and immigration status; yet most reported that they required support for income (71%), food and health support (40%), rent (31%), or the operation of a small business (27%) [3]. These and similar reports from other contexts worldwide indicate the critical importance of enacting policy changes to ensure that sex workers as equal members of society are afforded access to social protection schemes, along with rights-affirming health care and freedom from police repression and brutality.

At the same time, in 2020, we currently have the tools available to improve sex workers' health and human rights—for example, through 'treatment as prevention', PrEP, and other biomedical advances, we have the biomedical tools to stop HIV acquisition and transmission and achieve zero new infections, as per the UNAIDS goal for 2030. It is similarly possible to end unwanted pregnancies among sex workers. Yet sex workers continue to be left behind in the HIV response [4]. These goals cannot be achieved without addressing underlying and unaddressed gaps in reproductive health and mental health outcomes, exposure to violence, and drug use. Unfortunately, the structural factors shaping these outcomes have not declined in recent years—for example, criminalisation and stigma toward sex workers. In part, the lack of improvement is the result of limited investment by governments, global health organisations, and funding agencies. Current opportunities to intervene range from mitigating the effects of stigma on individuals and addressing stigma in healthcare settings to decreasing structural inequities through decriminalisation of sex work and drug use. Current steps to best support the health and human rights of sex workers necessitates moving from rhetoric to action in understanding and addressing the structural determinants of health and human rights outcomes among sex workers around the world.

Summary of Approach

This edited volume is underpinned by a unique academic–community partnership model, with each chapter reflecting the contributions of both academic and sex work community authors identified and contracted through the Global Network of Sex Work Projects (NSWP). This approach was developed to address the unequal power dynamics shaping dominant approaches to sex work-related research, service delivery, and policymaking. The meaningful involvement of sex workers and sex worker-led organisations in every stage is paramount, yet too often remains under-prioritised.

The author teams consisted of academic researchers, sex workers, and sex worker-led organisations, who were engaged to collaboratively develop chapters drawing upon the diverse perspectives within the author teams to synthesise research evidence as well as highlight evidence and lessons learned from the lived experiences of sex workers across different regions.

The NSWP policy team, in collaboration with regional networks, identified community authors from within member organisations, based on their experience and expertise in the topics relevant to sex workers to be covered by each of the chapters; bringing into each chapter a wealth of community evidence and knowledge. Initial discussions were then held with each potential community author to clarify roles, the scope of the work and expectations, and to explore their interest and capacity to undertake the work, and outline the technical support that could be offered by NSWP policy team to enable their effective participation in the project. The NSWP policy team then facilitated introductory calls between the community and academic co-leads for each chapter.

Community authors were involved in all stages of the chapter development. First, in developing the initial abstract with the academic authors, then in providing community-based contributions and perspectives (e.g. a community case study) on the specific theme of each chapter, illustrating the lived experiences of sex workers on national, regional, or global levels. Contributions from community authors were planned to complement the work of each academic author, who was responsible for synthesising findings of academic research by a review of the literature. Community authors were also asked to review and comment on the draft chapters submitted. Finally, the chapters were copyedited for plain English by NSWP's copyeditor to make this edited volume as accessible as possible to non-academics.

There are significant benefits to meaningfully involving sex workers as well as academics in a robust, participative, and empowering partnership approach—as shown by the formation of interdisciplinary teams by using this methodology, and by the insights it generated.

The chapters that follow are organised around three primary areas of inquiry. Part I aims to *describe the burden of different health and human rights inequities and lived experiences* of these inequities faced by sex workers in different contexts. This includes infectious diseases (e.g. HIV, STIs), violence, mental health, drug use, and sexual and reproductive health. Part II aims to *characterise the structural determinants of these health and human rights inequities*. This includes bringing together the perspectives of sex worker communities and academics regarding the roles of law and policy, law enforcement, community empowerment, migration, stigma, and health service delivery environments. Finally, Part III ultimately aims to *describe best practices and promising avenues for future research and interventions* to support the health and human rights of sex workers. This includes synthesis of academic evidence as well as drawing from key examples from the sex worker community on interventions and approaches at various levels of influence— ranging from individual to community to policy interventions (e.g. sex work decriminalisation).

Vancouver, BC, Canada   Shira M. Goldenberg
Edinburgh, UK   Ruth Morgan Thomas
Kensington, MD, USA   Anna Forbes
Baltimore, MD, USA   Stefan Baral

References

1. Platt L, Elmes J, Stevenson L, Holt V, Rolles S, Stuart R. Sex workers must not be forgotten in the COVID-19 response. Lancet. 2020;396(10243):9–11.
2. UNAIDS, NSWP. Sex workers must not be left behind in the response to COVID-19 [press release]. 8 Apr 2020.
3. Lam E. How are Asian and migrant workers in spas, holistic centres, massage parlours and the sex industry affected by the COVID-19 pandemic?. Butterfly (Asian and migrant Sex Workers Support Network); May 2020.
4. Shannon K, Crago A, Baral S, Bekker L, Kerrigan D, Decker M, et al. The global response and unmet actions for HIV and sex workers. Lancet. 2018;392(10148):698–710.

Acknowledgements

We thank all those who contributed their time and expertise to this book, particularly all of the community and academic authors, sex worker-led organisations, and others who contributed material and perspectives. We thank the administrative, editorial, and policy staff who supported this work, including Megan Bobetsis from the Centre for Gender and Sexual Health Equity (CGSHE) and consultants and staff from the Global Network of Sex Work Projects (NSWP) Secretariat. This book was supported by a grant from the Open Society Foundations Public Health Program (OR2018-43475) as well as the Simon Fraser University Open Access fund.

Contents

Contributors

Phelister Abdalla Kenya Sex Workers Alliance, Nairobi, Kenya

Gillian Abel University of Otago, Christchurch, New Zealand

Elena Argento Centre for Gender & Sexual Health Equity, Vancouver, BC, Canada
University of British Columbia, Vancouver, BC, Canada

Stefan Baral Center for Public Health and Human Rights, Department of Epidemiology, Johns Hopkins Bloomberg School of Public Health, Baltimore, MD, USA

Clare Barrington Department of Health Behavior, Gillings School of Global Public Health, University of North Carolina, Chapel Hill, NC, USA

Kholi Buthelezi Sisonke National Sex Worker Movement, Cape Town, South Africa

Carly Comins Center for Public Health and Human Rights, Department of Epidemiology, Johns Hopkins Bloomberg School of Public Health, Baltimore, MD, USA

Kate D'Adamo Reframe Health and Justice (RHJ), Baltimore, MD, USA

Putu Duff Centre for Gender and Sexual Health Equity, Vancouver, BC, Canada
Faculty of Medicine, University of British Columbia, Vancouver, BC, Canada

Allison R. Ebben School of Social Work, Columbia University, New York, NY, USA

Anna Forbes Independent Consultant, Kensington, MD, USA

Shira M. Goldenberg Faculty of Health Sciences, Simon Fraser University, Burnaby, BC, Canada

Centre for Gender and Sexual Health Equity, Vancouver, BC, Canada

Catherine Healy New Zealand Prostitutes Collective, Wellington, New Zealand

Liz Hilton and Empower Thailand Empower Foundation, Chiang Mai, Thailand

Jenny Iversen Kirby Institute for Infection and Immunity, Faculty of Medicine, UNSW Sydney, Sydney, NSW, Australia

Trachje Janushev The Red Edition – Sex Work Migrant Group, Vienna, Austria

Deanna Kerrigan Department of Prevention and Community Health, Milken Institute School of Public Health, George Washington University, Washington, DC, USA

Andrea Krüsi Department of Medicine, University of British Columbia, Vancouver, BC, Canada

Centre for Gender & Sexual Health Equity (CGSHE), Vancouver, BC, Canada

Patrick Lalor Sex Work Association of Jamaica, Kingston, Jamaica

Jamaica AIDS Support for Life, Kingston, Jamaica

Kandasi Levermore Jamaica AIDS Support for Life, Kingston, Jamaica

Carmen H. Logie Factor-Iwentash Faculty of Social Work, University of Toronto, Toronto, ON, Canada

Women's College Research Institute, Women's College Hospital, Toronto, ON, Canada

Pike Long St James Infirmary, San Francisco, CA, USA

Alexandra Lutnick Independent Researcher, San Francisco, CA, USA

Carrie E. Lyons Center for Public Health and Human Rights, Department of Epidemiology, Johns Hopkins Bloomberg School of Public Health, Baltimore, MD, USA

Lisa Maher Kirby Institute for Infection and Immunity, Faculty of Medicine, UNSW Sydney, Sydney, NSW, Australia

Burnet Institute, Melbourne, VIC, Australia

Andrea Mantsios Public Health Innovation & Action, New York, NY, USA

Bronwyn McBride Centre for Gender and Sexual Health Equity, Vancouver, BC, Canada

Interdisciplinary Studies Graduate Program, University of British Columbia, Vancouver, BC, Canada

Ruth Morgan Thomas The Matrix, Global Network of Sex Work Projects – NSWP, Edinburgh, UK

Anne M. Montgomery Department of Health Studies, Haverford College, Haverford, PA, USA

Cynthia Navarrete Gil APROASE, México City, Mexico

Manjula Ramaiah Ashodaya Samithi, Mysore, India

Amrita Rao Center for Public Health and Human Rights, Department of Epidemiology, Johns Hopkins Bloomberg School of Public Health, Baltimore, MD, USA

Marlise Richter Health Justice Initiative, Cape Town, South Africa

African Centre for Migration & Society, University of the Witwatersrand, Johannesburg, South Africa

School of Public Health & Family Medicine, University of Cape Town, Cape Town, South Africa

Justice Rivera Reframe Health and Justice, Baltimore, MD, USA

Sex Workers Outreach Project (SWOP), Washington, DC, USA

Sheree Schwartz Key Populations Program, Department of Epidemiology, Johns Hopkins School of Public Health, Baltimore, MD, USA

Ariel Sernick Centre for Gender & Sexual Health Equity (CGSHE), Vancouver, BC, Canada

Kate Shannon Centre for Gender & Sexual Health Equity, Vancouver, BC, Canada

University of British Columbia, Vancouver, BC, Canada

Ania Shapiro Sex Workers Outreach Project (SWOP-Tucson), Tucson, AZ, USA

Nikita Viswasam Key Populations Program, Center for Public Health and Human Rights, Department of Epidemiology, John Hopkins Bloomberg School of Public Health, Baltimore, MD, USA

Ying Wang Factor-Iwentash Faculty of Social Work, University of Toronto, Toronto, ON, Canada

Brooke S. West School of Social Work, Columbia University, New York, NY, USA

Davina Williams Jamaica AIDS Support for Life, Kingston, Jamaica

Kay Thi Win Asia-Pacific Network of Sex Workers (APNSW), Bangkok, Thailand

About the Editors

Shira M. Goldenberg, PhD (she/her), is an Assistant Professor in the Faculty of Health Sciences at Simon Fraser University in Burnaby, British Columbia (BC), Canada, and the Director of Research Education at the Centre for Gender and Sexual Health Equity (CGSHE). She is also adjunct faculty in the University of California, San Diego School of Medicine.

Dr. Goldenberg has conducted research on sexual health, violence, and human rights for im/migrants, sex workers, and young women since 2006. Her work has informed global policy initiatives and guidelines related to sex workers', women's, and im/migrants' health, including through consultation roles with the Joint United Nations Programme on HIV/AIDS (UNAIDS) and the International Association for Providers of AIDS Care.

Dr. Goldenberg's work has demonstrated the serious health and social inequities faced by marginalised im/migrant women in Canada and internationally, with a focus on sexual health, precarious labour conditions, gender-based violence, and access to health services. She is Principal Investigator (PI) of An Evaluation of Sex Workers' Health Access (AESHA), an ongoing longitudinal, community-based cohort study focused on sexual health, human rights, and access to care among women sex workers in Vancouver, BC. Dr. Goldenberg also leads the Evaluating Inequities in Refugee and Immigrant Women's Sexual and Reproductive Health Access (IRIS) Study with colleagues in BC. Her research employs qualitative, epidemiological, and community-based research approaches. Dr. Goldenberg is passionate about the role of community engagement and partnerships for ensuring ethical and effective approaches to research, programmes, and policy to advance the health and well-being of marginalised communities.

Ruth Morgan Thomas, BA (she/her), has been involved in sex work for 40 years: 8 years as a full-time sex worker, 2.5 years as an academic researcher looking at HIV-related risks in the sex industry and more than 30 years as a sex workers' rights advocate campaigning for, developing and maintaining services and support for sex workers within a human rights and labour framework.

Ruth was one of the 11 founding members of the Scottish Prostitutes Education Project (SCOT-PEP) set up in 1989 by sex workers for sex workers in Edinburgh, which she managed for 20 years.

In 2004, Ruth joined with other sex workers and allies across Europe to organise the European Conference on Sex Work, Human Rights, Labour and Migration and was Chair of the International Committee on the Rights of Sex Workers in Europe (ICRSE) until 2010.

Ruth was one of the founding members of the Global Network of Sex Work Projects (NSWP) in 1992 and has been employed as their Global Coordinator since 2010. She currently co-chairs the UNAIDS Steering Committee on HIV and Sex Work on behalf of the NSWP and represents NSWP in the recently formed Sex Worker Inclusive Feminist Alliance (SWIFA).

In 2012, Ruth coordinated the Sex Worker Freedom Festival: the alternative IAC2012 event for sex workers and their allies in protest at the legal travel restrictions imposed upon sex workers by the US government and is a member of the Core Group organising HIV2020 online for the same reason.

Anna Forbes, MSS (she/her), is an independent consultant. Her career as a community organiser, writer, public policy strategist, and women's health activist has been evolving since 1978. In 1985, she was hired by Philadelphia's first HIV/AIDS organisation as their first case manager. Over the next 13 years, she worked with local organisations, including Philadelphia's Health Department, to mobilise services and build understanding of HIV/AIDS. Her output ranged from a series of children's books on AIDS to a course on 'public policy through the lens of HIV' taught at Bryn Mawr College in Bryn Mawr, Pennsylvania. With ACT UP, Forbes was repeatedly arrested in civil disobedience actions highlighting the HIV/AIDS crisis.

In 1998, she joined the Global Campaign for Microbicides (GCM), an international effort to address women's urgent need for user-controlled HIV prevention tools. As Deputy Director, she worked with local GCM staff and civil society groups in Asia, Africa, North America, and Europe, building demand for microbicide research and development. She specialised in mobilising sex workers and young women, key constituencies particularly in need of such products. The 2012 International Microbicides Conference awarded her the Omololu Falobi Award for Excellence in HIV Prevention Research Community Advocacy.

Now a writer and consultant, her client list included UNAIDS; the Global Network of Sex Work Projects; University of the Witwatersrand Reproductive Health and HIV Institute in Johannesburg, South Africa; the US Department Health and Human Services; and Open Society Foundations, among many others. Currently, she is working to raise public awareness of how criminalising sex work both violates human rights and facilitates HIV transmission.

Stefan Baral, MD, MPH (he/him), is a physician epidemiologist and the Director of the Key Populations Program at the Center for Public Health and Human Rights in the Department of Epidemiology at the Johns Hopkins Bloomberg School of Public Health in Baltimore, Maryland.

Stefan completed his training at the University of Toronto in Community Medicine as a Fellow of the Royal College of Physicians and Surgeons of Canada and Family medicine with the Canadian Council of Family Physicians and provides clinical care through the Inner-City Health Associates in Toronto.

Through his role as the Director of the Key Populations Program in the Center for Public Health and Human Rights, Stefan has focused on trying to understand why people continue to be at risk for acquiring and transmitting HIV with a focus on the interactions of structural- and network-level determinants with individual-level proximal risks for HIV infection. Together with colleagues, Stefan focuses on using all scientific tools available to characterise the distribution of HIV risks including in countries with broadly generalised HIV epidemics. Consequently, this work has included studying the burden of HIV and HIV-related vulnerabilities among gay, bisexual, and other men who have sex with men, transgender women, people who use drugs, and sex workers in a range of HIV epidemic settings. In response to the disproportionate burden of HIV among populations with specific vulnerabilities, Stefan has participated in advancing the standardisation of methods and measures in HIV-related implementation research to study how best to implement programs serving marginalised communities.

Chapter 1
Overview and Evidence-Based Recommendations to Address Health and Human Rights Inequities Faced by Sex Workers

Shira M. Goldenberg, Ruth Morgan Thomas, Anna Forbes, and Stefan Baral

Based on a powerful combination of sex worker community and academic evidence, this edited volume highlights the unacceptable health and social inequities that sex workers in all their diversity continue to face across diverse global and policy contexts. The work presented here was guided by a unique community–academic partnership, developed to ensure that sex workers' voices were amplified in describing challenges, and presenting solutions and ways forward for research, service delivery, and policymaking. Interdisciplinary author teams comprised of academic researchers, sex workers, and sex worker-led organisations collaboratively developed each chapter to synthesise research evidence as well as highlight lessons learned from local-level experiences across different regions.

This edited volume aims to provide a comprehensive overview of health and human rights inequities faced by sex workers around the world. It aims to articulate structural determinants of sex workers' health and occupational outcomes (e.g. legislation, migration, healthcare delivery settings) and describe evidence-based interventions and 'best practices', including the roles of full decriminalisation of sex work, community empowerment models, and multi-level and integrated intervention

S. M. Goldenberg (✉)
Faculty of Health Sciences, Simon Fraser University, Burnaby, BC, Canada

Centre for Gender and Sexual Health Equity, Vancouver, BC, Canada
e-mail: Shira.Goldenberg@cgshe.ubc.ca

R. Morgan Thomas
The Matrix, Global Network of Sex Work Projects – NSWP, Edinburgh, UK
e-mail: ruth.morganthomas@nswp.org

A. Forbes
Independent Consultant, Kensington, MD, USA

S. Baral
Center for Public Health and Human Rights, Department of Epidemiology,
Johns Hopkins University, Baltimore, MD, USA
e-mail: sbaral@jhu.edu

© The Author(s) 2021
S. M. Goldenberg et al. (eds.), *Sex Work, Health, and Human Rights*,
https://doi.org/10.1007/978-3-030-64171-9_1

approaches. The chapters describe an elevated burden of HIV and sexually transmitted infections and drug-related harms; persistent and unacceptable experiences of violence and other human rights violations; and significant unmet sexual and reproductive health needs. Importantly, this edited volume also demonstrates that sex workers are not passive recipients of such structural inequity and violence, but rather actively resist and demonstrate tremendous resilience in the face of these harms. Sex workers across diverse global settings continue to mobilise to advocate for improved health, safety, and human rights conditions and policy changes—such 'community empowerment' interventions have been identified as a best practice for improving sex workers' health and labour rights.

Part I: Burden of Health and Human Rights Inequities Faced by Sex Workers Globally

In Chap. 2, authors *Viswasam, Rivera, Comins, Rao, Lyons,* and *Baral* draw on epidemiological studies and the lived experience of sex workers to describe the global HIV burden among sex workers and the factors that influence this. It also describes coverage of and gaps in interventions to reduce HIV-related inequities faced by sex workers over the past decade. This chapter shows that globally, sex workers face a disproportionate burden of HIV, and continue to face unacceptable gaps in access to HIV prevention, treatment, care, and support services. It also highlights current gaps in data, including limited research with communities of cis-men and transgender sex workers, as well as the need for further data focused on the harms of criminalisation and intersectional risks. Key recommendations include national action towards full decriminalisation of sex work and scale-up of community empowerment approaches, which remain vital alongside and in tandem with emerging biomedical HIV prevention approaches.

Although violence and other human rights violations are recognised as critical public health and human rights violations, global literature on violence against sex workers remains scant. In Chap. 3, authors *Argento, Win, McBride,* and *Shannon* illustrate this through a global overview of literature on violence and other human rights violations faced by sex workers, complemented by case studies from community partners in the Asia Pacific region. This chapter highlights the need for legislative reforms to decriminalise all aspects of sex work, end impunity for those who commit violence against sex workers, and ensure that sex workers have legally enforceable rights to occupational health and safety protections. The authors indicate the need for political commitment to reduce broader structural inequities, uphold anti-discrimination and other rights-respecting laws, and reduce stigma and exclusion. They also call for increased funding to support scale-up of community-led empowerment approaches and rights-based strategies to mitigate risk of violence, enable safer work environments, and uphold human rights among sex workers globally.

Chapter 4 addresses sex workers' lack of access to sexual and reproductive health and rights (SRHR). In this chapter, authors *Shapiro* and *Duff* draw on academic evidence and community consultations undertaken by NSWP with sex workers across ten countries to examine barriers to achieving SRHR for sex workers. Findings indicate that whereas HIV and STIs have been a primary focus of many sex worker services and interventions, sex workers face a high burden of unmet sexual and reproductive health services across diverse contexts. Multiple factors—including criminalisation of sex work, a lack of sex worker-specific SRHR models, and the stigmatisation of same-sex relationships and gender non-conformance—contribute to barriers to achieving SRHR. The authors recommend: increasing funding and support for comprehensive SRHR services designed to meet the needs of sex workers of all genders; ensuring access to safe, legal, affordable, and non-coercive SRHR services, including abortion; integrating SRHR with HIV and STI services as a 'one-stop-shop' model; promoting community-led SRH education programming for sex workers and their clients; and prioritising broader efforts towards full decriminalisation of sex work, community empowerment models of SRH care, and anti-stigma and discrimination efforts.

Work by *Logie, Wang, Lalor, Levermore,* and *Williams in* Chap. 5 addresses sex workers' mental health, examining mental health outcomes in relation to social cohesion among sex workers. In collaboration with two sex worker-led organisations in Jamaica, the findings generated from research with 340 women, men, and gender-diverse sex workers found that enhanced social cohesion was linked to reduced depressive symptoms and violence among participants, thus promoting their health and safety. Based on these findings and review of the literature, the authors describe an urgent need for full decriminalisation of sex work and same-gender sexual practices to advance health and human rights, alongside increased screening for mental health and scale-up of access to mental health services for mitigating the effects of structural stigmas.

In Chap. 6, authors *Iversen, Long, Lutnick,* and *Maher* evaluated the health needs of sex workers who use drugs, using a systematic review and community case studies from the St. James Infirmary in San Francisco. This systematic review of 86 studies conducted in 46 countries reveals a pooled prevalence of lifetime illicit drug use among sex workers of 35%, with 29% lifetime pooled prevalence among female sex workers. The authors note significant gaps existing in the data quality and availability in this review. Key recommendations included an urgent need for future research in partnership with sex workers to improve the quality and quantity of data on illicit drug use among sex workers and guide the creation, implementation, and evaluation of programmes and services that meaningfully address the needs of this population.

Part II: Structural Determinants of Health and Human Rights Inequities in Sex Work

Work by *Krüsi, D'Adamo,* and *Sernick* in Chap. 7 illustrates how the criminalisation and policing of sex work shapes sex workers' health and safety in the context of different legislative frameworks governing sex work around the world. Based on synthesis of research evidence and sex work community case studies from the global North and South, this chapter shows how sex workers' occupational health, safety, and human rights are violated and undermined under various criminalised models. These models include full criminalisation, as well as 'end-demand' models that criminalise clients and third parties but not sex workers directly. This chapter shows how numerous legislative frameworks sanction and perpetuate structural violence and negative health outcomes among sex workers. This chapter concludes with an evidence-based call for the full decriminalisation of all aspects of sex work, and also highlights the need to include sex workers from all segments of the sex industry, including those who are marginalised due to racialisation, im/migration status, and illicit substance use, in evidence-based policymaking.

In Chap. 8, authors *Richter* and *Buthelezi* describe experiences of stigma, denial of care, and other human rights violations faced by sex workers within health service delivery settings in Africa. They powerfully show that sex workers' negative experiences with health services act as a severe barrier to the right to health and quality health care—by inhibiting effective treatment, prevention and support for HIV and other health-related needs of sex workers, including sexual and reproductive health, preventative care, and mental health. In particular, stigmatising and discriminatory treatment by healthcare workers and non-clinical staff have a far-reaching negative impact on sex workers, undermining their wellbeing and access to care. In contrast, positive interactions with healthcare providers and health services empower sex workers, affirm sex worker dignity and agency, and assist in cultivating healthy behaviour and improved health outcomes. The authors conclude with recommendations for comprehensive, rights-affirming health programmes designed in partnership with sex workers, as well as programmes that focus on strategic and practical sex worker needs in the African context; these programmes should include structural interventions to shift away from outdated criminalised legal frameworks and implement violence prevention strategies, psycho-social support services, sex worker empowerment initiatives, and sex worker-led programmes.

Chapter 9 focuses on the health and social needs of women, men, and gender-diverse im/migrant sex workers. Authors *McBride* and *Janushev* draw on research evidence and community consultations in Europe to showcase the unique concerns of im/migrant workers in destination settings, based on their intersecting identities as sex workers as well as im/migrants. These concerns include racialised police harassment and surveillance, mandatory health testing, economic marginalisation, discrimination, and language barriers. Results of community consultations, primarily among male and gender-diverse im/migrant sex workers, illustrate a range of obstacles created by such social and structural exclusion, as well as the resilience of im/migrant workers in their efforts to resist them. Recommendations for policies and programmes include supporting safer indoor sex work environments, removal of punitive sex work, immigration, and public health laws and policies that affect im/migrant sex workers, and supporting non-stigmatising, sex worker-led education, outreach, and services.

Part III: Evidence-Based Services and Best Practices: Opportunities for Action

In Chap. 10, work by *Abel* and *Healy* draw on academic research and experiences of the New Zealand Prostitutes Collective to compellingly illustrate how New Zealand's national decriminalisation of sex work promotes best practices for occupational health, safety, and the broader social inclusion of sex workers. In stark contrast to criminalised settings, where sex workers fear coming forward to report violence due to mistrust of police and fear that they or their workplaces may be prosecuted, this work reports improved access to justice and police responsiveness to violence against sex workers under decriminalisation. Furthermore, this chapter reveals that decriminalisation promotes interagency collaboration to support safer indoor work environments and helps to ensure that new sex workers are well informed about safe and legal sex work practices. Nonetheless, gaps are noted, in particular for migrant workers who are not protected under this law. The authors conclude with recommending full decriminalisation of sex work that is also inclusive of im/migrant workers, so that all sex workers may benefit from improved occupational health, safety, and agency.

Chapter 11 describes the ways in which community empowerment and mobilisation strategies have, in the last few decades, become critical tools used by sex workers in many settings to confront the health and human rights challenges they face, including HIV, violence, discrimination, and labour rights abuses. In this chapter, authors *Navarrete Gil, Ramaiah, Mantsios, Barrington,* and *Kerrigan* review the literature on community empowerment and mobilisation, highlighting their effectiveness with case studies developed by sex work community organisations APROASE in Mexico and Ashodaya Samithi in India. The authors also identify several key evidence gaps, including a lack of systematic community empowerment-based approaches and evaluation of these efforts for male and transgender sex workers. Key recommendations include efforts to take community empowerment efforts to scale and to conduct additional longitudinal evaluation research assessing long-term changes across diverse contexts.

Features of sex workers' occupational environments are known to greatly shape health outcomes. In Chap. 12, authors *West, Hilton, Montgomery,* and *Ebben* describe the health and safety challenges, protective factors, and unique considerations and opportunities associated with indoor sex work. A case study from Empower in Thailand, a sex worker-led organisation, outlines the physical and policy components essential to ensuring sex workers' rights, occupational safety, and health in an indoor workplace. The authors conclude indoor venues pose important potential for establishing and implementing occupational health and safety standards in sex work, and also may provide substantial opportunity for collective organising given the close proximity of people working together. However, any efforts to improve the health and safety of sex workers must explicitly address the structural conditions that lead to power imbalances and which undermine sex worker agency and equality. Key recommendations include promoting occupational health and safety within indoor spaces, prioritising sex worker leadership and inclusion through community mobilisation and engagement efforts, and advocacy and policy reform to remove punitive policies.

Finally, in Chap. 13, *Schwartz, Viswasam,* and *Abdalla* highlight that the intersecting and multi-factorial factors that influence sex workers' health in most settings are too complex to be addressed with single disease-focused interventions. This chapter synthesises scientific evidence on existing approaches to designing and evaluating multi-level and integrated interventions to improve sex workers' health, which is complemented by sex work community perspectives from the Kenya Sex Workers Alliance (KESWA). This chapter highlights the necessity for integrated, multi-level public health approaches—including tailored combinations of structural, behavioural, and bio-medical interventions—to promote improved health outcomes for sex workers (e.g. HIV, gender-based violence, SRHR). The chapter also discusses challenges and considerations in the development and evaluation of such interventions, including the need for additional support and prioritisation for meaningful sex worker involvement. The chapter concludes with recommendations for further intervention research that incorporates and evaluates structural intervention components, as well as the critical need to support increased opportunities for leadership from the sex worker community in setting and implementing this research agenda.

Implications for Policy, Advocacy, and Programmes

Ten high-level, evidence-based recommendations for policy, programmes, and research informed by the chapters in this edited volume are presented in Box 1.1. We urge policymakers, service delivery organisations, researchers, community organisations, and other implementing partners to implement these recommendations in policy, programmes, and research efforts in the area of sex workers' health and human rights.

Box 1.1 Key Evidence-Based Recommendations of this Edited Volume

1. **Decriminalise all aspects of sex work.**
   Governments, policymakers, and advocates must actively pursue the full decriminalisation of sex work, including sex workers, clients and third parties, and the removal of all punitive laws and policies that increase the vulnerabilities of different sex worker sub-populations. Criminalisation is a primary driver of the stigma and discrimination experienced by sex workers when accessing health services and a major reason for why they continue to be disproportionately affected by HIV. Criminalisation also deters sex workers from reporting crimes to the police and exacerbates abuse and violence from law enforcement officers, as well as enabling

(continued)

Box 1.1 (continued)

impunity of all perpetrators of abuse and violence. Criminalisation of sex work, HIV transmission, and same-sex sexual activity increases stigma and discrimination and causes fear among sex workers that prevents them from seeking the health care they need. Decriminalisation of all aspects of sex work would significantly reduce the barriers to health for sex workers, in terms of both access to health care and meaningful involvement in the development of health services aimed at them. It would also enable occupational health and safety standards to be rolled out in ways that promote the safety, agency, and health of sex workers.

2. **Recognise sex work as work.**

   Governments should extend all legal protections and labour rights, to which all workers are entitled, to sex workers and remove legal and policy barriers that deny sex workers the protection of employment legislation, including health and safety protections and anti-discrimination, and access to social protection schemes.

3. **Ensure that healthcare services are accessible, non-coercive, and responsive to the diversity of sex workers' needs.**

   Health is not only the absence of illness, it is wellbeing, and sex workers in all their diversity need accessible, non-stigmatising access to health care that comprehensively fulfils their right to health. This includes access to non-coercive and non-discriminatory sexual and reproductive health services, psychological and psycho-social support, specialist health services, as well as access to justice and social protection. Sex workers are not vectors of disease and must not be treated as such by the health system; rather, they are on the frontlines of prevention and are contributing members of society. Integrated models of service delivery are often more convenient and less stigmatising than individual disease-oriented models that focus more narrowly on specific conditions (e.g. HIV).

4. **End police, immigration, and other state-sanctioned crackdowns, surveillance, and harassment of sex workers, third parties, and clients.**

   Alongside longer term efforts towards full decriminalisation, policies that address the harms of laws, policies, and practices surrounding sex work and immigration are urgently needed. There is a need for the implementation of local or regional-level 'non-harassment' and 'access without fear' policies that end police and immigration crackdowns, public health surveillance, arrests and prosecutions targeting im/migrant and non-migrant sex workers, third parties, and clients. This allows efforts to shift away from punitive measures that have been shown to severely undermine sex workers' health and violate their rights, towards community-led efforts that will reach and support those most in need.

(continued)

Box 1.1 (continued)

5. **Build trust and partnerships between the health system and sex worker-led organisations.**

   The organisation and delivery of healthcare services should treat sex workers as experts on their own lives and their health needs, and as potential service providers, not just service users. Non-stigmatising, non-discriminatory approaches are best developed by, for, and with sex workers and sex worker-led community organisations. To build more nuanced and non-stigmatising relationships between healthcare providers and sex workers, ongoing community-led training for providers regarding sex workers' lived experiences, expertise, and needs is recommended. Understanding health inequities and the needs of key populations, including sex workers, should also be core components of medical education.

6. **Prioritise community empowerment and mobilisation in research, programming, and policy.**

   Sex workers and sex worker-led organisations are the experts on their own lives and are ideally situated to inform approaches and deliver services that support their needs. Community-based and sex worker-led models of health and social services delivery are recognised 'best practices' for meeting sex workers' needs but are often not prioritised by funding agencies and health systems. Community empowerment and mobilisation should be implemented as critical strategies for advancing rights-affirming and evidence-based interventions including full decriminalisation, non-coercive occupational health and safety standards, addressing violence, ensuring access to justice and broader anti-stigma efforts.

7. **Support partnership and collaboration between sex worker-led organisations and academics, policymakers and programmers committed to addressing inequities across health, human rights, and justice.**

   These efforts are vital to ensuring balanced and inclusive perspectives across research, policymaking, and practice that meaningfully advance sex workers' health and human rights. It is often particularly relevant to collaborate with community-led organisations that work for other marginalised and criminalised groups that are disproportionally represented within sex work, such as im/migrants, people living with HIV, people who use drugs, lesbian, gay and bisexual, and transgender people, Black, Indigenous, and other People of Colour (BIPOC), and women that share the core values of the sex worker rights movement.

8. **Ensure access to health and social services and supports for sex workers, regardless of internal mobility or immigration status.**

   Sex workers require access to critical social services, including eligibility for housing, food support, basic income and employment insurance support, and other vital social services, including support for survivors of

(continued)

Box 1.1 (continued)

> violence. *Despite this need, im/migrant and mobile sex workers are often unjustly excluded from these due to restrictions on eligibility, stigma, and the lack of recognition of sex work as work. Urgent policy reforms are especially needed to ensure these protections for im/migrant and mobile workers, who are often unable to access health and social services and protection schemes that are dependent on local registration and/or immigration status.*

9. **Support sex worker-led, resilient, and evidence-based approaches.**
   Sex workers show individual and collective resilience, adaptability, and resistance in their work, lives, and advocacy efforts. Recognition of these strengths and efforts to build on sex worker communities knowledge and expertise in programmes, policy, and research are recommended. It is also important to ensure that research focused on health and social inequities faced by sex workers consider sex workers as agents and experts in their own lives.

10. **Ensure resources are made available to strengthen capacity among sex worker-led organisations to become meaningfully involved in research, policy, and programmes.**
    These efforts are vital to meaningful and successful community empowerment and mobilisation efforts, yet they remain woefully under-resourced. Many sex worker-led organisations are already engaging in these efforts and simply lack the funding to bolster them.

As we finalise this edited volume, we are living in a pandemic that has further exposed and exacerbated the inequities and vulnerabilities that confront sex workers of all genders around the world. Sex work is a work, and sex workers around the world have faced total or near-total loss of income in the context of the COVID-19 pandemic. Despite sex workers being recognised as informal workers by the international Labour Organisation, the criminalisation of sex work has resulted in many governments taking disproportionate repressive measures against sex workers in response to COVID-19, including increasing raids and arrests, compulsory testing, threats of deportation, and bulldozing their homes. In the United States, despite sex work being legal in some states, sex workers are explicitly excluded from social protection offered to other workers. It is imperative that states recognise sex workers, in all their diversity, and ensure that emergency social protection schemes are accessible to them.

Health inequities have long defined health and the healthcare access for sex workers around the world. The chapters show here that while there have been significant investments in clinical and epidemiologic research on sex workers, sex workers' health, and human rights continue to be hampered by limited attention and investment in structural interventions. As seen here, the average health and human rights indicators of sex workers remain suboptimal in 2020, a finding at least in part explained by inequity in access to health care and justice. In this context, COVID-19 has rapidly emerged as a major global threat to health. While it was initially thought that the pandemic would be the great equaliser as it would not discriminate, it is clear that COVID-19 incidence and mortality have rapidly reinforced health inequities drawn by historical and contemporary injustices. Throughout this book, we synthesised the data highlighting specific health and social inequities among sex workers driven by criminalisation and other structural factors. In the absence of major policy changes, such inequities will likely only be reinforced during COVID-19.

Ultimately, advancing the COVID-19 response and saving lives requires that we rapidly address inequities affecting sex workers rather than ignoring, or worse, reinforcing them. The COVID-19 pandemic provides a stark example of how sex workers are too often excluded from emergency responses and social protection schemes. COVID-19 has also clearly shown the critical contributions of sex worker-led organisations, who wherever and whenever possible, have launched and implemented emergency responses and mutual aid funds for their communities.

In April 2020, a joint statement was issued [1] by the Global Network of Sex Work Projects (NSWP) and the Joint United Nations Programme on HIV/AIDS (UNAIDS), which noted the severe inequities and hardships faced by sex workers during the current COVID-19 pandemic and called on countries to take the following comprehensive set of actions to mitigate these:

- Access to national social protection schemes for sex workers, including income support schemes.
- An immediate firewall between health services and immigration authorities in order to ensure that migrant sex workers can access health services.
- Emergency financial support for sex workers facing destitution, particularly migrants who are unable to access residency-based financial support.
- An immediate end to evictions and access to appropriate emergency housing for homeless sex workers.
- Stopping raids on sex workers' homes and sex work premises and ensuring that all measures to protect public health are proportionate.
- An immediate halt to arrests and prosecutions for sex work-related activity, moving away from punitive measures and criminalisation towards reaching and serving those most in need.
- An immediate end to the use of criminal law to enforce COVID-19-related restrictions, including forced COVID-19 testing and related prosecutions.
- Automatic extensions on visas due to expire as travel restrictions tighten. Immigration detention systems must support detainees in safe accommodation.
- The engagement of sex worker communities in responses—the meaningful involvement of sex worker-led organisations in emergency public health planning groups.

If we are to address the ongoing inequities highlighted throughout all the chapters in this edited volume, then sex worker's human rights must be protected, respected, and fulfilled. Fundamental changes are needed. Policymakers must be willing to listen to sex workers in all their diversity, and to review existing policy and legislation to ensure the harms identified in each chapter are eradicated. Sex workers' voices must be amplified and respected in decision-making that directly affects their lives and work. Policies and programmes must ensure that the agency and bodily autonomy, as well as the livelihoods of sex workers, are not undermined. It is essential that sex workers are meaningfully involved from the very start of processes to develop or review policies and programmes, to ensure existing harms are considered and mitigated. Change will also require the recognition of the critical role that sex worker-led organisations should play in addressing the inequities and identifying sustainable rights-affirming responses that uphold the value and dignity of sex workers, which must be appropriately resourced.

Reference

1. UNAIDS and NSWP. Sex workers must not be left behind in the response to COVID-19 [press release]; 8 Apr 2020.

Part I
Burden of Health and Human Rights Inequities Faced by Sex Workers Globally

Chapter 2
The Epidemiology of HIV Among Sex Workers Around the World: Implications for Research, Programmes, and Policy

Nikita Viswasam, Justice Rivera, Carly Comins, Amrita Rao, Carrie E. Lyons, and Stefan Baral

Introduction

The prevalence of HIV among sex workers is consistently high around the globe. The reasons for this high burden are complex, intersecting across lines of the behavioural, social, and structural realities experienced by sex workers of all genders. In this chapter, we build on systematic reviews of HIV among sex workers, as well as case studies rooted in the lived experience of sex workers and sex work organisations, to describe: (1) the global HIV burden among sex workers; (2) the factors and determinants that influence the HIV burden and risk; and (3) coverage of and gaps in interventions to reduce HIV-related inequities faced by sex workers over the past decade.

NV conceptualised the chapter, led the literature search, and drafted the sections on determinants of HIV, intervention coverage, research gaps; contributed to introduction, HIV burden, to literature review and overall editing of the chapter. CC contributed to the sections of intervention coverage, determinants of HIV, to conceptualisation of the chapter, the literature review, and to overall editing of the chapter. AR drafted the HIV global burden section, contributed to conceptualisation of the chapter, literature review, and overall editing of the chapter. CEL contributed to the structural determinants section and overall editing of the chapter. As community co-author, JR drafted community case studies featured in the introduction, drug use, determinants of HIV section and contributed to overall editing of the chapter. SDB contributed to conceptualisation of the chapter, conclusion, and overall editing of the chapter.

N. Viswasam (✉) · C. Comins · A. Rao · C. E. Lyons · S. Baral
Center for Public Health and Human Rights, Department of Epidemiology, Johns Hopkins Bloomberg School of Public Health, Baltimore, MD, USA
e-mail: nviswas@outlook.com; ccomins1@jhu.edu; arao24@jhu.edu; clyons8@jhmi.edu; sbaral@jhu.edu

J. Rivera
Reframe Health and Justice, Baltimore, MD, USA

Sex Workers Outreach Project (SWOP), Washington, DC, USA
e-mail: justice@reframehealthandjustice.com

© The Author(s) 2021
S. M. Goldenberg et al. (eds.), *Sex Work, Health, and Human Rights*,
https://doi.org/10.1007/978-3-030-64171-9_2

Epidemiological Data on the Global Burden of HIV Among Sex Workers

Despite overall reported progress towards the ambitious 90-90-90 targets in the general population, robust evidence continues to indicate severe unmet global need for HIV prevention, treatment, and care services among sex workers. As of 2019, sex workers continue to face a disproportionately high burden of HIV compared to other adults of reproductive age. A systematic review and meta-analysis by Shannon and colleagues published in 2018 found that cisgender women sex workers globally experience an HIV prevalence of 10.4% (95% Confidence Interval (CI): 9.5–11.5), with the highest regional HIV prevalence estimates reported in Eastern and Southern Africa (33.3%; CI: 29.2–37.6), followed by West and Central Africa (20.1%, CI: 16.7–23.8) [1]. As Shannon et al. report, this prevalence remains unacceptably high and is largely unchanged from data reported in 2014 [1]. Although there has been some progress, access to services and information is uneven across populations and hampered by social and structural barriers [1].

Following Shannon et al.'s meta-analysis reporting data from 2006 to 2017, 19 additional studies on HIV prevalence were published in 2018, primarily among cisgender women sex workers (Table 2.1). These prevalence data indicate overall patterns of HIV acquisition among female sex workers across regions that were similar to those noted in the previous reviews. We see the highest prevalence in Southern Africa: one study in Soweto, South Africa documented a prevalence of 53.6% (95% CI: 47.5–59.9) among 508 sex workers recruited through respondent-driven sampling (RDS) [21]. Another study of 2617 sex workers in 14 communities across Zimbabwe reported a prevalence of 59% overall, and saw a significantly lower burden among younger, compared to older, women sex workers (35% vs. 67%) [22]. Additional studies in other regions documented burdens similar to the estimated regional prevalence in Table 2.1—with 28% in Tanzania [23] and 31.4% in Uganda from the Eastern Africa region [24]; 11.5% in Togo from West Africa [2], in South America—Brazil: 5.3% [3, 4].

These results largely confirm those presented by Shannon and colleagues—that overall, the burden of HIV among cisgender women sex workers remains unchanged from what it was over a decade ago.

Differences in HIV prevalence among sex workers across regions partly reflect estimates of HIV prevalence among the general adult population in different regions. The Joint United Nations Programme on HIV/AIDS (UNAIDS) estimates that 70% of people living with HIV globally live in sub-Saharan Africa [1, 5]. Furthermore, in different regions, varying levels of poverty, education, HIV-related stigma, access to health care, and human rights violations including discrimination and violence, all affect uptake of HIV testing, awareness of status, and retention in care and treatment for those living with HIV—which limits the impact of treatment as prevention among sex workers [5, 6].

Data on cisgender men and transgender women and men sex workers, while growing, remain inadequate, especially as these data are often only available as

Table 2.1 HIV prevalence among sex workers reported in studies published in 2018

World region	Reported HIV prevalence (%)	Sex worker population	First author, year, citation
Asia and Pacific			
China	6.8	Cisgender women	Dong et al. (2018) [2]
	0.92–3.21	Cisgender women	Lai et al. (2018) [3]
	2.74	Cisgender women	Zhu et al. (2018) [4]
Thailand	8.8	Transgender women	Seekaew et al. (2018) [5]
	11	Cisgender men	Goldsamt et al. (2018) [6]
Eastern Europe and Central Asia			
Ukraine	6.3	Cisgender women	Dumchev et al. (2018) [7]
Middle East and North Africa			
Morocco	11	Cisgender women	Kouyoumjian et al. (2018) [8]
Eastern and Southern Africa			
Kenya	5.6	Cisgender women	Becker et al. (2018) [9]
Nigeria	25	Cisgender women	Awofala and Ogundele (2018) [10]
Malawi	62	Cisgender women	Herce et al. (2018) [11]
Angola	8	Cisgender women	Herce et al. (2018) [11]
Tanzania	28	Cisgender women	Vu and Misra (2018) [12]
Uganda	31.4	Cisgender women	Doshi et al. (2018) [13]
Zimbabwe	59	Cisgender women	Napierala et al. (2018) [14]
West and Central Africa			
Benin	41	Cisgender women	Diabate et al. (2018) [15]
Latin America and Caribbean			
Brazil	5.3	Cisgender women	Szwarcwald et al. (2018) [16]
	5.3	Cisgender women	Ferreira-Junior et al. (2018) [17]
Peru	3	Cisgender men	Degtyar et al. (2018) [18]
	19	Transgender women	Degtyar et al. (2018) [18]
Western and Central Europe, North America			
Europe	6.38	Cisgender men	Fernandez-Lopez et al. (2018) [19]
Portugal	14.9	Transgender women	Gama et al. (2018) [20]

sub-samples of cisgender men who have sex with men and transgender women. As part of a larger published work on transgender sex workers [7], Scheim and colleagues built on earlier reviews [21, 22] with a 2018 global review of HIV prevalence data among transgender sex workers. This review identified studies undertaken between 2008 and 2015, reporting prevalence estimates ranging 17–34% in majority-sex worker samples of transgender women, primarily in Asia and Latin America [10]. In Brazil, survey data stratified by lifetime sex work status found that transgender women sex workers had an HIV prevalence of 39%, compared to 19% of transgender women who did not report sex work [23]. A 2015 review of HIV among cisgender men sex workers found that approximately a third of the 52 countries that reported HIV prevalence data on men sex workers to the United Nations General Assembly reported an HIV prevalence of 12.5% or higher, noting that HIV burdens among men sex workers were consistently higher than in men in general [24]. Overall, more comprehensive HIV data are needed for cisgender men sex workers and transgender sex workers.

Engagement in Care and the HIV Treatment Cascade

The HIV treatment cascade begins with testing for HIV and, if diagnosed, linkage to HIV health services, initiating HIV antiretroviral therapy (ART)—and, in the absence of primary and secondary resistance to ART, staying on HIV treatment to remain on the path to viral suppression. Recent data demonstrate that there is no risk of onward HIV transmission when people have achieved viral suppression. Since 2010, multiple reviews have summarised available quantitative data on sex workers' engagement in HIV care and treatment [25–27]. These reviews, and updated data from studies published in 2018, reveal that 12 countries in total had data collected between 2011 and 2016 on cisgender women sex workers [28–35, 43]. One in Indonesia also contained data on transgender persons, though they did not report data for the subgroup of transgender sex workers [36].

Among sex workers aware of their HIV diagnosis, reports of being currently on treatment ranged from 33% in Burkina Faso and Togo to 84.4% in Papua New Guinea [37]. Viral suppression, where data were available, ranged from 23% in Indonesia and Cambodia to 77.8% in Zimbabwe [38]. While comparing cascade data is challenging because of the different definitions used to measure each cascade step across studies,[1] combined analyses in 2014 assessed ART uptake and adherence among cisgender women sex workers globally [39]. Pooled estimates found that about 38% (95% CI: 29–48) of sex workers living with HIV were currently on treatment, about 76% (95% CI: 68–83) were adherent,[2] and 57% (95% CI: 46–68) were virally suppressed [39]. While reported adherence levels were similar to women in the overall population [39], less than half of sex workers living with HIV were estimated to be on treatment, and two-thirds of them were virally suppressed.

Various studies have documented barriers throughout engagement in care and treatment, including intersecting stigmas, inadequate food, and substance use [40].

---

[1] Authors of the Mountain et al. analyses used the following definitions for the HIV treatment cascade: ART uptake was defined as the fraction of all HIV-infected individuals or the fraction of all ART-eligible individuals who either initiated ART in a specified follow-up period, currently use ART, or ever used ART. ART attrition: the fraction using ART who were either lost-to-follow-up, died or discontinued ART, or the fraction of treatment-experienced individuals no longer on ART. ART adherence: the fraction achieving a pre-defined threshold of adherence (e.g. ≥90%, ≥95%, 100%). Viral suppression: fraction with undetectable plasma viral load following ART initiation.

[2] ART adherence was defined by Mountain et al. as the fraction achieving a pre-defined threshold of adherence, e.g. ≥90%, ≥95%, 100%, which were available from nine studies.

Recent results have shown even larger gaps in care engagement among younger sex workers. In Zimbabwe, for example, a study comparing sex workers between the ages of 18 and 24 to those aged 25 or older found that younger women diagnosed with HIV were less likely to be previously aware of their status, to report being on treatment, and to be virally suppressed [41]. While HIV testing rates among sex workers has increased with knowledge of HIV, there are still documented gaps among sex workers in beginning voluntary HIV treatment, with those receiving continued support being more likely to stay on treatment and becoming virally suppressed.

Determinants of HIV Among Sex Workers

Broadly, structural determinants of HIV describe higher level, contextual factors that influence individual risks of HIV. Known structural determinants of HIV in the context of sex work include stigma, violence, criminalisation, and policing practices. Injecting and non-injecting drug use, also linked to structural determinants, play additional roles in HIV acquisition among sex workers.

Stigma

Stigma is a process by which an individual is labelled based on characteristics that may not adhere to socially accepted norms, resulting in reduced well-being and opportunities for that individual. Sex workers may experience stigma due to their engagement in sex work, HIV status, or other identities and behaviours (e.g. drug use, gender identity, sexual orientation, migration status) as well as the intersections of these characteristics. HIV-related stigma could be based on actual or perceived status of living with HIV. This can lead to fear or avoidance of health services (*anticipated stigma*) because they associate engaging in care with having experienced discrimination (*enacted stigma*) at the hands of healthcare providers. Mistreatment by healthcare providers may also affect the quality of care provided to sex workers. *Perceived, anticipated,* and *enacted stigmas* are major barriers to HIV prevention, testing, and care for all sex workers, which can also be exacerbated by multiple or intersecting stigmas [46, 47].

Identities are often multiple and intersecting, and therefore sex workers may overlap with other key populations, including people who use drugs and those with non-heteronormative sexual orientations and gender identities. The intersectional stigmas faced by more marginalised subgroups of sex workers are a powerful determinant of HIV, warranting further research attention. In Zimbabwe, nine out of ten sex workers reported experiencing stigma due to sex work. Those who reported experiencing stigma due to sex work also reported experiencing more HIV-related stigma than those who did not [42]. In Guatemala, MSM sex workers reported higher levels of discrimination than MSM non-sex workers, and transgender sex workers reported significantly higher proportions of discrimination compared to both MSM sex workers and MSM non-sex workers, suggesting intersecting stigmas due to both gender identity and sex work [49].

Interventions addressing stigma in the context of sex work are therefore critical for addressing the HIV burden faced by sex workers. A community intervention for female sex workers and healthcare providers in Senegal observed that teaching strategies for addressing stigma and discrimination reduced sex workers' fear of seeking health services and inclination to avoid health services [50]. This speaks to the need for sex work programmes to address stigma in combination with other factors to improve HIV prevention and care.

Criminalisation, Violence, and Policing

National policy-making around sex work has predominantly relied on criminal laws and legal frameworks, whether through criminalisation, containment, regulation, or eradication [6, 51]. In many settings that criminalise sex work, police arrest and harassment have often displaced sex workers and driven them into isolated working locations, disrupting support networks, service delivery, and opportunities for risk reduction [52]. This results in increased risk of physical and sexual violence and higher odds of HIV/STIs [52]. Furthermore, as the case studies in this chapter illustrate, sex work criminalisation has also led to the exacerbation of inequalities experienced by transgender persons, migrants, and sex workers who use drugs.

On the basis of human rights and health evidence, Amnesty International called for the full decriminalisation of sex work in 2014 and its separation from the definition of sex trafficking [53]. Decriminalisation of sex work refers to the absence of laws that criminalise selling sex, buying sex, the organisation of and facilitation of sex work [53], as well as the absence of other legal oppression [54]. Shannon and colleagues highlighted the potential HIV infections averted through decriminalisation's downstream effects on work environment, violence, and risk behaviours [55]. European countries which have partially legalised aspects of sex work displayed a lower HIV prevalence compared to those with full criminalisation [56]. Across sub-Saharan African countries, the odds of HIV among cisgender women sex workers in criminalised and non-protective settings was higher than in settings in which sex work is partially legalised. Furthermore, the effect of stigmas on HIV was higher in criminalised and non-protective settings compared to partially legalised settings [57]. However, partial legalisation policies in Sweden, Norway, and the UK, where clients of sex work and/or third-party managers are criminalised while the selling of sex is legal, have also been associated with many of the same HIV risks as full criminalisation, reinforcing the need for full decriminalisation to optimise health outcomes [58]. European countries with partial legalisation were shown to have higher HIV prevalence compared to the sole European country where buying, selling, *and* managing of sex work was legalised—Germany [25]. Ultimately, a larger sample size of countries with decriminalisation is needed to fully demonstrate quantitative differences in health outcomes by legislative model.

On a global level, individuals who undertake sex work are deeply affected by verbal, physical, and sexual violence perpetrated by clients, police, intimate partners, and others throughout their lifetime, both before their entry into sex work and during sex work [20, 59]. Violence increases their vulnerability to HIV, especially in cases of sexual violence. It also influences sexual risk behaviours, as well as one's access to prevention and care. Experiences of physical and sexual violence through a sex worker's lifetime are strongly associated with higher odds of unprotected sex and of acquiring HIV [3, 59–61].

Given the observed association between criminalisation of sex work and health outcomes, a recent systematic review and combined analyses undertaken by Platt and colleagues assessed 20 quantitative studies looking at the effect of sex work laws on health [52]. Repressive policing was linked to higher odds of experiencing physical or sexual violence by clients, intimate partners, police, or other parties. It was also related to higher odds of unprotected sex and twice the odds of living with HIV/STIs. It is particularly linked to the confiscation of needles/syringes, another factor increasing HIV risk [52]. Footer et al.'s systematic review of policing practices also found that experiencing sexual coercion, extortion, and arrest were each consistently associated with HIV or STI infection across studies, highlighting the role that policing, enabled by criminalisation, plays in HIV vulnerabilities [62]. The case study below illustrates some of these experiences.

Case Study 1 Sex Work, Violence, and HIV in Asia
Sex workers of all genders experience high rates of institutional, community-level, and interpersonal violence that negatively impact their physical, sexual, and mental health. A multi-country qualitative study by the United Nations Development Programme, United Nations Populations Fund, and *Asia-Pacific Network of Sex Workers* (2015) highlights gender-based violence as an important 'push' factor into sex work.

While at work, police violence—including raids and sexual extortion—increase the vulnerability of sex workers to client and community perpetrated violence as well as to HIV and STIs. Some workers contract STIs from sexual assaults, and others sacrifice condom use in exchange for immediate safety from police or client violence. An account of a female sex worker in Myanmar describes this.

> We had to do without one [a condom] because we couldn't go out late at nights to buy condoms if there was a police project [raid or crackdown]. Sometimes, I have many clients on that night and it's kind of urgent and didn't have time to find condoms. So I had to stay (to provide sexual services) with them without condoms (Female participant in Yangon). [26]

Frequently, sex workers who survive police and client violence do not report it, fearing that this may result in more violence towards themselves. They may also fear violence from healthcare settings and neighborhoods, especially where HIV infection is either actual or perceived. In addition to this institutional violence, most sex workers in the study reported experiencing intimate partner violence.

This case study further found that ciswomen sex workers were more likely to experience sexual violence related to a perception that they were challenging traditional gender roles. Transgender and cismen sex workers were more likely to experience physical violence related to challenging masculinity and heterosexual norms. Intervention outcomes that can reduce violence against sex workers include safe working environments, education on rights and safety, collectivisation, and access to stigma-free health care.

This data, along with qualitative work from New Zealand and New South Wales, Australia, where sex work is decriminalised, further demonstrates the need for full decriminalisation towards achieving better sex worker health and well-being [63, 64]. In Senegal, sex work is legalised but regulated through policies that mandate registration of sex workers and compliance to monthly health checks. A 2018 study noted both positive and negative effects of Senegal's sex work registration [65]. Overall, registered sex workers had higher average earnings due to more sex work activity, higher linkage to health services and lower STI prevalence. They had lower reported well-being, however, due to the still-prevalent social stigma associated with the disclosure of sex work status that came with registration. This reinforces Amnesty International's stance that any regulation of sex work should respect the agency of sex workers [53, 65]. Building on the efforts of sex worker movements and advocacy organisations as well as existing data, we reiterate the statements of Shannon and colleagues: the literature increasingly calls for full decriminalisation along with legal protections from exploitation and offers guidance on policy directions emphasising the health and human rights of sex workers [1, 51].

Migration

Migration, occurring between or within countries, is prevalent among sex workers, due to drivers such as economic needs, armed conflict, family separation, and a desire for social mobility or enhanced economic opportunities. Migration may influence HIV risk through sexual behaviours, economic vulnerability, and social capital through networks, as well as access to prevention and treatment services. Migration has been linked to a higher STI burden, likelihood of unprotected sex along with barriers to HIV care across settings, and to HIV acquisition in some settings [21, 66], though not all [67]. Migration status also interacts with other factors that can amplify the vulnerability of sex workers, as seen with undocumented sex workers in Europe in the case study below [68]. Overall, however, data suggest that migration has a complex relationship with health outcomes, with factors dependent on individual and local contexts [69–71].

Case Study 2 Migration and Mobility, TAMPEP International Foundation, 2009 and International Committee on the Rights of Sex Workers in Europe, 2016

In most European countries, residency permits and health insurance are bound to a person's employment. Sex workers living and working in countries that do not recognise sex work as work are structurally excluded from the public health system. Even where insurance is extended or health care is available, efforts to reach cultural minorities fall short in the absence of language translation services or availability of printed materials in multiple languages. Additionally, lack of protection from deportation reinforces migrant sex workers' fears of expulsion or residence restrictions. Lack of access to health care is compounded by stigma, racism, and sexism faced by many when attempting to access preventative services and treatment.

When looking at the case of undocumented sex workers, many of these factors converge to make them particularly vulnerable to HIV with less access to care, where "[r]epressive laws governing sex work paired with anti-immigration policies push many migrant sex workers into irregular migration situations which highly affects the range of health services available to them in their respective host country. The scope of health services granted to migrants in irregular situations is defined by national legislations (Surveilled. Exploited. Deported., 2016)."

In sum, strong evidence indicates the key role of structural factors in rendering sex workers particularly vulnerable to health inequities. For those living with HIV, overlapping structural factors often act as a barrier to accessing and being retained in care for sex workers. There remains a need for evidence-based structural interventions taking a multi-pronged approach, seeking to address healthcare provider discrimination, police repression, stigma, and experiences of violence to reduce the burden of HIV and barriers to HIV care.

Drug Use Among Sex Workers

Case Study 3 Sex Workers Who Use Drugs in Seattle, Washington, USA: Reframe Health and Justice, 2018

The prominent outdoor sex work market in Seattle is near the outskirts of the city, far away from where social services are concentrated downtown. Only one harm reduction agency exists along its track, and though Seattle harm reduction programmes provide medicated assisted therapy (MAT) or MAT referrals, this particular location is only open for a handful of hours each day, 4 days a week. Seattle is among the few US cities that prioritise an 'end-demand'[3] [72] approach to sex work, which has resulted in inconsistent diversion from arrest, expansion of

---

[3] End-demand is defined by the Global Network of Sex Work Projects (NSWP) as a legislative model that criminalises the purchase of sex work, while not criminalising the selling of sex work (NSWP, 2014).

anti-prostitution-oriented services, and decreases in clientele. The combination of a harsh sociopolitical environment and lack of services creates a perfect storm for an HIV outbreak, which occurred among street-based sex workers who inject drugs in this area just months after the passage of a 2018 federal US law restricting the availability of online advertising venues, thereby decreasing market prices and sex workers' ability to survive.

Sex workers in this area report experiencing high levels of overdose, as well as structural and interpersonal violence. They often must make a decision between having unprotected sex or experiencing withdrawal, sleeping on the street, or refusing a meal to their children. Some of these women, both cis and trans, know about the availability of Pre-exposure prophylaxis (PrEP), but cannot make it downtown during service hours because they must work and make money. Others do not have money for transportation or cannot find anywhere to store their belongings during the appointment. The lack of affordable housing, unavailability of hepatitis C treatment, and de-prioritisation of syringe service programmes across the state also negatively affect behavioural factors specific to this population, including high rates of stimulant use.

The overlap of sex work and drug use has been increasingly documented. The case study above illustrates the complex challenges facing sex workers who use drugs, including an elevated burden of HIV across diverse contexts, including Asia, Europe, and North America. Evidence has linked enhanced health-related harms among people who use drugs to structural factors—poor access to harm reduction and evidence-based drug treatment, criminalisation and repressive policing practices, stigma, and discrimination—as well as to individual factors, such as a higher risk of HIV transmission resulting from impaired decision-making in the context of sexual and drug use practices (e.g. unprotected sex, sharing of injecting equipment). Reported current drug use among sex workers, including the use of crack, ecstasy, cocaine, and injectable drugs including heroin, has been associated with 2–6 times the odds of HIV infection, compared to those reporting no drug use or former drug use [3, 73].

Cisgender African American women who reported trading sex for drugs alone had higher burdens of HIV than those who reported selling or trading sex for economic resources and drugs [74]. In Vietnam, 10% of sex workers sampled across ten provinces reported ever using drugs. In every province surveyed, sex workers who injected drugs had a higher HIV prevalence compared to those who did not, considering that parenteral transmission (through sharing injecting equipment) comes with a higher risk of HIV infection compared to sexual transmission [75]. The overlap of sex work and injecting drug use has also been linked to a higher likelihood of both drug-related and sexual risk behaviours, including sharing injection equipment and unprotected sex [73, 76, 77].

While studies directly linking drug use and HIV among transgender sex workers are limited, a New York area study of such sex workers found that a relationship between sex work and incident HIV/STI was significantly explained by interrelated effects of drug use, gender-related abuse,[4] and depression [78]. This highlights the interplay of social and structural determinants driving substance use and subsequent HIV outcomes among sex workers [78].

Repressive police practices play a key role in heightening HIV risk among sex workers who use drugs [52]. Abusive police practices—such as confiscating safe drug use supplies (obtained from harm reduction programmes) as well as condoms (considered evidence of sex work)—decrease the ability of sex workers who use drugs to practise safe drug use and safe sex. The experiences of sex workers in Seattle described at the opening of this section highlights this, and their personal statements, in particular, capture how police attitudes affect sex workers' ability to protect themselves against sexual and drug-related HIV risks:

'They are scared of them for some reason. They treat them like they are an uncapped needle when they aren't even open.' 'I had more than 3 condoms and was told that this meant that I was a hoe and could be arrested.' '[The police] used to take condoms and poke holes in them and still take me to jail. Said that condoms can be used as evidence of prostitution.' [27]

Coverage of Interventions Addressing HIV Burden

Community Empowerment Responses

While there have been many sex worker peer-based education programmes for HIV prevention, the past decade has also seen a growing emphasis on human rights-affirming community mobilisation approaches to improving health outcomes among sex workers [79, 80].These approaches recognise the economic and structural determinants affecting sex worker well-being. They depend on processes of empowerment and grassroots initiatives born from a collective identity in sex worker communities [81, 82].

For HIV prevention and care, this means local sex worker communities are part of the process of determining the needs of sex workers, identifying their specific barriers to engaging in HIV prevention and care, and leading the implementation of programmes designed to address these needs. Kerrigan and colleagues conducted a systematic review and meta-analysis of community empowerment responses to HIV among sex workers in low- and middle-income settings. They found that the combined effect of community empowerment approaches led to lower odds of gonorrhea, chlamydia, and syphilis, a 32% decrease in odds of HIV infection, and triple the odds of protected sex with clients, as previously described in the 2018 *Lancet* update [1, 79].

---

[4]Nuttbrock and colleagues defined measurement of "gender abuse" among study participants as reported experiences of verbal abuse and/or physical abuse during the previous 6 months that participants attributed to their gender identity or presentation [78].

In India, the *Sonagachi* project and *Avahan* initiative involved multiple community-based approaches, including provision of peer outreach, behaviour change communication, clinical prevention, and management services for STIs [81, 83–86]. This initiative also involved community mobilisation and structural interventions including formation of violence response teams, police sensitisation, journalist and legal training to peers, and establishment of community advisory committees who were given leadership and organisational development training [86].

A round of surveys indicated that women with high exposure to community mobilisation activities were more likely to have accessed HIV/STI services, to report having protected sex with a client during their last sexual encounter, and less likely to be infected with chlamydia or gonorrhea compared to women with low exposure [81].

In districts with *Avahan* programmes, 11,000 sex workers completed surveys and testing for HIV in 2005–2006, as did another 11,000 sex workers in 2008–2009. Stronger declines in HIV prevalence were seen in districts with larger increases in programme coverage between 2006 and 2008, though measures of mortality and HIV incidence, which can also contribute to an observed decline in HIV prevalence, were not reported [85].

Abriendo Puertas (Opening Doors) in the Dominican Republic and *Encontros* in Brazil provided combination structural and clinical STI/HIV prevention interventions to sex workers [87–89]. These included expanded clinic hours, sensitisation training of care providers to create a supportive and enabling environment for sex workers, individual- and community-level activities which included peer education, counselling, workshops, and social activities building relationships and dialogue among sex workers to promote social cohesion. Ten months into *Abriendo Puertas,* a survey of sex workers found that having taken part in the intervention resulted in higher odds of protected sex and of reported adherence to ART in the last 4 days, from the time of the survey [87]. Participants also reported lower rates of drug and alcohol use before sex and more engagement in care although viral load and level of retention in care did not change. Additionally, participants who reported higher social cohesion (feeling trust and mutual aid within the sex work community) had lower odds of having an STI [88]. *Encontros* programme participants had a higher odds of having protected sex with regular clients, and a non-significant two times lower odds of incident STI, compared to those who did not participate in the programme [89].

Overall, there exists only a handful of community empowerment interventions with documented effects on HIV outcomes, and these come with limited scale-up, demonstrating a need for greater adaptation and expansion of programmes. Wirtz and colleagues modelled the impact of expanding community empowerment interventions to 65–75% national coverage in the epidemic contexts of Kenya, Brazil, Thailand, and Ukraine [90]. They modelled two scenarios: one was a combination of empowerment interventions and universal ART expansion implemented on a national scale, and the other was the implementation of community empowerment interventions alone. The expansion of empowerment interventions was estimated to reduce new infections between 8% and 12% among sex workers across the four countries, and, combined with universal ART expansion, reduce new infections between 17% and 33% among sex workers across the four countries. These results paired with the above case studies demonstrate the powerful role community empowerment responses can play in addressing the burden of HIV among sex workers around the world.

Influence of Access to and Uptake of Biomedical HIV Prevention Tools on the Epidemiology of HIV

In response to growing calls for tailored combination HIV prevention among sex workers [1, 91], the epidemiology of HIV in sex work is also shaped by scale-up of traditional and emerging biomedical interventions such as HIV self-testing (HIVST), PrEP, sexual and reproductive health service integration with HIV, and vaginal and rectal microbicides. Though studies have documented promising feasibility and acceptability of many of these emerging biomedical interventions among sex workers, implementation challenges still exist, and further community engagement is needed to inform ethical and sustainable implementation and scale-up. Challenges described in the epidemiological literature include negative perceptions of PrEP and other tools at the community-, peer-, and individual-levels, clinical side effects, and experiences of violence and coercive testing that undermine acceptability, utilisation, and retention efforts [92–96].

HIV Self-Testing (HIVST)

Integration of voluntary access to HIVST within comprehensive HIV prevention services among sex workers can support the World Health Organization's (WHO) recommendation of frequent HIV testing for early HIV diagnosis and reduction in HIV acquisition [97]. In two HIVST randomised controlled trials implemented in Uganda [28] and Zambia [29], HIVST was considered acceptable among sex workers, achieved adequate HIV testing coverage, and was preferable to and substituted for facility-based HIV testing services [100].

As national and regional health programmes aim to reach 90% testing coverage of the 90-90-90 HIV care cascade targets (90% testing, 90% treatment, 90% viral suppression among people who live with HIV), HIVST may present an opportunity to address suboptimal HIV testing rates and the low proportion of sex workers who know their status. However, HIVST also comes with limitations and challenges.

Linkage to care among those testing positive in Zambia was lower in HIVST arms when compared to standard of care, illustrating that HIVST may not substantially improve gaps across the HIV care cascade, especially in contexts where HIV testing and linkage to care are already high [99].

A randomised controlled trial among ciswomen sex workers and men truck drivers in Kenya found that, while most participants who tested within the intervention arm chose the HIVST option, the cost to offering HIVST was double that of routine facility-based HIV testing, largely driven by the high price of test kits [101]. More efforts must be made to improve linkage to care following HIVST and reduce testing costs to improve the community-level effectiveness of HIVST among sex workers.

Pre-exposure Prophylaxis (PrEP)

Sex workers have shown high interest in oral PrEP [100] as a prevention strategy for HIV. PrEP has been shown to reduce HIV acquisition among heterosexual women by up to 79% in clinical trials, and up to 85% in those with detectable drug levels [102]. Furthermore, PrEP among sex workers in South Africa had an estimated service delivery cost of $136 per person-year, compared to $406 for early ART per person-year, demonstrating cost-effectiveness [103].

Clinical trial data, along with real-world implementation data collected among men who have sex with men [104, 105], have informed the WHO's guidelines to offer PrEP as part of a comprehensive HIV prevention package in HIV high-burden settings [106]. The success of PrEP as an HIV prevention tool depends on adherence. Modelling insights highlight that PrEP adherence by sex workers can achieve a level of effectiveness exceeding that of condoms, noting that PrEP will benefit reduction in HIV acquisition, even if condom use is reduced [107]. However, outside of status-disclosed, sero-discordant partnerships (where only one partner lives with HIV), sustained PrEP use by ciswomen sex workers and adult women overall has been limited, in both clinical trial and real-world settings [102, 108–111]. PrEP demonstration projects among sex workers, adolescent girls, and young women in South Africa [103, 112] and among the general population in Kenya [110], have shown that the proportion of PrEP maintenance is cut in half by 1-month after initiation and continues to decline during the first 6 months before stabilising [92, 112]. The Zimbabwe SAPPH-IRe study had an average PrEP retention period of 4 months among ciswomen sex workers enrolled [111], and obstacles to PrEP among sex workers have included provider- [103, 113], community- [114], and individual-level barriers [113–120]. Limited healthcare provider knowledge, communication, and support for PrEP for sex workers [113, 121]—as well as client-level concerns over side effects, PrEP-related stigma, awareness, and social pressure from partners and peers—have inhibited PrEP use [113, 115]. However, more research specific to sex workers is needed to identify and address limitations in the delivery of PrEP which prevent sex workers from continuing its sustained use. Modelling suggests that the uptake of HIV prevention products like PrEP could result in a decrease in the use of condoms in sex work due to a perceived reduction in the utility of condoms for HIV prevention though PrEP use alone does not prevent unintended pregnancy or STIs [119]. This reinforces the need for HIV prevention programming to be part of a health service package for sex workers which emphasises provision of STI screening and treatment services, reproductive health services offering contraception, and condom supply along with PrEP availability, to maintain their sexual and reproductive health.

Other Innovations

With growing recognition that pregnancy is common among ciswomen sex workers and the majority have at least one child [30–33], there is increasing awareness of the need to integrate sexual and reproductive health (SRH) services into sex workers' comprehensive HIV prevention service package [125, 126]. Yet access to a combined SRH service and HIV prevention innovation can be undermined by individual, social, and structural determinants, a dynamic exacerbated among sex workers in conflict-affected settings [127]. Generally, economic evidence on integrated HIV and SRH interventions among sex workers is limited, but, where available, integrated services are shown to be highly cost-effective [128].

For other innovative biomedical HIV prevention tools, such as oral PrEP and vaginal microbicides, the development of behaviourally congruent products can play a primary role in uptake and adherence [94, 129, 130]. Overall, the studies described demonstrate that improving comprehensive HIV prevention packages with innovative tools means integrating sexual and reproductive health services, multi-purpose prevention products, and awareness of structural determinants experienced by sex workers that affect engagement in care.

Research Gaps

Studies on the global HIV burden on sex workers and its determinants over the last decade have built a substantial body of evidence demonstrating the unmet health needs of sex workers. Much of these data have focused on cisgender women sex workers, with substantive gaps in data among transgender sex workers, as well cisgender men sex workers disaggregated from studies of men who have sex with men. Most assessments and interventions have focused on the horizontal transmission of HIV among sex workers' sexual networks and its impact on overall population prevalence. Very few have taken into account interrelated issues faced by sex workers as parents, including their reproductive health outcomes, and the healthcare access and health outcomes of children of sex workers [131]. More research on these topics is needed. Additionally, younger sex workers are also vulnerable to experiencing many of the same determinants and burdens of HIV/STIs as sex workers overall, but are largely understudied.

Studies have also discussed clients of sex workers as part of sexual transmission networks [34, 35], but there remains a dearth of data, particularly in sub-Saharan Africa, on the HIV/STI burden and determinants among sex work clients. Considering the role of clients in safe sex negotiations and experiences of violence, there is a need for more research, and particularly for the development of interventions tailored to reduce HIV/STI risks, violence, and onward transmission among clients [134–136].

There remains a need to better integrate HIV health services into more general health services for sex workers, including treatment and prevention services around obesity and diabetes, tuberculosis, other STIs, and sexual and reproductive health [126, 137, 138]. Key HIV comorbidities including tuberculosis, drug use, and chronic diseases require this approach, and research indicates that such integrated approaches may be most effective in reducing stigma and supporting the diverse array of health-related needs faced by sex workers.

Stigma, migration, criminalisation, violence, and associated policing practices remain major interrelated determinants of HIV, as well as barriers to engagement in the HIV prevention and care continuums among sex workers. Additional action must be taken through multilevel interventions that address structural determinants. While there have been interventions driven by community empowerment, further community-driven research on implementation strategies remains needed to improve, expand, and sustain programmes shown to have significant positive effects on health outcomes.

Conclusion

The global response to the HIV pandemic has come with many achievements. However, over the last decade, the global response has also increased inequities in the burden of HIV by largely limited investment in HIV prevention and treatment services specifically dedicated for sex workers of all genders and identities. In particular, evidence-based and rights-affirming programme and policy responses to the HIV prevention and treatment needs of sex workers remain limited. Though there has been more research detailing social and structural determinants of HIV among sex workers, there is a need for dedicated quantitative and qualitative studies disentangling the complex relationships between these factors, and translation of these findings into multilevel interventions for sex workers to improve HIV outcomes that move beyond the individual level alone.

Existing community mobilisation approaches to improve sex worker health and well-being are encouraging, and major multilateral donors can play a primary role in supporting civil society organisations in adapting and scaling up evidence-based, rights-affirming programming. However, criminalisation has reduced the ability of sex workers to consistently engage in health services and continues to limit the reach of sex work-specific programming. Policymakers must step up and respond to international and local community voices speaking of the harmful effects of criminalisation on sex workers and turn to a focus on their health and human rights. In the coming decades, the HIV burden among sex workers will continue to be tied to the larger HIV pandemic, and addressing the unmet needs of sex workers remains essential to the HIV pandemic response.

References

1. Shannon K, Crago AL, Baral SD, Bekker LG, Kerrigan D, Decker MR, et al. The global response and unmet actions for HIV and sex workers. Lancet (London, England). 2018;392(10148):698–710.
2. Coetzee J, Jewkes R, Gray GE. Cross-sectional study of female sex workers in Soweto, South Africa: factors associated with HIV infection. PLoS One. 2017;12(10):e0184775.
3. Napierala S, Chabata ST, Fearon E, Davey C, Hargreaves J, Busza J, et al. Engagement in HIV care among Young female sex Workers in Zimbabwe. J Acquir Immune Defic Syndr. 2018;79(3):358–66.
4. Vu L, Misra K. High burden of HIV, syphilis and HSV-2 and factors associated with HIV infection among female sex Workers in Tanzania: implications for early treatment of HIV and pre-exposure prophylaxis (PrEP). AIDS Behav. 2018;22(4):1113–21.
5. Doshi RH, Sande E, Ogwal M, Kiyingi H, McIntyre A, Kusiima J, et al. Progress toward UNAIDS 90-90-90 targets: a respondent-driven survey among female sex workers in Kampala. Uganda PloS one. 2018;13(9):e0201352.
6. Teclessou JN, Akakpo S, Gbetoglo D, Koumagnanou G, Singo A, Pitche P. HIV prevalence and behavioral studies among female sex workers in Togo in 2015. Bulletin de la Societe de pathologie exotique (1990). 2017;110(4):270–5.
7. Szwarcwald CL, Damacena GN, de Souza-Junior PRB, Guimaraes MDC, de Almeida WDS, de Souza Ferreira AP, et al. Factors associated with HIV infection among female sex workers in Brazil. Medicine. 2018;97(1S Suppl 1):S54–s61.
8. Szwarcwald CL, de Almeida WDS, Damacena GN, de Souza-Junior PRB, Ferreira-Junior ODC, Guimaraes MDC. Changes in attitudes, risky practices, and HIV and syphilis prevalence among female sex workers in Brazil from 2009 to 2016. Medicine. 2018;97(1S Suppl 1):S46–s53.
9. The Joint United Nations HIV and AIDS Programme. The gap report. Geneva: UNAIDS; 2014.
10. The Joint United Nations HIV and AIDS Programme. Miles to go: global AIDS update 2018. Geneva: The Joint United Nations HIV and AIDS Programme; 2018.
11. Nuttbrock L. Transgender sex work and society: Columbia University Press; 2018.
12. Poteat T, Scheim A, Xavier J, Reisner S, Baral S. Global epidemiology of HIV infection and related syndemics affecting transgender people. J Acquir Immune Defic Syndr. 2016;72(Suppl 3):S210–9.
13. Reisner SL, Poteat T, Keatley J, Cabral M, Mothopeng T, Dunham E, et al. Global health burden and needs of transgender populations: a review. Lancet (London, England). 2016;388(10042):412–36.
14. Scheim AWL, Marshall Z, Jeffries D, Baral S. The prevalence of HIV among transwomen sex workers: a review of current literature. In: Nuttbrock L, editor. Transgender sex work and society, vol. 1. New York: Harrington Park Press, LLC; 2018. p. 118.
15. Costa AB, Fontanari AMV, Jacinto MM, da Silva DC, Lorencetti EK, da Rosa Filho HT, et al. Population-based HIV prevalence and associated factors in male-to-female transsexuals from Southern Brazil. Arch Sex Behav. 2015;44(2):521–4.

16. Baral SD, Friedman MR, Geibel S, Rebe K, Bozhinov B, Diouf D, et al. Male sex workers: practices, contexts, and vulnerabilities for HIV acquisition and transmission. Lancet (London, England). 2015;385(9964):260–73.

17. Dong W, Zhou C, Jia MH, Zhou YJ, Chen X, Kang J, et al. HIV and syphilis infection and related medical treatment status of low-fee female sex workers in three provinces of China, 2012–2015. Zhonghua yu fang yi xue za zhi [Chinese journal of preventive medicine]. 2018;52(12):1239–42.

18. Lai J, Qin C, Nehl EJ, Jiang J, Huang Y, Liang B, et al. HIV prevalence among female sex workers in Guigang City, Guangxi, China: an 8-year consecutive cross-sectional study. BMC Public Health. 2018;18(1):450.

19. Zhu J, Yuan R, Hu D, Zhu Z, Wang N, Wang B. HIV prevalence and correlated factors of female sex workers and male clients in a border region of Yunnan Province, China. Int J STD AIDS. 2018;29(5):424–34.

20. Seekaew P, Pengnonyang S, Jantarapakde J, Sungsing T, Rodbumrung P, Trachunthong D, et al. Characteristics and HIV epidemiologic profiles of men who have sex with men and transgender women in key population-led test and treat cohorts in Thailand. PLoS One. 2018;13(8)

21. Goldsamt LA, Clatts MC, Giang LM, Le BQ, Colby DJ, Yu G. HIV and other STIs in male sex workers: findings from a sexual health promotion intervention in Vietnam. Int J STD AIDS. 2018;29(6):540–6.

22. Dumchev K, Sazonova Y, Salyuk T, Varetska O. Trends in HIV prevalence among people injecting drugs, men having sex with men, and female sex workers in Ukraine. Int J STD AIDS. 2018;29(13):1337–44.

23. Kouyoumjian SP, El Rhilani H, Latifi A, El Kettani A, Chemaitelly H, Alami K, et al. Mapping of new HIV infections in Morocco and impact of select interventions. Int J Infect Dis. 2018;68:4–12.

24. Becker ML, Bhattacharjee P, Blanchard JF, Cheuk E, Isac S, Musyoki HK, et al. Vulnerabilities at first sex and their association with lifetime gender-based violence and HIV prevalence among adolescent girls and young women engaged in sex work, transactional sex, and casual sex in Kenya. J Acquir Immune Defic Syndr. 2018;79(3):296–304.

25. Awofala AA, Ogundele OE. HIV epidemiology in Nigeria. Saudi journal of biological sciences. 2018;25(4):697–703.

26. Herce ME, Miller WM, Bula A, Edwards JK, Sapalalo P, Lancaster KE, et al. Achieving the first 90 for key populations in sub-Saharan Africa through venue-based outreach: challenges and opportunities for HIV prevention based on PLACE study findings from Malawi and Angola. J Int AIDS Soc. 2018;21:e25132.

27. Diabaté S, Chamberland A, Geraldo N, Tremblay C, Gonorrhea AM. Chlamydia and HIV incidence among female sex workers in Cotonou, Benin: a longitudinal study. PLoS One. 2018;13(5)

28. da Costa Ferreira-Júnior O, MDC G, Damacena GN, de Almeida WS, de Souza-Júnior PRB, Szwarcwald CL. Prevalence estimates of HIV, syphilis, hepatitis B and C among female sex workers (FSW) in Brazil, 2016. Medicine. 2018;97(1 Suppl)

29. Degtyar A, George PE, Mallma P, Diaz DA, Cárcamo C, García PJ, et al. Sexual risk, behavior, and HIV testing and status among male and transgender women sex workers and their clients in Lima, Peru. Int J Sex Health. 2018;30(1):81–91.

30. Fernàndez-López L, Reyes-Urueña J, Agustí C, Kustec T, Serdt M, Klavs I, et al. The COBATEST network: monitoring and evaluation of HIV community-based practices in Europe, 2014–2016. HIV Med. 2018;19:21–6.

31. Gama A, Martins MRO, Mendão L, Barros H, Dias S. HIV infection, risk factors and health services use among male-to-female transgender sex workers: a cross-sectional study in Portugal. AIDS Care. 2018;30(1):1–8.

32. Risher K, Mayer KH, Beyrer C. HIV treatment cascade in MSM, people who inject drugs, and sex workers. Curr Opin HIV AIDS. 2015;10(6):420–9.

33. Hakim AJ, MacDonald V, Hladik W, Zhao J, Burnett J, Sabin K, et al. Gaps and opportunities: measuring the key population cascade through surveys and services to guide the HIV response. J Int AIDS Soc. 2018;21(Suppl 5):e25119.
34. Mountain E, Mishra S, Vickerman P, Pickles M, Gilks C, Boily MC. Antiretroviral therapy uptake, attrition, adherence and outcomes among HIV-infected female sex workers: a systematic review and meta-analysis. PLoS One. 2014;9(9):e105645.
35. Braunstein SL, Umulisa MM, Veldhuijzen NJ, Kestelyn E, Ingabire CM, Nyinawabega J, et al. HIV diagnosis, linkage to HIV care, and HIV risk behaviors among newly diagnosed HIV-positive female sex workers in Kigali, Rwanda. J Acquir Immune Defic Syndr. 2011;57(4):e70–6.
36. Schwartz S, Lambert A, Phaswana-Mafuya N, Kose Z, McIngana M, Holland C, et al. Engagement in the HIV care cascade and barriers to antiretroviral therapy uptake among female sex workers in Port Elizabeth, South Africa: findings from a respondent-driven sampling study. Sex Transm Infect. 2017;93(4):290–6.
37. Schwartz SR, Papworth E, Ky-Zerbo O, Anato S, Grosso A, Ouedraogo HG, et al. Safer conception needs for HIV prevention among female sex workers in Burkina Faso and Togo. Infect Dis Obstet Gynecol. 2014;2014:296245.
38. Lafort Y, Greener R, Roy A, Greener L, Ombidi W, Lessitala F, et al. HIV prevention and care-seeking behaviour among female sex workers in four cities in India, Kenya. Mozambique and South Africa Tropical medicine & international health : TM & IH. 2016;21(10):1293–303.
39. Lancaster KE, Lungu T, Mmodzi P, Hosseinipour MC, Chadwick K, Powers KA, et al. The association between substance use and sub-optimal HIV treatment engagement among HIV-infected female sex workers in Lilongwe, Malawi. AIDS Care. 2017;29(2):197–203.
40. Zulliger R, Barrington C, Donastorg Y, Perez M, Kerrigan D. High drop-off along the HIV care continuum and ART interruption among female sex workers in the Dominican Republic. J Acquir Immune Defic Syndr. 2015;69(2):216–22.
41. Januraga PP, Reekie J, Mulyani T, Lestari BW, Iskandar S, Wisaksana R, et al. The cascade of HIV care among key populations in Indonesia: a prospective cohort study. The lancet HIV. 2018;5(10):e560–e8.
42. Muth S, Len A, Evans JL, Phou M, Chhit S, Neak Y, et al. HIV treatment cascade among female entertainment and sex workers in Cambodia: impact of amphetamine use and an HIV prevention program. Addict Sci Clin Pract. 2017;12(1):20.
43. Goldenberg SM, Muzaaya G, Akello M, Braschel M, Birungi J, Shannon K. High burden of previously undiagnosed HIV infections and gaps in HIV care cascade for conflict-affected female sex workers in northern Uganda. Int J STD AIDS. 2019;30(3):275–83.
44. Hakim AJ, Johnston LG, Dittrich S, Prybylski D, Burnett J, Kim E. Defining and surveying key populations at risk of HIV infection: towards a unified approach to eligibility criteria for respondent-driven sampling HIV biobehavioral surveys. Int J STD AIDS. 2018;29(9):895–903.
45. Lancaster KE, Cernigliaro D, Zulliger R, Fleming PF. HIV care and treatment experiences among female sex workers living with HIV in sub-Saharan Africa: a systematic review. African journal of AIDS research : AJAR. 2016;15(4):377–86.
46. Nyblade L, Reddy A, Mbote D, Kraemer J, Stockton M, Kemunto C, et al. The relationship between health worker stigma and uptake of HIV counseling and testing and utilization of non-HIV health services: the experience of male and female sex workers in Kenya. AIDS Care. 2017;29(11):1364–72.
47. Carrasco MA, Nguyen TQ, Barrington C, Perez M, Donastorg Y, Kerrigan D. HIV stigma mediates the association between social cohesion and consistent condom use among female sex workers living with HIV in the Dominican Republic. Arch Sex Behav. 2018;47(5):1529–39.
48. Hargreaves JR, Busza J, Mushati P, Fearon E, Cowan FM. Overlapping HIV and sex-work stigma among female sex workers recruited to 14 respondent-driven sampling surveys across Zimbabwe, 2013. AIDS Care. 2017;29(6):675–85.

49. Miller WM, Miller WC, Barrington C, Weir SS, Chen SY, Emch ME, et al. Sex work, discrimination, drug use and violence: a pattern for HIV risk among transgender sex workers compared to MSM sex workers and other MSM in Guatemala. Glob Public Health. 2019:1–13.

50. Lyons CE, Ketende S, Diouf D, Drame FM, Liestman B, Coly K, et al. Potential impact of integrated stigma mitigation interventions in improving HIV/AIDS service delivery and uptake for key populations in Senegal. J Acquir Immune Defic Syndr. 2017;74(Suppl 1):S52–s9.

51. Tandon t A-CG, Grover A. Sex work and trafficking: can human rights lead us out of the impasse? ; 2014.

52. Platt L, Grenfell P, Meiksin R, Elmes J, Sherman SG, Sanders T, et al. Associations between sex work laws and sex workers' health: a systematic review and meta-analysis of quantitative and qualitative studies. PLoS Med. 2018;15(12):e1002680.

53. Amnesty International. Policy on state oblication to respect, uphold and fulfil the human rights of sex workers. May. 2016;26

54. Krusi A, Kerr T, Taylor C, Rhodes T, Shannon K. They won't change it back in their heads that we're trash': the intersection of sex work-related stigma and evolving policing strategies. Sociol Health Illn. 2016;38(7):1137–50.

55. Shannon K, Strathdee SA, Goldenberg SM, Duff P, Mwangi P, Rusakova M, et al. Global epidemiology of HIV among female sex workers: influence of structural determinants. Lancet (London, England). 2015;385(9962):55–71.

56. Reeves A, Steele S, Stuckler D, McKee M, Amato-Gauci A, Semenza JC. Gender violence, poverty and HIV infection risk among persons engaged in the sex industry: cross-national analysis of the political economy of sex markets in 30 European and Central Asian countries. HIV Med. 2017;18(10):748–55.

57. Lyons CE, Schwartz SR, Murray SM, Shannon K, Diouf D, Mothopeng T, et al. The role of sex work laws and stigmas in increasing HIV risks among sex workers. Nat Commun 2020;11(1):1–10.

58. Krusi A, Pacey K, Bird L, Taylor C, Chettiar J, Allan S, et al. Criminalisation of clients: reproducing vulnerabilities for violence and poor health among street-based sex workers in Canada-a qualitative study. BMJ Open. 2014;4(6):e005191.

59. Decker MR, Lyons C, Billong SC, Njindam IM, Grosso A, Nunez GT, et al. Gender-based violence against female sex workers in Cameroon: prevalence and associations with sexual HIV risk and access to health services and justice. Sex Transm Infect. 2016;92(8):599–604.

60. Roberts ST, Flaherty BP, Deya R, Masese L, Ngina J, McClelland RS, et al. Patterns of gender-based violence and associations with mental health and HIV risk behavior among female sex workers in Mombasa, Kenya: a latent class analysis. AIDS Behav. 2018;22(10):3273–86.

61. Wirtz AL, Schwartz S, Ketende S, Anato S, Nadedjo FD, Ouedraogo HG, et al. Sexual violence, condom negotiation, and condom use in the context of sex work: results from two West African countries. J Acquir Immune Defic Syndr. 2015;68(Suppl 2):S171–9.

62. Footer KHA, Silberzahn BE, Tormohlen KN, Sherman SG. Policing practices as a structural determinant for HIV among sex workers: a systematic review of empirical findings. J Int AIDS Soc. 2016;19:20883.

63. Abel GF, Lisa, Brunton C. The impact of prostitution reform act on health and safety practices of sex workers. Christchurch, New Zealand: University of Otago; 2007.

64. Harcourt C, O'Connor J, Egger S, Fairley CK, Wand H, Chen MY, et al. The decriminalization of prostitution is associated with better coverage of health promotion programs for sex workers. Aust N Z J Public Health. 2010;34(5):482–6.

65. Ito S, Lepine A, Treibich C. The effect of sex work regulation on health and well-being of sex workers: evidence from Senegal. Health Econ. 2018;27(11):1627–52.

66. Duff P, Birungi J, Dobrer S, Akello M, Muzaaya G, Shannon K. Social and structural factors increase inconsistent condom use by sex workers' one-time and regular clients in Northern Uganda. AIDS Care. 2018;30(6):751–9.

67. Lasater ME, Grosso A, Ketende S, Lyons C, Pitche VP, Tchalla J, et al. Characterising the relationship between migration and stigma affecting healthcare engagement among female sex workers in Lome. Togo Global public health. 2019:1–14.
68. International Committee on the Rights of Sex Workers in Europe. Surveilled. Exploited. Deported. Rights Violations Against Migrant Sex Workers in Europe and Central Asia. November 2016:2016.
69. Platt L, Grenfell P, Fletcher A, Sorhaindo A, Jolley E, Rhodes T, et al. Systematic review examining differences in HIV, sexually transmitted infections and health-related harms between migrant and non-migrant female sex workers. Sex Transm Infect. 2013;89(4):311–9.
70. Goldenberg SM, Chettiar J, Nguyen P, Dobrer S, Montaner J, Shannon K. Complexities of short-term mobility for sex work and migration among sex workers: violence and sexual risks, barriers to care, and enhanced social and economic opportunities. J Urban Health. 2014;91(4):736–51.
71. Davey C, Dirawo J, Hargreaves JR, Cowan FM. Exploring the association between mobility and access to HIV services among female sex workers in Zimbabwe. AIDS Behav. 2020;24(3):746–61.
72. Global Network of Sex Work P. Sex work and the law: understanding legal frameworks and the struggle for sex work law reforms. 2014.
73. Wirtz AL, Peryshkina A, Mogilniy V, Beyrer C, Decker MR. Current and recent drug use intensifies sexual and structural HIV risk outcomes among female sex workers in the Russian Federation. Int J Drug Policy. 2015;26(8):755–63.
74. Dunne EM, Dyer TP, Khan MR, Cavanaugh CE, Melnikov A, Latimer WW. HIV prevalence and risk behaviors among African American women who trade sex for drugs versus economic resources. AIDS Behav. 2014;18(7):1288–92.
75. Le LV, Nguyen TA, Tran HV, Gupta N, Duong TC, Tran HT, et al. Correlates of HIV infection among female sex workers in Vietnam: injection drug use remains a key risk factor. Drug Alcohol Depend. 2015;150:46–53.
76. Bozinoff N, Luo L, Dong H, Krusi A, DeBeck K. Street-involved youth engaged in sex work at increased risk of syringe sharing. AIDS Care. 2019;31(1):69–76.
77. Nemoto T, Iwamoto M, Perngparn U, Areesantichai C, Kamitani E, Sakata M. HIV-related risk behaviors among kathoey (male-to-female transgender) sex workers in Bangkok, Thailand. AIDS Care. 2012;24(2):210–9.
78. Nuttbrock L. Sex work, high-risk sexual behavior, and incident HIV/STI among transwomen in New York City: a study of mediating factors. In: Nuttbrock L, editor. Transgender sex work and society. 1. New York: Harrington Park Press, LLC; 2018. p. 164–85.
79. Kerrigan D, Kennedy CE, Morgan-Thomas R, Reza-Paul S, Mwangi P, Win KT, et al. A community empowerment approach to the HIV response among sex workers: effectiveness, challenges, and considerations for implementation and scale-up. Lancet (London, England). 2015;385(9963):172–85.
80. World Health Organization. Implementing comprehensive HIV/STI programmes with sex workers: practical approaches from collaborative interventions. Geneva: World Health Organization.; 2013 October; 2013.
81. Beattie TS, Mohan HL, Bhattacharjee P, Chandrashekar S, Isac S, Wheeler T, et al. Community mobilization and empowerment of female sex workers in Karnataka State, South India: associations with HIV and sexually transmitted infection risk. Am J Public Health. 2014;104(8):1516–25.
82. Blanchard AK, Mohan HL, Shahmanesh M, Prakash R, Isac S, Ramesh BM, et al. Community mobilization, empowerment and HIV prevention among female sex workers in South India. BMC Public Health. 2013;13:234.
83. Ghose T, Swendeman D, George S, Chowdhury D. Mobilizing collective identity to reduce HIV risk among sex workers in Sonagachi, India: the boundaries, consciousness, negotiation framework. Soc Sci Med. 2008;67(2):311–20.

84. Cornish F, Campbell C. The social conditions for successful peer education: a comparison of two HIV prevention programs run by sex workers in India and South Africa. Am J Community Psychol. 2009;44(1–2):123–35.

85. Alary M, Banandur P, Rajaram SP, Thamattoor UK, Mainkar MK, Paranjape R, et al. Increased HIV prevention program coverage and decline in HIV prevalence among female sex workers in South India. Sex Transm Dis. 2014;41(6):380–7.

86. Avahan India AI. Avahan common minimum program for HIV prevention in India. Bill & Melinda Gates Foundation: New Delhi; 2010.

87. Kerrigan D, Barrington C, Donastorg Y, Perez M, Galai N. Abriendo Puertas: feasibility and effectiveness a multi-level intervention to improve HIV outcomes among female sex workers living with HIV in the Dominican Republic. AIDS Behav. 2016;20(9):1919–27.

88. Carrasco MA, Barrington C, Perez M, Donastorg Y, Kerrigan D. Social cohesion, condom use, and sexually transmitted infections among female sex workers living with HIV in the Dominican Republic. Int J STD AIDS. 2019;30(1):64–71.

89. Lippman SA, Chinaglia M, Donini AA, Diaz J, Reingold A, Kerrigan DL. Findings from Encontros: a multilevel STI/HIV intervention to increase condom use, reduce STI, and change the social environment among sex workers in Brazil. Sex Transm Dis. 2012;39(3):209–16.

90. Wirtz AL, Pretorius C, Beyrer C, Baral S, Decker MR, Sherman SG, et al. Epidemic impacts of a community empowerment intervention for HIV prevention among female sex workers in generalized and concentrated epidemics. PLoS One. 2014;9(2):e88047.

91. Bekker LG, Johnson L, Cowan F, Overs C, Besada D, Hillier S, et al. Combination HIV prevention for female sex workers: what is the evidence? Lancet (London, England). 2015;385(9962):72–87.

92. Eakle R, Gomez GB, Naicker N, Bothma R, Mbogua J, Cabrera Escobar MA, et al. HIV pre-exposure prophylaxis and early antiretroviral treatment among female sex workers in South Africa: results from a prospective observational demonstration project. PLoS Med. 2017;14(11):e1002444.

93. Restar AJ, Tocco JU, Mantell JE, Lafort Y, Gichangi P, Masvawure TB, et al. Perspectives on HIV pre- and post-exposure prophylaxes (PrEP and PEP) among female and male sex Workers in Mombasa, Kenya: implications for integrating biomedical prevention into sexual health services. AIDS education and prevention : official publication of the International Society for AIDS Education. 2017;29(2):141–53.

94. Peitzmeier SM, Tomko C, Wingo E, Sawyer A, Sherman SG, Glass N, et al. Acceptability of microbicidal vaginal rings and oral pre-exposure prophylaxis for HIV prevention among female sex workers in a high-prevalence US city. AIDS Care. 2017;29(11):1453–7.

95. Cowan FM, Delany-Moretlwe S, Sanders EJ, Mugo NR, Guedou FA, Alary M, et al. PrEP implementation research in Africa: what is new? J Int AIDS Soc. 2016;19(7(Suppl 6)):21101.

96. Giguere R, Frasca T, Dolezal C, Febo I, Cranston RD, Mayer K, et al. Acceptability of three novel HIV prevention methods among young male and transgender female sex Workers in Puerto Rico. AIDS Behav. 2016;20(10):2192–202.

97. Organization WH. Consolidated guidelines on HIV testing services; 5Cs: consent, confidentiality, counseling, correct results and connection. Geneva, Switzerland; 2015.

98. Ortblad K, Kibuuka Musoke D, Ngabirano T, Nakitende A, Magoola J, Kayiira P, et al. Direct provision versus facility collection of HIV self-tests among female sex workers in Uganda: a cluster-randomized controlled health systems trial. PLoS Med. 2017;14(11):e1002458.

99. Chanda MM, Ortblad KF, Mwale M, Chongo S, Kanchele C, Kamungoma N, et al. HIV self-testing among female sex workers in Zambia: a cluster randomized controlled trial. PLoS Med. 2017;14(11):e1002442.

100. Ortblad KF, Chanda MM, Musoke DK, Ngabirano T, Mwale M, Nakitende A, et al. Acceptability of HIV self-testing to support pre-exposure prophylaxis among female sex workers in Uganda and Zambia: results from two randomized controlled trials. BMC Infect Dis. 2018;18(1):503.

101. George G, Chetty T, Strauss M, Inoti S, Kinyanjui S, Mwai E, et al. Costing analysis of an SMS-based intervention to promote HIV self-testing amongst truckers and sex workers in Kenya. PLoS One. 2018;13(7):e0197305.
102. Thomson KA, Baeten JM, Mugo NR, Bekker LG, Celum CL, Heffron R. Tenofovir-based oral preexposure prophylaxis prevents HIV infection among women. Curr Opin HIV AIDS. 2016;11(1):18–26.
103. Eakle R, Gomez G, Naicker N, Bothma R, Mbogua J. Escobar M.A.C, et al., editors. PrEP and early ART for female sex workers in South Africa: the TAPS project. Conference on retroviruses and opportunistic infections; 2018; Boston. Massachusetts.
104. McCormack S, Dunn DT, Desai M, Dolling DI, Gafos M, Gilson R, et al. Pre-exposure prophylaxis to prevent the acquisition of HIV-1 infection (PROUD): effectiveness results from the pilot phase of a pragmatic open-label randomised trial. Lancet (London, England). 2016;387(10013):53–60.
105. Grinsztejn B, Hoagland B, Moreira RI, Kallas EG, Madruga JV, Goulart S, et al. Retention, engagement, and adherence to pre-exposure prophylaxis for men who have sex with men and transgender women in PrEP Brasil: 48 week results of a demonstration study. The lancet HIV. 2018;5(3):e136–e45.
106. WHO. Guideline on when to start antiretroviral therapy and on pre-exposure prophylaxis for HIV: World Health Organization; 2015.
107. Grant H, Mukandavire Z, Eakle R, Prudden H, Gomez Gabriela B, Rees H, et al. When are declines in condom use while using PrEP a concern? Modelling insights from a Hillbrow, South Africa case study. J Int AIDS Soc. 2017;20(1):21744.
108. Mboup A, Béhanzin L, Guédou FA, Geraldo N, Goma-Matsétsé E, Giguère K, et al. Early antiretroviral therapy and daily pre-exposure prophylaxis for HIV prevention among female sex workers in Cotonou, Benin: a prospective observational demonstration study. J Int AIDS Soc. 2018;21(11):e25208.
109. Fonner VA, Dalglish SL, Kennedy CE, Baggaley R, O'Reilly KR, Koechlin FM, et al. Effectiveness and safety of oral HIV preexposure prophylaxis for all populations. AIDS (London, England). 2016;30(12):1973–83.
110. Daniel Were, E. I, editors. PrEP scale up in Kenya: bridge to scale project. International AIDS Society Conference on HIV science; 2017. July 25, 2017; Paris, France.
111. Cowan FM, Davey CB, Fearon E, Mushati P, Dirawo J, Cambiano V, et al. The HIV care Cascade among female sex Workers in Zimbabwe: results of a population-based survey from the sisters antiretroviral therapy Programme for prevention of HIV, an integrated response (SAPPH-IRe) trial. J Acquir Immune Defic Syndr. 2017;74(4):375–82.
112. Gill KPT, Dietrich J, Gray G, Bennie T, Kayamba F, Myer L, Johnson L, Slack C, Strode A, Spiegel H, Elharrar V, Hosek S, Rooney J, Bekker L. A demonstration open label study to assess the acceptability, safety and use of Truvada pre-exposure prophylaxis in healthy, HIVUninfected adolescents, 15-19 years of age. 9th International AIDS Conference. 2017; Paris, France
113. Goparaju L, Praschan NC, Warren-Jeanpiere L, Experton LS, Young MA, Kassaye S. Stigma, partners, providers and costs: potential barriers to PrEP uptake among US women. Journal of AIDS & clinical research. 2017;8(9)
114. Mack N, Odhiambo J, Wong CM, Agot K. Barriers and facilitators to pre-exposure prophylaxis (PrEP) eligibility screening and ongoing HIV testing among target populations in Bondo and Rarieda. Kenya: results of a consultation with community stakeholders BMC health services research. 2014;14:231.
115. Goparaju L, Experton LS, Praschan NC, Warren-Jeanpiere L, Young MA, Kassaye S. Women want pre-exposure prophylaxis but are advised against it by their HIV-positive counterparts. Journal of AIDS & clinical research. 2015;6(11):1–10.
116. Eakle R, Bourne A, Jarrett C, Stadler J, Larson H. Motivations and barriers to uptake and use of female-initiated, biomedical HIV prevention products in sub-Saharan Africa: an adapted meta-ethnography. BMC Public Health. 2017;17(1):968.

117. Hartmann M, McConnell M, Bekker LG, Celum C, Bennie T, Zuma J, et al. Motivated reasoning and HIV risk? Views on relationships, trust, and risk from young women in Cape Town, South Africa, and implications for Oral PrEP. AIDS Behav. 2018;22(11):3468–79.

118. van der Straten A, Stadler J, Montgomery E, Hartmann M, Magazi B, Mathebula F, et al. Women's experiences with oral and vaginal pre-exposure prophylaxis: the VOICE-C qualitative study in Johannesburg, South Africa. PLoS One. 2014;9(2):e89118.

119. Quaife M, Vickerman P, Manian S, Eakle R, Cabrera-Escobar MA, Delany-Moretlwe S, et al. The effect of HIV prevention products on incentives to supply condomless commercial sex among female sex workers in South Africa. Health Econ. 2018;27(10):1550–66.

120. Deutsch MB, Glidden DV, Sevelius J, Keatley J, McMahan V, Guanira J, et al. HIV pre-exposure prophylaxis in transgender women: a subgroup analysis of the iPrEx trial. The lancet HIV. 2015;2(12):e512–e9.

121. Kambutse I, Igiraneza G, Ogbuagu O. Perceptions of HIV transmission and pre-exposure prophylaxis among health care workers and community members in Rwanda. PLoS One. 2018;13(11):e0207650.

122. Scorgie F, Chersich MF, Ntaganira I, Gerbase A, Lule F, Lo YR. Socio-demographic characteristics and behavioral risk factors of female sex workers in sub-saharan Africa: a systematic review. AIDS Behav. 2012;16(4):920–33.

123. Beckham SW, Shembilu CR, Brahmbhatt H, Winch PJ, Beyrer C, Kerrigan DL. Female sex workers' experiences with intended pregnancy and antenatal care services in southern Tanzania. Stud Fam Plan. 2015;46(1):55–71.

124. Papworth E, Schwartz S, Ky-Zerbo O, Leistman B, Ouedraogo G, Samadoulougou C, et al. Mothers who sell sex: a potential paradigm for integrated HIV, sexual, and reproductive health interventions among women at high risk of HIV in Burkina Faso. J Acquir Immune Defic Syndr. 2015;68(Suppl 2):S154–61.

125. Duff P, Evans JL, Stein ES, Page K, Maher L. High pregnancy incidence and low contraceptive use among a prospective cohort of female entertainment and sex workers in Phnom Penh, Cambodia. BMC Pregnancy Childbirth. 2018;18(1):128.

126. Lafort Y, Greener L, Lessitala F, Chabeda S, Greener R, Beksinska M, et al. Effect of a 'diagonal' intervention on uptake of HIV and reproductive health services by female sex workers in three sub-Saharan African cities. Tropical medicine & international health : TM & IH. 2018;23(7):774–84.

127. Ferguson A, Shannon K, Butler J, Goldenberg SM. A comprehensive review of HIV/STI prevention and sexual and reproductive health services among sex Workers in Conflict-Affected Settings: call for an evidence- and rights-based approach in the humanitarian response. Confl Heal. 2017;11:25.

128. Rinaldi G, Kiadaliri AA, Haghparast-Bidgoli H. Cost effectiveness of HIV and sexual reproductive health interventions targeting sex workers: a systematic review. Cost effectiveness and resource allocation : C/E. 2018;16:63.

129. Pines HA, Strathdee SA, Hendrix CW, Bristow CC, Harvey-Vera A, Magis-Rodriguez C, et al. Oral and vaginal HIV pre-exposure prophylaxis product attribute preferences among female sex workers in the Mexico-US border region. Int J STD AIDS. 2019;30(1):45–55.

130. Pines HA, Semple SJ, Strathdee SA, Hendrix CW, Harvey-Vera A, Gorbach PM, et al. Vaginal washing and lubrication among female sex workers in the Mexico-US border region: implications for the development of vaginal PrEP for HIV prevention. BMC Public Health. 2018;18(1):1009.

131. Schwartz SR, Papworth E, Ky-Zerbo O, Sithole B, Anato S, Grosso A, et al. Reproductive health needs of female sex workers and opportunities for enhanced prevention of mother-to-child transmission efforts in sub-Saharan Africa. J Fam Plann Reprod Health Care. 2017;43(1):50–9.

132. Papworth E, Ceesay N, An L, Thiam-Niangoin M, Ky-Zerbo O, Holland C, et al. Epidemiology of HIV among female sex workers, their clients, men who have sex with men and people who inject drugs in west and Central Africa. J Int AIDS Soc. 2013;16(Suppl 3):18751.

133. Subramanian T, Gupte MD, Paranjape RS, Brahmam GN, Ramakrishnan L, Adhikary R, et al. HIV, sexually transmitted infections and sexual behaviour of male clients of female sex workers in Andhra Pradesh, Tamil Nadu and Maharashtra, India: results of a cross-sectional survey. AIDS (London, England). 2008;22(Suppl 5):S69–79.
134. Kohli A, Kerrigan D, Brahmbhatt H, Likindikoki S, Beckham J, Mwampashi A, et al. Social and structural factors related to HIV risk among truck drivers passing through the Iringa region of Tanzania. AIDS Care. 2017;29(8):957–60.
135. Matovu JK, Ssebadduka NB. Knowledge, attitudes & barriers to condom use among female sex workers and truck drivers in Uganda: a mixed-methods study. Afr Health Sci. 2013;13(4):1027–33.
136. Pitpitan EV, Chavarin CV, Semple SJ, Magis-Rodriguez C, Strathdee SA, Patterson TL. Hombre Seguro (Safe Men): a sexual risk reduction intervention for male clients of female sex workers. BMC Public Health. 2014;14:475.
137. Steiner RJ, Aquino G, Fenton KA. Enhancing HIV/AIDS, viral hepatitis, sexually transmitted disease, and tuberculosis prevention in the United States through program collaboration and service integration: the case for broader implementation. Sex Transm Dis. 2013;40(8):663–8.
138. Haldane V, Legido-Quigley H, Chuah FLH, Sigfrid L, Murphy G, Ong SE, et al. Integrating cardiovascular diseases, hypertension, and diabetes with HIV services: a systematic review. AIDS Care. 2018;30(1):103–15.

Chapter 3
Global Burden of Violence and Other Human Rights Violations Against Sex Workers

Elena Argento, Kay Thi Win, Bronwyn McBride, and Kate Shannon

Introduction

Every person possesses the right to freedom from torture, inhumane treatment, and the right to recognition before the law. These rights are not invalidated if a person sells sex or is suspected of a crime. However, globally, sex workers continue to experience disproportionate rates of violence and other human rights violations. A systematic review in 2014 identified a staggeringly high lifetime prevalence of physical, sexual, or combined workplace violence against women sex workers—from 45% to 75% [1]. Although these violations of sex workers' rights remain largely overlooked within international agendas on violence prevention, over the last decade, sex workers and advocates have upheld the human rights framework to document them [2–4]. As a result, increasingly, the unacceptable violence faced by sex workers is being addressed in international guidelines [5–7].

The intersection of macro-structural factors (e.g. laws/policies, stigma, poverty, racism, transphobia/homophobia, cultural norms) and community-level factors (e.g. policing, working conditions, access to health, and peer-led services) influences the risks of experiencing violence among sex workers and their access to recourse on a global level [8–11]. A recent systematic review identified major structural factors—the criminalisation of sex work and resulting punitive policing, work environments, and gender and economic inequities—as shaping the vulnerability of sex workers [1]. Criminalisation is a key determinant of sex workers' access to safer indoor work

E. Argento · B. McBride · K. Shannon (✉)
Centre for Gender & Sexual Health Equity, Vancouver, BC, Canada

University of British Columbia, Vancouver, BC, Canada
e-mail: elena.argento@bccsu.ubc.ca; bronwyn.mcbride@cgshe.ubc.ca; Dr.Shannon@cgshe.ubc.ca

K. T. Win
Asia-Pacific Network of Sex Workers (APNSW), Bangkok, Thailand
e-mail: kaythi@apnsw.info

© The Author(s) 2021
S. M. Goldenberg et al. (eds.), *Sex Work, Health, and Human Rights*,
https://doi.org/10.1007/978-3-030-64171-9_3

environments, supportive third parties, and labour and police protections [1]. Criminalisation also contributes to the devaluing of sex workers' social status, which increases their vulnerability to violent perpetrators. Sex workers often hesitate to report incidents to police, due to deep-rooted mistrust and fear of criminal charges, stigma, or further abuse [12–16]. This inability to access justice enables perpetrators to abuse sex workers with impunity, perpetuating high levels of violence [16–20].

Guided by a structural determinants framework [8], this chapter provides an overview of the socio-structural factors shaping violence against sex workers. We summarise findings from academic research, and feature examples of sex workers' lived experiences as well as case studies from Asia-Pacific Network of Sex Workers (APNSW), a sex worker initiated and led organisation representing sex worker organisations in Asia and the Pacific. In recognising the right to live and work free from violence as a human right, we aim to provide an evidence base to inform the development of policy and public health interventions to promote safety for sex workers worldwide.

Interpersonal Violence from Clients and Intimate/Non-paying Partners

Globally, sex workers of all genders experience elevated rates of violence. Among women sex workers working mostly in street-based settings, an estimated 32–55% experienced workplace violence by any perpetrator in the last year [9].

Violence experienced by sex workers varies substantially in nature and degree, depending on their working environment (e.g. managerial and policy features of venues) and community-level factors (e.g. empowerment) [9]. In many settings, sex workers experience physical and sexual violence perpetrated by clients and by predators posing as clients, often during negotiation around the use of condoms. This is a violation of sex workers' labour rights and increases their risk of exposure to HIV and sexually transmitted infections (STIs) [21–28]. Sex workers also suffer violence from intimate partners, including threats of exposure to police as a form of domination and control [29, 30]. Global estimates of combined physical and sexual violence by intimate partners over lifetime range from 4% to 73% [9], and the homicide rate among sex workers in the USA is approximately 17 times the rate of the general population [29]. In Canada's worst serial murder case, 67 women—most of whom were sex workers, and many of whom were Indigenous—were murdered or went missing from Vancouver between 1997 and 2002. This case received widespread scrutiny regarding inaction on the part of police and the judicial system, reflecting pervasive stigma and the devaluing of marginalised women involved in sex work [12].

The following community case study conducted by APNSW describes how violence from various perpetrators has become normalised a sex workers. This is how one sex worker described an experience of severe physical/sexual client violence in Bangladesh:

> *I am 30 years old. I am a sex worker over the last 8 years in Dhaka. Violence is part of our daily lives. We face violence from police, clients, boyfriends, family and the public. There is not a single day we don't face violence. However, two months ago I faced serious violence from some clients. A group of 4 people took me in a night in an under-construction building. They all were on drugs and also took sex drugs. The first person did sex with me a minimum of one hour and I was feeling pain and after the second person, I told them I cannot do sex anymore. They were very angry and they forced me to do sex. After the third client I had severe pain. I was crying and told them to allow me to go. They become very angry and bit me seriously. At one point they pushed a beer bottle in my vagina. I felt serious pain. After that I was crying, and then security people came and sent me to home. I was feeling pain for two days in my abdomen. I could not tell anyone that inside my body was a bottle. Then I called my sex worker friend. She took me to a clinic. The doctor said situation is so serious and I needed an operation. It was expensive but my friend helped me to do the operation. I am so grateful to my friend.*

Qualitative research among street-based sex workers has documented pervasive gender inequality and their experiences of psychological dominance by males within intimate partnerships. This work underscores the impact of gendered power imbalances directly influencing women's agency and their ability to safeguard themselves against risky sexual behaviours. Such behaviour also normalises violence within the context of multiple forms of oppression such as poverty, racism, and economic dependence on partners [31–35]. Qualitative research from India among men, trans, and women sex workers has described the ways in which collectivisation and community empowerment can reduce violence from clients and police, but also indicates an increase in violence from sex workers' male intimate partners, attributed to those partners feeling threatened by shifts in the balance of power in their relationships [36].

The Impacts of Criminalisation

Punitive, enforcement-based approaches continue to undermine the health of sex workers [5, 8, 37]. A Lancet review determined that rights violations against sex workers are most profound where aspects of sex work are criminalised [29]. Under criminalisation, violence occurring in the context of sex work (i.e. as a workplace hazard/harm) is not monitored by any formal bodies; due to this omission, few to no legal protections are afforded to sex workers [38]. Violence against sex workers often goes unreported and is seldom registered as an offence. In some cases, it is perpetrated by police, exacerbating trauma and further restricting sex workers from accessing justice, health, or social services [9, 26, 39].

Violence against sex workers is largely shaped by criminalisation and contemporaneous stigma, discrimination, and social marginalisation [8, 29, 40]. These structural factors impact health access and outcomes, leading to heightened physical risks (e.g. violence, injury, death, HIV/STIs) [9, 38, 41] and mental health harms (e.g. addiction, depression, anxiety, post-traumatic stress disorder) [42–44]. Criminalisation also hinders collectivisation among sex workers, a factor critical to building capacity among sex workers and which enables them to negotiate safety in the workplace, advocate for labour protections and demand equal access to health and social services [36, 37, 45–47].

International bodies including the World Health Organization, UNAIDS, and Amnesty International have endorsed the full decriminalisation of sex work as necessary to promoting sex workers' human rights [5, 7, 48]. Despite this, the dominant socio-legal response to sex work remains criminalisation through punitive law. Criminalisation models can prohibit all aspects of sex work, or certain aspects, such as soliciting, advertising, collective working, or third party involvement [49]. Legalisation models—implemented in parts of Australia, Switzerland, Turkey, Hungary, Germany, the Netherlands, Nevada (USA), and Mexico—typically feature regulatory conditions (e.g. mandatory licencing or registration, mandatory HIV/STI testing) that are often discriminatory and enforced through criminal law [29, 49]. In 1999, Sweden criminalised the purchasing of sexual services (but not the selling of sex). This approach focuses on targeting clients and third parties and has generated a global wave of such "end-demand" legislation. Initial evidence on the impacts of end-demand laws suggest that even policies purportedly designed to criminalise only clients and third parties continue to indirectly criminalise sex workers and undermine sex workers' labour conditions, health, and human rights.

Research evaluating the impact of Canada's new end-demand laws (Protection of Communities and Exploited Persons Act; PCEPA) in Vancouver found that sex workers had significantly reduced access to health and community-led services as a result of the implementation of end-demand criminalisation [50]. Qualitative findings from Sweden and Canada underscore that criminalising clients reproduces the harms of full criminalisation models [51, 52]. Similarly, research from France found that end-demand laws undermined sex workers' safety and overall living conditions—exacerbating, rather than reducing, the harms associated with the previous laws against soliciting [53]. Conversely, evidence from New Zealand, which decriminalised sex work in 2003 (but only for New Zealand citizens), and New South Wales, Australia, has highlighted improved workplace safety, working conditions, and access to police protections for sex workers under full decriminalisation [54–56].

In Bangladesh, where sex work is legalised and regulated, sex workers face a lack of recourse after experiencing violence. The following APNSW case study illustrates how a sex worker and "ghorwali" (third party who provides space to sex workers and takes commissions) did not feel she could report violence and extortion to police.

It was a Friday evening at 8:00 pm; 4 young people entered my house. They said that I'm a bad woman and I take clients. At that time, in my house were two girls (sex workers) and 3 clients. They asked me who are those girls and boys...and started to be slapping the boys. The clients were scared and started to cry. The girls were scared too. They took money by force from clients... They were shouting and slapping me...telling me if I give them 20,000 BDT [Bangladeshi taka] and allow them to have sex with the girls then they will leave my house. All 4 young boys did sex with girls by force and we were scared so we could not protect them. However, after sex they again asked for 20,000 BDT. In this point, I started to cry and...the house owner heard. At this point, they left without money from me.

One night a week later, my client came to my house. All 4 bad boys again entered my house. The boys start to slap [my client] and asked 10,000 BDT. They threatened to take naked pictures and post on Facebook. The client was scared and gave them 5000 BDT. After that, they saw my 15-year-old daughter... they demanded to have sex with my daughter. My daughter was scared and started to cry. I called Morzina (HARC [HIV/AIDS Research and Welfare Centre] paralegal) and told her to come with police. At this point the bad boys... said we will go if I gave them 5000 BDT. As they were asking for my daughter, I was scared. I gave them 5000 and they left.

After that, I went to HARC office for next steps. They gave me two suggestions, one to do a general diary to the police station mentioning their names, or to change house as now everybody knew that I was involved in sex work. I took the second option and moved to a new house. I am continuing work but not sure what will happen next. I told the house owner that I work at HARC office...but I'm not sure how long I can stay in this house.

Police Repression, Extortion, and Abuse

Criminalisation enables police abuses against sex workers, for example, harassment and threats; fines, bribes, or other financial extortion; confiscation of condoms; assault; extorting sex under threat of arrest, all of which have been documented in diverse contexts [14, 16, 57–63]. Such punitive policing practices have been reported by sex workers globally as proxies for enforcement of sex work laws, dynamically influencing experiences of violence and the ability of sex workers to negotiate safer sexual transactions with clients [22, 24, 64–71]. Trans sex workers are especially vulnerable to being targeted by police and are subjected to discrimination and greater levels of violence [25, 72, 73].

Among sex workers in Canada, violence by police and enforced displacement to isolated outdoor locations are independently associated with their experiences of violence from clients [65]. Studies evaluating policing guidelines that prioritised targeting clients and third parties over arrest of sex workers in Vancouver, Canada, found increased likelihood of rushed negotiations with clients due to police presence [74], and no reductions in violence [70, 74].

Globally, police are primary perpetrators of violence against sex workers, further undermining their access to criminal justice systems. Gang rape and forced unprotected sex by police officers while being arrested and detained have been documented among sex workers of all genders [21, 28, 30, 39, 75–78]. Estimates of police-perpetrated sexual violence vary widely from 7% to 89% [9, 21, 29, 67, 75, 78]. Police further violate sex workers' rights by extorting money or sex, frequently under threat of arrest [39, 75, 79]. Police harassment has also been independently associated with increased odds of workplace violence among sex workers in Canada, Ivory Coast, and India [65, 67, 80], and a meta-analysis demonstrated that sex workers who have been exposed to repressive policing were significantly more likely to experience violence from clients and others [49].

The following APNSW case study excerpts describe sex workers' lived experiences with extortion, severe violence, and detainment by police across diverse countries. These narratives underscore the urgency of addressing punitive policing practices to improve the safety of sex workers.

Over the last 7 years, I faced many different types of violence, but the terrible experiences were with police. I was arrested 2 times. The first time was 5 years ago. Police asked me to give money but I had no money. After that I was in police station for a night and then transferred to court. I had no one to help me, I couldn't even understand what type of allegation was against me but had to go to jail for 15 days. I had a 1-year-old daughter and she faced serious problems. One of my relative took care of her, but she was poor too, so, my daughter could not get proper food for many days. After 15 days when I came back from jail, I was afraid to work too, so I spent many days without food. Second time I was arrested 2 years ago, with a client. Police only arrested me and did not say anything to the client. However, when police put me in the car going to the police station, I jumped from the moving car and ran away. We have many experiences but there is no one to listen to our issues. We are also human, we have also rights to live like other women, but we cannot because we are sex workers.—sex worker, India

In my sex worker life, I've experienced many different types of violence. Now, the biggest problem is police violence. Police usually arrest us on Friday night, then keep us in the police station where there is no food, no water, no toilet, no shower facilities. We often need to do sex with police there too. They keep us for two days just to get money and sex. Finally, police transfer to court on Sunday. I was arrested on Friday and was in the station for two nights. I did sex with two policemen. However, just before transfer to court on Sunday morning, my pimp released me from the police station. He told me he spent 10,000 (125 USD) and I have to pay 15,000 (200 USD) in a year. I could not pay because my income was not that high. Finally, I gave back 22,000 (300 USD) in two years. I had to do so much work just to give back money, and often I could not eat properly.—sex worker, Bangladesh

I was arrested by police 3 times. First time when I was only 20 years old and just 6 months after starting sex work. Police arrested me and kept me in the station for 3 days. I had sex with 6/7 police in those 3 days and was in jail for one year. I had to do sex in jail with jail police too. After coming back, I started sex work and within a year I got arrested again by police, same situation, 3 days in the police station and sex with many police. That time I was in jail for 3 months. After coming back, I stopped sex work. I thought, I cannot go to jail again as it's painful. So I got married and thought to continue housewife life. After 2 years I got divorced, I had a son, so again I was in a bad situation. I started sex work again. Finally, I got arrested in February 2018. After arrest, I called my relatives to loan money to get out. One gave money to police so I got released. Now I feel to stop sex work, but on the other hand, I need food, and there is no alternative work for me because I am not educated.—sex worker, Myanmar

Impact of Violence on HIV/STIs

The failure of the state to protect sex workers from violence and other human rights abuses has shaped epidemic rates of violence and HIV/STIs against sex workers globally [9, 49]. Violence by any offender reduces the ability of sex workers to safely negotiate transactions (e.g. types of sex acts, condom use), constrains their choices and heightens vulnerability [38]. Violence—physical and sexual—is the most influential determinant of HIV/STI risk among sex workers, associated with inconsistent condom use and refusal by clients to use condoms [45, 81–83].

Violence from the state, clients, individuals posing as clients, or intimate partners—together with unlawful arrest, detention, and discrimination—have severe effects on the HIV/STI-related inequities faced by sex workers. Punitive approaches to sex work hinder HIV prevention [84, 85], criminalisation, incarceration, and legal restrictions on sex work constrain sex workers' agency and access to safe working conditions. They also elevate HIV/STI exposure through increased violence [29, 76, 83]. In Argentina, India, and China, arrest, extortion, condom confiscation, and physical/sexual violence by police have been shown to significantly reduce condom use with clients and intimate partners [64, 66, 68, 86]. A global meta-analysis demonstrated that sex workers who experienced police violence faced a significantly higher HIV and STI burden [49]. In contrast, modelling estimates indicate that decriminalisation of sex work (i.e. removal of all laws targeting the sex industry) could avert up to 46% of new HIV infections among sex workers and their clients over a period of 10 years [8].

In criminalised contexts, the structural violence of stigma and discrimination (e.g. from police and healthcare providers) prevent sex workers from carrying condoms and hinder efforts to increase sex workers' access to health services [21, 77, 87, 88]. Police surveillance limits sex workers' ability to negotiate client condom use by forcing sex workers to rush transactions and client screening and displaces sex workers to isolated locations, increasing their vulnerability [34, 52, 89].

Alarmingly, across global contexts, police use possession of condoms as evidence of sex work to justify arrest, making it difficult for sex workers to safely access needed HIV/STI prevention supplies [38, 56, 76]. Condoms have also been used as evidence to target third parties and sex work businesses, which can undermine sex workers' access to condoms in the workplace [90].

Community perspectives from ANSWP echo these concerns. For example, the following case study describes a sex worker's experience of police using possession of condoms to justify arrest and abuse in Papua New Guinea:

A female sex worker was thoroughly checked by police [...] when she was dressed to go to a nightclub to do her sex work. A police car drove by and all of a sudden, stopped and reversed to where she was. Two policemen came out with a gun and pointed it at her and asked where she was going. One got hold of her small ladies' bag and opened it up, and saw condoms and her makeup. They asked her to get into the car and drove her to the police station, locked her up and raped her, and one took photos and videos. She was also asked to use her condoms to blow and make balloons and play with them. We finally found out the next day after one sex worker called me, the vocal person. When we tried to file the matter and take the police to court, the lawyer who was engaged to hear the case never showed up. We are still trying to carry out the case, but the sex worker told me she's scared of the policemen in case they will murder her if she's found alone. My advice to her is that; if we take them to court, they will not do that to us and if we ignore, we will face this for the rest of our lives.

Forced Rehabilitation and Mandatory Testing

Forced or mandatory 'rehabilitation' and detention of sex workers often occur under the guise of anti-trafficking efforts which conflate sex work (consensual exchange of sexual services) with forced sexual labour. Sex workers have faced rape and other physical violence during forced rehabilitation (i.e. programmes designed to force sex workers to exit/leave sex work) [91], and police have been documented as using forced HIV testing as a means of exploitation and harassment, including during detention and following police raids [75, 92]. In China, Cambodia, and India, sex workers have faced forced confinement, forced labour, forced HIV/STI testing, and poor treatment, including unhygienic conditions and denial of medical services [91, 93, 94]. In China, sex workers and clients have been detained for up to 2 years without trial in the so-called education and rescue centres and subjected to forced labour [93], sharply highlighting the hypocrisy of attempts to "rescue" sex workers from what the state deems to be exploitative labour. Mandatory HIV testing of sex workers is considered a rights violation by the UN Refugee Agency and UNAIDS, as it creates barriers to accessing services by facilitating discrimination against sex workers living with HIV [49]. In Nevada, USA, sex workers who test positive for HIV can face up to 10 years in prison [95].

Strategies for Change: A Human Rights Framework and Community-Led Interventions

To achieve human rights objectives and address violations such as unacceptable levels of violence against sex workers, a human rights framework and an approach using structural determinants are required [29, 83]. This means targeting punitive laws, policies, and resulting repressive policing. It also requires the promotion of enabling environments fostering community empowerment and partnerships, whereby sex workers can take collective ownership of programmes to address social and structural barriers to health, safety, and human rights [47].

Robust evidence has demonstrated that sex work criminalisation forces sex workers into adversarial relationships with police, increasing their vulnerability and restricting their access to legal protections [8, 37, 64, 96]. As such, the full decriminalisation of sex work, reform of policing practices, and facilitation of access to safer work environments are urgently needed. In South India, successful community-led approaches to reducing violence and HIV, improving access to justice, and challenging institutional stigma offer examples of what can be achieved with sustained funding and support [36, 46, 77, 78, 97].

Building on evaluations of community-led HIV prevention interventions conducted in lower-middle income countries (namely India, Dominican Republic, and Brazil [47]), community-based and biomedical HIV interventions should be integrated to ensure human rights outcomes and consider rights-related barriers to success. Sex workers of all genders should have meaningful roles in these efforts.

Case Study: Response to Violence in Asia Pacific

The End Violence against Sex Workers (EVASW) project in Myanmar is a sex worker-led, community-based initiative which has proven successful and cost-effective in addressing factors that contribute to sex workers' vulnerability to abuse (see Box 3.1). However, broader structural changes, such as legal reform, are necessary to facilitate the work of community-led organisations.

Box 3.1 Ending Violence Against Sex Workers in Myanmar

Violence against female and trans sex workers is pervasive in Myanmar, and police are both primary perpetrators of violence and key gatekeepers to sex workers' rights. This project aims to improve the safety of and promote access to justice for sex workers in four cities across Myanmar, and also aims to reduce discrimination and stigma against them, by February 2020. It aims to increase sex workers' knowledge of their rights, empower collective action to prevent and respond to violence, and advocate for structural change to reduce sex workers' vulnerability. Key factors to successful reduction of violence include greater collective agency among sex workers, enhanced self-efficacy contributing to greater use of crisis response mechanisms, and relationship-building with stakeholders. In a South-South partnership between APNSW members Ashodaya and Aye Myanmar Association (AMA), this approach has been adapted to Myanmar's context and implemented with support from APNSW. Because sex work is criminalised in Myanmar, special measures for ethics and safety have been taken.

Sex workers have learned about human rights through legal literacy and court process workshops hosted by AMA. A violence response team, made up of a core cadre of sex worker leaders, has been created. AMA encourages sex workers to report violence through the response team and by using technology called iMonitor+: a mobile app that sex workers can use to document violence with photos and videos. When sex workers report information using iMonitor+, the violence response team responds with action. AMA also continues to work to establish institutional partnerships between the community and police to address stigma and discrimination. Through sensitisation workshops and advocacy meetings, law enforcement officers gain an enhanced appreciation of violence against sex workers, and of their own roles and capacity in response. These strategies are in the process of being systematically implemented within interventions to reduce violence against sex workers in Myanmar. Successes include meetings with police and the uptake of reporting and documenting violence against sex workers. AMA has received reports of some officers assisting sex workers after learning more about sex workers' lives.

APNSW and its members have developed a rapid-response programme which was pioneered in Myanmar and is now being adapted and implemented in four countries in Asia (see Box 3.2). The following excerpts describe how the programme in Myanmar (AMA) has provided legal assistance and protection for sex workers who have been incarcerated.

I learned about the AMA program 4 months ago when I met with outreach workers downtown. I learned that AMA helps sex workers from violence and if police arrest them, they help them to get released without any money. After this I was thinking about my past. When I was 30 years old, police arrested me. I was in jail for one year. I had a 3-year-old boy when I went to jail. After release, I could not find my son. Until today, I don't know where my son is! At that time, there was no program, no communication system with anyone from jail. Now, the situation is totally changed. I was arrested again in February, and I called my outreach workers. The police sent me to court; the AMA legal officer was there and she talked for me in court. I got released but my case is still active. I need to go to court twice a month but I am free and can work like any other sex worker. Now I think, if this project was here 20 years ago, I would not have lost my son. This project is a great help for sex workers.—sex worker, Myanmar

I've done sex work for the last 8 years. In the past, I was arrested by police and got released by spending over 500,000 MMK (500 USD). However, I was arrested in 2017 and the court sent me to jail. My case was not finished so I had to come to court twice a month from jail. I got an AMA hotline card in jail from another sex worker. I sent the hotline number to my daughter, who called and requested help. In January when I came to court, the AMA legal officer talked in court about my case. I got released. Now I am free and living with my family. My case is still active, but I have no problem because I can work like others. I am so happy with AMA; if AMA didn't help me, I could be in jail for a long time. AMA is saving the lives of sex workers in Myanmar.—sex worker, Myanmar

---

Box 3.2 Ending Violence Against Sex Workers in Bangladesh, Indonesia, Myanmar, and Nepal

Safety First is a programme to reduce violence against sex workers, comprised of human rights documentation, legal rights training, legal services, and a crisis hotline. APNSW implements the Safety First project with four established partner organisations: HIV AIDS Research and Welfare Centre (HARC, Bangladesh), Organisasi Perubahan Sosial Indonesia (OPSI, Indonesia), Aye Myanmar Association (AMA, Myanmar), and Jagriti Mahila Mahasang Sanghta (JMMS, Nepal). Over the last 2 years, APNSW has provided intensive technical support to all four organisations.

Safety First uses rights-based interventions designed by female sex workers, based on their recommendations for the most effective local interventions. It involves four peer-led service components, including a safe space, outreach, a hotline, and legal services.

Safety First starts with know-your-rights trainings and legal education held in the safe space. Sex workers trained to be paralegals offer legal counselling in the safe space every working day. Legal counsellors also document human rights violations and proceed with representation in court or pursuing legal

(continued)

Box 3.2 (continued)

action on behalf of sex workers. The sex worker community experts developed a violence reporting form during the regional training. Each quarter, a lawyer will come to the partner organisation's office to meet sex workers and explain court procedures, the rights of a person who has been arrested, and how sex workers should respond to police harassment/arrest. A lawyer is always standing by in court to assist sex workers with pro-bono representation and legal advice.

Outreach is conducted in sex work venues by peer educators to promote Safety First's services. Each partner organisation has recruited three peer outreach workers for a Rapid Action Team (RAT), who all carry mobile phones. Sex workers call the hotline or outreach workers when they experience or witness violence. The RAT responds to hotline calls, goes to police stations and court when sex workers are arrested, and documents violence using the form developed during the regional meeting.

The RAT also conducts advocacy and sensitisation meetings with police, building on earlier police advocacy work. These sessions aim to reduce the number of sex workers being arrested, by sensitising police to the marginalisation, stigmatisation, and harassment facing sex workers. Additional advocacy meetings take place with high-level commanding officers to create opportunity for meaningful exchanges between law enforcement and sex workers.

Safety First team members accompany sex workers who have experienced violence when they seek health care, and OPSI, the Indonesian Safety First partner, has successfully advocated in medical settings for confidentiality around being a sex worker and HIV status.

Safety First has demonstrated success in reducing violence against sex workers. In Myanmar, the RAT receives an average of 20 calls each month, in addition to calls to the hotline. Sex workers who received legal advice and representation from Safety First experienced better outcomes in court. The success of Safety First programming demonstrates that community-based programmes can effectively reduce violence and its impacts on HIV transmission within an enabling environment. This programme also demonstrates the need to involve higher level stakeholders including governments, NGOs, and law enforcement to increase safety for sex workers.

Box 3.3 Lessons Learned from APNSW

APNSW works to end violence by empowering sex workers and encouraging collective action, and this approach has demonstrated to generate positive results. For example, sex workers now inform one another about police movements by mobile phone, and when police arrest any sex worker, others call the hotline to inform paralegals to take necessary action. When police arrest sex

(continued)

Box 3.3 (continued)

workers, other sex workers go to the police and try to help them to get released. In the past, sex workers would never dare question or confront the police.

As violence is a multi-dimensional issue, multiple partnerships are critical. In all four countries, APNSW built meaningful partnerships with government, police, and the National AIDS Programme (NAP) under the Ministry of Health. NAP clinics in project areas agreed to provide health services to sex workers after they have experienced assault. Within the Government sector, during township-level inter-governmental meetings, NAP staff strongly highlighted the issue of violence against sex workers. These statements also helped when it came to advocacy work with police. Global experience shows that partnership with Ministries of Health and other stakeholders are essential to bring about sustainable institutional change to address violence against sex workers.

Access to legal services have direct impacts on community empowerment, confidence-building, and overall reduction of violence. Outreach workers of APNSW partners found that sex workers at the community level are now aware of legal aid services. In Myanmar, community members follow the progress of legal cases in the courts through informal sex worker networks. These cases build confidence among sex workers, who realise that they are not alone—there are people to help them—and this realisation itself is empowering. Now, after being arrested, 65% sex workers are released, either before being taken to the police station or from the station.

There has been excellent uptake of our hotline and direct calls to outreach workers, where sex workers report experiences of violence. APNSW is also working with media to promote positive, non-stigmatising reporting about sex workers, and is documenting rights violations against sex workers. Over 745 cases in each country have been documented, and we qualitatively analysed each case for use in advocacy with journalists and in Government meetings. This process of documenting human rights violations helps to amplify community voices.

A 2015 UN and APNSW sex worker-led, multi-country study in Asia Pacific produced recommendations on the reduction of violence against sex workers [98]. It underscored the need to end impunity among violent predators; strengthen sex workers' access to justice, and improve sex workers' access to non-discriminatory health, HIV/STI, and violence crisis services.

Recommendations for Programming and Policies [98]:

1. Reform punitive laws and law enforcement practices to uphold sex workers' right to be free of violence
2. End impunity for those who commit violence against sex workers by holding perpetrators accountable for crimes

3. Strengthen sex workers' access to justice and support sex worker-led legal advocacy
4. Recognise sex work as legitimate work and ensure that sex workers have legally enforceable rights to occupational health and safety protections
5. Improve sex workers' access to sexual and reproductive health, HIV and gender-based violence services
6. Full decriminalisation of sex work to ensure labour rights for sex workers
7. Uphold anti-discrimination and other rights-respecting laws
8. Ensure available, accessible, and acceptable health services for sex workers
9. Address violence against sex workers in all health and HIV programmes
10. Support community empowerment and sex worker-led programming and remove laws restricting sex workers' ability to formally organise

Conclusions and Future Directions

Academic literature and lived experiences of sex workers and sex worker-led organisations overwhelmingly indicate that there remains an urgent need to improve the safety and human rights of sex workers worldwide. Criminalisation, stigma, and discrimination interact to reproduce sex workers' exposure to violence, and hinder efforts to enact change. Community empowerment approaches that facilitate sex worker organising are effective strategies to promote sex workers' rights. Interdisciplinary, mixed-method and participatory research is needed to further document the impacts of criminalisation and violence on sex workers' health and their access to health and legal services, as well as to inform context-specific interventions. Legislative reforms to decriminalise all aspects of sex work; political commitment to reduce structural inequalities, stigma, and exclusion; and funding to scale up sex worker-led services are evidence-based, rights-based strategies proven to mitigate risk of violence, to ensure safer work environments, and to uphold human rights among sex workers globally.

References

1. Deering KN, Amin A, Shoveller J, Nesbitt A, Garcia-Moreno C, Duff P, et al. A systematic review of the correlates of violence against sex workers. Am J Public Health. 2014;104(5):42–54.
2. Ditmore MH, Allman D. An analysis of the implementation of PEPFAR's anti-prostitution pledge and its implications for successful HIV prevention among organizations working with sex workers. J Int AIDS Soc. 2013;16:17354.
3. FIDA. Documenting human rights violation of sex workers in Kenya. Nairobi: FIDA; 2008.
4. International Committee on the Rights of Sex Workers in Europe. Sex workers in Europe manifesto. Brussels: International Committee on the Rights of Sex Workers in Europe; 2005.
5. World Health Organization. Prevention and treatment of HIV and other sexually transmitted infections for sex workers in low- and middle-income countries - recommendations for a public health approach [Internet]. Geneva; 2012 [cited 2017 Sep 6]. Available from: http://www.who.int/hiv/topics/sex_worker/en/.

6. UNAIDS. UNAIDS guidance note on HIV and sex work. WHO Libr Cat Data [Internet]. 2009 [cited 2018 Jan 17];(2009):23. Available from: http://www.unaids.org/sites/default/files/media_asset/JC2306_UNAIDS-guidance-note-HIV-sex-work_en_0.pdf.

7. Global Commission on HIV and the Law. Risks, rights & health. New York: Global Commission on HIV and the Law; 2012.

8. Shannon K, Strathdee SA, Goldenberg SM, Duff P, Mwangi P, Rusakova M, et al. Global epidemiology of HIV among female sex workers: influence of structural determinants. Lancet. 2015;385(9962):55–71.

9. Deering KN, Amin A, Shoveller JA, Nesbitt A, Garcia-Moreno C, Duff P, et al. A systematic review of the global magnitude and drivers of violence against sex workers. Am J Public Health. 2014;104(5):e42–54.

10. Operario D, Soma T, Underhill K. Sex work and HIV status among transgender women - systematic review and meta-analysis. J Acquir Immune Defic Syndr. 2008;48(1):97–103.

11. Baral SD, Friedman MR, Geibel S, Rebe K, Bozhinov B, Diouf D, et al. Male sex workers: practices, contexts, and vulnerabilities for HIV acquisition and transmission. Lancet. 2015;385:260–73.

12. Oppal WT. Forsaken: The Report of the Missing Women Commission of Inquiry Executive Summary [Internet]. Vancouver; 2012 [cited 2018 Aug 14]. Available from: http://www.missingwomeninquiry.ca/wp-content/uploads/2010/10/Forsaken-ES-web-RGB.pdf.

13. Strega S, Janzen C, Morgan J, Brown L, Thomas R, Carriére J. Never innocent victims. Violence Against Women. 2014;20(1):6–25. https://doi.org/10.1177/1077801213520576.

14. Global Network of Sex Work Projects. The impact of criminalisation on sex workers' vulnerability to HIV and violence [Internet]. 2017. Available from: http://www.nswp.org/sites/nswp.org/files/impact_of_criminalisation_pb_prf01.pdf.

15. PION. The convention to eliminate all forms of discrimination against women 2017 forms of discrimination against women 2017 - a shadow Report by PION; 2017.

16. Lim S, Peitzmeier S, Cange C, Papworth E, LeBreton M, Tamoufe U, et al. Violence against female sex workers in Cameroon. J Acquir Immune Defic Syndr. 2015;68:S241–7. Available from: http://content.wkhealth.com/linkback/openurl?sid=WKPTLP:landingpage&an=00126334-201503011-00022.

17. Dewey S, St. Germain T. "It depends on the cop:" street-based sex workers' perspectives on police patrol officers. Sex Res Soc Policy. 2014;11(3):256–70.

18. Ganju D, Saggurti N. Stigma, violence and HIV vulnerability among transgender persons in sex work in Maharashtra, India. Cult Health Sex. 2017;1058(March):1–15. https://doi.org/10.1080/13691058.2016.1271141.

19. Goldenberg SM, Krüsi A, Zhang E, Chettiar J, Shannon K. Structural determinants of health among im/migrants in the indoor sex industry: experiences of workers and managers/owners in metropolitan Vancouver. PLoS One. 2017;12(1):e0170642. https://doi.org/10.1371/journal.pone.0170642.

20. Lam E. Behind the rescue: how anti-trafficking investigations and policies harm migrant sex workers. Toronto: Butterfly Asian and Migrant Sex Workers Support Network; 2018.

21. Mayhew S, Collumbien M, Qureshi A, Platt L, Rafiq N, Faisel A, et al. Protecting the unprotected: mixed-method research on drug use, sex work and rights in Pakistan's fight against HIV/AIDS. Sex Transm Infect. 2009;85(Suppl 2):ii8–16.

22. Decker MR, Wirtz AL, Baral SD, Peryshkina A, Mogilnyi V, Weber RA, et al. Injection drug use, sexual risk, violence and STI/HIV among Moscow female sex workers. Sex Transm Infect. 2012;88(4):278–83. Available from: http://search.ebscohost.com/login.aspx?direct=true&AuthType=cookie,ip,shib&db=rzh&AN=104435877&site=ehost-live.

23. Goldenberg SM, Rangel G, Vera A, Patterson TL, Abramovitz D, Silverman JG, et al. Exploring the impact of underage sex work among female sex workers in two Mexico-US border cities. AIDS Behav. 2012;16(4):969–81.

24. Deering KN, Bhattacharjee P, Mohan HL, Bradley J, Shannon K, Boily M, Ramesh B, et al. Violence and HIV risk among female sex workers in southern India. Sex Transm Dis. 2013;40(2):168–74.

25. Nemoto T, Boedeker B, Iwamoto M. Social support, exposure to violence and transphobia, and correlates of depression among male-to-female transgender women with a history of sex work. Am J Public Health. 2011;101(10):1980–8.
26. Simić M, Rhodes T. Violence, dignity and HIV vulnerability: street sex work in Serbia. Sociol Health Illn. 2009;31(1):1–16.
27. Surratt HL, Kurtz SP, Chen M, Mooss A. HIV risk among female sex workers in Miami: the impact of violent victimization and untreated mental illness. AIDS Care. 2012;24(5):553–61.
28. Okal J, Chersich MF, Tsui S, Sutherland E, Temmerman M, Luchters S. Sexual and physical violence against female sex workers in Kenya: a qualitative enquiry. AIDS Care. 2011;23:612–8.
29. Decker MR, Crago AL, Chu SKH, Sherman SG, Seshu MS, Buthelezi K, et al. Human rights violations against sex workers: burden and effect on HIV. Lancet. 2015;385(9963):186–99. https://doi.org/10.1016/S0140-6736(14)60800-X.
30. Scorgie F, Vasey K, Harper E, Richter M, Nare P, Maseko S, et al. Human rights abuses and collective resilience among sex workers in four African countries: a qualitative study. Glob Health. 2013;9(1):33.
31. Bourgois P, Prince B, Moss A. The everyday violence of hepatitis C among young women who inject drugs in San Francisco. Hum Organ. 2004;63(3):253–64.
32. Maher L. Sexed work: gender, race and resistance in a Brooklyn drug market (Clarendon studies in criminology). Oxford: Clarendon Press; 1997. 279 p.
33. Rhodes T, Wagner K, Strathdee S, Shannon K, Davidson P, Bourgois P. Structural violence and structural vulnerability within the risk environment: theoretical and methodological perspectives for a social epidemiology of HIV risk among IDU and SW. In: O'Campo P, Dunn J, editors. Rethinking social epidemiology: towards a science of change. Toronto: University of Toronto Press; 2012.
34. Shannon K, Kerr T, Allinott S, Chettiar J, Shoveller JA, Tyndall MW. Social and structural violence and power relations in mitigating HIV risk of drug-using women in survival sex work. Soc Sci Med. 2008;66:911–21.
35. Syvertsen JL, Bazzi AR. Sex work, heroin injection, and HIV risk in Tijuana: a love story. Anthropol Conscious. 2015;26(2):182–94.
36. Argento E, Reza-Paul S, Lorway R, Jain J, Bhagya M, Fathima M, et al. Confronting structural violence in sex work: lessons from a community-led HIV prevention project in Mysore, India. AIDS Care. 2011;23(1):69–74.
37. Csete J, Cohen J. Health benefits of legal services for criminalized populations: the case of people who use drugs, sex workers and sexual and gender minorities. J Law Med Ethics. 2010;38(4):816–31.
38. Shannon K, Csete J. Violence, condom negotiation, and HIV/STI risk among sex workers. JAMA. 2010;304(5):573. https://doi.org/10.1001/jama.2010.1090.
39. Rhodes T, Simic M, Baros S, Platt L, Zikic B. Police violence and sexual risk among female and transvestite sex workers in Serbia: qualitative study. BMJ. 2008;337(7669):560–3.
40. Krüsi A, Chettiar J, Ridgway A, Abbott J, Strathdee SA, Shannon K. Negotiating safety and sexual risk reduction with clients in unsanctioned safer indoor sex work environments: a qualitative study. Am J Public Health. 2012;102(6):1154–9.
41. World Health Organization. Global and regional estimates of violence against women: prevalence and health effects of intimate partner violence and non-partner sexual violence. Geneva: World Health Organization; 2013.
42. World Health Organization. Preventing suicide: a global imperative. Geneva: World Health Organization; 2014.
43. Zhang L, Li X, Wang B, Shen Z, Zhou Y, Xu J, et al. Violence, stigma and mental health among female sex workers in China: a structural equation modeling. Women Health. 2016;57(6):685–704.
44. Roxburgh A, Degenhardt L, Copeland J. Posttraumatic stress disorder among female street-based sex workers in the greater Sydney area, Australia. BMC Psychiatry. 2006;6(24):1–12.

45. Argento E, Duff P, Bingham B, Chapman J, Nguyen P, Strathdee SA, et al. Social cohesion among sex workers and client condom refusal in a Canadian setting: implications for structural and community-led interventions. AIDS Behav. 2016;20(6):1275–83. Available from: http://www.ncbi.nlm.nih.gov/pubmed/26499335.

46. Blanchard AK, Mohan HL, Shahmanesh M, Prakash R, Isac S, Ramesh BM, et al. Community mobilization, empowerment and HIV prevention among female sex workers in south India. BMC Public Health. 2013;13:234.

47. Kerrigan D, Kennedy CE, Morgan-Thomas R, Reza-Paul S, Mwangi P, Win KT, et al. A community empowerment approach to the HIV response among sex workers: effectiveness, challenges, and considerations for implementation and scale-up. Lancet. 2015;385(9963):172–85.

48. Amnesty International. Sex worker's rights are human rights. London: Amnesty International; 2015.

49. Platt L, Grenfell P, Meiksin R, Elmes J, Sherman SG, Sanders T, et al. Associations between sex work laws and sex workers' health: a systematic review and meta-analysis of quantitative and qualitative studies. PLOS Med. 2018;15(12):e1002680. https://doi.org/10.1371/journal.pmed.1002680.

50. Argento E, Goldenberg SM, Braschel M, Machat S, Strathdee SA, Shannon K. The impact of end-demand legislation on sex workers' access to health and sex worker support services: a community-based prospective cohort study in Canada. PLoS One. 2020;15(4):e0225783.

51. Levy J, Jakobsson P. Sweden's abolitionist discourse and law: effects on the dynamics of Swedish sex work and on the lives of Sweden's sex workers. Criminol Crim Justice. 2014;14(5):593–607.

52. Krüsi A, Pacey K, Bird L, Taylor C, Chettiar J, Allan S, et al. Criminalisation of clients: reproducing vulnerabilities for violence and poor health among street-based sex workers in Canada - a qualitative study. BMJ Open. 2014;4:e005191.

53. Le Bail H, Giametta C. What do sex workers think about the French Prostitution Act? A study on the impact of the law from 13 April 2016 against the "prostitution system" in France. Paris; 2018.

54. Jeffrey LA, Sullivan B. Canadian sex work policy for the 21st century: enhancing rights and safety, lessons from Australia. Can Polit Sci Rev. 2009;3(1):57–76.

55. Abel GM, Fitzgerald LJ, Brunton C. The impact of decriminalisation on the number of sex workers in New Zealand. J Soc Policy. 2009;38(03):515–31.

56. Bruckert C, Hannem S. Rethinking the prostitution debates: transcending structural stigma in systemic responses to sex work. Can J Law Soc. 2013;28(01):43–63.

57. Decker MR, Pearson E, Illangasekare SL, Clark E, Sherman SG. Violence against women in sex work and HIV risk implications differ qualitatively by perpetrator. BMC Public Health. 2013;13:876. Available from: http://ovidsp.ovid.com/ovidweb.cgi?T=JS&PAGE=reference&D=emed15&NEWS=N&AN=604576750.

58. Research for Sex Work. Sex work, HIV/AIDS, public health and human rights [Internet]. Amsterdam; 2003 [cited 2018 Aug 15]. Available from: https://childhub.org/fr/system/tdf/library/attachments/research_for_sex_work_no_6_.pdf?file=1&type=node&id=16708.

59. Ndondo HM, Maseko S, Ndlovu S. Sexual and physical violence against sex workers: a qualitative survey to explore experiences of violence perpetrated by police among sex workers in Victoria Falls, Zimbabwe, 2012. Sex Transm Infect. 2013;89:A312.

60. Popoola BI. Occupational hazards and coping strategies of sex workers in Southwestern Nigeria. Health Care Women Int. 2013;34(2):139–49. https://doi.org/10.1080/07399332.2011.646366.

61. Strathdee SA, Lozada R, Martinez G, Vera A, Rusch M, Nguyen L, et al. Social and structural factors associated with HIV infection among female sex workers who inject drugs in the Mexico-US border region. PLoS One. 2011;6(4):e19048. Available from: http://www.ncbi.nlm.nih.gov/pubmed/21541349.

62. Baral S, Beyrer C, Muessig K, Poteat T, Wirtz AL, Decker MR, et al. Burden of HIV among female sex workers in low-income and middle-income countries: a systematic review and

meta-analysis. Lancet Infect Dis. 2012;12(7):538–49. Available from: http://linkinghub.elsevier.com/retrieve/pii/S147330991270066X.

63. Sherman SG, Footer K, Illangasekare S, Clark E, Pearson E, Decker MR. "What makes you think you have special privileges because you are a police officer?" A qualitative exploration of police's role in the risk environment of female sex workers. AIDS Care. 2015;27(4):473–80. https://doi.org/10.1080/09540121.2014.970504.

64. Pando MA, Coloccini RS, Reynaga E, Rodriguez Fermepin M, Gallo Vaulet L, Kochel TJ, et al. Violence as a barrier for HIV prevention among female sex workers in Argentina. PLoS One. 2013;8(1):e54147.

65. Shannon K, Kerr T, Strathdee SA, Shoveller J, Montaner JS, Tyndall MW. Prevalence and structural correlates of gender based violence among a prospective cohort of female sex workers. BMJ. 2009;339:b2939. Available from: http://www.bmj.com.proxy.lib.sfu.ca/content/339/bmj.b2939.full.

66. Zhang C, Li X, Hong Y, Zhou Y, Liu W, Stanton B. Unprotected sex with their clients among low-paying female sex workers in Southwest China. AIDS Care. 2013;25(4):503–6.

67. Erausquin JT, Reed E, Blankenship KM. Police-related experiences and HIV risk among female sex workers in Andhra Pradesh, India. J Infect Dis. 2011;204(5):S1223–8.

68. Erausquin JT, Reed E, Blankenship KM. Change over time in police interactions and HIV risk behavior among female sex Workers in Andhra Pradesh, India. AIDS Behav. 2015;19(6):1108–15.

69. Platt L, Grenfell P, Bonell C, Creighton S, Wellings K, Parry J, et al. Risk of sexually transmitted infections and violence among indoor-working female sex workers in London: the effect of migration from Eastern Europe. Sex Transm Infect. 2011;87(5):377–84.

70. Prangnell A, Shannon K, Nosova E, DeBeck K, Milloy M-J, Kerr T, et al. Workplace violence among female sex workers who use drugs in Vancouver, Canada: does client-targeted policing increase safety? J Public Health Policy. 2018;39(1):86–99. https://doi.org/10.1057/s41271-017-0098-4.

71. Lyons CE, Grosso A, Drame FM, Ketende S, Diouf D, Ba I, et al. Physical and sexual violence affecting female sex workers in Abidjan, Côte d'Ivoire. J Acquir Immune Defic Syndr. 2017;75(1):9–17. Available from: http://insights.ovid.com/crossref?an=00126334-201705010-00002.

72. Lyons T, Krüsi A, Pierre L, Kerr T, Small W, Shannon K. Negotiating violence in the context of transphobia and criminalization: the experiences of trans sex workers in Vancouver, Canada. Qual Health Res. 2015;27:182–90.

73. Poteat T, Wirtz AL, Radix A, Borquez A, Silva-Santisteban A, Deutsch MB, et al. HIV risk and preventive interventions in transgender women sex workers. Lancet. 2015;385(9964):274–86.

74. Landsberg A, Shannon K, Krüsi A, DeBeck K, Milloy MJ, Nosova E, et al. Criminalizing sex work clients and rushed negotiations among sex Workers who use drugs in a Canadian Setting. J Urban Health. 2017;94(4):563–71.

75. Sex Workers' Rights Advocacy Network. Arrest the violence: human rights abuses against sex workers in Central and Eastern Europe and Central Asia. New York: Open Society Foundations; 2009.

76. Open Society Foundations. Criminalizing condoms: how policing practices put sex workers and HIV services at risk in Kenya, Namibia, Russia, South Africa, USA, and Zimbabwe. Sexual Health and Rights Project. New York: Open Society Foundations; 2012.

77. Reza-Paul S, Lorway R, O'Brien N, Lazarus L, Jain J, Bhagya M, et al. Sex worker-led structural interventions in India: a case study on addressing violence in HIV prevention through the Ashodaya Samithi collective in Mysore. Indian J Med Res. 2012;135(1):98–106.

78. Beattie TSH, Bhattacharjee P, Ramesh BM, Gurnani V, Anthony J, Isac S, et al. Violence against female sex workers in Karnataka state, south India: impact on health, and reductions in violence following an intervention program. BMC Public Health. 2010;10:476.

79. Abad N, Baack BN, O'Leary A, Mizuno Y, Herbst JH, Lyles CM. A systematic review of HIV and STI behavior change interventions for female sex workers in the United States. AIDS Behav. 2015;19:1701–19.

80. Lyons CE, Grosso A, Drame FM, Ketende S, Diouf D, Ba I, et al. Physical and sexual violence affecting female sex workers in Abidjan, Côte d'Ivoire: prevalence, and the relationship with the work environment, HIV, and access to health services. J Acquir Immune Defic Syndr. 2017;75(1):9–17. Available from: http://insights.ovid.com/crossref?an=00126334-201705010-00002.

81. Lazarus L, Chettiar J, Deering K, Nabess R, Shannon K. Risky health environments: women sex workers' struggles to find safe, secure and non-exploitative housing in Canada's poorest postal code. Soc Sci Med. 2011;73(11):1600–7.

82. Platt L, Grenfell P, Fletcher A, Sorhaindo A, Jolley E, Rhodes T, et al. Systematic review examining differences in HIV, sexually transmitted infections and health-related harms between migrant and non-migrant female sex workers. Sex Transm Infect. 2012;(3):1–10.

83. Shannon K, Strathdee SA, Shoveller J, Rusch M, Kerr T, Tyndall MW. Structural and environmental barriers to condom use negotiation with clients among female sex workers: implications for HIV-prevention strategies and policy. Am J Public Health. 2009;99(4):659–65.

84. Beyrer C, Crago AL, Bekker LG, Butler J, Shannon K, Kerrigan D, et al. An action agenda for HIV and sex workers. Lancet. 2015;385(9964):287–301.

85. Argento E, Goldenberg S, Shannon K. Preventing sexually transmitted and blood borne infections (STBBIs) among sex workers: a critical review of the evidence on determinants and interventions in high-income countries. BMC Infect Dis. 2019;19:212.

86. Beattie TS, Bhattacharjee P, Isac S, Mohan HL, Simic-Lawson M, Ramesh BM, et al. Declines in violence and police arrest among female sex workers in Karnataka state, South India, following a comprehensive HIV prevention programme. J Int AIDS Soc. 2015;18(1):1–16.

87. Lazarus L, Deering KN, Nabess R, Gibson K, Tyndall MW, Shannon K. Occupational stigma as a primary barrier to health care for street-based sex workers in Canada. Cult Health Sex. 2012;14(2):139–50.

88. Beattie TSH, Bhattacharjee P, Suresh M, Isac S, Ramesh BM, Moses S. Personal, interpersonal and structural challenges to accessing HIV testing, treatment and care services among female sex workers, men who have sex with men and transgenders in Karnataka state, South India. J Epidemiol Community Health. 2012;66(2):II42–8.

89. Goldenberg SM, Duff P, Krusi A. Work environments and HIV prevention: a qualitative review and meta-synthesis of sex worker narratives. BMC Public Health. 2015;15(1):1241. Available from: http://www.biomedcentral.com/1471-2458/15/1241.

90. Anderson S, Shannon K, Li J, Lee Y, Chettiar J, Goldenberg S, et al. Condoms and sexual health education as evidence: impact of criminalization of in-call venues and managers on migrant sex workers access to HIV/STI prevention in a Canadian setting. BMC Int Health Hum Rights. 2016;16(1):1–10.

91. Human Rights Watch. Off the streets: arbitrary detention and other abuses against sex workers in Cambodia; 2010.

92. Dimitrov S. In focus Macedonia alert: police raids, detentions, involuntary STI tests; 2008.

93. Asia Catalyst. "Custody and education": arbitrary detention for female sex workers in China; 2013.

94. Magar V. Rescue and rehabilitation: a critical analysis of sex workers' antitrafficking response in India. Signs (Chic). 2012;37(3):619–44.

95. Brents BG, Hausbeck K. Violence and legalized brothel prostitution in Nevada: examining safety, risk, and prostitution policy. J Interpers Violence. 2005;20(3):270–95.

96. Socías ME, Deering K, Horton M, Nguyen P, Montaner JS, Shannon K. Social and structural factors shaping high rates of incarceration among sex workers in a Canadian setting. J Urban Health. 2015;92(5):966–79.

97. Jana S, Basu I, Rotheram-Borus MJ, Newman PA. The Sonagachi Project: a sustainable community intervention program. AIDS Educ Prev. 2004;16(5):405–14.

98. Bhattacharjya M, Fulu E, Murthy L, Seshu M, Cabassi J, VallejoMestres M. The right(s) evidence: sex work, violence and HIV in Asia: a multi-country qualitative study. Bangkok; 2015.

Chapter 4
Sexual and Reproductive Health and Rights Inequities Among Sex Workers Across the Life Course

Ania Shapiro and Putu Duff

Sexual and Reproductive Health: A Fundamental Human Right

The highest attainable standard of sexual and reproductive health (SRH) is a fundamental human right [1–4], affirmed through numerous international and national laws and mandates including the Universal Declaration of Human Rights [5], the International Conference on Population and Development [6], and the Convention on the Elimination of All Forms of Discrimination against Women [1]. Sexual and reproductive rights recognise the basic rights of all individuals to access information, SRH services, and the means and supports to make informed decisions about their SRH, including the spacing and timing of children [1]. All individuals are entitled to exercise their SRH rights free from coercion, discrimination, and violence [6]. SRH and rights continue to be featured prominently on the international agenda, including in the United Nations' Sustainable Development Goal number 5, which strives to ensure universal access to SRH and rights [7].

Data SourceMuch of the information, including the methods and results contained in this chapter, were based on the Global Network of Sex Work Projects' Briefing paper, entitled "Sex Workers' Access to Comprehensive Sexual and Reproductive Health Services" available at: https://www.nswp.org/sites/nswp.org/files/bp_sws_access_to_comp_srh_-_nswp_2018.pdf

A. Shapiro
Sex Workers Outreach Project (SWOP-Tucson), Tucson, AZ, USA

P. Duff (✉)
Centre for Gender and Sexual Health Equity, Vancouver, BC, Canada

Faculty of Medicine, University of British Columbia, Vancouver, BC, Canada
e-mail: putu.duff@cgshe.ubc.ca

Structural Determinants of Sexual and Reproductive Health Access for Sex Workers

Sex workers experience a multitude of overlapping structural barriers that impede their fundamental SRH rights, including access to SRH care. SRH care encompasses a range of services such as: maternal and newborn care (e.g. antenatal, perinatal, and postnatal care); family planning services (e.g. contraceptives, fertility services, and safe abortions); and services that address HIV/STIs, HPV-related cancer prevention, and other reproductive-tract morbidities. The criminalisation of sex work is one of the most formidable barriers to SRH care, as it limits access to and use of health services [8–10] on the part of sex workers, and undermines their access to condoms, including the right to carry condoms and negotiate their use [9, 11, 12], either independently or as part of the practice of using dual contraceptive methods [13]. Criminalisation can also undermine HIV testing [14], access to social services and support [15]; plus, it increases the incidence of HIV/STIs and physical/sexual violence [9, 16].

In many settings, the harmful impacts of the criminalisation of sex work are compounded by other rights-violating laws and policies, including the criminalisation of HIV, of same-sex relationships, and of gender non-conformance, e.g. laws against "crossdressing" or "impersonating the opposite sex", which further exacerbate SRH inequities among transgender and male sex workers [17].

The widespread criminalisation of sex work is often based on portrayals of sex workers as either dangerous, immoral individuals, or as helpless victims—and often as victims of human trafficking. Criminalisation, together with the prevalence of vilifying depictions of sex workers, has far-reaching implications, perpetuating stigma, violence [16], and fueling the exclusion of organisations serving sex workers from receiving HIV and health funding. A striking example of this is the U.S. President's Emergency Plan for AIDS Relief (PEPFAR's) Anti-Prostitution Loyalty Pledge, which, until 2013, funded only US organisations (and their foreign sub-grantees) opposing prostitution, and which continues to restrict funding, to organisations outside of the United States.

The SRHR of sex workers are further undermined by policies restricting women's SRHR more broadly, including the criminalisation of abortion, and other policies and efforts which restrict access to safe abortion. In 2017, the Mexico City policy—known also as the Global Gag rule—was expanded to include all US government aid, preventing organisations from receiving US funding if they engage in any abortion-related activities, including offering abortion information, services, referrals, and/or advocating for abortion law reform. Furthermore, organisations are excluded from receiving funding even if abortion-related information and services are provided by another donor.

The criminalisation and stigmatisation of sex work influence community perceptions of sex workers, reinforcing stigma and discrimination both in healthcare settings and in day-to-day life [18]. As a result, sex workers are often denied equal access to quality health services and may experience difficulties accessing SRH care across their life course [19–24]. Together, these overlapping structural barriers contribute to a lack of targeted services, thus violating the right of sex workers to comprehensive and appropriate SRH care.

Gaps in Comprehensive Sexual and Reproductive Health Services Across the Life Course

While sex workers are entitled to the full spectrum of SRH rights, for this population, critical gaps in the provision of SRH services remain. Closing the gap in SRHR for sex workers continues to be a global priority, with the 2016 Committee on Economic, Social and Cultural Rights' recommendations underscoring the need to protect sex workers from violence, coercion, and discrimination, and to ensure their access to sexual and reproductive healthcare services across the life course [2].

Nonetheless, at the expense of this population's broader SRH needs, the dominant view on the part of public health authorities of sex workers as "vectors of disease" [25] has perpetuated a narrow focus on the prevention, testing, and treatment interventions of HIV and sexually transmitted infection (STI). While sex workers are particularly vulnerable to HIV and other STIs, they often lack access to routine SRH screening, including reproductive-tract screening. Female sex workers, for example, are disproportionately affected by high-risk strains of the human papillomavirus (HPV) [26] and cervical cancer [27], but cervical screening among sex workers remains low [28, 29].

The gap in SRH screening is particularly pronounced for male sex workers, whose SRH needs are poorly understood and are often conflated with those of gay men and men who have sex with men (MSM) [30]. The paucity of data on male sex workers' health has contributed to the near-complete absence of targeted SRH services, including screening for anorectal STIs and anal cancers [31].

Similarly, while transgender sex workers bear a high burden of STIs [32], including HIV (estimates from 2012 placed the global prevalence at 19%) [33], the holistic SRH needs of transgender sex workers are seldom acknowledged. Data available on transgender sex workers focus almost exclusively on STIs and HIV [34, 35], and are often limited by small sample sizes and/or failure to disaggregate transgender women from MSM. The near-complete lack of data on the SRH needs of sex working transgender men means the SRHR of these workers remain even less visible. Transgender sex workers contend with myriad social and structural forces driving SRH inequities, including pervasive violence, and gender-related stigma and discrimination, which can occur within health settings [36]. Gender-sensitive SRH care, including counselling and referrals to or provision of hormone therapy, and other gender-affirming services, are essential SRH services for transgender sex workers [37, 38]. Such services remain scarce and, where available, are rarely integrated into existing SRH programming.

Globally, sex workers experience high rates of unintended pregnancies [39, 40]. For example, 53% of sex workers in a Colombian study reported having had at least one induced abortion [41]. In a study conducted in Uzbekistan [42], roughly a quarter of sex workers reported having had three or more abortions. Such high rates of unintended pregnancies have been attributed to a number of structural factors, including criminalisation, gender-based violence, and difficulties negotiating client condom use [39–42]. In poorly resourced settings in particular, there is significant unmet need for effective contraceptive methods [43–47], especially voluntary access to long-acting reversible contraceptives such as intrauterine devices and implants. For instance, while 53% of sex workers in a Colombian study reported having had an abortion, 17% reported using no contraceptive methods at all [41]. In Cambodia, only 10% of sex workers reported using hormonal contraceptives [43]. Similarly, a study across three Russian cities documented that only one-third of sex workers used contraceptive methods other than condoms [45].

Significant challenges to accessing effective contraception include the availability and cost of services, plus the distances involved in accessing them. Due to limited access to family planning and contraceptive counselling services, sex workers may also receive less information about the effective use and potential side effects of contraceptives [48]. In some cases, sex workers are not even offered the full range of effective contraceptives [25].

Many sex workers also lack access to safe and affordable abortion procedures [49–52], particularly in contexts where abortion is criminalised. For example, a qualitative study in Brazil revealed that most sex workers seeking abortions used illegally acquired misoprostol, and many of these procedures resulted in serious health complications including haemorrhaging and the need for hospitalisation [50]. There remains a near-dearth of data when it comes to sex workers on the subject of their needs or requirements for care post-abortion, despite the high rates of (often unsafe) abortion in this population.

The SRH needs of sex workers who are pregnant, parenting, or who wish to become pregnant, also remain unmet, including access to essential services such as prenatal, delivery, and postnatal care [53]. The SRHR needs of pregnant and parenting SWs remain inadequately addressed in both health systems and research, partly owing to public perceptions of sex workers as unlikely or unfit parents. However, sex work and parenthood are intimately entwined: many sex workers have children, and many support dependent children. One study among Kenyan sex workers reported that almost 90% had dependent children [54]. Emerging evidence suggests sex workers have pregnancy intentions similar to women in other occupations [55, 56]. However, numerous social and structural barriers—the criminalisation of sex work [57], stigma, and lack of appropriate, low-barrier services—create challenges for parenting sex workers by limiting access to and engagement with pregnancy-related SRH services. Reduced access to safe conception services (including pre-conception counselling), as well as pre- and postnatal care, may result in serious SRH and rights violations at a critical time in the reproductive lives of sex workers [56]. Furthermore, personal accounts reveal serious violations to their reproductive choices, including coerced sterilisation and abortions, as well as the disproportionate removal of children from sex workers, due to their parents' occupation [13].

This chapter draws from research conducted by the Global Network of Sex Work Projects (NSWP) for its Briefing Paper, "Sex Workers' Access to Comprehensive Sexual and Reproductive Health Services" [58]. NSWP uses a methodology that ensures the grassroots voices of sex workers and sex worker-led organisations are heard. While identifying global trends, this process documents issues faced by sex workers at local, national, and regional levels. The NSWP Secretariat manages the production of briefing papers and conducts consultations among its members to document evidence. To do this, NSWP contracts:

- Global Consultants to undertake desk research and global e-consultations with NSWP member organisations, coordinate and collate inputs from National Consultants, analyse regional differences, and draft the global briefing papers.
- National Consultants to gather information and document country case studies

This chapter presents excerpts gathered from in-depth interviews, focus group discussions, and a global e-consultation conducted by NSWP with member organisations in September to October of 2017. National consultants conducted in-depth interviews and focus group discussions (FGDs) with 171 male, female, and transgender sex workers across ten countries (Austria, Bahamas, Canada, El Salvador, Indonesia, Kyrgyzstan, Namibia, Nepal, Peru, and Rwanda), using a standardised interview/FGD questionnaire designed to elicit the experiences of sex workers when accessing SRH services. The same questionnaire was distributed throughout the NSWP network, garnering 13 responses from NSWP member organisations.

Responses gathered from the interviews, focus groups, and e-consultation were analysed to identify global trends, and organised by theme. In this chapter, we present the most prominent themes emerging from this consultation, alongside representative quotes illustrating each theme. All quotes and findings presented in this chapter originate from the NSWP Briefing Paper, "Sex Workers' Access to Comprehensive Sexual and Reproductive Health Services", and its accompanying research.

Barriers to Accessing SRH Services and Rights: Findings from In-Depth Interviews and Focus Groups

Widespread Criminalisation, Discrimination, and Stigmatisation in Healthcare Settings

The direct and indirect criminalisation of sex work was found to simultaneously increase the vulnerability of sex workers to violence, unintended pregnancies, and HIV and STI transmission, while decreasing their access to SRH services. Fearing legal repercussions such as arrest, detention, and loss of child custody, sex workers were found to avoid seeking vital SRH care at critical moments across their life course. A Rwandan sex worker described how the criminalisation of sex work in Rwanda prevented her from accessing post-exposure prophylaxis, as well as legal recourse, after being raped by police officers.

> *Late one night, I was arrested by two police officers who asked me to have sex with them in case I wanted to be set free. When I refused, one of them forced himself on me and raped me. I had nowhere to report since sex work is illegal under the Rwandan penal code. Because of this, I couldn't even get post-exposure prophylaxis that is offered to all rape victims. Thankfully, I didn't get pregnant... But I tested HIV positive. I couldn't believe it since I had tried to protect myself against HIV all the years I was in sex work. I went back for another test, which confirmed my status. To get infected through rape was heartbreaking.*—Female sex worker, Rwanda

Criminalisation was also found to fuel stigma and discrimination among healthcare providers, coalescing with moral judgements surrounding sexuality, gender, and parenthood. Stigma and discrimination were particularly prevalent in public SRH care settings, where medical staff seldom receive sensitivity training surrounding sex workers' health concerns. Upon disclosure or outing of their profession, many sex workers reported changes in the attitude of staff towards them, lower quality of care, or even denial of services.

> *I went to the ER with a lot of abdominal pain and was denied services because I was a sex worker. They told me they had to finish with the rest of their patients first before providing me with assistance.*—Female sex worker, Peru

> *I was sent back number of times by the health providers when I went in for family planning because most of the time I was drunk and a very well-known sex worker. I was told to change the person I am, and only then can I be helped.*—Female sex worker, Namibia

Due to widespread homophobia and transphobia, male and transgender sex workers face even greater stigma and discrimination in SRH care settings.

> *... The doctor... lifted up my pullover and noticed that I had no breasts. She started telling me that my lifestyle was wrong. I was born a man and thus I should be a man. I shouldn't wear skirts or use makeup... After that incident I am really scared of going to a clinic.*—Transgender sex worker, Kyrgyzstan

As a result, many sex workers chose not to disclose their profession to healthcare workers, or they avoided seeking care altogether.

Lack of Tailored and Integrated SRH Services

By and large, the NSWP community consultation confirmed that the healthcare available to sex workers remained limited in scope and failed to address the population-specific SRH concerns. Comprehensive SRH services, including pregnancy care, reproductive cancer screening, and hormone therapy, were rarely integrated with HIV and STI programmes, requiring sex workers to travel to multiple locations to address their various concerns. Moreover, as public health services were aimed towards the general population, and specialised non-governmental SRH programmes remained scarce, critical gaps persisted in the coverage of sex workers' SRH care.

In Nepal, where a large portion of female sex workers have been affected by cervical cancer, the lack of information and accessible SRH services was reported to contribute to higher mortality rates.

> ... (Sex workers) are not very aware of treatment for cervical cancer, as they think that it cannot be detected in advance. They have seen that many female sex workers have died of cervical cancer... There are only a few clinics for female sex workers that are providing free cervical screenings, and they are difficult to reach from residential areas.—Jagriti Mahila Maha Sangh, Nepal

The unique SRH needs of male and transgender sex workers were rarely addressed in both public and non-governmental health settings, exacerbating inequities and isolation for these populations. As one male sex worker described,

> In SRH services, we male sex workers have no type of access... because we are not considered within the health care system... We are struggling to be included in health care programs specific to our work activities and our masculinities. We can only access health care as MSM (men who have sex with men), and only from a pathologized approach in HIV/AIDS, not in an integrated way.—Asociación Goover, Ecuador

The lack of targeted, non-judgemental SRH care also increased sex workers' reliance on self-medication. Due to the unavailability of supervised hormone therapy and other gender-affirming treatments, many transgender sex workers chose to self-medicate, risking long-term health consequences such as thromboembolism, liver dysfunction, breast cancer, and coronary artery disease. The sharing and reusing of injection supplies may also put transgender sex workers at greater risk of HIV and Hepatitis C transmission.

> We, trans women ... have to buy syringes used by veterinarians so that we can inject hormones, since in our country, in our region, there is no hormone treatment.—Transgender sex worker, Peru

Harmful and Coercive SRH Policies

Mandatory testing and treatment of HIV and STI occur in many regions of the world where sex work is legalised and criminalised. This violates the bodily integrity of sex workers and reinforces unequal power dynamics between provider and patient. In Austria, sex workers explained that, in order to work legally, they were required to undergo weekly STI tests and quarterly HIV tests at government-run facilities. This policy eroded their trust in healthcare systems, and discouraged sex workers from speaking openly about their SRH concerns.

> This (testing) center is more of a (means) to control sex workers' bodies than it is a healthcare and counseling space.—Sex worker, Austria

Even in the absence of formal mandatory testing and treatment policies, coercive practices were still widespread. In Ecuador, health centres frequently required sex workers to take HIV and STI tests in order to receive free condoms—undermining the concept of voluntary testing and further restricting access to already-limited sexual health supplies.

In our country there is a practice to obtain condoms, which is to force us to take a voluntary test, and only then can we access condoms. There is also a shortage of (prevention) supplies and many problems to obtain them.—Coalición de Trabajadores Sexuales de Quito, Ecuador

In other cases, healthcare professionals forced or coerced sex workers into undergoing abortions or sterilisation procedures, blatantly infringing upon their bodily integrity and right to bear children. At the same time, in regions of the world where abortion is prohibited or restricted, sex workers may risk their lives and health by using illegal service providers. While the criminalisation of abortion affects all women, sex workers may be particularly impacted by this due to their increased susceptibility to sexual violence and reduced access to contraceptives.

Every type of abortion is punishable and sex workers, if they want to practice, have to go to clandestine clinics where they risk their lives and health.—Asociacion de Mujeres Las Golondrinas, Nicaragua

Logistical and Practical Barriers to SRH Care

Given that the majority of SRH services available to sex workers are offered at public healthcare centres targeting the general population, the location of clinics, their opening hours, and the fees they charged were often found to be incompatible with the reality of sex workers' lives.

A typical situation is such that after working at night, sex workers sleep during the day, and the opening hours, for example, of the state dermatovenereological center, are only until 3pm.—Tais Plus, Kyrgyzstan

To address their various needs, many sex workers needed to travel long distances due to SRH services being scattered across multiple locations. Sex workers explained that this factor could result in reduced uptake and adherence, as well as income loss. For individuals living in rural or poorly resourced areas, these logistical barriers were compounded.

A very small percentage of (sex workers) referred to HIV testing centers from general clinics will actually arrive there at the end of the day.—Avenir Jeune de l'Ouest, Cameroon

Some sex workers described accessing select SRH services at mobile health clinics located near their places of work. While convenient, some of these clinics were poorly designed, with inadequate consideration given to sex workers' privacy. As a result, sex workers who relied on these clinics for their SRH care may not have been afforded the same level of confidentiality as patients from the general population.

I receive my results in the corner of the room and I'm scared that the others will hear some-thing about me... when we do VCT (voluntary counseling and testing) in this facility they should partition the room... not give us our results in the corner of an open room where others can listen.—Female sex worker, Indonesia

Costs for comprehensive SRH care, including non-barrier contraceptives, mater-nity care, abortion, hormone therapy, PrEP, and other medications, were found to be prohibitive for some sex workers. Even where affordable subsidised SRH care was available, many sex workers lacked the necessary identification, residency, or employment documents to benefit from these programmes. In countries where sex work is a regulated profession, such as Austria, mandatory national health insurance costs were found to be inaccessible for some sex workers, and did not always cover essential services such as maternity care.

Some months, I don't earn so much. I can't afford to pay the bill (the Social Security Service) sends me.—Sex worker, Austria

Supporting the SRH Rights and Needs of SWs: Community Recommendations

Grounded in the lived experiences of sex workers globally, these narratives shed light on the tremendous impact that overlapping structural barriers play in con-straining sex workers' access to comprehensive, rights-based SRH services. Echoing international guidelines, the sex workers and sex worker-led organisations partici-pating in the NSWP consultation highlighted a number of recommendations to bet-ter support the SRH needs and rights of sex workers [58]:

1. *"Decriminalize sex work, HIV transmission, and same-sex sexual activity, and depathologize transgender identities"*. [58]
   The criminalisation of sex work, same-sex relationships, and HIV continues to trigger a cascade of harms, including reduced access to SRH services due to fears of legal repercussions, judgement, or harassment. As such, participants pointed to the decriminalisation of sex work as essential to improving sex work-ers' SRH and rights [58].
   A decriminalised legal framework can promote the SRH and rights of sex workers in a number of ways. Alongside mitigating the harms of stigma within communities and healthcare settings, the legal empowerment of sex workers, LGBTQ people, and people living with HIV can support sex workers' ability to organise and advocate for conditions and SRH services that best suit their needs [59]. Decriminalisation of sex work can facilitate the implementation of sex worker-led structural SRH interventions, including access to safer indoor work-places. Such access may subsequently enable the provision of rights-based SRH services at or close to sex work venues, confer protection from client-perpetrated violence, and offer a level of control and privacy necessary to fulfil sex workers' reproductive rights [60, 61]. The Global Network of Sex Work Projects has

advocated for the decriminalisation of sex work for 25 years. Numerous international organisations have followed suit in recommending decriminalisation, including WHO, UNAIDS, UNFPA, UNDP, and Amnesty International [62].

2. *"Remove barriers to accessing public health care systems for migrant sex workers, as well as individuals who cannot provide formal proof of income or employment"*. [58]

Restrictions surrounding public health services prevent sex workers from accessing essential SRH care. As a result, migrant sex workers may depend on limited NGO programming or emergency-room services for their SRH needs.

3. *"Eliminate mandatory and coercive HIV and STI testing and treatment policies"*. [58]

The pervasive stigma around sex work, including portrayals of sex workers as vectors of disease, often manifests as mandatory and/or coercive HIV/STI testing policies [63]. Coercive HIV testing, or the surreptitious testing for HIV by healthcare workers or police without obtaining consent from sex workers [64–66], violates sex workers' rights to bodily integrity. Such practices also foster their distrust in authorities and further excludes sex workers from vital SRH services. Similarly, mandatory HIV/STI testing policies also undermine the right of sex workers to make autonomous choices regarding their own SRH.

Sex workers when consulted recommended the elimination of mandatory and coercive HIV/STI testing and treatment policies, including HIV/STI testing and treatment without consent. These recommendations strongly align with the WHO and UNAIDS statement on HIV testing and counselling, which opposes mandatory and coercive HIV and STI testing, and emphasises the importance of adhering to the "5 C's"—consent, confidentiality, counselling, correct test results, and connection/linkage to prevention care and treatment [67].

4. *"Address the stigma and discrimination that female, male and transgender sex workers experience from mainstream SRH services"*. [58]

Stigma and discrimination remain pervasive in SRH health settings, particularly mainstream services, and continue to hamper access to and retention in, care. To support the SRH rights of sex workers, healthcare providers should receive specialised training focused on providing non-judgemental and gender-sensitive care tailored to the needs of the sex workers of all genders. Qualitative findings from Argentina suggest that specialised healthcare provider training focused on the needs of cis and transgender sex workers has improved provider–patient relationships and has contributed to increased uptake and continued engagement in HIV care [65].

Addressing stigma and discrimination within SRH care settings is crucial. However, multilevel interventions, including structural interventions, are essential to stemming stigma relating to sex work, gender, and HIV status within the community.

A promising policy intervention to reduce gender-based stigma towards transgender sex workers is Argentina's "Gender Identity Law", rolled out 2012, which acknowledges the basic right of transgender individuals to personhood. The law recommends universal coverage for transition-related health care and allows individuals to change their name on legal documents (e.g. identity cards and birth certificates). Since this law was enacted, reports from transgender sex workers suggest improved patient–provider attitudes and relationships, and improved access to health care [66], including retention in HIV care. Acknowledging that a shift in attitudes on the part of the community and care providers takes time, there is an immediate need for the development of sex worker-led systems to redress the ongoing stigma experienced by sex workers within healthcare settings [58].

5. *"Increase funding and support for comprehensive SRH services and programs designed to meet the needs of sex workers of all genders"*. [58]
   Advance a holistic approach to comprehensive SRH services for sex workers that extends beyond HIV and STI testing and treatment. [58]

   In line with UNAIDS recommendations [66], there is a need to improve funding for and access to comprehensive, sex worker-specific SRH services, which should be integrated with other essential services, including HIV/STI programming. Moving away from a strict focus on HIV/STI services, there is a need for comprehensive services that holistically address sex workers' broader SRH needs and rights, as defined in the Sex Worker Information Tool (SWIT) [38].

6. *"Ensure access to safe, legal, and affordable abortion and post-abortion services"*. [58]

   Action is needed to ensure access to safe and affordable abortion and post-abortion care for sex workers. Restrictions on abortion may lead women to risk their health through the use of informal methods of termination.

7. *"Integrate SRH care with HIV and STI services in line with a 'one-stop-shop' model"*. [58]

   To address logistical barriers to accessing services, including the need to travel long distances to obtain fragmented services, sex workers highlighted the need for SRH services to be integrated into HIV and STI services in a "one-stop-shop" model. While questions remain regarding the best model for SRH service integration, and more evaluations of the effectiveness of integrated SRH models are needed [53], emerging research suggests such an approach could improve uptake of broader SRH services [49, 68, 69].

8. *"Promote SRH education programming for sex workers and their clients"*. [58]

   Targeted SRH information is essential to fulfiling the right of sex workers to informed SRH decisions and improving their access to SRH services. SRH education targeting clients, particularly surrounding safe sex practices, is also critical, and reduces the burden of educating clients that sex workers currently shoulder.

9. *"Prioritize funding for community empowerment models of SRH services"*. [58]

   It is imperative that the voices of sex workers steer the development and implementation of SRH programmes and services affecting them. Community-led SRH models can take many forms, including outreach programmes, drop-in centers, peer educators and navigators, and sensitisation trainings for medical personnel, with sex workers' collective ownership being a hallmark of these initiatives. Community-led HIV/STI approaches have been linked to positive

SRH outcomes, including reduced HIV/STIs and increased condom use by clients, while also addressing social and structural barriers to SRH and rights [58].

Sex worker-led interventions that empower sex workers and foster community engagement with key stakeholders have also been found to help reduce stigma and violence towards sex workers [68, 69]. In collaboration with Durbar Mahila Samanwaya Committee, the Sonagachi project in Kolkata is an example of such an approach. The multifaceted intervention included a number of key components, including community-level interventions that: articulated sex workers' rights; involved sex workers as staff, programme leaders, key decision-makers; and facilitated the sex workers' organisation as an occupational employment group [70]. Together, these initiatives contributed to improving sex workers' collective social power and reducing stigma [70]. Another important feature of Sonagachi's success and sustainability included the involvement of and careful negotiations between sex workers and influential "non-sex worker" interest groups, for example, madams, local clubs, healthcare providers, and funding agencies. Acknowledging and managing existing power relations in this manner has had numerous benefits, including the reduction of stigma [71]. This important work is being continued by the Durbar Mahila Samanwaya Committee.

Despite the immense promise that community-empowerment models hold, increased political and financial support for community-led SRH models is urgently needed, alongside the removal of regressive policies (e.g. PEPFAR APLO, Mexico City Policy) and laws (e.g. the criminalisation of sex work), which impede sex workers' ability to organise, and limit the funding and scope of sex worker-led SRH services [58].

Conclusion

Sex workers around the world continue to face serious SRH inequities, which are shaped by a lack of comprehensive, integrated, and non-judgemental SRH care tailored to their diverse needs. To date, the broader SRH needs of sex workers have been neglected, with existing efforts focused narrowly on HIV/STI prevention. Limited access for sex workers to comprehensive and integrated SRH services represents a serious violation of their fundamental right to obtain the highest attainable standards of SRH. This limitation points to the urgent need for political action to close these gaps. Such efforts need to tackle the structural barriers that drive gaps in the SRH of sex workers, including criminalisation and other rights-violating policies, stigma, and violence. At the same time, these efforts must empower sex workers to shape and lead the SRH policies and programming that affect them.

Conflicts of Interest The authors have no conflicts of interest to declare.

References

1. UN General Assembly. Convention on the elimination of all forms of discrimination against women; 1979.
2. UN Committee on Economic, Social, and Cultural Rights. General Comment No. 22 (2016) on the right to sexual and reproductive health (article 12 of the International Covenant on Economic, Social, and Cultural Rights); 2016.
3. Women Fourth World Conference on Women. Beijing declaration and platform for action; 1995. p. 93–7.
4. Eleventh International Conference of the International Coordinating Committee of National Institutes for the Promotion and Protection of Human Rights. Amman Declaration and Programme of Action; 2012.
5. UN General Assembly. Universal declaration of human rights; 1948.
6. International Conference on Population and Development. Programme of action; 1994.
7. UN General Assembly. Transforming our world: the 2030 Agenda for Sustainable Development; 2015.
8. Shannon K, Rusch M, Shoveller J, Alexson D, Gibson K, Tyndall MW. Mapping violence and policing as an environmental-structural barrier to health service and syringe availability among substance-using women in street-level sex work. Int J Drug Policy. 2008;19(2):140–7.
9. Platt L, Grenfell P, Meiksin R, Elmes J, Sherman SG, Sanders T, et al. Associations between sex work laws and sex workers' health: a systematic review and meta-analysis of quantitative and qualitative studies. PLoS Med. 2018;15(12):e1002680.
10. Lyons T, Krusi A, Pierre L, Smith A, Small W, Shannon K. Experiences of trans women and two-spirit persons accessing women-specific health and housing services in a downtown neighborhood of Vancouver, Canada. LGBT Health. 2016;3(5):373–8.
11. Duff P, Birungi J, Dobrer S, Akello M, Muzaaya G, Shannon K. Social and structural factors increase consistent condom use by sex workers' one-time and regular clients in Northern Uganda. AIDS Care. 2018;30(6):751–9.
12. Shannon K, Strathdee SA, Goldenberg SM, Duff P, Mwangi P, Rusakova M, et al. Global epidemiology of HIV among female sex workers: influence of structural determinants. Lancet. 2015;385(9962):55–71.
13. Iran Official Calls for Sterilization for Sex Workers, Homeless Drug Addicts. Radio free Europe; 2017.
14. Qiao S, Li X, Zhang C, Zhou Y, Shen Z, Tang Z, et al. Psychological fears among low-paid female sex workers in southwest China and their implications for HIV prevention. PLoS One. 2014;9(10):e111012.
15. Anderson S, Shannon K, Li J, Lee Y, Chettiar J, Goldenberg S. Condoms and sexual health education as evidence: impact of criminalisation of in-call venues and managers on migrant sex workers access to HIV/STI prevention in a Canadian setting. BMC Int Health Hum Rights. 2016;16(1):30.
16. Deering KN, Amin A, Shoveller J, Nesbitt A, Garcia-Moreno C, Duff P, et al. A systematic review of the correlates of violence against sex workers. Am J Public Health. 2014;104(5):e42–54.
17. Baral S, Holland CE, Shannon K, Logie C, Semugoma P, Sithole B, et al. Enhancing benefits or increasing harms: community responses for HIV among men who have sex with men, transgender women, female sex workers, and people who inject drugs. J Acquir Immune Defic Syndr. 2014;66(Suppl 3):S319–28.
18. Krüsi A, Kerr T, Taylor C, Rhodes T, Shannon K. 'They won't change it back in their heads that we're trash': the intersection of sex work-related stigma and evolving policing strategies. Sociol Health Illn. 2016;38(7):1137–50.
19. Rocha-Jimenez T, Morales-Miranda S, Fernandez-Casanueva C, Brouwer KC, Goldenberg SM. Stigma and unmet sexual and reproductive health needs among international migrant sex workers at the Mexico-Guatemala border. Int J Gynaecol Obstet. 2018;143(1):37–43.

20. King EJ, Maman S, Bowling JM, Moracco KE, Dudina V. The influence of stigma and discrimination on female sex workers' access to HIV services in St. Petersburg, Russia. AIDS Behav. 2013;17(8):2597–603.
21. Lazarus L, Deering KN, Nabess R, Gibson K, Tyndall MW, Shannon K. Occupational stigma as a primary barrier to health care for street-based sex workers in Canada. Cult Health Sex. 2012;14(2):139–50.
22. Crowell TA, Keshinro B, Baral SD, Schwartz SR, Stahlman S, Nowak RG, et al. Stigma, access to healthcare, and HIV risks among men who sell sex to men in Nigeria. J Int AIDS Soc. 2017;20(1):21489.
23. Nnko S, Kuringe E, Nyato D, Drake M, Casalini C, Shao A, et al. Determinants of access to HIV testing and counselling services among female sex workers in sub-Saharan Africa: a systematic review. BMC Public Health. 2019;19(1):15.
24. Scorgie F, Nakato D, Harper E, Richter M, Maseko S, Nare P, et al. 'We are despised in the hospitals': sex workers' experiences of accessing health care in four African countries. Cult Health Sex. 2013;15(4):450–65.
25. Dhana A, Luchters S, Moore L, Lafort Y, Roy A, Scorgie F, et al. Systematic review of facility-based sexual and reproductive health services for female sex workers in Africa. Glob Health. 2014;10(1):46.
26. Soohoo M, Blas M, Byraiah G, Carcamo C, Brown B. Cervical HPV infection in female sex workers: a global perspective. Open AIDS J. 2013;7:58–66.
27. Mak R. Cervical smears and human papillomavirus typing in sex workers. Sex Transm Infect. 2004;80(2):118–20.
28. Duff P, Ogilvie G, Shoveller J, Amram O, Chettiar J, Nguyen P, et al. Barriers to cervical screening among sex workers in Vancouver. Am J Public Health. 2016;106(2):366–73.
29. Jeal N, Salisbury C. Self-reported experiences of health services among female street-based prostitutes: a cross-sectional survey. Br J Gen Pract. 2004;54(504):515–9.
30. Baral SD, Friedman MR, Geibel S, Rebe K, Bozhinov B, Diouf D, et al. Male sex workers: practices, contexts, and vulnerabilities for HIV acquisition and transmission. Lancet. 2015;385(9964):260–73.
31. GNP+ and Network of Sex work Projects (NSWP). Advancing the sexual and reproductive health and human rights of sex workers living with HIV; 2010.
32. MacCarthy S, Poteat T, Xia Z, Roque NL, Hyun Jin Kim A, Baral S, et al. Current research gaps: a global systematic review of HIV and sexually transmissible infections among transgender populations. Sex Health. 2017;14(5):456–68.
33. Baral SD, Poteat T, Stromdahl S, Wirtz AL, Guadamuz TE, Beyrer C. Worldwide burden of HIV in transgender women: a systematic review and meta-analysis. Lancet Infect Dis. 2013;13(3):214–22.
34. Shannon K, Crago AL, Baral SD, Bekker LG, Kerrigan D, Decker MR, et al. The global response and unmet actions for HIV and sex workers. Lancet. 2018;392(10148):698–710.
35. Reisner SL, Poteat T, Keatley J, Cabral M, Mothopeng T, Dunham E, et al. Global health burden and needs of transgender populations: a review. Lancet. 2016;388(10042):412–36.
36. Poteat T, Scheim A, Xavier J, Reisner S, Baral S. Global epidemiology of HIV infection and related syndemics affecting transgender people. J Acquir Immune Defic Syndr. 2016;72(Suppl 3):S210–9.
37. Reisner SL, Bradford J, Hopwood R, Gonzalez A, Makadon H, Todisco D, et al. Comprehensive transgender healthcare: the gender affirming clinical and public health model of Fenway Health. J Urban Health. 2015;92(3):584–92.
38. World Health Organization, UNFP, Joint United Nations Programme on HIV/AIDS, Global Network of Sex Work Projects, The World Bank. Implementing comprehensive HIV/STI programmes with sex workers: practical approaches from collaborative interventions. Geneva: WHO; 2013.
39. Ampt FH, Willenberg L, Agius PA, Chersich M, Luchters S, Lim MSC. Incidence of unintended pregnancy among female sex workers in low-income and middle-income countries: a systematic review and meta-analysis. BMJ Open. 2018;8(9):e021779.

40. Delvaux T, Crabbe F, Seng S, Laga M. The need for family planning and safe abortion services among women sex workers seeking STI care in Cambodia. Reprod Health Matters. 2003;1(21):88–95.
41. Bautista CT, Mejia A, Leal L, Ayala C, Sanchez JL, Montano SM. Prevalence of lifetime abortion and methods of contraception among female sex workers in Bogota, Colombia. Contraception. 2008;1(3):209–13.
42. Todd CS, Alibayeva G, Sanchez JL, Bautista CT, Carr JK, Earhart KC. Utilization of contraception and abortion and its relationship to HIV infection among female sex workers in Tashkent, Uzbekistan. J Womens Health. 2006;1(4):318–23.
43. Duff P, Evans JL, Stein ES, Page K, Maher L, Young Women's Health Study Collaborative. High pregnancy incidence and low contraceptive use among a prospective cohort of female entertainment and sex workers in Phnom Penh, Cambodia. BMC Pregnancy Childbirth. 2018;1(1):128.
44. Khan MR, Turner AN, Pettifor A, Van Damme K, Rabenja NL, Ravelomanana N, et al. Unmet need for contraception among sex workers in Madagascar. Contraception. 2009;1(3):221–7.
45. Martin CE, Wirtz AL, Mogilniy V, Peryshkina A, Beyrer C, Decker MR. Contraceptive use among female sex workers in three Russian cities. Int J Gynaecol Obstet. 2015;1(2):156–60.
46. Todd CS, Nasir A, Raza Stanekzai M, Scott PT, Strathdee SA, Botros BA, et al. Contraceptive utilization and pregnancy termination among female sex workers in Afghanistan. J Womens Health. 2010;1(11):2057–62.
47. Zhang XD, Kennedy E, Temmerman M, Li Y, Zhang WH, Luchters S. High rates of abortion and low levels of contraceptive use among adolescent female sex workers in Kunming, China: a cross-sectional analysis. Eur J Contracept Reprod Health Care. 2014;1(5):368–78.
48. Luchters S, Bosire W, Feng A, Richter ML, King'ola N, Ampt F, et al. "A baby was an added burden": predictors and consequences of unintended pregnancies for female sex workers in Mombasa, Kenya: a mixed-methods study. PLoS One. 2016;1(9):e0162871.
49. Schwartz S, Papworth E, Thiam-Niangoin M, Abo K, Drame F, Diouf D, et al. An urgent need for integration of family planning services into HIV care: the high burden of unplanned pregnancy, termination of pregnancy, and limited contraception use among female sex workers in Cote d'Ivoire. J Acquir Immune Defic Syndr. 2015;1:S91–8.
50. Madeiro AP, Diniz D. Induced abortion among Brazilian female sex workers: a qualitative study. Cien Saude Colet. 2015;1(2):587–93.
51. Erickson M, Goldenberg SM, Akello M, Muzaaya G, Nguyen P, Birungi J, et al. Incarceration and exposure to internally displaced persons camps associated with reproductive rights abuses among sex workers in northern Uganda. J Fam Plann Reprod Health Care. 2017;1(3):201–9.
52. Feldblum PJ, Nasution MD, Hoke TH, Van Damme K, Turner AN, Gmach R, et al. Pregnancy among sex workers participating in a condom intervention trial highlights the need for dual protection. Contraception. 2007;1(2):105–10.
53. Schwartz SR, Baral S. Fertility-related research needs among women at the margins. [Review]. Reprod Health Matters. 2015;1(45):30–46.
54. Elmore-Meegan M, Conroy RM, Agala CB. Sex workers in Kenya, numbers of clients and associated risks: an exploratory survey. Reprod Health Matters. 2004;1(23):50–7.
55. Duff P, Shoveller J, Feng C, Ogilvie G, Montaner J, Shannon K. Pregnancy intentions among female sex workers: recognising their rights and wants as mothers. J Fam Plann Reprod Health Care. 2015;1(2):102–8.
56. Schwartz SR, Papworth E, Ky-Zerbo O, Anato S, Grosso A, Ouedraogo HG, et al. Safer conception needs for HIV prevention among female sex workers in Burkina Faso and Togo. Infect Dis Obstet Gynecol. 2014;1:296245.
57. Global Commission on HIV and the law. HIV and the law: risks, rights, & health; 2012.
58. Global Network of Sex Work Projects. Briefing Paper: Sex workers' access to comprehensive sexual and reproductive health services; 2018.
59. Kerrigan D, Kennedy CE, Morgan-Thomas R, Reza-Paul S, Mwangi P, Win KT, et al. A community empowerment approach to the HIV response among sex workers: effectiveness, challenges, and considerations for implementation and scale-up. Lancet. 2014;6736(14):1–14.

60. Goldenberg SM, Duff P, Krusi A, Shannon K. Work environments and HIV prevention: a qualitative review and meta-synthesis of sex worker narratives. BMC Public Health. 2015;15:1241.
61. Duff P, Shoveller J, Dobrer S, Ogilvie G, Montaner J, Chettiar J, et al. The relationship between social, policy and physical venue features and social cohesion on condom use for pregnancy prevention among sex workers: a safer indoor work environment scale. J Epidemiol Community Health. 2015;69(7):666–72.
62. WHO, UNFPA, UNAIDS, NSWP. Prevention and treatment of HIV and other sexually transmitted infections for sex workers in low- and middle-income countries. Geneva, Switzerland: WHO, UNFPA, UNAIDS, NSWP; 2012.
63. Tokar A, Broerse JEW, Blanchard J, Roura M. HIV testing and counseling among female sex workers: a systematic literature review. AIDS Behav. 2018;22(8):2435–57.
64. Duff P, Supriyadinata C, Rowe C, Maher L, Nanditha N, Sarahdita T, et al. Supporting patient rights and informed consent in the context of HIV testing and treatment scale-up: experiences of female sex workers living with HIV in Bali, Indonesia. International AIDS Society Conference, Amsterdam; 2018.
65. Zalazar V, Cardozo N, Socias E, Aristegui I, Frola C, Antonini C, et al. Community perspectives on supporting the ethical scale-up of HIV services among transgender women in Argentina in the context of Treatment as Prevention. International AIDS Conference, Paris, France; 2017.
66. Aristegui I, Radusky P, Zalazar V, Romero M, Schwartz J, Sued O. Impact of the Gender Identity Law in Argentinean transgender women. Int J Transgenderism. 2017;18(4):446–56.
67. World Health Organization. Statement on HIV testing and counseling: WHO, UNAIDS reaffirm opposition to mandatory HIV testing. World Health Organization. 2012. Available from: https://www.who.int/hiv/events/2012/world_aids_day/hiv_testing_counselling/en/.
68. Beattie TSH, Bhattacharjee P, Ramesh BM, Gurnani V, Anthony J, Isac S, et al. Violence against female sex workers in Karnataka state, south India: impact on health, and reductions in violence following an intervention program. BMC Public Health. 2010;10:476.
69. Reza-Paul S, Beattie T, Syed HU, Venukumar KT, Venugopal MS, Fathima MP, et al. Declines in risk behaviour and sexually transmitted infection prevalence following a community-led HIV preventive intervention among female sex workers in Mysore, India. AIDS. 2008;22(Suppl 5):S91–100.
70. Jana S, Basu I, Rotheram-Borus MJ, Newman PA. The Sonagachi project: a sustainable community intervention program. AIDS Educ Prev. 2004;16(5):405–14.
71. Cornish F, Ghosh R. The necessary contradictions of 'community-led' health promotion: a case study of HIV prevention in an Indian red light district. Soc Sci Med. 2007;64(2):496–507.

Chapter 5
Exploring the Protective Role of Sex Work Social Cohesion in Contexts of Violence and Criminalisation: A Case Study with Gender-Diverse Sex Workers in Jamaica

Carmen H. Logie, Ying Wang, Patrick Lalor, Kandasi Levermore, and Davina Williams

Background

Sex workers experience stigma and marginalisation across global contexts. With claims of sex work being among the oldest professions in the world [1], there is a long history of stigma directed towards sex workers [2–4]. Stigma contributes to the precarious nature of sex work, producing social, legal, and work environments that increase exposure to violence while reducing access to legal support and health care [5–7]. The convergence of stigma and violence targeting sex workers contributes to disparities when it comes to their mental and sexual health. Client violence and stigma have been associated with depression among sex workers [8]. A systematic review examining HIV vulnerabilities among transgender (trans) sex workers noted that the convergence of violence and stigma against sex workers compromises sexual health [5].

Sex work is criminalised in many countries across the world [9, 10]. The criminalisation of sex work presents profound barriers to sex workers when it comes to accessing healthcare services and legal support [7]. Due to a lack of legal protections,

C. H. Logie (✉)
Factor-Iwentash Faculty of Social Work, University of Toronto, Toronto, ON, Canada

Women's College Research Institute, Women's College Hospital, Toronto, ON, Canada
e-mail: carmen.logie@utoronto.ca

Y. Wang
Factor-Iwentash Faculty of Social Work, University of Toronto, Toronto, ON, Canada

P. Lalor
Sex Work Association of Jamaica, Kingston, Jamaica

Jamaica AIDS Support for Life, Kingston, Jamaica

K. Levermore · D. Williams
Jamaica AIDS Support for Life, Kingston, Jamaica

© The Author(s) 2021
S. M. Goldenberg et al. (eds.), *Sex Work, Health, and Human Rights*,
https://doi.org/10.1007/978-3-030-64171-9_5

sex workers may experience violence from clients, community members, police and/ or intimate partners, with little recourse to justice [11]. This may be exacerbated for sexually and gender-diverse sex workers in contexts such as Jamaica, where not only sex work but also same-gender sexual practices are criminalised [12]. Studies from China report high prevalence of gender-based violence among sex workers, with associated harms including physical (e.g. chronic pain and injury), reproductive (e.g. unwanted pregnancy) and mental (e.g. post-traumatic stress disorder and depression) health outcomes [13]. A study from India reported that physical, verbal, and sexual violence from intimate partners and others were associated with suicide attempts and self-harm on the part of sex workers [14]. The convergence of violence and mental health challenges can reduce the ability of sex workers to negotiate safer sex practices, such as condom use [14–16].

Sex workers have identified that community-based empowerment interventions—initiated and led by sex workers—number among effective strategies towards reducing barriers to their health and well-being [17]. These strategies can provide education and peer-support. There is an evidence-base documenting the association between improved health among sex workers and sex worker social cohesion [17, 18]. Social cohesion is a complex concept that emphasises "sense of belonging" among people within a given society or community, and which may be leveraged to reduce violence and challenge injustices, including criminalisation and human rights violations [19]. Within this context of social cohesion, social support and mutual respect can facilitate knowledge sharing and other social norms that work towards promoting health. Social cohesion can also reduce barriers to accessing healthcare services [20].

Social cohesion when it comes to sex work is multifaceted and includes mutual aid and support. Social cohesion among sex workers is associated with increased odds of condom use and reduced HIV acquisition in countries including India [18], Swaziland [17], and Canada [16]. A study in Eswatini (Swaziland) [17] found that social cohesion among sex workers was associated with increased condom use, reduced social discrimination, and reduced police violence [17].

As several studies have reported in China [13, 21], India [14], and Jamaica [15], violence against sex workers contributes to mental health challenges and reduced condom use. Fewer studies have explored associations between social cohesion among sex workers and their mental health outcomes, which is important to examine, considering that social cohesion appears to have mental health benefits among general populations. A cross-national analysis of World Values surveys spanning 69 countries studied the associations between social capital and trust within a country and the health of its citizens [22]. Among some European countries, higher social capital was associated with improved health outcomes [22]. A longitudinal analysis in South Wales, UK [23] examined the correlation between social cohesion in neighbourhoods and individual mental health. They found that neighbourhoods with higher social cohesion were linked with the improved mental health of individuals. It is plausible that social cohesion among sex workers would similarly be associated with improved mental health outcomes in this group.

This chapter address the knowledge gaps regarding associations between social cohesion among sex workers and improved mental health and reduced exposure to violence. We provide a case example from Jamaica, a salient context within which to examine the experiences of cisgender men and trans women sex workers, who experience both sex work criminalisation and criminalisation of same-gender sexual practices [12]. The objectives of this chapter are to: (1) explore a case study reflecting the lived experiences of a sex worker in Jamaica; (2) examine findings from a community-based study among gender-diverse sex workers in Jamaica (cisgender men and women, and transgender (trans) women) that assesses social cohesion among sex workers and its associations with stigma against sex work, mental health, harassment and arrest by police, and exposure to violence; and (3) discuss implications for activists, researchers, and service providers working with sex workers in diverse global contexts. This chapter begins with the case study, followed by empirical findings from a community-based research project. We end by discussing implications for practice and future research.

Case Study: Human Rights Violations Experienced by a Sex Worker in Jamaica

The following case study was compiled following in-depth conversations with members of the Sex Worker Association of Jamaica (SWAJ), conducted by chapter author Patrick Lalor of SWAJ. Largely based on the narrative of one person, the overall goal of this case study is to share a snapshot of the life of a sex worker, with a focus on human rights experiences and social cohesion among sex workers. It cannot and does not aim to capture the lived experiences of all sex workers in Jamaica and may only reflect some elements of the realities shared by cisgender women sex workers in this country. The narrative is written in the third person to reflect the retelling of these lived experiences by practitioners and academics.

In the heart of Kingston, Jamaica, in an inner-city community called "Back to", a single mother struggled to support seven children. Her eldest daughter, Maria,[1] could not regularly attend school as she needed to care for her younger siblings while her mother worked. Maria started doing sex work when she was 18 years old, having dropped out of school when she became pregnant at 16. Although she became pregnant as a minor, despite the fact that sex with minors is an offence under Jamaican law, there were no legal consequences. A decade ago, when she was 20, Maria migrated from Kingston to Montego Bay to advance her sex work career. Over this decade Maria has had three other children, and reports experiences of abuse, legal involvement, rape and other forms of violence.

On a cold dark night in 2011 on the streets of Montego Bay, Maria was at her regular spot sourcing clients when a car pulled up and the driver asked if she was

---

[1] Name changed to a pseudonym to protect privacy.

doing business. After negotiating, she got into the car and the client drove to a remote location and then ordered her to get out. They went into what appeared to be an abandoned building and to her surprise there were three other men there waiting. One of them pulled out a gun and ordered her to remove her clothes. He informed her that if she did not comply, he would kill her. She did as she was ordered, and all four men raped her. She begged them not to kill her and did everything they commanded. After they were finished, one of the men searched her purse, took all of the money she had on her, including payments from two prior clients, and also took her phone. The men all left in the car. Maria was distraught, and in a strange and unknown place. She wandered in the dark until she saw a familiar landmark. She managed to hail a cab with a driver that she was familiar with, and he dropped her home.

Maria confirmed that, even though many sex workers in Jamaica face serious and commonplace incidences of violence and abuse, they never go to the police. She recounted experiences of three of her colleagues: the first, Mary,[2] went to the police to report being raped and was subsequently arrested for engaging in sex work. Angela[3] was raped by the police and told if that she tried to report this, she would be arrested, as sex work was illegal. The body of another colleague, Jacky,[4] was found on a beach after she had left her regular spot with an unknown client. In the midst of this trauma, in 2014, Maria lost custody of two of her children when she was declared an 'unfit mother' by child protective services, after the father of one of her children reported that she was a sex worker. There was no evidence indicating that she was endangering her children or causing them any harm—according to Maria, her children were removed due to the stigma of her being a sex worker. Maria visits her children, who are in state care, monthly but feels deep grief and loss every time she visits, as she is forced to leave them behind.

Maria reported that she had a nervous breakdown in 2015. So much was happening in her life, and she had no one to talk to. She found solace in meeting with fellow sex workers who gather nightly to share stories and frustrations. These meetings often involve alcohol, cigarettes and marijuana while waiting for the next clients. While these regular meetings help to ease the pain of struggles in everyday life, going back to reality is often challenging.

In 2016, a sex work club was raided, and Maria was the only sex worker arrested. A friend of Maria's, Gloria,[5] was familiar with the Sex Work Association of Jamaica (SWAJ) and contacted SWAJ who then intervened on Maria's behalf. Maria reported that the officer who arrested her had sex with her on numerous occasions and refused to pay. He warned Maria that if she refused to have sex with him, he would arrest her. A couple of weeks earlier, Maria had been standing on the corner with other sex workers when this same officer pulled up in a private vehicle and asked

---

[2] Name changed to a pseudonym to protect privacy.

[3] Name changed to a pseudonym to protect privacy.

[4] Name changed to a pseudonym to protect privacy.

[5] Name changed to a pseudonym to protect privacy.

her to get in. Maria refused, and when he tried to force her, the other sex workers began arguing and fighting him. He left, promising Maria that he would 'get her' for this. With SWAJ's assistance, Maria was not charged. Yet later that year, Maria was arrested by the same officer and charged for loitering in a public place; she pleaded guilty and was fined and released. At this point Maria began feeling suicidal. She started to engage with SWAJ, and describes this as a turning point in her life. Maria attends legal literacy sessions for sex workers with SWAJ; in these sessions she first heard the phrase "sex workers have rights too". Maria met sex workers who were empowered—they filed police reports, sought justice and advocated for sex workers' human rights.

Maria began receiving psycho-social support from SWAJ via support groups and sessions with a psychologist, and she describes this as what "keeps her going". She shares her experiences of violence and abuse with others at the sex worker support groups at SWAJ, where she has the opportunity to meet others with similar experiences. Maria describes SWAJ as 'her family'. Through her involvement with SWAJ, Maria is more aware of the laws that criminalise sex work. She still lives in fear of losing her two other children to state custody due to the existence of laws that criminalise living off the earnings of prostitution and being habitually in the company of a prostitute, resulting in direct implications for her children. Maria has witnessed many sex workers' children removed to state custody, and having this personal experience herself, she understands the resulting mental health impacts. Recently, Maria described being chastised by a nurse at a public health facility for engaging in sex work. She left the facility without receiving the services she required and returned accompanied by a SWAJ representative. While advocating for her own rights, Maria continues to provide support to, and receive support from, other sex workers.

Findings from a Community-Based Research Study with Sex Workers in Jamaica

We conducted a community-based research project in collaboration with the SWAJ and Jamaica AIDS Support for Life, with a peer-driven recruitment sample of cisgender men, trans women, and cisgender women sex workers in Kingston, Montego Bay, Ocho Rios, and surrounding areas. We hired and trained sex workers, including trans women, cisgender women, and cisgender men, as peer research assistants. Peer research assistants helped to refine the survey through pilot testing, distributed the study information to their networks, and conducted a tablet-based, cross-sectional survey of 30–40 min in duration to explore social and structural factors associated with health and well-being. Inclusion criteria comprised the following: self-identifying as a sex worker (exchanging sex for money or goods); living in Jamaica, residing in or nearby Kingston, Ocho Rios, and Montego Bay; and being 18 years of age and older. We used multiple convenience sampling methods, including venue-based recruitment through advertising the study via word-of-mouth at Jamaica AIDS Support for Life and SWAJ. We also used snowball sampling by notifying participants that they could invite other sex workers in their networks to participate. No print advertisement was used. The study was approved by research ethics boards at the University of Toronto and the University of the West Indies.

Measures

The primary explanatory variable was sex work social cohesion, using a 14-item sex work social cohesion scale [24] (range: 15–54; Cronbach's alpha = 0.78 in this study). Examples of items included the following: On a scale of 1 (strongly disagree) to 4 (strongly agree), you can count on your colleagues if you need to:

"borrow money"
"ask someone to accompany you to the doctor or hospital"
"help you deal with a violent or difficult client"

Outcome variables included depressive symptoms, violence from clients and intimate partners, and police harassment/arrest. Depressive symptoms in the last 2 weeks were measured continuously with the two-item Patient Health Questionnaire-2 (PHQ-2) (range 2–8) [25]. Client violence was measured with the item: *"Have you experienced violence (verbal, physical or sexual) from a sex work client in the last 6 months?"* An affirmative answer was coded as having recent client violence experience. Intimate partner violence was measured with the item: *"In your life, have you ever experienced violence from a partner (boyfriend, girlfriend)?"* Participants who reported "yes" were coded as having intimate partner violence experience. Police harassment and arrest [11] was assessed by using the following items: *"On a scale of 1 (never) to 3 (many times), how often have the police: (1) thrown you in jail/lockup; (2) sexually harassed you (called your names/groped you); (3) beaten you up; (4) robbed you of money or drugs; (5) raped you or bribed you (give a "thing") to keep working; or (6) arrested you/charged you?"* Participants who reported having had any of the preceding experiences were coded as having experienced police harassment/arrest. The final value for types of violence/harassment experienced was calculated from the previously mentioned scores for client violence, intimate partner violence, and police harassment/arrest, to produce a score ranging from 0 to 3 types of violence/harassment.

Potential mediators included sex work stigma and binge drinking. Sex work stigma was measured based on a 4-item scale adapted from Lazarus et al.'s "Occupational Sex Work Stigma Scale" [26] (Examples: *"Do you hide involvement in sex work from family and friends"*; *"Do you hide involvement in sex work from your home community"*; and *"Do you hide involvement in sex work from your doctor or healthcare provider"*; and *"Do you believe sex work is shameful")* (range: 0–8, Cronbach's alpha = 0.71). Binge drinking was measured by: *"How many drinks do you usually have per sitting/outing?"* Participants who reported having five drinks or more were coded as binge drinking. Socio-demographic characteristics were examined as covariates: age (continuous), education level (dichotomous: less than high school vs. high school or higher), and monthly income (continuous).

Statistical Analysis

We first conducted descriptive analyses of all variables for the whole sample. Bivariate analysis was performed to identify the difference of socio-demographic characteristics by gender (cisgender men, cisgender women, trans women). We conducted an explanatory factor analysis (EFA) and confirmatory factor analysis (CFA) to determine the validity of the latent construct of sex work social cohesion using the social cohesion scale [24], as this measure had not previously been used in the Jamaican context. Structural equation modelling (SEM) using weighted least squares estimation methods was conducted to examine the direct and indirect effect of the latent construct of sex work social cohesion on types of violence/harassment experienced (clients, intimate partners, police) and depressive symptoms, testing the potential mediating effects of sex work stigma and binge drinking. Model fit was assessed using: Chi-square, Root Mean Square Error of Approximation (RMSEA), and Comparative Fit Index (CFI). A significance level for Chi-square of <0.05, a score of <0.05 for RMSEA with 90% confidence interval between 0.02 and 0.08, and a score greater than 0.90 for CFI indicate acceptable model fit. Statistical significance was set at the $p<0.05$ level. Missing responses were excluded from the analyses. All statistical analyses were performed using Stata (version 14.0).

Results

Table 5.1 reports the socio-demographic characteristics for the whole sample and the differences by gender among 340 sex worker participants (mean age: 25.77, SD = 5.71, range: 17–57) across three sites in Jamaica (Kingston, Ocho Rios, Montego Bay). These included 124 (36.47%) who identified as cisgender men, 101 (29.71%) trans women, and 115 (33.82%) cisgender women. Approximately three-quarters of the sample ($N = 266$, 78.24%) had completed high school or higher. The mean weekly income received was USD 119.92 (SD = 131.50). More than half of the participants (173/338, 51.18%) reported having ever experienced police harassment/arrest (including being locked up, sexually harassed, beaten up, robbed, raped, or arrested by police). More than one-third ($N = 116$, 36.14%) reported having experienced violence from clients in the last 6 months. Nearly half ($N = 167$, 49.41%) reported having ever experienced intimate partner violence. Trans women were more likely to report police and client violence than cisgender women and cisgender men, and cisgender women were more likely to report intimate partner violence than trans women or cisgender men.

Table 5.1 Socio-demographic characteristics among sex workers in Jamaica ($N = 340$)

Characteristics	Total N (%)/ mean (SD, range)	Missing	Cisgender men sex workers N (%)/mean (SD, range)	Cisgender women sex workers N (%)/mean (SD, range)	Transgender women sex workers N (%)/mean (SD, range)	p (ANOVA/ Chi-square)
Total	$N = 340$		$N = 124$ (36.47%)	$N = 115$ (33.82%)	$N = 101$ (29.71)	
Age	25.77 (5.71, 17–57)	13	24.72 (4.11, 17–38)	28.07 (6.54, 17–57)	24.57 (5.75, 17–51)	<0.001
Weekly income in USD	119.92 (131.50, 0–1580)		95.03 (84.62, 0–711)	152.64 (166.64, 0.079–1580)	109.84 (126.72, 0.079–790)	<0.01
Education: completed high school or higher	266 (78.24)		106 (85.48)	81 (70.43)	79 (78.22)	<0.05
City						<0.001
Kingston	101 (29.71)		21 (16.94)	27 (23.48)	53 (52.48)	
Montego Bay	72 (21.18)		30 (24.19)	32 (27.83)	10 (9.90)	
Negril	20 (5.88)		12 (9.68)	7 (6.09)	1 (0.99)	
Spanish Town	25 (7.35)		5 (4.03)	8 (6.96)	12 (11.88)	
Ocho Rios	71 (20.88)		34 (27.42)	27 (23.48)	10 (9.90)	
Others	51 (15.00)		22 (17.74)	14 (12.17)	15 (14.85)	
Relationship status		3				<0.001
Married or living together	43 (12.76)		13 (10.57)	22 (19.13)	8 (8.08)	
Dating-not living together	58 (17.21)		18 (14.63)	17 (14.78)	23 (23.23)	
Casual dating	45 (13.35)		24 (19.51)	11 (9.57)	10 (10.10)	
No current partner	96 (28.49)		42 (34.15)	32 (27.83)	22 (22.22)	
Multiple partners/ polyamorous	95 (28.19)		26 (21.14)	33 (28.70)	36 (36.36)	
Police harassment (ever)	173 (51.18)	2	52 (41.94)	55 (47.83)	66 (66.67)	<0.01
Intimate partner violence (ever)	167 (49.41)	2	51 (41.13)	70 (60.87)	46 (46.46)	<0.01
Client violence (past 6 months)	116 (36.14)	19	32 (27.83)	37 (34.58)	47 (47.47)	<0.05

(continued)

Table 5.1 (continued)

Characteristics	Total N (%)/ mean (SD, range)	Missing	Cisgender men sex workers N (%)/mean (SD, range)	Cisgender women sex workers N (%)/mean (SD, range)	Transgender women sex workers N (%)/mean (SD, range)	p (ANOVA/ Chi-square)
Binge drinking	79 (23.24)		23 (18.55)	27 (23.48)	29 (28.71)	0.199
Sexual orientation		18				<0.001
Heterosexual	119 (36.96)		9 (7.83)	80 (74.77)	30 (30.00)	
Bisexual	86 (26.71)		53 (46.09)	25 (23.36)	8 (8.00)	
Gay/lesbian	111 (34.47)		51 (44.35)	2 (1.87)	58 (58.00)	
Queer	6 (1.86)		2 (1.74)	0	4 (4.00)	

Table 5.2 Univariate and multivariate linear regressions on depressive symptoms and types of violence among sex workers in Jamaica ($N = 340$)

Variables	Depressive symptoms		Types of violence	
	Unadjusted coefficient (95% CI)	Adjusted coefficient (95% CI)*	Unadjusted coefficient (95% CI)	Adjusted coefficient (95% CI)*
Sex work social cohesion	−0.05 (−0.08 to −0.03***)	−0.04 (−0.07 to −0.02)	−0.04 (−0.05 to −0.03)***	−0.02 (−0.04 to 0.01)**
Sex work stigma	0.12 (0.03 to 0.21)**	0.06 (−0.04 to 0.15)	0.21 (0.16 to 0.26)***	0.17 (0.12 to 0.22)***
Binge drinking	0.75 (0.29 to 1.20)**	0.40 (−0.07 to 0.87)	0.68 (0.40 to 0.96)	0.27 (−0.01 to 0.54)

Note: *$p < 0.05$, **$p < 0.01$, ***$p < 0.001$. Covariates include: age, weekly income, education level, relationship status, and gender identity

Table 5.2 displays the results of univariate and multivariate linear regression analysis on depressive symptoms and types of violence among sex workers in Jamaica. We found that, when adjusting for socio-demographic factors (age, income, education, relationship status, gender identity), lower sex work social cohesion was associated with: higher depression symptoms (Acoef: −0.04, 95% CI: −0.07 to −0.02), increased violence and harassment, (Acoef: −0.02, 95% CI: −0.04 to −0.01), and increased sex work stigma (Acoef: 0.17, 95% CI: 0.12–0.22). Taken together, this suggests that increasing social cohesion among sex workers could *reduce* depression, risks of violence, and sex work stigma.

The structural equation modelling analyses examined the direct and indirect effects of sex work social cohesion on depressive symptoms and experiences of violence. Final model fit indices suggested that the model fit the data well ($\chi^2[7] = 10.28$, $p = 0.173$; CFI = 0.983; RMSEA = 0.044; SRMR = 0.026). Table 5.3

Table 5.3 Final path analysis for sex work social cohesion on depressive symptoms and violence among sex workers in Jamaica ($N = 340$)

Parameter	Coefficient (SE)	Critical ratio	p	Standardized estimate
Depressive symptoms ON				
Sex work social cohesion	−0.046 (0.013)	−3.50	<0.001	−0.231 (0.065)
Sex work stigma	0.045 (0.048)	0.96	0.339	0.649 (0.068)
Binge drinking	0.370 (0.241)	1.53	0.125	0.101 (0.065)
Types of violence ON				
Sex work social cohesion	−0.028 (0.008)	−3.58	<0.001	−0.208 (0.058)
Sex work stigma	0.199 (0.028)	7.00	<0.001	0.418 (0.056)
Binge drinking	0.111 (0.144)	0.77	0.440	0.045 (0.058)
Binge drinking ON				
Sex work social cohesion	−0.007 (0.004)	−2.00	<0.05	−0.132 (0.065)
Sex work stigma	0.488 (0.012)	3.92	<0.001	0.256 (0.064)
Sex work stigma ON				
Sex work social cohesion	−0.094 (0.017)	−5.46	<0.001	−0.333 (0.058)

Covariates include: age, weekly income, education level, relationship status, and gender identity

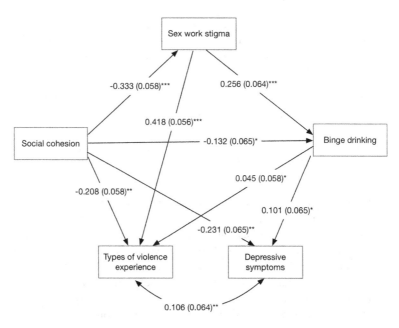

Fig. 5.1 Pathways between sex worker social cohesion, sex work stigma, and depression among sex workers in Jamaica

displays the results of the final model and Fig. 5.1 illustrates the model with standard coefficients and the significance levels of each pathway.[6] Standard errors are included in parenthesis. In the final model, sex work social cohesion was associated with fewer depressive symptoms ($\beta = -0.046$ for direct effect, $p < 0.001$; -0.009 for indirect effect, $p < 0.001$) and less violence ($\beta = -0.028$ for direct effect, $p < 0.001$; -0.020 for indirect effect, $p < 0.001$). Sex work stigma partially mediated these relationships: social cohesion among sex workers reduced experiences of sex work stigma; in turn, lower sex work stigma resulted in lower depression and fewer experiences of violence. Sex work social cohesion, therefore, emerged as important to promoting mental health and reducing violence among sex workers in this study.

The case example and community-based study have limitations. First, study authors developed a case study based on in-depth conversations with sex workers at SWAJ. This case study is limited in representing one perspective from a cisgender woman sex worker; generating additional cases with cisgender women, cisgender men, and trans women would provide additional richness of understanding these lived experiences. Second, the experiences of trans men sex workers remain unexplored in this study. Third, the survey was cross-sectional with non-random sampling, limiting the ability to generalise findings or ascertain causality. Finally, we used single items to assess client violence and intimate partner violence.

More detailed measures could have provided information to tailor violence prevention strategies, and would have allowed us to create latent constructs for each type of violence rather than one latent violence construct for combined experiences of violence. Such an approach would allow exploration of pathways between sex work social cohesion and each type of violence. Despite these limitations, this study included over 300 sex workers in Jamaica—a context in which sex work and same-gender sexual practices are criminalised. It also provides novel information about the importance of sex work social cohesion and measures to address sex work stigma for better understanding mental health, violence, and harassment among sex workers.

Discussion: Implications for Researchers, Service Providers, and Activists

This chapter has considered the associations between sex work social cohesion and reduced experiences of violence, harassment, and depression among sex workers in Jamaica. The case study narrative provides insight into the lived experiences of poly-victimisation of a cisgender woman sex worker in Jamaica, and the ways that sex work criminalisation exacerbated her abuse by police and clients while simultaneously

---

[6] The standard coefficient indicated that with a standard deviation of increase of the independent variable, the dependent variable would increase by x standard deviation, holding all other variables constant.

reducing her access to justice. The case study also points to the ways in which stigma targeting sex workers can result in the forced removal of children to child protective services, and the harmful mental health impacts of such violence and loss. Finally, this case study illuminated the ways that sex workers share experiences and provide informal support with one another to build community, as well as the formal rights-based programming that a sex worker collective such as the Sex Work Association of Jamaica can provide to advance human rights and access to health services among sex workers.

The empirical data from a cross-sectional survey in Jamaica corroborated and expanded on the case study by including cisgender men, cisgender women, and trans women sex workers. Findings reveal that trans women sex workers are particularly impacted by police harassment/arrest and client violence, while cisgender women sex workers are disproportionately affected by intimate partner violence. These findings have implications for rights-based programming, gender-tailored support, and violence reduction programmes by and for sex workers. Extending beyond Jamaica, these findings can inform research, service provision, and activism with sex workers in global contexts, particularly where sex work and same-gender sexual practices are criminalised. Sex work social cohesion is a strengths-based construct that shows the powerful role support and care among sex workers have on well-being.

Research Implications Taken together, these findings corroborate prior research that demonstrates the deleterious impacts of sex work criminalisation on the health and human rights of sex workers [7], including violence and harassment from police, clients, and intimate partners [11, 14, 27]. The prevalence of violence reported by sex workers in our study was comparable to that gathered from a global systematic review [7] (which omitted Caribbean studies), in which sex workers reported lifetime physical/sexual violence prevalence of 45–75% and past year workplace violence prevalence of 32–55%. Our findings also corroborate prior work with cisgender women sex workers in Jamaica highlighting rape by clients [28]. These findings signal the need for research that includes cisgender and transgender sex workers, assesses and reduces multiple forms of violence (for instance, by police, partners, clients), and applies a strengths-focused approach centering sex work social cohesion.

Future research can also explore the shared and differential needs and experiences among sex workers by intersecting identities such as gender, age, socioeconomic status, and sexual orientation. While we found gender identity differences in experiences across client violence, intimate partner violence, and police harassment/arrest, we were not able to ascertain how support services could be tailored to meet the diverse needs of sex workers. Qualitative studies could provide further understanding of experiences of social cohesion among sex workers and provide their recommendations for rights-based programming.

Service Provision Implications Social cohesion among sex workers emerged as a protective factor associated with reduced sex work stigma, reduced depression, reduced experiences of violence and harassment and, in the case study, increased access to health care and legal literacy. This corroborates findings that social support is health-promoting and can reduce barriers when it comes to accessing health care among general populations [20]. Similar to a study in Eswatini (formerly known as Swaziland), we found that sex work social cohesion was associated with reduced odds of experiencing stigma, violence, harassment, and arrest [17]. Findings also contribute to the knowledge base regarding social cohesion among sex workers and their rates of mental health. Similar to findings with non-sex work specific populations [23], we found social cohesion to be associated with reduced depression. Taken together, these findings can contribute to trauma-informed mental health programmes by, with, and for sex workers, that build opportunities and resources for mutual aid, advocacy, and social support. In addition to providing counselling, service providers can offer training and resources to support the development of sex workers' sustainable rights-based and solidarity-oriented programmes and groups.

Implications for Activism Findings point to the urgent need to end sex work criminalisation across global contexts and provide sex workers with legal rights and protections. Similar to prior research in four Sub-Saharan African countries, the case study pointed to fears of reporting violence to police due to punishment, arrest, and further violence [29]. The quantitative data also provided evidence that sex workers in Jamaica experience harassment and arrest by police, as they do in other contexts [7, 11, 27]. Yet sex work social cohesion combined with advocacy and education about legal rights, as described in the case study, has the potential to provide recourse to justice for sex workers. In the quantitative data, sex work social cohesion was also linked with reduced violence, harassment, and arrest, suggesting the importance of community-engaged and rights-based interventions by and for gender-diverse sex workers [30]. Community empowerment approaches must be coupled with changes at a structural level such as (a) the decriminalisation of sex work and same-gender sexual practices, and (b) training and policies to reduce intersectional stigma (towards sex workers and lesbian, gay, bisexual, and transgender persons) among healthcare and social service providers, police, communities, and within intimate partnerships. Such approaches can also advance HIV prevention. A conceptual model with cisgender women sex workers in Jamaica, for example, positions sexual decision-making constraints within the sex work environment of criminalisation [31]. In fact, estimates suggest that the decriminalisation of sex work could prevent 33–46% of new HIV infections in the next 10 years [11]. Future research could assess the mental health benefits of sex work decriminalisation, and the potential role of sex work social cohesion in decriminalisation efforts and mental health promotion.

This chapter advances understanding of multiple forms of violence experienced by sex workers in Jamaica, and the protective role of sex work social cohesion. It also furthers an intersectional approach [6, 32] that points to the importance of considering gender identity in shaping life experiences. Prior research with trans women [15] and gay, bisexual, and other men who have sex with men [12] in Jamaica reported higher levels of stigma and rape among those who were involved in sex work.

The study detailed in this chapter found different experiences of violence based on gender identity, with a particularly high burden of police harassment and client violence experienced by trans women sex workers in comparison to their cisgender women and men counterparts. This necessitates an intersectional approach with sex workers to violence and stigma reduction strategies that identify gender-specific experiences, needs, and priorities. It also highlights the urgent need for decriminalisation of sex work and same-gender sexual practices in Jamaica to advance health and human rights.

Conflict of Interest and Source of Funding The authors have no conflicts of interest to declare. This research was funded by the Canadian Institutes of Health Research (CIHR) Operating Grant 0000303157; Fund: 495419, Competition 201209. Dr. Logie's efforts were in part supported by an Ontario Ministry of Research and Innovation Early Researcher Award, a Canada Research Chair in Global Health Equity and Social Justice with Marginalized Populations, and the Canada Foundation for Innovation.

References

1. Benoit C, Jansson SM, Smith M, Flagg J. Prostitution stigma and its effect on the working conditions, personal lives, and health of sex workers. J Sex Res. 2018;55(4–5):457–71.
2. Jiao S, Bungay V. Intersections of stigma, mental health, and sex work: how Canadian men engaged in sex work navigate and resist stigma to protect their mental health. J Sex Res. 2019;56(4–5):641–9.
3. Herek GM, Widaman KF, Capitanio JP. When sex equals AIDS: symbolic stigma and heterosexual adults' inaccurate beliefs about sexual transmission of AIDS. Soc Probl. 2005;52(1):15–37.
4. Zarhin D, Fox N. "Whore stigma" as a transformative experience: altered cognitive expectations among Jewish-Israeli street-based sex workers. Cult Health Sex. 2017;19(10):1078–91.
5. Poteat T, Wirtz AL, Radix A, Borquez A, Silva-Santisteban A, Deutsch MB, et al. HIV risk and preventive interventions in transgender women sex workers. Lancet. 2015;385(9964):274–86.
6. Logie CH, James L, Tharao W, Loutfy MR. HIV, gender, race, sexual orientation, and sex work: a qualitative study of intersectional stigma experienced by HIV-positive women in Ontario, Canada. PLoS Med. 2011;8(11):e1001124.
7. Deering KN, Amin A, Shoveller J, Nesbitt A, Garcia-Moreno C, Duff P, et al. A systematic review of the correlates of violence against sex workers. Am J Public Health. 2014;104(5):e42–54.
8. Carlson CE, Witte SS, Pala AN, Tsai LC, Wainberg M, Aira T. The impact of violence, perceived stigma, and other work-related stressors on depressive symptoms among women engaged in sex work. Glob Soc Welf. 2017;4(2):51–7.
9. NSWP. Global mapping of sex work laws [Internet]. Global Network of Sex Work Projects; 2019 [cited 2020 May 13]. Available from: https://www.nswp.org/sex-work-laws-map.
10. Vanwesenbeeck I. Sex work criminalization is barking up the wrong tree. Arch Sex Behav. 2017;46(6):1631–40.
11. Shannon K, Strathdee SA, Goldenberg SM, Duff P, Mwangi P, Rusakova M, et al. Global epidemiology of HIV among female sex workers: influence of structural determinants. Lancet. 2015;385(9962):55–71.
12. Logie CH, Lacombe-Duncan A, Kenny KS, Levermore K, Jones N, Baral SD, et al. Social-ecological factors associated with selling sex among men who have sex with men in Jamaica: results from a cross-sectional tablet-based survey. Glob Health Action. 2018;11(1):1424614.

13. Hail-Jares K, Chang RCF, Choi S, Zheng H, He N, Huang ZJ. Intimate-partner and client-initiated violence among female street-based sex workers in China: does a support network help? PLoS One. 2015;10(9):e0139161.
14. Shahmanesh M, Wayal S, Cowan F, Mabey D, Copas A, Patel V. Suicidal behavior among female sex workers in Goa, India: the silent epidemic. Am J Public Health. 2009;99(7):1239–46.
15. Logie CH, Wang Y, Lacombe-Duncan A, Jones N, Ahmed U, Levermore K, et al. Factors associated with sex work involvement among transgender women in Jamaica: a cross-sectional study. J Int AIDS Soc. 2017;20(1):21422.
16. Argento E, Duff P, Bingham B, Chapman J, Nguyen P, Strathdee SA, et al. Social cohesion among sex workers and client condom refusal in a Canadian setting: implications for structural and community-led interventions. AIDS and Behavior. 2016;20(6):1275–83.
17. Fonner VA, Kerrigan D, Mnisi Z, Ketende S, Kennedy CE, Baral S. Social cohesion, social participation, and HIV related risk among female sex workers in Swaziland. PLoS One. 2014;9(1):e87527.
18. Jana S, Basu I, Rotheram-Borus MJ, Newman PA. The Sonagachi project: a sustainable community intervention program. AIDS Educ Prev. 2004;16(5):405–14.
19. Langer A, Stewart F, Smedts K, Demarest L. Conceptualising and measuring social cohesion in Africa: towards a perceptions-based index. Soc Indic Res. 2017;131(1):321–43.
20. Chuang Y-C, Chuang K-Y, Yang T-H. Social cohesion matters in health. Int J Equity Health. 2013;12:87.
21. Hong Y, Xiaoyi F, Xiaoming L, Liu Y, Li M, Tai-Seale T. Self-perceived stigma, depressive symptoms, and suicidal behaviors among female sex workers in China. J Transcult Nurs. 2009;21(1):29–34.
22. Jen MH, Sund ER, Johnston R, Jones K. Trustful societies, trustful individuals, and health: an analysis of self-rated health and social trust using the World Value Survey. Health Place. 2010;16(5):1022–9.
23. Fone D, White J, Farewell D, Kelly M, John G, Lloyd K, et al. Effect of neighbourhood deprivation and social cohesion on mental health inequality: a multilevel population-based longitudinal study. Psychol Med. 2014;44(11):2449–60.
24. Lippman SA, Donini A, Díaz J, Chinaglia M, Reingold A, Kerrigan D. Social-environmental factors and protective sexual behavior among sex workers: the Encontros intervention in Brazil. Am J Public Health. 2010;100(Suppl 1):S216–23.
25. Kroenke K, Spitzer RL, Williams JBW. The Patient Health Questionnaire-2: validity of a two-item depression screener. Med Care. 2003;41(11):1284–92.
26. Lazarus L, Deering KN, Nabess R, Gibson K, Tyndall MW, Shannon K. Occupational stigma as a primary barrier to health care for street-based sex workers in Canada. Cult Health Sex. 2012;14(2):139–50.
27. Beattie TS, Bhattacharjee P, Ramesh B, Gurnani V, Anthony J, Isac S, et al. Violence against female sex workers in Karnataka state, south India: impact on health, and reductions in violence following an intervention program. BMC Public Health. 2010;10:476.
28. Eldemire-Shearer D, Bailey A. Determinants of risk behaviour of sex-workers in Jamaica. A qualitative approach. West Indian Med J. 2008;57(5):450–5.
29. Scorgie F, Vasey K, Harper E, Richter M, Nare P, Maseko S, et al. Human rights abuses and collective resilience among sex workers in four African countries: a qualitative study. Glob Health. 2013;9(1):33.
30. Logie CH, Lacombe-Duncan A, Kenny KS, Levermore K, Jones N, Marshall A, et al. Associations between police harassment and HIV vulnerabilities among men who have sex with men and transgender women in Jamaica. Health Hum Rights. 2017;19(2):147–54.
31. Bailey A, Figueroa JP. A framework for sexual decision-making among female sex workers in Jamaica. Arch Sex Behav. 2016;45(4):911–21.
32. Turan JM, Elafros MA, Logie CH, Banik S, Turan B, Crockett KB, et al. Challenges and opportunities in examining and addressing intersectional stigma and health. BMC Med. 2019;17(1):7.

Chapter 6
Patterns and Epidemiology of Illicit Drug Use Among Sex Workers Globally: A Systematic Review

Jenny Iversen, Pike Long, Alexandra Lutnick, and Lisa Maher

Introduction

Potential harms associated with illicit drug use in the context of sex work include increased vulnerability to: infectious disease such as HIV and other sexually transmitted infections (STI), violence, stigma and discrimination, criminalisation, and exploitation [1–10]. For example, both illicit and licit drug use have been associated with increased exposure to violence against sex workers. The perpetrators of this violence include clients, police, and strangers, and the violence occurs in a range of settings [11, 12]. An early US study found that injecting heroin and trading sex at a crack house were significantly associated with client-perpetrated violence [13]. A Russian study observed that recent injection drug use was significantly associated with police-perpetrated sexual violence against sex workers [14], and in China sex workers who reported drug use were more likely than those who did not report violence by clients [15]. However, major gaps remain in the

J. Iversen
Kirby Institute for Infection and Immunity, Faculty of Medicine, UNSW Sydney, Sydney, NSW, Australia
e-mail: jiversen@kirby.unsw.edu.au

P. Long
St James Infirmary, San Francisco, CA, USA
e-mail: ms.pike.long@gmail.com

A. Lutnick
Independent Researcher, San Francisco, CA, USA
e-mail: alix.lutnick@gmail.com

L. Maher (✉)
Kirby Institute for Infection and Immunity, Faculty of Medicine, UNSW Sydney, Sydney, NSW, Australia

Burnet Institute, Melbourne, VIC, Australia
e-mail: lmaher@kirby.unsw.edu.au

© The Author(s) 2021
S. M. Goldenberg et al. (eds.), *Sex Work, Health, and Human Rights*,
https://doi.org/10.1007/978-3-030-64171-9_6

epidemiological data on violence and other health and social inequities faced by sex workers who use drugs. In particular, limited data exist about male and transgender sex workers.

Sex workers who use drugs face unique challenges as a population experiencing health and human rights inequities. No country in the world has decriminalised both drug use and sex work, and people who use drugs and sell sex remain globally criminalised [16]. Legal and regulatory environments in which people who sell sex and use drugs are criminalised promote stigmatisation and discrimination [5]. Mathematical modelling by Shannon et al. [4] indicated that decriminalising sex work could significantly reduce HIV, averting 33–46% of HIV infections globally through reduced violence and police harassment, and access to safe work environments. A recent analysis of data from 27 European countries found that countries where sex work is fully or partly legalised had a lower burden of HIV among female sex workers than countries where sex work was criminalised [17]. Not only is decriminalisation supported by the WHO, the United Nations, and the Global Commission on HIV and Law [16, 18, 19], but, as Shannon et al. [5] have noted, "The criminalisation of sex work continues to provide cover and sanction to state-sponsored human rights abuses against sex workers and sex worker human rights defenders" [5]. Most recently, a range of countries including Canada, France, and Ireland have introduced end-demand or Nordic model criminalisation laws [5]. While data on this regulatory model are scarce, some evidence suggests that it produces harm similar to full criminalisation [20–22].

Although the prevalence of drug use among sex workers is generally believed to be higher than in the general population, the literature is dominated by studies of street-based sex workers, particularly ciswomen, many of whom engage in sex work to support their drug use. Street-based sex workers often have complex health and social needs due to high prevalence of heroin, cocaine, and injection drug use, poor treatment outcomes, high levels of morbidity and mortality, including mental and physical health outcomes, and exposure to sexual and physical violence and homelessness. Less is known about drug use among other sub-groups of sex workers, including those who work in settings such as bars and clubs, massage parlours and private homes [23], or among non-street-based male or transgender sex workers. Functional or occupational drug use by sex workers, including alcohol and amphetamine-type stimulant (ATS) use is also less researched. Some suggest that stimulants may be used by some sex workers to remove the need for food and rest, and to remain alert and awake while working long hours [24].

This chapter reviews what is known about the prevalence of illicit drug use among sex workers. Acknowledging the diversity of populations and contexts in which drug use and sex work overlap, we aimed to estimate the prevalence of lifetime illicit drug use among sex workers overall, by gender (cis, trans, and nonbinary), and by sub-region.

Methods

Search Strategy

In 2018, we searched electronic databases (EMBASE, Pub Med, Web of Science, Sociological Abstracts, and PsychInfo) to identify journal articles published in the preceding decade (2009–2018). Search terms comprised a combination of Medical Subject Headings (MESH) and free text ((sex work*, prostitut*, erotic service, erotic dancer, massage parlour, massage parlour, strip club, OR brothel) AND (substance us*, drug us*, heroin, opioid*, cocaine, methamphetamine, amphetamine, cannabis OR marijuana)) contained within the title, abstract, or keyword.

Inclusion/Exclusion Criteria

The search used a broad definition of sex work, including commercial and transactional sex, in a wide range of settings and venues, including brothels, massage parlours, clubs, bars, streets, parks, and private homes. UNAIDS has recently argued that "Transactional sex is not sex work but refers to non-marital, non-commercial sexual relationships motivated by an implicit assumption that sex will be exchanged for material support or other benefits. Most women and men involved in transactional sex relationships consider themselves as partners or lovers rather than sellers or buyers" ([25]: page 2). However, our review, conducted prior to the publication of the UNAIDS report, included two studies which explicitly included people engaged in transactional sex. We included original studies that measured prevalence of illicit drug use (defined as any use of illicit psychoactive drugs) among sex workers, using either biological markers or self-report. We did not exclude studies on the basis of study design and the review was not restricted according to demographic characteristics (biological sex, gender identity, age, race, or ethnicity), blood-borne viral status of study participants, or the timeframe studies used to define sex work or drug use. However, publications with additional sample inclusion criteria, for example, alcohol, drug or injection drug use, pregnancy or mental health disorders, were excluded due to potential sample bias. Where there were multiple studies from the same sample with estimates of the same outcome, only the most comprehensive study in terms of sample size was included.

Data Extraction and Synthesis

Search results in the form of citations were imported into EndNote (a reference management software programme) and duplicates were removed. Titles and abstracts were screened for relevance and for those considered relevant, full texts were retrieved and further screened. Screening was done by one author (JI), with screening of a subset of references (10%) by a second author (LM), revealing no discrepancies between the two lists of accepted references. The following data were extracted from the selected studies: study location, study period, design, and lifetime and recent prevalence of (a) illicit drug use and (b) injection drug use. Although data were extracted about recent illicit drug and recent injection drug use, there was inconsistency in the timeframes used to define "recent" (range past 1 day to 12 months).

Where publications involved duplicate study populations, including from longitudinal or open cohort studies, the review retained the publication with the largest sample (typically the most recent publication) containing data on the outcome of interest. Where publications reported data from studies repeated across multiple years, data was extracted for only the most recent survey round where this was available. Most studies did not specify specific drugs used or injected, however, in studies where illicit drug or injection drug use prevalence data was separately listed for a range of individual drugs and where there was potential for overlap due to participants using more than one type of drug, data from the most commonly used or injected drug was extracted.

The review combined data from multiple studies to derive pooled prevalence estimates and 95% confidence intervals (CIs) of lifetime illicit drug use among sex workers, using a random effects model. Countries were categorised into geographic sub-regions according to UN Standard Country or Area Codes for Statistical Use [26]. Sub-regional pooled prevalence estimates of lifetime illicit drug use among female sex workers were also generated. Tableau software (version 2018.3 Tableau, Seattle, WA, USA) was used to map sub-regional prevalence of lifetime illicit drug use among female sex workers, noting that recent illicit drug use data was used as a proxy for lifetime use in three sub-regions where estimates of lifetime illicit drug use were not available. An asterisk "*" is used to denote these three sub-regions on the map. Statistical analyses were conducted using STATA software (version 14.2 Stata Corporation, College Station, TX, USA).

Results

Our search generated 2889 publications (Fig. 6.1). After removal of duplicates ($n = 1334$), 1555 publications were retained for abstract review. The abstract review excluded 1264 publications, with 291 publications retained for further screening via full text review. Of these publications, 38 were conference posters or review articles, 7 did not present data on the population of interest, 52 did not present data on the outcome of interest, 20 included drug use as sample recruitment criteria, and 87 publications used the same study or sample as another retained publication (duplicates). One study was excluded because prevalence of lifetime illicit drug use in the sample was <1%, lower than prevalence in the general population. A total of 86 publications were kept and included in this review.

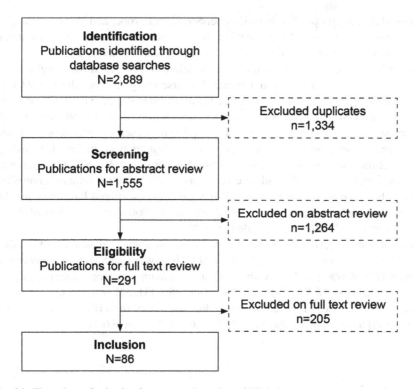

Fig. 6.1 Flow chart of selection for systematic review of illicit drug use among sex workers

Among the $n = 86$ review studies where prevalence of illicit drug use or injection drug use was reported among sex workers, the majority of studies ($n = 70$, 40 countries) reported prevalence among female sex workers, 13 studies (10 countries) reported prevalence among male sex workers, 6 studies (5 countries) reported prevalence among transgender including kathoey (defined as male to female transgender), and hijra (defined as people whose birth sex is male but who identify as female or non-binary sex workers), and 5 studies (5 countries) reported prevalence among combined population groups. Six publications reported prevalence among more than one subpopulation of sex workers. Of the six studies that included transgender sex workers, all were transwomen, and only one specifically focused on this group (100% of participants). Transwomen sex workers accounted for a minority of participants in the other five studies, ranging from 7.8% to 43% of participants, with these samples primarily comprised of female ($n = 4$ studies; range 34.5%–87.5% of participants) or male ($n = 1$; 57% of participants) sex workers. No studies included transmen.

The studies identified in the review were from 46 countries, encompassing the Americas (sub-regions Caribbean, Central America, South America, Northern America), Asia (sub-regions Central Asia, Eastern Asia, South-eastern Asia, Southern Asia, and Western Asia), Africa (Eastern Africa, Western Africa, and Southern Africa),

Europe (Eastern Europe, Northern Europe, Southern Europe, and Western Europe), and Oceania (Australia and New Zealand and Melanesia). No studies were identified from the sub-regions of Northern Africa, Middle Africa, or Micronesia.

Included studies used different criteria to define current sex work (ranging from the last 4 months to 5 years) and recent drug use (ranging from the last 24 h to 12 months). Studies varied considerably in sample size (range 31–18,475, median 401) and methods of recruitment (venue and street outreach $n = 59$; respondent-driven sampling (RDS) $n = 12$; snowball sampling $n = 6$, service attenders $n = 6$, and web-based recruitment $n = 3$). A range of study designs were included, including cross-sectional studies ($n = 71$, 83%), cohort studies ($n = 10$, 12%), randomised controlled trials ($n = 3$, 3%), and case series ($n = 2$, 2%). The randomised controlled trials, cohort and case series studies all reported cross-sectional baseline data. All studies identified in the review were conducted from 2000 onward, with most (60%, $n = 52$) conducted in the past decade (from 2009).

Global pooled prevalence of lifetime illicit drug use among sex workers (39 studies from 23 countries) was 35% (95% CI 30–41%). There was significant heterogeneity or diversity ($I^2 > 90.0\%$, $P < 0.01$), with prevalence of lifetime and recent drug use ranging from 1.2% [27] to 84% [28, 29] and 1.7% [30] to 98% [31, 32], respectively. Similarly, prevalence of lifetime and recent injection drug use varied from 0% [33] to 82% [34] and 0% [35] to 48% [14], respectively (Tables 6.1, 6.2, 6.3, and 6.4).

Table 6.1 Review studies: Prevalence of illicit drug use and injection drug use among female sex workers

Region	Source	Study period	Design	Illicit drug use		Injection drug use	
				Lifetime % (n/N)	Recent % (n/N)	Lifetime % (n/N)	Recent % (n/N)
AFRICA							
Eastern Africa							
Ethiopia	Bugssa, 2015	2013	CS	16.6 (53/319)	–	–	–
Kenya	Tegang, 2010	2007	CS	71.0 (211/297)	–	–	–
Malawi	Lancaster, 2016	2014	CS	–	23.9 (33/138)[C]	–	–
Mauritius	Johnston, 2012	2010	CS	–	28.3 (86/299)[3a]	37.4 (120/299)[a]	30.5 (99/299)[3a]
Tanzania	Leddy, 2018	2005–2006	RCT	6.9 (34/496)	–	–	–
Uganda	Bukenya, 2013	2008–2009	C	–	21.2 (192/905)[1]	–	–
Southern Africa							
Swaziland	Berger, 2018	2011	CS	–	31.1 (101/325)[12]	–	–
Western Africa							
Nigeria	Okafor, 2017	2010	CS	–	–	–	4.3 (78/1796)[U]
AMERICAS							
Caribbean							
Dominican Republic	Kerrigan, 2016	2016	CaS	25 (57/228)	15.4 (35/228)[6]	–	–
Jamaica	Duncan, 2010	2005	CS	56.6 (245/450)	–	3.6 (16/439)	–
Central America							
Mexico	Robertson, 2012	2004–2006	CaS	–	32.1 (297/924)[1b]	13.4 (124/924)	–
Mexico	Chen, 2012a	2009–2010	CS	52.5 (105/200)	–	–	–
Mexico	Semple, 2015	2011–2013	RCT	–	–	–	10.3 (110/1089)[1]
Mexico	Semple, 2016	2011–2013	RCT	–	10.6 (106/1001)[1]	–	–
Mexico	Conners, 2018	2013–2014	C	61.0 (182/301)	38.2 (115/301)[6]	–	23.6 (71/301)[6]
Panama	Hakre, 2013	2009–2011	CS	26.2 (262/999)	–	–	–
South America							

(continued)

Table 6.1 (continued)

Region	Source	Study period	Design	Illicit drug use		Injection drug use	
				Lifetime % (n/N)	Recent % (n/N)	Lifetime % (n/N)	Recent % (n/N)
Argentina	Bautista, 2009	2000–2002	CS	20.8 (157/625)	–	–	–
Brazil	Fernandes, 2014	2009–2011	CS	–	35.7 (169/402)[Ua]	–	1.2 (5/402)[U]
Brazil	Devóglio, 2016	2014	CS	–	51.8 (43/83)[U]	–	–
Colombia	Hooi, 2018	2014	CS	6.9 (5/76)	–	–	–
Northern America							
United States	Martin, 2010	2006–2007	CS	83.8 (98/117)	–	–	–
United States	Reuben, 2011	2008–2009	CS	–	97.7 (42/43)[3]	–	46.51 (20/43)[3]
United States	Terplan, 2018	2013	CS	–	43.8 (42/96)[6]	–	8.3 (8/96)[6]
ASIA							
Central Asia							
Uzbekistan	Todd, 2009	2004–2005	CS	–	–	5.2 (17/329)	–
Eastern Asia							
China	Lau, 2010	2004	CS	–	–	40.4 (118/293)	–
China	Xu, 2013	2006–2007	CS	15.9 (261/1642)	–	–	7.4 (122/1642)[3]
China	Wang, 2012a	2006–2009	C	12.9 (265/2051)	–	6.8 (140/2051)	–
China	Liao, 2012a	2008[c]	CS	13.2 (152/1150)	–	0.4 (5/1150)	–
China	Li, 2017	2008–2009	CS	–	7.4 (118/1604)[12]	–	0.9 (15/1604)[12]
China	Chen, 2012b	2009	C	–	–	–	0.3 (20/7083)[U]
China	Wang, 2012b	2009	CS	1.2 (4/345)	–	–	–
China	Liao, 2012b	2009[c]	CS	13.9 (60/431)	–	1.2 (5/431)	–
China	Yang, 2011	2009[c]	CS	–	3.2 (13/411)[12]	–	–
China	Cai, 2013	2009–2012	CS	4.1 (67/1653)	–	–	–
China	Zhang, 2014	2010[c]	CS	–	1.7 (7/404)[3]	–	–
China	Zhang, 2016	2012	CS	–	8.7 (27/310)[12]	–	–

Country	Author, Year	Design				
China	Liao, 2016	CS	36.0 (144/400)	–	0.0 (0/400)	–
China	Zhou, 2014	CS	–	–	–	3.9 (30/1115)[6]
China	Zhang, 2015	CS	3.4 (12/358)	–	–	–
South-eastern Asia						
Cambodia	Couture, 2012	C	40.6 (65/160)	25.0 (40/160)[3]	1.2 (2/160)	0.0 (0/160)[3]
Cambodia	Wadhera, 2015	C	27.3 (60/220)	27.3 (60/220)[3]	–	–
Malaysia	Wickersham, 2017	CS	–	23.2 (114/492)[1]	–	–
Myanmar	Hail-Jares, 2016	CS	–	31.7 (32/101)[C]	–	1.0 (1/101)[6]
Philippines	Urada, 2014	CS	–	20.4 (34/167)[U]	–	–
Thailand	Nemoto, 2013	CS	–	22 (45/205)[12]	–	–
Vietnam	Nguyen, 2009	CS	8.9 (35/394)	–	–	–
Vietnam	Tran, 2014	CS	3.5 (70/1998)	–	1.3 (26/1998)	–
Vietnam	Le, 2015	CS	9.9 (523/5298)	–	5.2 (273/5298)	3.7 (195/5298)[1]
Southern Asia						
Afghanistan	Todd, 2010	CS	6.9 (36/520)	–	0.4 (2/520)	–
Bangladesh	Hengartner, 2015	CS	–	30.9 (80/259)[U]	–	–
India	Medhi, 2012	CS	25.1 (107/426)	–	5.6 (24/426)	–
Iran	Karamouzian, 2017	CS	71.6 (642/871)	–	14.6 (127/871)	–
Iran	Kazerooni, 2014	CS	69.9 (195/278)	–	11.5 (32/278)	–
Iran	Shokoohi, 2019	CS	–	24.9 (335/1347)[1]	–	4.3 (58/1347)[1]
Nepal	Kakchapati, 2017	CS	6.2 (369/5958)	–	–	–
Pakistan	Melesse, 2016	CS	–	–	–	10.1 (296/2927)[6]
Western Asia						
Lebanon	Mahfoud, 2010	CS	–	–	0.0 (0/135)	–
EUROPE						
Eastern Europe						
Moldova	Zohrabyan, 2013	CS	–	–	12.0 (79/658)	4.6 (30/658)[12]
Russian Federation	Decker, 2012	CS	–	–	82.3 (121/147)	–

(continued)

Table 6.1 (continued)

Region	Source	Study period	Design	Illicit drug use		Injection drug use	
				Lifetime % (n/N)	Recent % (n/N)	Lifetime % (n/N)	Recent % (n/N)
Russian Federation	Odinokova, 2014	2007–2008	CS	71.3 (639/896)	57.3 (513/896)[1]	–	47.5 (426/896)[0.03]
Russian Federation	Wirtz, 2015	2011	CS	–	–	21.6 (163/754)	10.7 (81/754)[6]
Ukraine	Lakunchykova, 2017	2013	CS	–	–	–	6.0 (286/4764)[C]
Northern Europe							
United Kingdom	Platt, 2011	2008–2009	CS	41.4 (103/249)	–	–	–
Southern Europe							
Portugal	Dias, 2015	2011	CS	31.1 (265/853)	–	5.6 (48/853)	–
Croatia	Stulhofer, 2010	2008	CS	–	–	35.7 (55/154)	–
Western Europe							
The Netherlands	van Veen, 2007	2002–2005	CS	–	18.1 (88/487)[6]	9.4 (46/487)	–
OCEANIA							
Australia and New Zealand							
Australia	Tang, 2013	2002–2011	CS	–	–	–	10.3 (443/4296)[U]
Australia	Read, 2012	2009–2011	CS	–	–	0.8 (13/1540)	–
Australia	Callander, 2018	2009–2015	C	–	–	–	4.6 (846/18,475)[12]
Melanesia							
Papua New Guinea	Bruce, 2010	2003	CS	–	54.4 (43/79)[0.25]	–	–

Acronyms: *CS* cross-sectional study, *C* cohort study, *RCT* randomised control trial, *CaS* case series

–, Data not available

Superscript denotes drug use/injection timeframe in months or defined as C (current); R (regular); U (timeframe unspecified)

[a]Adjusted

[b]During/before sex

[c]Most recent year data extracted

Table 6.2 Review studies: Prevalence of illicit drug use and injection drug use among male sex workers

Region	Source	Study period	Design	Illicit drug use Lifetime % (n/N)	Recent % (n/N)	Injection drug use Lifetime % (n/N)	Recent % (n/N)
AFRICA							
Eastern Africa							
Kenya	McKinnon, 2014	2009–2012	C	–	11.8 (60/507)[C]	–	–
AMERICAS							
Northern America							
United States	Grov, 2015	2013	CS	–	43.5 (170/391)[12]	–	–
United States	Underhill, 2014	2013–2014	CS	–	67.7 $(21/31)^{0.25}$	–	46.2 (24/52)[6]
ASIA							
Central Asia							
Uzbekistan	Todd, 2009	2004–2005	CS	–	–	7.0 (3/43)	–
Eastern Asia							
China	Liu, 2012	2009	CS	–	19.9 (83/418)[6]	0.2 (1/418)	–
South-eastern Asia							
Vietnam	Biello, 2014	2010	CS	–	15.6 (45/288)[1]	–	–
Vietnam	Yu, 2015	2010–2011	CS	46.0 (327/710)	–	8.0 (57/710)	–
Southern Asia							
Pakistan	Shaw, 2010	2005–2006	CS	–	5.9 (68/1162)[6]	–	–
Pakistan	Melesse, 2016	2011	CS	–	–	–	0.8 (24/2808)[6]
EUROPE							
Eastern Europe							
Czech Republic	Bar-Johnson, 2015	2011	CS	–	42.5 (17/40)[R]	–	–
Russian Federation	Baral, 2010	2005–2006	C	16.0 (8/50)	–	8.0 (4/50)	–
Southern Europe							
Portugal	Dias, 2015	2011	CS	68.9 (73/106)	–	9.4 (10/106)	–
Spain	Ballester-Arnal, 2017	2015	CS	–	38.7 (31/80)[C]	–	–

Acronyms: CS (cross-sectional study); C (cohort study)
–, Data not available
Superscript denotes drug use/injection timeframe in months or defined as C (current); R (regular)

Table 6.3 Review studies: Prevalence of illicit drug use and injection drug use among transgender sex workers

Region	Source	Study period	Design	Illicit drug use Lifetime % (n/N)	Illicit drug use Recent % (n/N)	Injection drug use Lifetime % (n/N)	Injection drug use Recent % (n/N)
ASIA							
South-eastern Asia							
Thailand	Nemoto, 2012	2006	CS	–	53.6 (60/112)[12a]	–	–
Malaysia	Wickersham, 2017	2014	CS	–	18.6 (36/193)[1]	–	–
Southern Asia							
Pakistan	Shaw, 2010	2005–2006	CS	–	4.9 (75/1532)[6]	–	–
Pakistan	Melesse, 2016	2011	CS	–	–	–	2.2 (61/2748)[6]
EUROPE							
Southern Europe							
Portugal	Dias, 2015	2011	CS	46.9 (38/81)	–	3.7 (3/81)	–
Western Europe							
The Netherlands	van Veen, 2007	2002–2005	CS	0	5.7 (4/70)[6]	5.7 (4/70)	–

Acronyms: CS cross-sectional study
–, Data not available
Superscript denotes drug use/injection timeframe in months
[a]During/before sex

The majority of studies reporting prevalence of lifetime illicit drug use were conducted among female sex workers (32 studies from 20 countries), and global pooled prevalence among this sub-group was 29% (95% CI 24–34%). The review identified significant geographic variation in lifetime illicit drug use among female sex workers (Fig. 6.2), with pooled prevalence higher in Northern America (84%, 95% CI 76–90%) and Eastern Europe (71%, 95% CI 68–74%) compared to Eastern Asia (12%, 95% CI 7–17%) and South-eastern Asia (16%, 95% CI 11–22%). Insufficient studies were identified to generate pooled estimates of lifetime illicit drug use among male (3 studies) and transgender (1 study) sex workers.

Table 6.4 Review studies: Prevalence of illicit drug use and injection drug use among combined sex worker populations

Region	Source	Study period	Design	Illicit drug use Lifetime % (n/N)	Recent % (n/N)	Injection drug use Lifetime % (n/N)	Recent % (n/N)
AFRICA							
Southern Africa							
South Africa	Poliah, 2017	2015	CS	82.6 (128/153)	–	–	–
AMERICAS							
Northern America							
Canada	Goldenberg, 2017	2010–2014	C	–	67.6 (513/759)[6]	–	39.3 (298/759)[6]
EUROPE							
Eastern Europe							
Hungary	Moro, 2013	2010	CS	84.3 (430/510)	0	–	–
Southern Europe							
Serbia	Ilić, 2010	2006–2007	CS	–	98.4 (188/191)[U]	–	15.7 (30/191)[U]
OCEANIA							
Australia and New Zealand							
Australia	Cregan, 2013	2008	CS	–	90.7 (97/107)[R]	–	–

Acronyms: *CS* cross-sectional study, *C* cohort study
–, Data not available
Superscript denotes drug use/injection timeframe in months or defined as R (regular); U (timeframe unspecified)

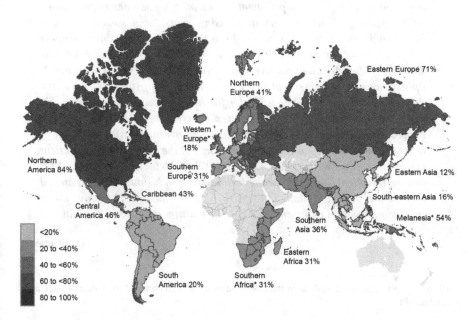

Fig. 6.2 Lifetime illicit drug use among female sex workers by sub-region

Box 6.1 Case Studies[1]
Our case studies from the St. James Infirmary (SJI) illustrate the diversity of experiences among sex workers who use drugs. Founded in San Francisco in 1999 and operated by current and former sex workers, SJI aims to provide compassionate and non-judgemental prevention, treatment and social services for all sex workers.

1. Abdul
   Abdul is an attractive, softly spoken, 24-year-old cisgender gay Arab-American man. His religious family emigrated from the Middle East when he was a baby. At 19, in his first year of college, he was "outed" as gay to his parents, who threw him out of their home and threatened to have him killed. He dropped out of school and fled to a major city several hundred miles away where he hoped his parents couldn't reach him. Alone and unable to reach out to his existing networks for fear of being located, he began engaging in transactional sex with mostly older men in order to earn money and have safe places to stay. It was at this time that he was introduced to both poppers and methamphetamine, both of which are common in gay male "party and play" (P&P) interactions. They increase libido, sexual stamina, and receptivity in anal sex. In fact, he found that much of the sex work available to gay men is predicated on such arrangements, whereby clients supply the drugs and invite younger men over to engage in long-lasting, drug-fueled sexual encounters, often involving multiple partners.
   Abdul was able to eventually find a full-time job working with LGBT youth. It does not pay well since he lacks a college degree. He still engages in occasional sex work to supplement his income, sometimes opportunistically (meeting clients in bars or cruising spots), and sometimes more intentionally by placing ads online. Even though Abdul does not routinely use drugs (aside from nicotine), he finds it difficult to pass up P&P sessions since they are often relatively lucrative, with clients booking for multiple hours or even several days at a time. Unfortunately, once the "partying" begins, it is much harder for him to negotiate or enforce his rates, sexual boundaries, or safer sex practices. Last month, a client invited him over, got him high, and kept him overnight with promises of more and more money as the night wore on, but the next morning the client threw him out without paying him at all. When Abdul tried to demand his money, the client, a wealthy white businessman in his mid-50s, threatened to call the police. Abdul didn't push back because he felt that police involvement would make an already bad situation even worse for him.

(continued)

---

[1]All names and personal identifiers in the case studies have been changed to protect privacy and confidentiality.

Box 6.1 (continued)

2. *Cassie*

Cassie, a 25-year-old black transgender woman, was taken away from her birth parents when she was a toddler. Both her parents struggled with addiction to crack cocaine, and both died of AIDS early in Cassie's life. After several years in foster care, she was adopted by an extremely strict, religious family. Her adoptive father died soon after, leaving her adoptive mother to raise three children alone in a small town. Her mother became emotionally, verbally, and physically abusive towards Cassie, oftentimes for presenting as effeminate. Cassie is still impacted by these emotional wounds. She also experienced sexual abuse by an uncle and several older male cousins.

Cassie escaped her difficult childhood by disappearing into books; her avid reading helped her become a good student. However, by the end of tenth grade, her abusive home life had become unbearable, so Cassie dropped out of high school and ran away to San Francisco where she could live as a woman and make her own way. At 16, she started taking feminising hormones and quickly realised she could support herself through street-based sex work; she often found that her clients made her feel beautiful and validated as a woman in ways the rest of the world often did not. Her hormones also meant that she was largely reliant on black market "performance enhancing" prescription drugs such as Viagra and Cialis to be able to provide the kind of sexual experience her clients were looking for. She often had to "check out" of her body to engage in this kind of work.

In spite of lifetime struggles with depression and other PTSD symptoms, Cassie developed a tight network of other young transwomen friends, quickly emerging as a natural leader among her peers. However, ongoing bouts with homelessness led her to start smoking methamphetamine to stay awake at night, which helped protect her from being robbed or assaulted in her sleep—this had happened several times to her at shelters, so she quickly stopped staying in them. When she smoked meth, she found that the ongoing crushing sense of doom plaguing her disappeared. The drug made her feel "euphoric" and "invincible". She began using methamphetamine more regularly, prompting increasingly erratic behaviours. She found herself engaging in high-risk sexual activity while high, considering it a minor miracle that she remains HIV-negative, especially given how many of her friends have sero-converted.

Cassie became trapped in cycles of short-term incarceration and release; when incarcerated, she was sober and able to stabilise on her psychiatric medications, and would revert back to the witty, empathetic person she had been before, in spite of the oppressive conditions of jail. As soon as she was released (usually back to the street, as she was still homeless) she would decompensate, self-medicate with methamphetamine, and start the

(continued)

Box 6.1 (continued)

cycle anew. After a recent arrest, she is now facing a multi-year prison sentence since her record is one of missed court dates and increasingly serious charges. Although she has gained valuable skills that would make her employable, Cassie is so ashamed of her ongoing struggles with drugs and incarceration that she does not engage with the organisations where she previously found support, making her increasingly reliant on sex work to earn money.

Cassie wants to become a professional makeup artist, and has the looks, talent, and charisma to make a career of it, if given the support to meet her mental health and addiction needs. However, engaging her in long-term therapy has proven elusive thus far, and permanent housing to help her stabilise is now out of reach since she's no longer eligible for the youth housing programmes she relied on when she was younger. The short-term housing that is available is abstinence-only, and since she is not ready to give up using meth, she is not eligible to stay there.

3. *Roxanne*

Roxanne is a 53-year-old white cisgender woman. She grew up in San Francisco, and started drinking, smoking marijuana, and using PCP and hallucinogens with friends when she was 13. During that time, she was living at home with her parents and siblings. After graduating high school, she moved into a house with some friends and pieced together jobs to earn enough money for rent. After partying all night with her friends, she would mix some amphetamines into her morning coffee to help her get through the workday. Roxanne looks back on this time of her life with fondness.

When Roxanne was 25, a man she was dating turned her on to crack, which quickly became the most important thing in her life. She realised that to support her habit she needed to find additional ways to make money. Roxanne started doing sex work, learning from other women working the streets. Between drug use and sex work, she went to jail close to 40 times. Sometimes this was for possession charges, other times it was for solicitation or loitering with the intent to engage in prostitution.

When Roxanne was 45 she decided she was tired of using and of engaging in sex work to support her use. She went into a programme at a drop-in centre which she knew other women had successfully used to get sober. After maintaining a year of sobriety, she met a man and they started dating. She knew he was dealing drugs, but she thought she would be able to date him and stay sober. However, once she moved in with him, the proximity to crack was too much for her and she started using again. Initially, he was giving her crack for free but then told her she would have to pay for it. Roxanne found herself back in the position of needing to sell sex to support her habit.

By the time Roxanne was almost 50, she knew she wanted to change. She was worn out and tired. She realised she had missed time with her five

(continued)

Box 6.1 (continued)

children, four of whom were now adults and had not spent time with her two grandkids. Over the years, Roxanne gave her children to other family members because she knew she was not capable of taking care of them. As she described it, crack was in the way of everything. Roxanne went back to the drop-in centre she had used years before and they helped her get into a residential treatment programme. She was in that programme for a year before moving into a transitional living house. During that time, she started to rebuild relationships with her family.

Still new in her recovery, Roxanne is taking it slow and trying not to put too much pressure on herself. She feels as if she is starting life all over again. She and her roommate are hoping to move out of San Francisco; she wants a break from all the noise and to be closer to her children. She's also upset that men will approach her outside her apartment building and ask if she smokes (referring to crack). She knows she does not want to use again, but when people ask her that, she initially wants to say yes. Although she would prefer to not do sex work, both her criminal record and inconsistent legal work history make it hard for her to find employment. When necessary, Roxanne will do sex work to get a little extra money. If someone is presentable and has some money, she is willing to perform oral sex or give them a hand job but longer has vaginal sex with clients. That is something she never wanted to do, and only did to support her crack use.

4. *Claire*

   Claire is a 38-year-old Asian American bisexual cisgender woman. Claire started engaging in erotic massage work in her early 20s to help pay her way through college and started working full-time as a dominatrix at a professional dungeon after she finished school. After a few years at the dungeon, she "went independent", finding clients via online ad platforms. She found that the flexible hours and relatively high hourly pay allowed her to spend time making art, volunteering at a local animal shelter, and eventually earning her Master's degree in psychotherapy. Since completing her degree, Claire has leveraged her unique understanding of sexual issues to carve out a niche for herself as a sex therapist, helping people develop greater comfort with their bodies and sexuality. She finds this work both fulfilling and financially rewarding, and she now balances her "above-board" therapy practice with a continued (yet separate) career as a successful professional Dominatrix.

   Claire has a large, close-knit circle of friends which includes other sex workers, people in tech, and a number of artists and musicians. On weekends, she indulges in a number of "party drugs", such as ketamine, GHB and MDMA, often going out to dance all night to electronic music or hosting friends at the home she co-owns with her husband (also a sex worker) and several others. She also uses marijuana, usually to unwind at night. Although she enjoys getting high, she has very strong boundaries around her engagement with clients, and has strict policies about keeping her personal and professional lives separate: when it comes to clients, the only thing she indulges in is an occasional glass of wine if out to dinner with a submissive.

Our case studies indicate that the existing literature fails to adequately capture the complexity and needs of sex workers. Nuances regarding types of sex work, differences between types and patterns of sex work, sex work trajectories, working conditions and contexts, and the full spectrum of gender and other demographic factors are erased by studies that fail to account for these complexities. In order to design programmes that will best serve sex workers' needs, different sub-populations targeted by such programming need to be given the tools, resources, and support to design programmes specific to their circumstances. For example, the needs of full-service, street-based transgender sex workers will be very different from the needs of relatively well-to-do, independent indoor escorts, which in turn will differ widely from the needs of gay men who are dancers in a strip club.

Discussion

We identified 86 studies from 46 countries, encompassing the Americas, Asia, Africa, Europe, and Oceania. Most studies were cross-sectional in design (80%) and conducted in the last decade (60%). The majority of studies ($n = 70$) reported prevalence among "female" sex workers, with only 13 studies reporting prevalence among male sex workers, 6 reporting prevalence among transgender sex workers, and 5 studies which reported prevalence among combined population groups. However, because most studies only identified participants as "female", "male", or "transgender", we were unable to estimate prevalence by gender identity (cis, trans, or non-binary).

Global pooled prevalence of lifetime illicit drug use was 35%, with prevalence of lifetime and recent drug use ranging from 1.2% to 84% and 1.7% to 98%, respectively. Similarly, prevalence of lifetime and recent injection drug use varied from 0% to 82% and 0% to 48%, respectively. The majority of studies reporting prevalence of lifetime illicit drug use were conducted among female sex workers and global pooled prevalence among this sub-group was 29%. Pooled prevalence was higher in Northern America (84%) and Eastern Europe (71%) compared to Eastern Asia (12%) and South-eastern Asia (16%).

Despite the fact that more than a third of sex workers in our review reported lifetime use of illicit drugs, there is no specific guidance on the delivery of services for people who sell sex and use drugs [36]. Most programmatic interventions for sex workers are HIV-informed, and few interventions specific to this population exist for drug use. The only systematic review of interventions targeting illicit drug use in (street-based) sex workers concluded that there was no strong evidence for the effectiveness of interventions to reduce illicit drug use among street-based female sex workers with problematic drug use [37]. Nonetheless, a recent review concluded that interventions that combined structural approaches (as opposed to only focusing on the individual), harm reduction, safer sex interventions, and access to sex work-specific health services were more successful than single interventions which did not, highlighting the need for multi-component approaches [38].

Evidence-based harm reduction, including drug treatment such as opioid agonist therapy (OAT), remains difficult to access for drug users, including sex workers who use drugs, particularly in low- and middle-income countries [39]. Sex work, harm reduction, and drug treatment services often operate separately from each other and few programmes are tailored to people who both use drugs and sell sex. This is particularly important in the context of the current opioid overdose crisis in North America [40], where integrated service provision for sex workers who use drugs will be key to effective scale-up of interventions designed to reduce morbidity and mortality. Barriers to service access are further accentuated for this population because of the compounded stigma surrounding both drug use and sex work, and the prevailing legal and policy environments in most countries that criminalise aspects of one or both.

Our review has limitations. Grey literature and non-peer-reviewed publications were not included. There was inconsistency in the timeframes used to define "recent" drug and injection drug use. Because we were unable to distinguish between mono and poly drug use among studies that reported drug use by drug type, we extracted data from the illicit drug most commonly used, which may have resulted in an under-estimate of prevalence in some studies. On the other hand, because our review esti-mated lifetime prevalence of any illicit drug use, it is not possible to draw meaningful correlations between drug use and sex work, as most studies did not differentiate between different types of drugs (i.e. opioids versus stimulants), or different patterns of use (occasional vs. habitual, long ago or in the present).

Most included studies were also from low-middle income countries (78%, 67 of 86 studies), with no studies included from the sub-regions of Northern Africa, Middle Africa, and Micronesia. Although we found high diversity between studies, there was no evidence to suggest that this was explained by geographical region. Geographic mapping of pooled prevalence used lifetime illicit drug use; however, "recent" illicit drug use was used as a proxy for three sub-regions where estimates of lifetime use were not available, which also likely results in an underestimate in prevalence for these sub-regions. The cross-sectional design and convenience sam-pling of most included studies limits the strength of the evidence and highlights the need for more rigorous research, including a standardised approach to data collec-tion and measurement to document prevalence.

Our review did not identify sufficient data to provide pooled prevalence esti-mates of lifetime illicit drug use among male and transgender sex workers, limiting our ability to make comparisons between sex workers. Limited data on transwomen sex workers, and a global scarcity of data on drug use among transmen engaged in sex work, is both a limitation and a finding of our review. Few studies specified cis, trans, or non-binary gender identity, and it is possible that some studies of "female" and "male" sex workers included cis- and transgender sex workers. Given that gen-der and sexual identity have been identified as key factors influencing vulnerability to harmful drug use [39, 41], the inability to classify results by gender identity reduces our understanding of these issues. The scarcity of data on male and trans-gender sex workers, particularly transmen, is a key gap that should be addressed in future research.

Our review also included estimates from two studies of sex workers which explicitly included people engaged in transactional sex [31, 35]. A recent UNAIDS report which focuses on adolescent girls and young women in sub-Saharan Africa argues that sex workers and people who engage in transactional sex are distinct populations, that interventions for sex workers will not reach people engaged in transactional sex, and that programmes need to take care not to conflate transactional sex and sex work when designing interventions [25].

Finally, our review of the prevalence literature was unable to capture lived experiences of drug use and sex work and therefore cannot speak to the ways in which many sex workers manage to balance illicit drug use and sex work with a high level of day-to-day functionality and life meaning. However, our case studies provide insights into these lived experiences and demonstrate that the characteristics, circumstances, drug use and needs of people engaged in sex work can and do vary widely. The epidemiological literature has often treated sex workers as a monolith, focusing predominantly on cisgender women who offer "full service" sex work, either on the streets or in brothel settings. By overlooking the diversity of experiences of people who do sex work, a huge swathe (in fact, according to St. James Infirmary, the majority) of sex workers' needs are unknown and unaccounted for. Also lost is the ability for practitioners to apply lessons learned from sex workers who have kept themselves safe and healthy—often while using illicit drugs—by studying their lives from a strengths-based, harm reduction approach. In the absence of a fuller picture of the intersections between drug use and sex work, it is impossible to gain an accurate understanding of the various factors leading people to engage in either, and the ways in which they do and do not interact with one another.

Conclusions

Using data from 86 studies in 46 countries, we estimated global pooled prevalence of lifetime illicit drug use in sex workers of 35%, with estimates ranging from 1.2% to 84%. The majority of studies included in the review reported prevalence of lifetime illicit drug use among female sex workers (32 studies from 20 countries), and global pooled prevalence among this sub-group was 29%. Insufficient data precluded the generation of global pooled prevalence of illicit drug use among cismen and transgender sex workers.

Our review also aimed to determine whether illicit drug use was more prevalent in sex work populations than the general population. While we identified 39 studies from 24 countries which provided a measure of recent illicit drug use, including 27 which estimated recent use and 12 which estimated recent injection, these had varying definitions and timeframes. These limitations meant that it was not possible to compare global estimates of prevalence among sex workers with normative data, such as the estimates published in the UNODC's World Drug Report [42]. In 2016, UNODC estimated recent (last 12 months) global prevalence of illicit drug use (defined as use of drugs controlled under the international drug control conventions) in the general population (15–64 years) at 5.6% [42].

Our review highlights a lack of data on the diversity of populations involved in sex work (see case studies, Box 6.1). Current estimates of prevalence provide insufficient data on sex work settings and fail to differentiate between illicit drug use while doing sex work and drug use outside the sex work context. Significant gaps in the availability of data, as well as differences in the timeframes and measures used to estimate prevalence, create a mandate for future research and, specifically, for studies which estimate prevalence in ciswomen, cismen, and transgender sex workers.

Our findings in relation to these data gaps are also consistent with the literature. A recent review of morbidity and mortality data in four overlapping socially excluded populations (homeless people, individuals with drug use disorders, prisoners, and sex workers) found extremely high excess mortality and noted that while people with drug use disorders were the most studied sub-group (42.1% of data points), followed by prisoners (27.1%) and homeless people (26.6%), sex workers (4.2%) were the least well studied [43].

Our results indicate an urgent need to improve the quality and quantity of data on illicit drug use among sex workers. Most studies have focused on cis women, including women who sell sex to support their drug use, and less is known about cis men and transgender sex workers [44]. There is a need for both more robust epidemiological methods and increased measurement rigour to estimate prevalence by sex work population and setting, as well as qualitative research that explores the lived experience of sex work and the intersection of sex work and illicit drug use.

However, such research needs to be guided and, where feasible, conducted by sex workers. We recognise that criminalisation, violence, and stigmatisation present barriers to finding and counting sex workers, let alone expecting them to provide honest answers about their drug use. Research initiated by and/or in partnership with sex worker-led organisations using reliable and ethical methods to capture the diversity and lived experience of sex work populations is necessary to inform rigorous estimates of prevalence, identify differences in risk and exposures, and inform the evaluation and optimisation of evidence-based, human-rights informed, targeted interventions designed to improve the lives of sex workers.

At a programmatic level, while sex workers and people who inject drugs are now recognised as key populations in the global HIV response, funding remains inadequate. As NSWP and INPUD have recently pointed out, "this recognition often fails to translate into funding commitments of appropriate scale and reach, and at times results in health programmes that are not implemented from a rights-based perspective" [45]. Policy and programmatic efforts need to remain mindful that, as a community spanning two key populations, sex workers who use drugs may be at increased risk of harms, including HIV and violence, compared to people who only sell sex or only use drugs [36].

Finally, efforts both to address data gaps and inform public health responses remain hampered by punitive laws and policies governing sex work globally. The criminalisation of both sex work and drug use and the stigmatisation of sex workers who use drugs impedes the development and delivery of effective and accessible services, including drug treatment. Recent research indicates that sex workers who were unable to access drug treatment were at higher risk for physical violence, including violence perpetrated by clients [46]. Legislative and policy reform is needed to remove punitive laws and policies relating to sex work and drug use/possession. This needs to be accompanied by research on proposed, as well as enacted, sex work and drug use reforms, and their impacts using both public health and human rights frameworks.

Acknowledgements We acknowledge the contributions of sex worker communities to the studies reported here and are grateful to Rachel McCleave for assistance with formatting and referencing.

References

1. Decker MR, Wirtz AL, Moguilnyi V, Peryshkina A, Ostrovskaya M, Nikita M, et al. Female sex workers in three cities in Russia: HIV prevalence, risk factors and experience with targeted HIV prevention. AIDS Behav. 2014;18(3):562–72.
2. Maher L, Dixon TC, Phlong P, Mooney-Somers J, Stein ES, Page K. Conflicting rights: how the prohibition of human trafficking and sexual exploitation infringes the right to health of female sex workers in Phnom Penh, Cambodia. Health Hum Rights. 2015;17(1):102–13.
3. Rekart ML. Sex-work harm reduction. Lancet. 2005;366(9503):2123–34.
4. Shannon K, Strathdee SA, Goldenberg SM, Duff P, Mwangi P, Rusakova M, et al. Global epidemiology of HIV among female sex workers: influence of structural determinants. Lancet. 2015;385(9962):55–71.
5. Shannon K, Crago AL, Baral SD, Bekker LG, Kerrigan D, Decker MR, et al. The global response and unmet actions for HIV and sex workers. Lancet. 2018;392(10148):698–710.
6. Shannon K, Csete J. Violence, condom negotiation, and HIV/STI risk among sex workers. JAMA. 2010;304(5):573–4.
7. Baral S, Beyrer C, Muessig K, Poteat T, Wirtz AL, Decker MR, et al. Burden of HIV among female sex workers in low-income and middle-income countries: a systematic review and meta-analysis. Lancet Infect Dis. 2012;12(7):538–49.
8. Oldenburg CE, Perez-Brumer AG, Reisner SL, Mattie J, Barnighausen T, Mayer KH, et al. Global burden of HIV among men who engage in transactional sex: a systematic review and meta-analysis. PLoS One. 2014;9(7):e103549.
9. Deering KN, Amin A, Shoveller J, Nesbitt A, Garcia-Moreno C, Duff P, et al. A systematic review of the correlates of violence against sex workers. Am J Public Health. 2014;104(5):E42–54.
10. Lutnick A, Harris J, Lorvick J, Cheng H, Wenger LD, Bourgois P, et al. Examining the associations between sex trade involvement, rape, and symptomatology of sexual abuse trauma. J Interpers Violence. 2015;30(11):1847–63.
11. Wirtz AL, Peryshkina A, Mogilniy V, Beyrer C, Decker MR. Current and recent drug use intensifies sexual and structural HIV risk outcomes among female sex workers in the Russian Federation. Int J Drug Policy. 2015;26(8):755–63.
12. Dunne EM, Dyer TP, Khan MR, Cavanaugh CE, Melnikov A, Latimer WW. HIV prevalence and risk behaviors among African American women who trade sex for drugs versus economic resources. AIDS Behav. 2014;18(7):1288–92.
13. El-Bassel N, Witte SS, Wada T, Gilbert L, Wallace J. Correlates of partner violence among female street-based sex workers: substance abuse, history of childhood abuse, and HIV risks. AIDS Patient Care STDS. 2001;15(1):41–51.

14. Odinokova V, Rusakova M, Urada LA, Silverman JG, Raj A. Police sexual coercion and its association with risky sex work and substance use behaviors among female sex workers in St. Petersburg and Orenburg, Russia. Int J Drug Policy. 2014;25(1):96–104.
15. Hong Y, Zhang C, Li XM, Liu W, Zhou YJ. Partner violence and psychosocial distress among female sex workers in China. PLoS One. 2013;8(4):e62290.
16. WHO. Guidance on prevention of viral hepatitis B and C for people who inject drugs. World Health Organisation [Internet]. 2012. https://apps.who.int/iris/bitstream/handle/10665/75357/9789241504041_eng.pdf;jsessionid=85C2769A59B24E204D049307 1E26030B?sequence=1. Accessed 20 Mar 2019.
17. Reeves A, Steele S, Stuckler D, McKee M, Amato-Gauci A, Semenza JC. National sex work policy and HIV prevalence among sex workers: an ecological regression analysis of 27 European countries. Lancet HIV. 2017;4(3):E134–E40.
18. UNAIDS. Guidance note on HIV and sex work. 2012. http://www.unaids.org/en/media/unaids/ contentassets/documents/unaidspublication/2009/JC2306_UNAIDSguidance-note-HIV-sex-work_en.pdf. Accessed 22 Mar 2019.
19. Global Commission on HIV and the Law. Risks, rights & health. UNDP: New York; 2012.
20. Medecins du Monde. What do sex workers think about the French Prostitution Act. 2018. https://www.medecinsdumonde.org/sites/default/files/ENGLISH-Synth%C3%A8se-Rapport-prostitution-BD.PDF. Accessed 27 Mar 2019.
21. International AIDS Society. Studies raise concerns about policies seeking to "end demand" for sex work. 2018. http://www.aids2018.org/Media-Centre/The-latest/Press-releases/ ArticleID/192/Studies-raise-concerns-about-policies-seeking-to-%E2%80%9Cend-demand%E2%80%9D-for-sex-work. Accessed 27 Mar 2019.
22. Dennermalm N. Resistance to the Swedish model through LGBTQ and sex work community collaboration and online intervention. Digital Culture & Education [Internet]. 2014. http://www.digitalcultureandeducation.com/uncategorized/dennermalm_html/. Accessed 27 Mar 2019.
23. Goldenberg SM, Duff P, Krusi A. Work environments and HIV prevention: a qualitative review and meta-synthesis of sex worker narratives. BMC Public Health. 2015;15:1241.
24. Dixon TC, Ngak S, Stein E, Carrico A, Page K, Maher L. Pharmacology, physiology and performance: occupational drug use and HIV risk among female entertainment and sex workers in Cambodia. Harm Reduct J. 2015;12:33.
25. UNAIDS. Transactional sex and HIV risk: from analysis to action. Geneva: Joint United Nations Programme on HIV/AIDS and STRIVE; 2018.
26. United Nations. Statistics Division of the United Nations Secretariat, Standard Country or Area Codes for Statistical Use (M49). 1999. https://unstats.un.org/unsd/methodology/m49/. Accessed 14 Feb 2019.
27. Wang JJ, Zhu ZB, Yang X, Wu J, Wang HB, Feng L, Ding GW, Norris JL, Wang N. (b). Herpes simplex virus type 2 risks in female sex workers in the China-Vietnam border county of Hekou. Biomed Environ Sci. 2012;25(6):706–10.
28. Martin L, Hearst MO, Widome R. Meaningful differences: comparison of adult women who first traded sex as a juvenile versus as an adult. Violence Against Women. 2010;16(11):1252–69.
29. Moro L, Simon K, Sarosi P. Drug use among sex workers in Hungary. Soc Sci Med. 2013;93:64–9.
30. Zhang L, Liang S, Lu W, Pan SW, Song B, Liu Q, et al. HIV, syphilis, and behavioral risk factors among female sex workers before and after implementation of harm reduction programs in a high drug-using area of China. PLoS One. 2014;9(1):e84950.
31. Reuben J, Serio-Chapman C, Welsh C, Matens R, Sherman SG. Correlates of current transactional sex among a sample of female exotic dancers in Baltimore, MD. J Urban Health. 2011;88(2):342–51.
32. Ilic D, Sipetic S, Bjegovic V. Risk of HIV infection among indoor and street sex workers and their use of health services in Belgrade, Serbia. Srp Arh Celok Lek. 2010;138(3–4):219–24.

33. Mahfoud Z, Afifi R, Ramia S, El Khoury D, Kassak K, El Barbir F, et al. HIV/AIDS among female sex workers, injecting drug users and men who have sex with men in Lebanon: results of the first biobehavioral surveys. AIDS. 2010;24(Suppl 2):S45–54.

34. Decker MR, Wirtz AL, Baral SD, Peryshkina A, Mogilnyi V, Weber RA, et al. Injection drug use, sexual risk, violence and STI/HIV among Moscow female sex workers. Sex Transm Infect. 2012;88(4):278–83.

35. Couture MC, Evans JL, Sothy NS, Stein ES, Sichan K, Maher L, et al. Correlates of amphetamine-type stimulant use and associations with HIV-related risks among young women engaged in sex work in Phnom Penh, Cambodia. Drug Alcohol Depend. 2012;120(1–3):119–26.

36. Ditmore MH. When sex work and drug use overlap: considerations for advocacy and practice. London: Harm Reduction International; 2013.

37. Jeal N, Macleod J, Turner K, Salisbury C. Systematic review of interventions to reduce illicit drug use in female drug-dependent street sex workers. BMJ Open. 2015;5(11):e009238.

38. Awungafac G, Delvaux T, Vuylsteke B. Systematic review of sex work interventions in sub-Saharan Africa: examining combination prevention approaches. Tropical Med Int Health. 2017;22(8):971–93.

39. Iversen J, Page K, Madden A, Maher L. HIV, HCV, and health-related harms among women who inject drugs: implications for prevention and treatment. J Acquir Immune Defic Syndr. 2015;69:S176–S81.

40. Haegerich TM, Jones CM, Cote PO, Robinson A, Ross L. Evidence for state, community and systems-level prevention strategies to address the opioid crisis. Drug Alcohol Depend. 2019;204:107563.

41. Reisner SL, Poteat T, Keatley J, Cabral M, Mothopeng T, Dunham E, et al. Global health burden and needs of transgender populations: a review. Lancet. 2016;388(10042):412–36.

42. UNODC. World drug report 2018. 2018. https://www.unodc.org/wdr2018/. Accessed 20 Mar 2019.

43. Aldridge RW, Story A, Hwang SW, Nordentoft M, Luchenski SA, Hartwell G, et al. Morbidity and mortality in homeless individuals, prisoners, sex workers, and individuals with substance use disorders in high-income countries: a systematic review and meta-analysis. Lancet. 2018;391(10117):241–50.

44. Opeiario D, Soma T, Underhill K. Sex work and HIV status among transgender women - systematic review and meta-analysis. J Acquir Immune Defic Syndr. 2008;48(1):97–103.

45. NSWP/INPUD. Sex workers who use drugs: ensuring a joint approach. 2013. https://www.nswp.org/sites/nswp.org/files/Joint%20Briefing%20Paper%20Sex%20Workers%20Who%20Use%20Drugs%2C%20NSWP%20INPUD%20-%20October%202015.pdf. Accessed 27 Mar 2019.

46. Shannon K, Kerr T, Strathdee SA, Shoveller J, Montaner JS, Tyndall MW. Prevalence and structural correlates of gender based violence among a prospective cohort of female sex workers. Br Med J. 2009;339:b2939.

Part II
Structural Determinants of Health and Human Rights Inequities in Sex Work

Chapter 7

Criminalised Interactions with Law Enforcement and Impacts on Health and Safety in the Context of Different Legislative Frameworks Governing Sex Work Globally

Andrea Krüsi, Kate D'Adamo, and Ariel Sernick

Background

Sex workers are a highly diverse group who solicit and service clients in a variety of settings, including on the internet, through escort agencies, in third-party owned spaces such as brothels or massage parlours, or in public space. Globally, sex work is highly stigmatised, and the dominant policy approach has been criminalisation and police enforcement. Intersecting regimes of criminalisation and stigmatisation perpetuate poor labour conditions that render sex workers at increased risk for violence and poor health, denying sex workers the ability to fully realise their human rights, including access to occupational health and safety, police protection, and legal recourse.

There is now a well-established body of epidemiological and social science research showing that criminalisation of sex work negatively impacts sex workers' human rights, increases experiences of violence, and exacerbates health risks, including vulnerability to HIV and STI infections among sex workers [1–10]. Yet the criminalisation of some or all aspects of sex work remains the dominant legislative approach [1, 9]. Various models of criminalisation persist, in stark contrast to the significant body of empirical evidence and clear international guidelines by a variety of policy and human rights bodies including the World Health Organization, NSWP, UNAIDS, UNDP, UNFPA, and Amnesty International calling for the full decriminalisation of sex work as necessary to promote the health and human rights

A. Krüsi (✉)
Department of Medicine, University of British Columbia, Vancouver, BC, Canada

Centre for Gender & Sexual Health Equity (CGSHE), Vancouver, BC, Canada
e-mail: Andrea.Krusi@cgshe.ubc.ca

K. D'Adamo
Reframe Health and Justice (RHJ), Baltimore, MD, USA

A. Sernick
Centre for Gender & Sexual Health Equity (CGSHE), Vancouver, BC, Canada

© The Author(s) 2021   121
S. M. Goldenberg et al. (eds.), *Sex Work, Health, and Human Rights*,
https://doi.org/10.1007/978-3-030-64171-9_7

of sex workers. Indeed, an ever growing body of research suggests that much of what has been identified as harmful in sex work is not an inherent characteristic of the work, but rather of the social and structural factors that shape the working conditions of sex workers. Prohibitive sex work legislation, punitive policing, stigma, poverty, restrictive immigration policies, and gender inequity [1, 2, 11, 12] all constrain and negatively shape the circumstances surrounding them and the options that people have when trading sex—meaning that sex workers have fewer options to work under conditions which would provide more safety and autonomy, as well as fewer avenues for redress when they face violence and victimisation. Ironically, the conflation of sex work and these experiences of victimisation, including sexual exploitation, remain a significant barrier to reforming punitive laws and creating safer work environments for sex workers, including migrant sex workers [13].

Regimes of Regulating Sex Work

The judicial regulation of sex work globally can be broadly categorised in three different approaches: (1) Criminalisation, including End-Demand Criminalisation, (2) Legalisation, and (3) Decriminalisation. In this chapter, we review three dominant legislative approaches to the regulation of sex work and provide country spotlights to show how different legislative frameworks and law enforcement approaches shape sex workers' lived experiences of occupational health, safety, and human rights in different places globally.

Full and Partial Criminalisation

Full and partial criminalisation of sex work includes environments where some or all aspects of selling sex, buying sex, and organising for the aforementioned objectives are criminalised; this includes end-demand criminalisation, a form of partial criminalisation that we will discuss in more detail below [14]. Full and partial criminalisation of sex work is the dominant policy response to sex work globally and has been combined into one category because of the similar impacts and outcomes. Full criminalisation exists as the dominant legal regime in many settings including in most of the USA (except parts of Nevada),[1] South Africa, Sri Lanka, Cameroon, and Uganda. Partial criminalisation models are those in which neither the selling nor buying of sex is illegal per se, but most aspects surrounding sex work, such as solicitation and brothel keeping, remain illegal. This exists in various jurisdictions, including India and the United Kingdom (UK). Increasingly, end-demand crimi-

---

[1] Recently, legislation to decriminalize sex work has been introduced in several US States, including Washington, DC, New York, Maine, and Massachusetts.

nalisation where the purchase of sex is criminalised while the selling of sex is legal has been implemented in various settings, including in Sweden, Norway, Canada, and France. A growing body of research has demonstrated that prohibition of sex work in policy and law is not effective in culling sex work [15]. Prohibitory approaches to sex work reflect how moralistic attitudes discriminating against and stigmatising sex workers are manifested in law [15, 16]. In criminalised settings, policing strategies can include surveillance, crackdowns, arrests, or threats of arrest, intimidation, and sexual and physical violence by police. These acts of violence can be frequent and largely go unreported to law enforcement [6, 17–20].

Links Between Client Violence, Criminalisation, and Policing

Criminalisation and repressive policing strategies have consistently been linked to an elevated risk of violence and a reduced ability on the part of sex workers to negotiate safer sex work transactions [6–9, 21]. The risk of violence by clients and from law enforcement is amplified for the most marginalised and visible sex workers, specifically those soliciting clients primarily in street-based settings, those living in poverty, racialised sex workers, sex workers who use illicit drugs, and sex workers of gender minorities [20, 22, 23]. In an effort to avoid police, to meet and service clients, sex workers often move to secluded areas where there are few to no protections from violence and abuse—such as peer networks or even something as simple as good lighting—circumstances which can lead to reduced ability to refuse unwanted clients or services, including client demands for sex without a condom; also, due to the fact that help is not readily available, violent perpetrators can assault sex workers with impunity [17, 20, 24–26]. Criminalisation and policing force sex workers—in order to avoid police detection—to rush or forgo screening prospective clients or negotiating the terms of sexual transactions before engaging with clients or entering a vehicle, placing sex workers at increased risk of physical or sexual violence [17, 27, 28]. Because criminalisation also targets the people around sex workers and clients, broadly written and applied laws against "pimping", "pandering," and "promoting" also create a barrier for sex workers to working with others or employing other protection [29–31]. The impact of criminalisation also stretches beyond the experience of arrest and incarceration itself. Evidence from the UK and India indicate that sex workers who have been arrested or imprisoned at one point in their lives were more likely to have experienced client violence [27, 32].

Criminalisation also causes increased vulnerability to negative health outcomes, as sex workers are less likely to disclose victimisation and must take on risks with clients to mitigate the risk of arrest. Physical and sexual violence against sex workers is linked to the transmission of sexually transmitted infections (STIs) and HIV through coercive unprotected sex and a reduced capacity to negotiate sexual risk reduction with clients [6–9, 21, 28, 33]. There is also evidence that, more broadly, legislation criminalising sex work constitutes a significant barrier to accessing health services, including primary care, HIV treatment and prevention, and sexual health services [25, 34–36].

Violence by Police

In criminalised settings, interactions with police perpetuate both direct and indirect harms on sex workers and their safety. Direct violence perpetrated by police, as well as the fear caused by police presence and the resulting need to operate clandestinely without access to help in case of violence, cement the institutional violence of sex work criminalisation [14, 37]. In criminalised settings, interactions between sex workers and police are frequent and can be violent [6, 18, 38–40]. In Nairobi, Kenya, for example, a change in policing policy in 2017 banned the conduct of sex work in the Central Business District, forcing sex workers to increasingly resort to bribery in that lucrative area to avoid arrest by police [41].

In India, police violence and coercion, including sexual assault, confiscation of condoms, raiding of workplaces, and arrest, were associated with increased experiences of physical or sexual violence by clients [42]. Among sex workers who experienced sexual violence in the past year in India, 6.6% reported that the main perpetrators were the police [43]. In Russia, sex workers in street-based settings were more likely to experience sexual violence by police than from clients [38]. Similarly, in Serbia, sex workers perceived police violence as a more serious threat than client-perpetrated physical violence, as they felt more able to manage their clients' behaviours. The police were routinely feared for abuse of their powers and for causing physical harm, for stealing, and for acts of public humiliation [8]. Moreover, criminalisation was also identified as undermining sex workers' human rights, including the right to police protection and legal recourse [16, 29]. Sex workers in criminalised settings are fearful of reporting violence to the police as they may face criminal prosecution or other ramifications, such as negative consequences regarding their im/migration status, or risk increased police surveillance and harassment after disclosing that they trade sex [16, 29]. This highlights the indirect consequences of criminalisation on the violence experienced by sex workers in an environment of impunity for the violent perpetrators targeting sex workers.

Intersections of Criminalisation

The negative effects of the criminalisation of sex work are amplified for sex workers who are racialised, im/migrants, live in poverty, use illicit drugs, work in outdoor venues, or identify as a sexual or gender minority [44–46]. Multiple layers of criminalisation intersect with racism and cis/hetero normativity and are engrained in policy and law—worsening the health and safety of many sex workers with various racialised and gendered identities. Furthermore, poverty, marginal housing, and homelessness undermine health equity and safety among sex workers [47].

Communities and people who are already marginalised based on their identities experience higher levels of violence, even in the context of violence against sex workers. Racialised sex workers experience the most brutal and relentless police violence and as a result have worsened health outcomes [6, 48]. Activists and researchers have highlighted the centrality of race in the organisation of sex industry labour, with non-racialised workers often holding better paying jobs in safer working environments with reduced risk of police detection and criminal sanctions, and racialised sex workers experiencing more vulnerability to violence by police and clients [49]. In Canada, Indigenous women are disproportionately targeted by police and have a reduced capacity to negotiate sexual risk, which is linked to their elevated rates of violence and HIV [50]. Furthermore, im/migrant sex workers also experience increased risk of violence and reduced access to sexual and reproductive health services. Research conducted among migrant Latin American women highlights the ties between im/migrant status and negative health outcomes and healthcare access [51]. Broadly, negative health outcomes are especially evident for racialised and im/migrant sex workers who experience language barriers, restrictive immigration policies, unstable housing, racism, xenophobia, and barriers to accessing employment within and outside the sex industry.

Criminalisation and enforcement also disproportionately target sex workers who solicit clients in outdoor settings and those experiencing insecurity regarding housing, due to their increased visibility and reduced cultural, social, and economic capital [20, 22, 23, 52]. Sex workers who live in poverty are more visible as they are more likely to work in street-based settings, making them more likely to be subjected to police intervention [19, 47]. A growing body of literature has delineated the impact of different venues where sex workers engage clients on sexual health, violence, and policing [53–56].

Many of the sex workers engaged in the lowest paying street-based sex work settings have a history of illicit drug use and thus are not only criminalised due to their income-generating activities, but also on charges related to their drug use, such as drug and paraphernalia possession. A high concentration of harms, including increased risk of violence and ill health, have consistently been documented in settings where street-based sex work and illicit drug markets co-exist [18, 20, 22, 57–60]. The intersecting negative effects of criminalising both sex work and illicit drug use compound sex workers' ability to negotiate transactions and their ability to report violence to police [20, 61, 62]. Research from Russia has identified binge illicit drug use as increasing the risk of sexual violence by clients and police [38].

Sex workers with greater income security are more likely to have the resources to use safety measures, including the time required to screen new clients, more control and discernment over their physical location, and the ability to hire drivers or security personnel, and security cameras. These harm reduction techniques are meant to not only protect sex workers from client violence, but also from police detection [39, 63].

Research that focuses on the experiences of trans sex workers with sex work criminalisation is somewhat limited [33, 64, 65]. However, it is clear that trans, two spirit, and gender non-binary (T2SGNB) sex workers face additional risks in their interactions with police in the context of criminalisation [64, 66]. Globally, T2SGNB peoples face economic and social exclusion that both limit the breadth of work opportunities and exacerbate violence and discrimination within those settings, including sex work [64, 67–69]. Stigma against trans people compounds the stigma placed on sex workers and further exacerbates the negative effects of criminalisation

[64]. Much of the existing research related to trans sex workers in criminalised settings highlights a disproportionate burden of violence perpetrated by police, including rape and other forms of physical violence [65, 70]. In Vancouver, Canada, for example, moving to new locations in order to avoid police contributed to trans workers facing increased experiences of violence perpetrated by clients. Spaces where sex workers solicit clients are often segregated by gender identity, even within the same city. As trans sex workers were pushed into other locations where clients traditionally only found cisgender sex workers, clients who were unaware of a workers' gender identity sometimes exhibited transphobic violence [64]. Similarly, in Serbia, coercive policing practices were associated with reduced condom use among trans sex workers, due to their reduced capacity to negotiate sexual safety in order to avoid police detection [6].

There is a lack of understanding of how evolving sex work legislation and policing practices shape the occupational health, safety, and labour rights among cis and trans men and gender non-binary sex workers [71–73]. Men sex workers have been largely erased from the public discourse about sex work laws. Historically, laws that frame sex work have not been the primary mechanism relied upon to regulate men sex workers, due to the close connection between the criminalisation of homosexuality and men who sell sex [74]. As a result of gendered assumptions on the part of law enforcement, men sex workers are often viewed, treated, and ultimately charged differently than women and femme presenting workers. Findings from Canada and elsewhere highlight a shift among men sex workers from primarily street-based work to online solicitation, linked in part to efforts to avoid police detection and harassment [72, 75]. Given the targeted criminalisation of third parties in many settings, including punitive approaches to control the advertising of sexual services, men sex workers are also directly affected by criminalisation that limits sex workers' access to their clients via the internet. There is a critical need to explore the lived experiences of cis and trans men who engage in sex work, including how various regimes of criminalisation—including the ongoing criminalisation of homosexuality in some settings—shape their health and safety in street settings and elsewhere.

> **Box 7.1 Country Spotlight Full Criminalisation: Cameroon**
> Over 60% of sex workers in Cameroon report experiencing physical or sexual violence in their lifetime [36]. Selling sex is illegal, with a punishment of jail time ranging from 6 months to 5 years and a fine of approximately 34–85 USD [76]. Also outlawed are third parties, brothel keeping, and solicitation in public spaces [77]. In qualitative interviews in collaboration with a local sex worker organisation, workers not only pointed to criminalisation as encouraging harm and violence against the community, but also the stigma that manifests around the sex trade. As a member of a local sex worker organisation described, "sex workers are constantly subject to corrective rapes, refusals of care in health facilities, insults after the sexual act from their clients who do not want to pay" [76].

(continued)

Box 7.1 (continued)

The police brutalise us out there

Sex workers highlighted that policing is a major source of harm, even when it doesn't lead to an arrest. In addition to laws which criminalise sex work, sex workers are often unfairly detained for not having an identification card and are forced to bribe the officers for release [78]. Sex workers frequently experience sexual and physical violence enacted by police. One sex worker described, "You take them like all the rest of your clients but when a uniformed man takes you, they are always brutal. He doesn't want to do you in a way that should be done. He wants to assault you as if he is saying 'ah here's a woman from the street. I should destroy her this one time'" [79]. Even when sex workers report violence to the police, they may be brushed off or not taken seriously. "[W]hen we have problems here, you will go complain maybe if you go to complain they won't take your problems into consideration because we are prostitutes!" one worker noted. "The police don't intervene on our behalf when we have problems because we are waka [pidgin English word meaning 'prostitute']!" [36]. Worse, these encounters may lead to even more acts of violence. For example, a young woman who was a member of a sex worker organisation had been physically assaulted by a client after he demanded she give the money back. However, encounters with law enforcement only compounded the harm done. "When the police arrived at the scene on the alert of the entourage, they brought [her] and her client to the police station to hear them. Once at the station, the community member was taken to an office by 3 policemen who forced her to have sex with them in exchange for her freedom. Having no choice, she gave way". [76].

Beyond direct criminalisation, sex workers in Cameroon pointed to "stigma, discrimination and social rejection" [76] as major barriers to accessing services, including health services. This stigma both promotes policing and state violence, while also being reinforced by it, making it harder for sex workers to access healthcare services for information and the tools to prevent HIV/STIs. Additionally, financial penalties of criminalisation and arrest such as court fines and fees also contribute to the inability to access the full range of healthcare services. Beyond bribery, a conviction for sex work can also have long-lasting financial consequences: "Many sex workers are students who are asked to do this activity in order to finance their studies", notes a member of a local sex worker organisation. "When they are convicted because of sex work, their criminal records [exclude them] from the opportunity to ... gain access to certain jobs". [76]

When asked what would change the situation for sex workers in Cameroon, sex workers provided varied answers, including police accountability, decriminalisation, increases in social services and a safe place where they could connect with other sex workers [36].

End-Demand Criminalisation

Over the past decade, in a growing number of places there has been increased interest in attempting to eradicate sex work through end-demand criminalisation, a form of prohibition that criminalises the purchase, but not the selling, of sexual services under some circumstances. Sweden, Norway, Iceland, and more recently France, Canada, and Northern Ireland, among other countries, have opted for end-demand criminalisation, despite the lack of evidence that this legal framework succeeds in either eradicating or reducing sex work or sexual exploitation. End-demand criminalisation was first implemented in Sweden in 1999, and it is often referred to as the Nordic model, despite the fact that the countries involved differ slightly from each other in its implementation. The primary objective of this approach is to eradicate sex work by eliminating demand through criminal sanctions targeting sex buyers and third parties, such as receptionists, venue owners/managers, drivers, and peers working collectively. Many countries that have adopted this model have layered the criminalisation of clients onto the continued criminalisation of sex workers and third parties, and thus continue to criminalise many sex workers, including im/migrant sex workers and street-based sex workers [80]. Recent evidence from Canada, Sweden, and France indicates that end-demand criminalisation is unsuccessful in meeting its objective of eradicating sex work and has resulted in continued violations of sex workers' human rights and limited their access to safe working conditions [30, 31, 81–84].

In some circumstances, moving away from criminalising sex workers themselves marks a conceptual shift from seeing sex workers as exclusively "risky" and as criminals—the view that underlies prohibitionist approaches to the regulation of sex work. Instead, this shift characterises sex workers as "at risk" of exploitation and sexual violence thus in need of intervention and state control for their protection, and the sex trade as inherently comprising spaces of harm [11, 37]. Although the "end demand" rhetoric in some settings claims to prioritise women sex workers' safety, its main goal remains the eradication of sex work through criminal sanctions.

Increasing epidemiological and social science evidence from Sweden, France, and Canada indicates that criminalisation and policing strategies targeting clients and third parties—such as receptionists, security personnel, and drivers—effectively reproduce the harms created by other forms of criminalisation of sex workers outlined above. In particular, this approach heightens risks for violence and abuse and contributes to the precarity of sexual labour and human rights abuses [30, 31, 82, 84, 85].

Box 7.2 Country Spotlight End-Demand Criminalisation: Canada

In 2013, the Canadian Supreme Court struck down the laws criminalising sex work as unconstitutional, citing the country's Charter of Rights and Freedoms which protects the security of the person. After several years of fierce deliberation, Canada passed the Protection of Communities and Exploited Persons Act (PCEPA), which implemented an "End-Demand" style of criminalisation where buying sexual services is illegal but the selling of sexual services is not criminalised, unless it takes place in the proximity of schools, daycare centres, or playgrounds. Additionally, PCEPA also criminalises third parties who gain material benefits, such as receptionists, managers, drivers, spotters, and advertisers and continues to criminalise im/migrant sex workers [79, 86].

In the 5 years since the law's enactment, research from various parts of Canada has reported harms in sex workers' relationships with law enforcement and in their safety as being similar to what was previously experienced under prohibitive sex work legislation [30, 82, 85, 87, 88]. One cisgender woman sex worker who predominantly solicited clients in street-based settings said: "Harassing the clients is exactly the same as harassing the women. You harass the clients and you are in exactly the same spot you were before. I'm staying on the streets and I am in jeopardy of getting raped, hurt" [29]. Similarly, research with sex workers from Eastern Canada indicated that law enforcement continued to enact violence, engage in intimidation and threats, conduct illegal searches, commit extortion and "out" individuals to community and family members [87]. Even if the criminal penalty for selling sex under some circumstances has been removed, ultimately, the legal reform has not improved sex workers' occupational conditions. A study from Vancouver, BC, found that 72% of "respondents said the [law] didn't improve their working conditions, while over a quarter reported negative changes" [82]. These findings underscore that end-demand legislation did not advance sex workers' occupational health and safety. Im/migrant workers in formal indoor work settings (e.g. massage parlours) as well as sex workers who already face high rates of criminalisation (e.g. due to illicit drug use) were most likely to report negative changes after the implementation of the PECPA [82]. These findings highlight that the implementation of end-demand legislation in Canada has resulted in further marginalising the most precarious groups of sex workers. Many sex workers interviewed in Vancouver have indicated that these laws merely reproduce the harms of other forms of criminalisation [29].

Most at risk of policing and abuse were racialised and immigrant sex workers [82, 87]. As one sex worker described, "Indigenous sex workers or Black, African-Caribbean sex workers are most targeted within the work they do; they're most visible, and even when sex workers are not working" [87]. Migrant workers on open work permits still face criminalisation for selling sex, and immigration infractions could lead to eventual deportation. Asian sex workers are regularly profiled and targeted by police. As one immigration law

(continued)

Box 7.2 (continued)

advocate explained, "If I'm a white American up here without status doing sex work, I'll be fine. If I'm an Asian woman working at a massage parlour and I have a work permit that says I shouldn't do sex work, I'm in grave danger". [87]

Despite the claims of some PECPA's supporters that it would reduce the abuse and criminalisation of sex workers, this has not been the case. Sex workers still experience harm and are forced to adapt their behaviour to the detriment of their safety and health. Sex workers report a variety of ways they structure their work to avoid interacting with police, including employing screening techniques, avoiding visibility by staying in more isolated locales, adopting irregular hours and work schedules, moving to secluded locations or working alone. All of these behaviours can also contribute to vulnerability to interpersonal violence with potential clients. As rational decision-makers, sex workers are prioritising avoiding arrest over avoiding risk of assault. One sex worker described, "I find it's almost equal avoiding cops versus avoiding aggressors; it almost takes from keeping an eye on tricks when you've got to watch for police now, who might be trying to set you up" [87]. Sex workers are also forced to adapt their behaviours in order to address their clients' fear of law enforcement, and many of these techniques carry with them new layers of vulnerability to violence. "A lot of the johns that I'm talking to now are so nervous and it seems almost like it's dangerous", one sex worker noted, "they want to meet you in dark alleyways, because they're scared of the cops now, because it's only them that get in trouble" [87].

The criminalisation of third parties, a central aspect of end-demand legislation, harms sex workers. Research has demonstrated that it is inaccurate to generalise that all third parties are exploitative male "pimps". The majority of third-party workers in indoor sex work environments were actually found to be either current or former women sex workers. Sex workers reported that these "third parties" provided client screening, security, and sexual health resources to sex workers; yet criminalisation under end-demand models restricted the availability of condoms and constrained access to police protections in case of violence or fraud, thereby undermining sex workers' health, safety, and human rights [88]. These findings showed that the criminalisation of third parties reproduced the unsafe working conditions experienced under other forms of sex work criminalisation [88]. Under end-demand legislation, the threat of police raids and inspections continued to deter condom availability in indoor sex work venues due to fears that condoms may be used as evidence to confirm that sex work takes place in a particular locale [46, 89]. The physical absence of condoms onsite, issues concerning sex workers' immigration status (e.g. fear of arrest or deportation), limited English proficiency, gendered power imbalance, and poverty, have all been found to interact to reduce women's ability to negotiate transactions and negotiate their health and safety in massage parlours [46, 89, 90].

(continued)

Box 7.2 (continued)

Additionally, end-demand legislation continues to constitute one of the main reasons sex workers are targeted for abuse. It is still apparent that sex workers remain unlikely to contact law enforcement if they are victimised. Elene Lam, an organiser of Chinese migrant sex workers, explained how the consequences of immigration status make sex workers less likely to reach out for law enforcement assistance, and this reality is yet another factor increasing their vulnerability. "We see people in other cities who target sex workers, especially migrant sex workers, because they know that they will not report to the police, and then they are organising to get money, or rob or rape. Some sex workers were robbed four times a week by a group of people" [87]. Despite all of this, sex workers across Canada are continuing to organise and advocate. Finding strength and survival in their communities and networks, they continue to push for renewed law reform that decriminalises sex work.

Legalisation

Legalisation is a regulatory model wherein sex work as well as sex workers are offered limited legal status based on various structural identities, including immigration status, age, work environment, and geographic location [91]. This model of regulating sex work takes a different form compared to other prohibitionist regimes, but is predicated on similar moralistic principals treating sex work as distinct from the mainstream service industry, and continues to undermine sex workers' human rights and health [91].

Regulatory models to govern sex work have been implemented in diverse settings including in the Netherlands, Germany, Guatemala, Switzerland, parts of Australia, Mexico, and Senegal [14, 92, 93]. These legalised settings have been lauded by some for being in contrast to purely prohibition-based approaches. But the legalisation of sex work in these settings is predicated on the ability and willingness of workers to adhere to exceptional and moralistic assumptions about the sex industry. It generally regulates government-mandated health and HIV/STI testing and compliance, curfews, and public registration [91]. Some of these requirements, including mandatory testing among sex workers, are based on public health regulations that aim to protect "the public" by treating sex workers as vectors for disease [94]. In these settings, these controlling health regulations prioritise certain citizens while undermining the health and safety of sex workers [95].

Legalisation restricts the occupational autonomy of sex workers, including where and when they can work. In a survey conducted among sex workers working in Amsterdam, only 2% of sex workers supported changes to work environments proposed in the city's primary sex work settings. Under legalisation, sex workers have little control or agency in negotiating the specifics of their work environments [96]. Legalisation in the Netherlands in recent years has shown to be a tool for the gradual encroachment on the rights and autonomy of sex workers, through legislative reform

and decentralised legal authority that controls the regulation of sex work in munici-
palities [92]. Regional differences in the way sex work is regulated can create confu-
sion and may leave sex workers vulnerable to judiciary action or fines. Evidence from
the Netherlands has demonstrated that legalisation has not been sufficient in eliminating the structural violence experienced by those working in this industry and is insufficient in conferring full citizenship rights for sex workers [97]. Recent amendments
to sex work laws in this setting have failed to address stigma or remedy a lack of
social rights, and migrant workers remained barred from this industry in part due to
the conflation of sex work and trafficking for the purpose of sexual exploitation [97].

Evidence from Senegal has demonstrated that models of legalisation may create
new vulnerabilities for sex workers by legalising some aspects of sex work while
failing to address stigmatising attitudes towards this form of labour [98]. In Senegal,
sex workers must register and carry a copy of their registration with them, as well as
attend compulsory sexual health testing. Fears of stigma and social isolation are
cited as the primary barriers, causing over 80% of sex workers in Senegal to avoid
registration, thereby forfeiting the associated legal protections [98]. Moreover,
legalisation status contributes to the growing inequity between sex workers who
have access to legal protection and those who do not. In the Netherlands, for example, foreign workers who are not eligible for legal protection in an otherwise legal
setting experience exaggerated forms of structural violence by employers and clients, including blackmail [97].

The regulation of sex work under a legalisation paradigm includes, in many settings, mandatory STI and HIV testing for workers. This practice is clearly flagged as
a human rights violation by sex workers' rights organisations as well as global policy
bodies such as WHO and UNAIDS. Research in various settings has demonstrated
that forced HIV/STI testing undermines more successful voluntary prevention methods [99, 100]. It also exacerbates stigma, interferes with relationships between
healthcare providers and sex workers, and may contribute to criminalisation of sex
workers who test positive [100]. In this way, mandatory testing creates new opportunities to criminalise and control sex workers within supposedly legal settings [91].

**Box 7.3 Country Spotlight Legalised Model: Australia (Except New
South Wales and the Northern Territory)**
In Australia, each state or territory has its own system of regulation and criminalisation of sex work using legalised models; however, in contrast to other
states and territories, New South Wales and the Northern Territory have
decriminalised sex work entirely. One worker (who asked that her organisation and location not be disclosed) described how, in states with regulation in
the context of a legalised model, there remains a significant fear of criminalisation among sex workers. *"Our main problem is coercion for fear of being
reported for breaking one of the myriad impossible laws around sex work in
our state. It is difficult to screen, difficult to negotiate and nearly impossible
to report assault when you are scared of being charged for offering illegal*

(continued)

Box 7.3 (continued)

services... State law prohibits private workers from working with anyone else in any capacity. No doubles, no phone message taker, no driver, no security, no sharing of spaces. They do police this law and it is a criminal offence (anti-pimping law...). This leaves workers incredibly open to violence from clients. I have worked under many different legislative models and this kind of regulation is the one I find the most difficult". [101]

Research conducted in Australia, where some states have implemented mandatory STI and HIV testing for sex workers, demonstrates that mandatory testing devalues effective prevention methods already in use among sex workers, unnecessarily overburdens the healthcare system and contributes to stigmatising conceptions of sex workers as unable or unwilling to take effective control over their health [99].

Decriminalisation

Decriminalisation is a model wherein sex work is regulated under existing labour laws and processes rather than through exceptional measures, as is the case with legalised models. Decriminalised sex work environments contribute to the wellbeing, health, and safety of sex workers. Significantly, various global human rights and policy bodies such as the World Health Organization, UNAIDS, UNDP, UNFPA, NSWP, and Amnesty International consistently reinforce the need to decriminalise sex work as a best practice to promote the health and human rights of sex workers. Estimates suggest that the decriminalisation of sex work is among the most substantive actions that can be taken to address the global burden of HIV, averting an estimated 33–46% of HIV infections in the next decade [102]. Yet decades of advocacy and campaigning by sex workers have resulted in dramatically few decriminalised environments, with New Zealand, and New South Wales and the Northern Territory in Australia being rare exceptions to the more common restrictive approaches, including end-demand criminalisation and legalisation observed globally [103].

Box 7.4 Country Highlight Decriminalisation: New Zealand
In New Zealand, where sex work has been decriminalised since 2003, workplace health and safety standards have been established in consultation with sex workers, and sex workers can bring employment complaints to governing bodies [81]. The New Zealand Prostitution Reform Act treats sex workers as full citizens with rights and occupational responsibilities. Sex work is regulated in the same manner as any other business by regulating its commercial practice through standard employment Health and Safety regulations; regulating the location of commercial sex establishments through zoning by-laws; and specifying the health and safety obligations of managers and workers. Regulating sex work as any

(continued)

Box 7.4 (continued)

other business in the service industry has significantly reduced the structural stigma of sex work in New Zealand [11]. Despite these gains, migrant sex workers in New Zealand remain criminalised, and still suffer many of the harms perpetuated in criminalised settings [104]. Although decriminalisation of sex work is by no means a panacea, in New Zealand it has created improved working conditions for sex workers overall, including increased ability to report violence to police and recourse in case of workplace regulation violations [15].

Decriminalisation has positive impacts on the health, safety, and human rights of sex workers [103]. In many settings, sex workers, especially women sex workers, are a key population in addressing the global burden of STIs and HIV [102]. Evidence from decriminalised settings has firmly indicated that these settings support access to better working conditions and increased occupational health and safety among sex workers [105].

Conclusion

Intersecting regimes of criminalisation, policing, and stigmatisation shape sex workers' occupational health and safety and experiences of violence and victimisation. A wealth of evidence demonstrates a growing consensus among sex workers and academics towards the need for decriminalisation as the only option for protecting the health and human rights of sex workers [21, 30, 37, 102, 106–108]. There is a critical need to include the expertise of sex workers from all segments of the sex industry, including those who are most marginalised due to racialisation, im/migration status, and illicit substance use, in evidence-based policy making [109]. Globally, the failures of sex work law stem from failure of governments and law makers to take seriously strong evidence produced by sex workers, human rights advocates and academics. The evidence shows that existing laws are creating and exacerbating devastating harms to the safety, health, and human rights of sex workers, including violence and poor health. Indeed, an ever growing body of research suggests that much of what has been identified as harmful in sex work is a product, not of the inherently dangerous or violent character of sex work, but rather of the social and structural factors that shape the working conditions of sex workers, such as criminalisation and punitive policing, stigma, poverty, and gender inequity [1, 2, 11, 12].

References

1. Gruskin S, Ferguson L, Alfven T, Rugg D, Peersman G. Identifying structural barriers to an effective HIV response: using the National Composite Policy Index data to evaluate the human rights, legal and policy environment. J Int AIDS Soc. 2013;16:18000.
2. Gruskin S, Williams Pierce G, Ferguson L. Realigning government action with public health evidence: the legal and policy environment affecting sex work and HIV in Asia. Cult Health Sex. 2013;16:14–29.

3. Muldoon KA, Akello M, Muzaaya G, Simo A, Shoveller J, Shannon K. Policing the epidemic: high burden of workplace violence among female sex workers in conflict-affected northern Uganda. Glob Public Health. 2017;12(1):84–97.
4. Platt L, Jolley E, Rhodes T, Hope V, Latypov A, Reynolds L, et al. Factors mediating HIV risk among female sex workers in Europe: a systematic review and ecological analysis. BMJ Open. 2013;3(7):e002836.
5. Platt L, Rhodes T, Judd A, Koshkina E, Maksimova S, Latishevskaya N, et al. Effects of sex work on the prevalence of syphilis among injection drug users in 3 Russian cities. Am J Public Health. 2007;97(3):478–85.
6. Rhodes T, Simic M, Baros S, Platt L, Zikic B. Police violence and sexual risk among female and transvestite sex workers in Serbia: qualitative study. BMJ. 2008;337:a811.
7. Shannon K, Csete J. Violence, condom negotiation, and HIV/STI risk among sex workers. JAMA. 2010;304(5):573–4.
8. Simić M, Rhodes T. Violence, dignity and HIV vulnerability: street sex work in Serbia. Sociol Health Illn. 2009;31(1):1–16.
9. WHO U, UNICEF. Global HIV/AIDS response: epidemic update and health sector progress towards universal access. Geneva: WHO, UNICEF; 2011.
10. Sanders T, Campbell R. Criminalization, protection and rights: global tensions in the governance of commercial sex. Criminol Crim Just. 2014;14(5):535–48.
11. Bruckert C, Hannem S. Rethinking the prostitution debates: transcending structural stigma in systemic responses to sex work. Can J Law Soc. 2013;28(01):43–63.
12. Zatz ND. Sex work/sex act: law, labor, and desire in constructions of prostitution. Signs. 1997;22:277–308.
13. Kotiswaran P. Beyond the allures of criminalization: rethinking the regulation of sex work in India. Criminol Crim Just. 2014;14(5):565–79.
14. Platt L, Grenfell P, Meiksin R, Elmes J, Sherman SG, Sanders T, et al. Associations between sex work laws and sex workers' health: a systematic review and meta-analysis of quantitative and qualitative studies. PLoS Med. 2018;15(12):e1002680.
15. Abel G, Fitzgerald L, Brunton C. The impact of decriminalisation on the number of sex workers in New Zealand. J Soc Policy. 2009;38(3):515–31.
16. Baratosy R, Wendt S. "Outdated Laws, Outspoken Whores": exploring sex work in a criminalised setting. Women's Stud Int Forum. 2017;62:34–42.
17. Okal J, Chersich MF, Tsui S, Sutherland E, Temmerman M, Luchters S. Sexual and physical violence against female sex workers in Kenya: a qualitative enquiry. AIDS Care. 2011;23(5):612–8.
18. Rekart ML. Sex-work harm reduction. Lancet. 2006;366(9503):2123–34.
19. Sanders T. The risks of street prostitution: punters, police and protesters. Urban Stud. 2004;41(9):1703–17.
20. Shannon K, Kerr T, Allinott S, Chettiar J, Shoveller J, Tyndall MW. Social and structural violence and power relations in mitigating HIV risk of drug-using women in survival sex work. Soc Sci Med. 2008;66(4):911–21.
21. Shannon K, Montaner JG. The politics and policies of HIV prevention in sex work. Lancet Infect Dis. 2012;12(7):500–2.
22. Lowman J. Violence and the outlaw status of (street) prostitution in Canada. Violence Against Women. 2000;6(9):987–1011.
23. Sanders T, Campbell R. Designing out vulnerability, building in respect: violence, safety and sex work policy. Br J Sociol. 2007;58(1):1–19.
24. Krüsi A, Chettiar J, Ridgway A, Abbott J, Strathdee SA, Shannon K. Negotiating safety and sexual risk reduction with clients in unsanctioned safer indoor sex work environments: a qualitative study; 2012. Report No.: 0090-0036 Contract No.: 6.
25. Maher L, Mooney-Somers J, Phlong P, Couture M-C, Stein E, Evans J, et al. Selling sex in unsafe spaces: sex work risk environments in Phnom Penh, Cambodia. Harm Reduct J. 2011;8(1):30.

26. Shannon K, Strathdee SA, Shoveller J, Rusch M, Kerr T, Tyndall MW. Structural and environmental barriers to condom use negotiation with clients among female sex workers: implications for HIV-prevention strategies and policy. Am J Public Health. 2009;99(4):659–65.
27. Deering KN, Bhattacharjee P, Mohan HL, Bradley J, Shannon K, Boily MC, et al. Violence and HIV risk among female sex workers in Southern India. Sex Transm Dis. 2013;42(2):168–74.
28. Shannon K, Kerr T, Strathdee SA, Shoveller J, Montaner JS, Tyndall MW. Prevalence and structural correlates of gender based violence among a prospective cohort of female sex workers. BMJ. 2009;339(7718):b2939.
29. Krusi A, Pacey K, Bird L, Taylor C, Chettiar J, Allan S, et al. Criminalisation of clients: reproducing vulnerabilities for violence and poor health among street-based sex workers in Canada-a qualitative study. BMJ Open. 2014;4(6):e005191.
30. McBride B, Goldenberg SM, Murphy A, Wu S, Braschel M, Krusi A, et al. Third parties (venue owners, managers, security, etc.) and access to occupational health and safety among sex workers in a Canadian Setting: 2010–2017. Am J Public Health. 2019;109(5):792–8.
31. McBride B, Shannon K, Duff P, Mo M, Braschel M, Goldenberg SM. Harms of workplace inspections for im/migrant sex workers in in-call establishments: enhanced barriers to health access in a Canadian setting. J Immigr Minor Health. 2019;21:1290–9.
32. Platt L, Grenfell P, Bonell C, Creighton S, Wellings K, Parry J, et al. Risk of sexually transmitted infections and violence among indoor-working female sex workers in London: the effect of migration from Eastern Europe. Sex Transm Infect. 2011;87(5):377–84.
33. Decker M, Beyrer C, Sherman S. Ending the invisibility of sex workers in the US HIV/AIDS surveillance and prevention strategy. AIDS. 2014;28(15):2325–7.
34. Boynton P, Cusick L. Sex workers to pay the price: UK plans to cut street prostitution will threaten sex workers' health. BMJ. 2006;332(7535):190–1.
35. Lazarus L, Deering KN, Nabess R, Gibson K, Tyndall MW, Shannon K. Occupational stigma as a primary barrier to health care for street-based sex workers in Canada. Cult Health Sex. 2012;14(2):139–50.
36. Decker M, Lyons C, Billong S, Njindam I, Grosso A, Nunez G, et al. Gender-based violence against female sex workers in Cameroon: prevalence and associations with sexual HIV risk and access to health services and justice. Sex Transm Infect. 2016;92(8):599–604.
37. Krusi A, Kerr T, Taylor C, Rhodes T, Shannon K. 'They won't change it back in their heads that we're trash': the intersection of sex work-related stigma and evolving policing strategies. Sociol Health Illn. 2016;38(7):1137–50.
38. Odinokova V, Rusakova M, Urada LA, Silverman JG, Raj A. Police sexual coercion and its association with risky sex work and substance use behaviors among female sex workers in St. Petersburg and Orenburg, Russia. Int J Drug Policy. 2014;25(1):96–104.
39. Sanders T. A continuum of risk? The management of health, physical and emotional risks by female sex workers. Sociol Health Illn. 2004;26(5):557–74.
40. Shannon K, Rusch M, Shoveller J, Alexson D, Gibson K, Tyndall MW. Mapping violence and policing as an environmental-structural barrier to health service and syringe availability among substance-using women in street-level sex work. Int J Drug Policy. 2008;19(2):140–7.
41. Lorway R, Lazarus L, Chevrier C, Khan S, Musyoki HK, Mathenge J, et al. Ecologies of security: on the everyday security tactics of female sex workers in Nairobi, Kenya. Glob Public Health. 2018;13(12):1767–80.
42. Erausquin JT, Reed E, Blankenship KM. Police-related experiences and HIV risk among female sex workers in Andhra Pradesh, India. J Infect Dis. 2011;204(Suppl 5):S1223–8.
43. Beattie TS, Bhattacharjee P, Ramesh BM, Gurnani V, Anthony J, Isac S, et al. Violence against female sex workers in Karnataka state, south India: impact on health, and reductions in violence following an intervention program. BMC Public Health. 2010;10:476.
44. Katsulis Y. Sex work and the city: the social geography of health and safety in Tijuana, Mexico. Austin: University of Texas Press; 2008.
45. Sausa LA, Keatley J, Operario D. Perceived risks and benefits of sex work among transgender women of color in San Francisco. Arch Sex Behav. 2007;36(6):768–77.

46. Anderson S, Xi Jia J, Liu V, Chettier J, Krusi A, Allan S, et al. Violence prevention and municipal licensing of indoor sex work venues in the Greater Vancouver Area: narratives of migrant sex workers, managers and business owners. Cult Health Sex. 2015;17(7):825–41.
47. Lazarus L, Chettiar J, Deering K, Nabess R, Shannon K. Risky health environments: women sex workers' struggles to find safe, secure and non-exploitative housing in Canada's poorest postal code. Soc Sci Med (1982). 2011;73(11):1600–7.
48. Nemoto T, Bödeker B, Iwamoto M. Social support, exposure to violence and transphobia, and correlates of depression among male-to-female transgender women with a history of sex work. Am J Public Health. 2011;101(10):1980–8.
49. Van der Meulen E, Dursin E, Love V. Introduction. In: van der Meulen E, Dursin E, Love V, editors. Selling sex: experience, advocacy, and research on sex work in Canada. Vancouver, BC: UBC Press; 2013.
50. Bingham B, Leo D, Zhang R, Montaner J, Shannon K. Generational sex work and HIV risk among indigenous women in a street-based urban Canadian setting. Cult Health Sex. 2014;16(4):440–52.
51. Rocha-Jiménez T, Brouwer KC, Silverman JG, Morales-Miranda S, Goldenberg SM. Migration, violence, and safety among migrant sex workers: a qualitative study in two Guatemalan communities. Cult Health Sex. 2016;18(9):965–79.
52. Bruckert C. The mark of "disreputable" labour. In: Hannem S, Bruckert C, editor. Stigma revistited: implications of the mark. Ottawa: University of Ottawa Press; 2012.
53. Chen X-S, Liang G-J, Wang Q-Q, Yin Y-P, Jiang N, Zhou Y-J, et al. HIV prevalence varies between female sex workers from different types of venues in southern China. Sex Transm Dis. 2012;39(11):868–70.
54. Gaines TL, Rusch ML, Brouwer KC, Goldenberg SM, Lozada R, Robertson AM, et al. Venue-level correlates of female sex worker registration status: a multilevel analysis of bars in Tijuana, Mexico. Glob Public Health. 2013;8(4):405–16.
55. Jain AK, Saggurti N. The extent and nature of fluidity in typologies of female sex work in southern India: implications for HIV prevention programs. J HIV/AIDS Soc Serv. 2012;11(2):169–91.
56. Safika I, Johnson TP, Levy JA. A venue analysis of predictors of alcohol use prior to sexual intercourse among female sex workers in Senggigi, Indonesia. Int J Drug Policy. 2011;22(1):49–55.
57. Cusick L. Widening the harm reduction agenda: from drug use to sex work. Int J Drug Policy. 2006;17(1):3–11.
58. Deering KN, Boily MC, Lowndes CM, Shoveller J, Tyndall MW, Vickerman P, et al. A dose-response relationship between exposure to a large-scale HIV preventive intervention and consistent condom use with different sexual partners of female sex workers in southern India. BMC Public Health. 2011;11:S8.
59. Harcourt C, Beek I, Heslop J, McMahon M, Donovan B. The health and welfare needs of female and transgender street sex workers in New South Wales. Aust N Z J Public Health. 2001;25(1):84–9.
60. Harcourt C, Donovan B. The many faces of sex work. Sex Transm Infect. 2005;81(3):201–6.
61. Aral SO, Lawrence JSS. The ecology of sex work and drug use in Saratov Oblast, Russia. Sex Transm Dis. 2002;29(12):798–805.
62. Shannon K, Bright V, Allinott S, Alexson D, Gibson K, Tyndall MW. Community-based HIV prevention research among substance-using women in survival sex work: The Maka Project Partnership. Harm Reduct J. 2007;4(1):20.
63. Deering KN, Lyons T, Feng CX, Nosyk B, Strathdee SA, Montaner JS, et al. Client demands for unsafe sex: the socioeconomic risk environment for HIV among street and off-street sex workers. J Acquir Immune Defic Syndr. 2013;63(4):522–31.
64. Lyons T, Krusi A, Pierre L, Kerr T, Small W, Shannon K. Negotiating violence in the context of transphobia and criminalization: the experiences of trans sex workers in Vancouver, Canada. Qual Health Res. 2017;27(2):182–90.

65. Decker MR, Crago A-L, Chu SKH, Sherman SG, Seshu MS, Buthelezi K, et al. Burden and HIV impact of human rights violations against sex workers. Lancet. 2015;385(9963):186–99.
66. Cohan D, Lutnick A, Davidson P, Cloniger C, Herlyn A, Breyer J, et al. Sex worker health: San Francisco style. Sex Transm Infect. 2006;82:418–22.
67. Hotton AL, Garofalo R, Kuhns LM, Johnson AK. Substance use as a mediator of the relationship between life stress and sexual risk among young transgender women. AIDS Educ Prev. 2013;25(1):62–71.
68. Bhattacharjya M, Fulu E, Murthy L, Seshu MS, Cabassi J, Vallejo-Mestres M. The right(s) evidence – sex work, violence and HIV in Asia: a multi-country qualitative study. United Nations Population Fund (UNFPA), United Nations Development Programme (UNDP), Asia Pacific Network of Sex Workers (CASAM): Bangkok; 2015.
69. Poteat T, Wirtz AL, Radix A, Borquez A, Silva-Santisteban A, Deutsch MB, et al. HIV risk and preventive interventions in transgender women sex workers. Lancet. 2015;385(9964):274–86.
70. Wilson E, Pant SB, Comfort M, Ekstranda M. Stigma and HIV risk among Metis in Nepal. Cult Health Sex. 2011;13(3):253–66.
71. Baral S, Friedman M, Geibel S, Rebe K, Bozhinov B, Diouf D, et al. Male sex workers: practices, contexts, and vulnerabilities for HIV acquisition and transmission. Lancet. 2015;385(9964):260–73.
72. Minichiello V, Scott J, Callander D. New pleasures and old dangers: reinventing male sex work. J Sex Res. 2013;50(3–4):263–75.
73. Minichiello V, Scott J, Cox C. Commentary: Reversing the agenda of sex work stigmatization and criminalization: signs of a progressive society. Sexualities. 2017;21(5–6):730–5.
74. Crofts T. Regulation of the male sex industry. In: Minichiello V, Scott J, editors. Male sex work and society. New York: Harrington Park Press; 2014.
75. Argento E, Taylor M, Jollimore J, Taylor C, Jennex J, Krusi A, et al. The loss of Boystown and transition to online sex work: strategies and barriers to increase safety among men sex workers and clients of men. Am J Mens Health. 2018;12(6):1994–2005.
76. D'Adamo K. Interview conducted in 2017.
77. Sexuality, Poverty and Law Programme. Sex work law: countries. http://spl.ids.ac.uk/sexworklaw/countries.
78. African Regional Correspondent. Sex work in Cameroon: NSWP 2014. https://www.nswp.org/news/sex-work-cameroon.
79. Lim S, Peitzmeier S, Cange C, Papworth E, LeBreton M, Tamoufe U, et al. Violence against female sex Workers in Cameroon: accounts of violence, harm reduction, and potential solutions. J Acquir Immune Defic Syndr. 2015;68:S241–S7.
80. McBride B, Shannon K, Braschel M, Mo M, Goldenberg SM. Lack of full citizenship rights linked to heightened client condom refusal among im/migrant sex workers in Metro Vancouver (2010–2018). Glob Public Health. 2020; https://doi.org/10.1080/17441692.2019.1708961.
81. Goodyear M, Weitzer R. International trends in the control of sexual services. In: Dewey S, Kelly P, editors. Policing pleasure: sex work, policy and the state in global perspective. New York: New York University Press; 2011. p. 16–30.
82. Machat S, Shannon K, Braschel M, Moreheart S, Goldenberg SM. Sex workers' experiences and occupational conditions post-implementation of end-demand criminalization in Metro Vancouver, Canada. Can J Public Health. 2019;110(5):575–83.
83. Argento E, Muldoon KA, Duff P, Simo A, Deering KN, Shannon K. High prevalence and partner correlates of physical and sexual violence by intimate partners among street and off-street sex workers. PLoS One. 2014;9(7):e102129.
84. Hélène Le Bail CG, Rassouw N. What do sex workers think about the French Prostitution Act?: a study on the impact of the law from 13 April 2016 against the 'Prostitution System' in France. [Research Report]. Médecins du Monde; 2019. p.96.
85. Argento E, Goldenberg S, Braschel M, Moreheart S, Strathdee S, Shannon K. The impact of end-demand legislation on sex workers' utilization of HIV care, health and community-led support services in a Canadian setting. PLoS One. 2020;15(4):e0225783.

86. Protection of Communities and Exploited Persons Act; 2014.
87. Network CHAL. The perils of "protection": sex workers' experiences of law enforcement in Ontario; 2019.
88. McBride B, Shannon K, Murphy A, Mo M, Wu S, Erickson M, Goldenberg SM, Krüsi A. Harms of third party criminalisation under end-demand legislation: undermining sex workers' safety and rights. Cult Health Sex. 2020; https://doi.org/10.1080/13691058.2020.1767305.
89. Handlovsky I, Bungay V, Kolar K. Condom use as situated in a risk context: women's experiences in the massage parlour industry in Vancouver, Canada. Cult Health Sex. 2012;14(9):1007–20.
90. Bungay V, Halpin M, Atchison C, Johnston C. Structure and agency: reflections from an exploratory study of Vancouver indoor sex workers. Cult Health Sex. 2011;13(1):15–29.
91. Vanwesenbeeck I. Sex work criminalization is barking up the wrong tree. Arch Sex Behav. 2017;46(6):1631–40.
92. Heumann S, Coumans SV, Shiboleth T, Ridder-Wiskerke M. The Netherlands: analysing shifts and continuities in the governing of sexual labour. In: Ward E, Wylie G, editors. Feminism, prostitution and the state: the politics of neo-abolitionism, Routledge studies in gender and global politics. 1st ed. New York: Routledge; 2017.
93. Rocha-Jimenez T, Morales-Miranda S, Fernandez-Casanueva C, Brouwer K, Goldenberg SM. Stigma and unmet sexual and reproductive health needs among international migrant sex workers at the Mexico-Guatemala border. Int J Gynaecol Obstet. 2018;143(1):37–43.
94. Rocha-Jiménez T, Brouwer K, Silverman J, Morales-Miranda S, Goldenberg SM. Exploring the context and implementation of public health regulations governing sex work: a qualitative study with migrant sex workers in Guatemala. J Immigr Minor Health. 2016;19:1235–44.
95. Goldenberg S, Brouwer K, Rocha Jimenez T, Morales Miranda S, Rivera Mindt M. Enhancing the ethical conduct of HIV research with migrant sex workers: human rights, policy, and social contextual influences. PLoS One. 2016;11(5):e0155048.
96. Weitzer R. Researching prostitution and sex trafficking comparatively. Sex Res Soc Policy. 2015;12(2):81–91.
97. Outshoorn J. Policy change in prostitution in the Netherlands: from legalization to strict control. Sex Res Soc Policy. 2012;9(3):233–43.
98. Ito S, Lepine A, Treibich C. The effect of sex work regulation on health and well-being of sex workers: evidence from Senegal. Health Econ. 2018;27(11):1627–52.
99. Jeffreys E, Fawkes J, Stardust Z. Mandatory testing for HIV and sexually transmissible infections among sex workers in Australia: a barrier to HIV and STI prevention. World J AIDS. 2012;2:203–11.
100. Decker M, Crago A-L, Chu SH, Sherman S, Seshu M, Buthelezi K, et al. Human rights violations against sex workers: burden and effect on HIV. Lancet. 2015;385(9963):186–99.
101. D'Adamo K. Interview conducted in 2017.
102. Shannon K, Strathdee SA, Goldenberg SM, Duff P, Mwangi P, Rusakova M, et al. Global epidemiology of HIV among female sex workers: influence of structural determinants. Lancet. 2015;385(9962):55–71.
103. Armstrong L. From law enforcement to protection? Interactions between sex workers and police in a decriminalized street-based sex industry: table 1. Br J Criminol. 2016;57:azw019.
104. NSWP. Briefing Paper: Migrant sex workers. 2017. https://www.nswp.org/resource/briefing-paper-migrant-sex-workers.
105. Harcourt C, O'Connor J, Egger S, Fairley CK, Wand H, Chen MY, et al. The decriminalization of prostitution is associated with better coverage of health promotion programs for sex workers. Aust N Z J Public Health. 2010;34(5):482–6.
106. Howard S. Better health for sex workers: which legal model causes least harm? BMJ. 2018;361:k2609. https://doi.org/10.1136/bmj.k2609.

107. Deering KN, Amin A, Shoveller J, Nesbitt A, Garcia-Moreno C, Duff P, et al. A systematic review of the correlates of violence against sex workers. Am J Public Health. 2014;104(5):e42–54.

108. Socias ME, Deering K, Horton M, Nguyen P, Montaner JS, Shannon K. Social and structural factors shaping high rates of incarceration among sex workers in a Canadian Setting. J Urban Health. 2015;92(5):966–79.

109. Dewey S, Kelly P. Introduction: sex work and the politics of public policy. In: Dewey S, Kelly P, editors. Policing pleasure sex work, policy and the state in global perspective. New York: New York University Press; 2011. p. 1–16.

Chapter 8
Stigma, Denial of Health Services, and Other Human Rights Violations Faced by Sex Workers in Africa: "My Eyes Were Full of Tears Throughout Walking Towards the Clinic that I Was Referred to"

Marlise Richter and Kholi Buthelezi

I felt so humiliated. I felt that I hated myself. I was crying. My eyes were full of tears throughout walking towards the [public health] clinic that I was referred to. Because of the way that the nurse [at the general hospital] shouted at me. I didn't know what I did wrong by coming to the clinic for a consultation [...]

So, in that way if sex workers continued to be treated in this way; it drives them away [from healthcare facilities]. It drives them away—Penelope Zulu[1] (female sex worker, aged 45, inner-city Johannesburg, South Africa)

Introduction

In 1993, one of South Africa's academic health journals, the *South African Medical Journal*, published an article entitled "Prevention of sexually transmitted disease. The Shurugwi sex-workers project" [1]. While this article describes an intervention that is more than 30 years old and which was limited to a small rural town in sub-Saharan Africa, it unfortunately reflects contemporary features of the health sector's general approach to sex workers and to sex work in many areas of the world. This

---

[1] Pseudonym.

M. Richter (✉)
Health Justice Initiative, Cape Town, South Africa

African Centre for Migration & Society, University of the Witwatersrand, Johannesburg, South Africa

School of Public Health & Family Medicine, University of Cape Town, Cape Town, South Africa
e-mail: marlise.richter@gmail.com

K. Buthelezi
Sisonke National Sex Worker Movement, Cape Town, South Africa

© The Author(s) 2021
S. M. Goldenberg et al. (eds.), *Sex Work, Health, and Human Rights*,
https://doi.org/10.1007/978-3-030-64171-9_8

work described a 1988 health intervention that took place in a small mining town in the Midlands province of Zimbabwe, in which sex workers were framed as "a reservoir and transmission of sexually transmitted disease (STDs)"in Zimbabwe. The project—called the Shurugwi experiment—included the formation of an STD Committee consisting of health workers that "resolved at its first meeting that all sex-workers in the town should convene a general meeting. The sex-workers were then given a lecture on STDs and their possible complications, especially for women" and were subsequently warned about "becoming reservoirs and spreaders of STDs". Sex workers were requested to form their own committee that would work with the STD committee. The author noted:

> At the general meeting, it was also resolved that a card system for sex-workers would be introduced. To qualify for the card, a sex-worker had to undergo a physical examination by the medical officers in the committee. Those who required psychiatric counselling, e.g. for AIDS pre-testing, were referred to the nurse responsible. No sex-worker could enter a beer garden, where most clients are available, without the health card. Since all beerhalls are manned by security guards, these were informed of the committee's resolution [...] The card holders were examined on a monthly basis. A special government stamp was put on the cards of those free from disease. Those found to have a disease had their cards withdrawn until such time they were free from disease [...]. The researcher gave lectures on STDs and their complications in all beerhalls... ([1], p. 40)

Unfortunately, the intervention described in, and the content and tone of, the above publication [1] did not recognise sex workers or sex workers' health as having intrinsic value—and in many ways this context has hardly changed. Moreover, the fraught setting of sex work and the oppressive context in which the above HIV/STI prevention project took place in 1988 in Zimbabwe still persist today. While it would seem to be understood that if sex workers were diagnosed with an infection, they would be referred for treatment, no details or reference to treatment was described as part of the intervention. Rather, the approach appeared to be strongly underpinned by themes of blame, the need for compulsory policing, reprisal, and "lectures", as well as moral superiority. Similarly, the intervention had been imposed in a top-down manner, contained very little incentives, and did not respect sex worker agency or autonomy. While the author concluded the article by calling for law reform (in this case in the form of legalisation) and recommended that sex workers be consulted in the planning of prevention programmes, no evidence was provided that sex workers had, in fact, any input on either the programme or the resolutions taken on how to manage their health, work, or well-being.

In this chapter, we aim to describe contemporary sex worker experiences with health services and the health system in Africa as documented in the literature and supported by sex workers' lived experiences. We will highlight how stigma, discrimination, and sexual moralism impact on health workers' engagement with sex workers and their families, and how this inhibits sex workers from keeping themselves safe and healthy. We will conclude with an encouraging example from South Africa where the Department of Health, in partnership with civil society, has taken leadership in rolling-out specialised services for sex workers to proactively address healthcare worker prejudices, and to provide health care for sex workers that is respectful and participatory.

Sex Work and Health in Africa

Much of the research on sex work in Africa describes the perilous position of sex workers, and usually relates it to poor health outcomes and, in particular, to HIV transmission. The dangers that African sex workers face are by no means unique, and criminalisation and an oppressive legal system, high levels of violence, repressive law-enforcement, dangerous clients, and a prejudiced public constitute challenges that sex workers face on all continents. Yet, in many African countries these challenges are particularly severe due to a number of interlocking factors including the following: sex work is strongly stigmatised from religious, cultural, and gender perspectives; extreme levels of poverty combined with the lack of adequate social safety nets push many women into the informal sector, which includes exchanging sex for resources; healthcare and social services are under resourced; there is little legal recourse for human rights violations; and sex worker collectivisation did not begin to gain much momentum until 2009, with the formation of the African Sex Worker Association (ASWA) [2]. In fact, the criminalisation of adult consensual sex is a popular strategy adopted by many of the 55 states on the African continent. The vast majority of countries in Africa criminalise some aspects of sex work [3, 4]. Same-sex practices are criminalized in 33 countries, with the death penalty still applicable in Mauritania, Sudan, Northern Nigeria, and Southern Somalia [5], and between 27 and 30 countries in Sub-Saharan Africa criminalise aspects of HIV [6, 7]. The far-reaching, negative consequences of using the blunt tool of the criminal law to regulate adult consensual sexual behaviour has been well-documented—particularly so within the literature on HIV [8]. The health system and healthcare workers are often first responders, required to meet the recurring support and care needs of individuals who are directly affected by these criminal laws and their concomitant stigmatisation and violence; thus they are in an important position to document these issues [9] and be vocal patient advocates.

A recent systematic review of healthcare services for female sex workers in Africa found that these were limited in coverage, included only a narrow scope of services, and were poorly coordinated [10]. Health programmes associated with sex work were specialised and mostly focused on HIV and STIs rather than providing comprehensive health services, including sexual and reproductive health. In fact, contraception was only available in 7 sites out of the 54 found in the systematic review. Only 6 of them offered urine pregnancy tests and not one of the sites offered termination of pregnancy services (a number of African countries criminalise termination of pregnancies) [11]. The funding of all the sites was provided by international donors, not by governments, and the focus was research-driven rather than the implementation of much-needed, large-scale service-delivery programmes.

Disappointingly, the review also noted that there were few structural interventions targeting the sex work context. The structural interventions documented included gender-based violence services in only two countries (Zambia and South Africa); one project that provided legal literacy (South Africa); and one facility teaching violence prevention techniques such as the development of personal plans to reduce risk (South Africa). For example, in Zambia, local clinics would arrange referrals for legal assistance as part of gender-based violence interventions. Limited programmes in Malawi and Kenya included micro-enterprise to support additional income generation for sex workers.

The findings of the systemic review are deeply distressing, against a backdrop in which more than a third of female sex workers in Sub-Saharan Africa (37%) are living with HIV [10]. This is three times the global HIV prevalence among female sex workers [10]. Unaddressed HIV risk has led to large-scale illness and death, as well as increased stigmatisation and human rights violations among the various sex work communities in Africa. One modelling study suggested that, of the 106,000 deaths from HIV in 2011 linked to female sex work globally, 98,000 occurred in Sub-Saharan Africa [12]. Clear, rigorous scientific evidence [13–16] and a long history of calls by sex workers and allies support expansion of interventions to support the health, well-being, and rights of sex workers and to mitigate HIV [17–19]. Among these are the removal of criminal laws surrounding sex work, scaling up of treatment, prevention and care programmes, and violence prevention and stigma reduction programmes. Yet these are not being implemented, or at best, are not implemented to scale. It is also very troubling that, despite far-reaching inroads into the AIDS epidemic globally [20], HIV rates among female sex workers at a global level remain "largely unchanged" today [15]. Finally, HIV data on transgender and male sex work as well as on sex work clients—groups which have traditionally been overlooked—remain scant but are increasingly being collected [15]. It is vital that this research is expanded to inform programmes and services that serve these groups and to address their particular needs and concerns.

How Do Sex Workers Experience Existing Healthcare Services?

Moving from country-level to individual-level, we now turn to exploring how sex workers in Africa experience the healthcare services available to them. A range of problems have been documented, and the paternalism and stigma described in the opening paragraph of this chapter unfortunately still characterise how some healthcare services approach sex workers and the sex work context.

The issues of discrimination and prejudice remain key themes in sex workers' interactions with health care, and healthcare settings are, alarmingly, still a significant site of human rights violations [21]. Research with male, female, and transgender sex workers in Uganda, South Africa, Kenya, and Zimbabwe, for example, has documented a range of problems experienced by sex workers within healthcare settings: poor treatment, stigmatisation, and discrimination by healthcare workers; having to pay bribes to obtain services or treatment; being humiliated by healthcare workers; and, the breaching of confidentiality [22, 23].

Conservative beliefs held by healthcare workers combined with the deeply unequal power differentials between healthcare workers and sex workers often result in the latter being particularly poorly treated. Some sex workers report avoiding healthcare services as much as possible rather than to be subjected to prejudice and disrespect. It should be noted that healthcare worker approaches to sex work are shaped by broader societal, cultural, and religious beliefs bolstered by the criminalisation of sex work. Structural reform including the decriminalisation of sex work and addressing the stigma that attaches to sex work is a vital component of the social change necessary to support sex worker health and well-being, which will, in turn, shape positive and empathetic healthcare worker approaches.

Let us look at specific examples:

At the first African Sex Worker conference in 2009, delegates from different countries spoke about sex workers' experiences with health services. The country representative from Malawi noted a colleague's experience with seeking ARV treatment in a hospital in Zomba, who had received the following response from a nurse:

> Why do you bother us? It's better for people like you to die. Why should the government waste money treating people like you rather than giving the medication to important people? ([2], p. 12)

The notion that sex workers are undeserving of services or treatment, and the experience of healthcare workers bluntly articulating offensive views that sex workers should rather be dead than treated, are also described in Scorgie's study, where a sex worker in Uganda related:

> We are despised in the hospitals. They [healthcare providers] say, "We don't have time for prostitutes" and they also say that if one prostitute dies then the number reduces. (Belinda, 27-year-old female, Kampala) ([23], p. 6.)

Delegates at the African Sex Worker conference from Botswana and Zimbabwe also noted the intense hostility and discrimination on the part of healthcare workers. Examples cited from Botswana included breaches of privacy and medical ethics, such as conducting HIV testing without consent. Scorgie and colleagues documented forced HIV testing or HIV testing without the patient's knowledge in two clinical sites in South Africa and one in Uganda. In contrast, some participants in the same study noted that they were denied HIV testing when they had requested it.

Binagwaho related the experience of a female sex worker in Rwanda who noted that she was refused treatment reputedly because of personal vindictiveness or jealousy on the part of healthcare workers:

> I live in the center of town, where most health workers live, and I run into them all the time. [At the clinic,] if they know you haven't given up prostitution, they can refuse to serve you, because they suspect you've been with their husbands. They keep grabbing other people's files and passing you over, because you're a prostitute. ([24], p. 92)

Sex workers have noted how healthcare workers have interrogated them unnecessarily about sexual practices, while male and transgender sex workers, in particular, have been held up as curiosities by staff. Boyce's study with male sex workers noted how participants have been publicly humiliated:

> Nurses often call each other when they find out about being a male sex worker saying: "we have never had such a case" or "come look at what his type of STD, we have never had it at this hospital before" ([25], p. 20)

Following a gang rape by clients, a transgender participant in the Scorgie study painfully described the secondary victimisation by healthcare workers in the following way:

> I go to report to the police, they told me to go to the hospital and I was still wearing my jeans, wig and with my breasts. When the doctor examined me and find out that I am a she-male, he called other doctors and nurses. They left their work to come and see that a man got raped. It was like a mockery.... The doctor told me I was not raped but I was sodomised because I am a man. The way I was dressing they said "what kind of a woman [are you]?" I just walked [away] from the hospital without being treated. It was not fair because I was raped the whole night. ([23], p. 6)

Transphobia, homophobia, and xenophobia often overlap and strengthen prejudices toward sex work, and some of these dynamics are described by Boyce and Isaacs as "intercommunity hostility" ([26], p. 300). Xenophobia, racism, migration status, homelessness, gender identity, sexual orientation, and drug-use are all factors that can compound discrimination in the healthcare setting, and leave populations that are often most in need of social, legal, and wellness support without services, thus ultimately compounding their marginalisation.

Sex workers often report that they would rather avoid health care than expose themselves to additional stigmatisation or rights violations. Alternatively, they may choose not to inform healthcare workers that they are sex workers, which Scorgie points out could lead to sub-optimal medical treatment. In a study by Fobosi and colleagues on truck-stop clinics in South Africa, sex workers articulated this reticence as being "shy" about seeking treatment at public hospitals [27]. Sex workers who register their "shyness" seem to distort the problem of healthcare avoidance as an individual failing or a personal lack of assertiveness, rather than placing the focus on broader systemic issues within health and society.

Some healthcare workers' attitudes toward sex work are informed by conservative and religious perceptions of sex work—views that often label sex worker livelihoods as immoral. Baleta relates an experience of a female sex worker in Lesotho who was refused treatment for a badly infected wound on her leg in the following way:

> She had her leg bandaged at the hospital but the health-care providers accompanying her informed staff that she was a sex worker, which was recorded on her health card. The doctor's response was, 'Well you are a sex worker, you are going to die in the next 3 months. There is nothing more we can do for you, and I have a waiting room full of people who are not morally corrupt like you' and sent her home. ([28], p. e1)

These distressing attitudes manifest not only in the provision of medical treatment to sex workers, but also limit the reach and effectiveness of other services and supports, including psycho-social support, disease prevention, and health promotion. In some healthcare settings where male condoms are provided free-of-charge, sex workers reported only being allowed to take a few condoms each, or alternatively, being expected by unscrupulous healthcare workers to trade sex or money for the allegedly free condoms [23, 29]. Some healthcare workers erroneously believe that by providing condoms to sex workers, they are "promoting" sex work—an assumption in line with early opposition to making free condoms available to youth because, rather than reducing their HIV risk, it would simply increase their sexual activity. Research has thoroughly debunked this argument [30, 31].

Conservative attitudes about sexual and relationship constellations also manifest in healthcare worker insistence that female sex workers bring their husbands or sexual partners along to the clinic. Otherwise they will not provide treatment to sex workers. Scorgie quotes a 25-year-old female sex worker from Kampala who said:

> When you go to the hospital the health workers say, "We will not treat you unless you come with your husband". We don't have husbands, so we go to drug shops and buy some drugs to relieve us from the pain. ([23], p. 6)

While research on sex workers' healthcare-seeking behaviour beyond the public health sector is limited, some studies mention sex worker self-treatment: purchasing over-the-counter remedies from pharmacies, seeking services in the very expensive private sector and/or consulting with traditional healers [10, 23, 25]. Anecdotal evidence suggests that some sex workers experience traditional healers as less judgemental than healthcare workers. A respondent in the Scorgie study noted that:

> It's tough, especially when you suffer from an STI, they treat you like you just got what you deserve, and we end up using some traditional herbs because the traditional healers don't ask too many questions. (Thuli, 35-year-old female, Bulawayo) ([23], p. 10)

An under-explored issue is how sex workers' negative experiences in the healthcare settings may impact on their family members' access of these services. Sex worker avoidance strategies may include a reluctance to bring their children or adult dependents to health facilities, leading to poor health outcomes, not just at the individual level but at the family level, too. Scorgie notes that:

> Discriminatory treatment was applied even at times to family members of sex workers who accompanied them to health facilities. One participant recounted being pushed to the end of the queue when bringing her child for treatment and was attended to only after all other patients had been seen ([23], p. 10).

Significantly, while many sex workers support dependents, including children, the systematic review by Dhana and colleagues found only one general clinic in Uganda that specifically offered health care for the children of female sex workers [10].

In addition to documented concerns regarding negative treatment by healthcare workers, the prejudices of non-clinical staff employed in health systems, such as receptionists, security guards, cleaners, porters, and administrators, also contribute to sex worker mistrust, fear, and avoidance of healthcare facilities. This, however, is often overlooked as a barrier to services. A 2018 study in South Africa on access to health care for Key Populations noted the following:

> [...] it was widely reported that health facility staff express stigmatising attitudes towards key populations. Although these were said to occur from all cadres of staff, a majority of assessment participants singled out non-clinical staff, especially security guards, but also clerks and cleaners, as the most problematic; one reason being that they are rarely, if ever, involved in training and sensitisation activities provided for their clinical colleagues. Research findings bolster these observations, particularly for MSM [Men who have sex

with Men] and for foreign migrants (Rispel et al., 2011; Vearey, 2014). As a further example, peer educators working with PWID [people who inject drugs] described how their clients are frequently barred from facilities by security guards, either because of their appearance or because it has become known that they are a PWID. ([32], p. 23)

In view of the fact that non-clinical staff often serve as gate-keepers to health care, it is vital that they are routinely included in sensitivity training.

The Power of Positive Experiences

Studies documenting sex worker experiences within healthcare services also describe positive and encouraging engagements with health care although these tend to be the minority of experiences. Respondents in the Scorgie study spoke about some healthcare workers as being "friendly and respectful", having a "good attitude" and as affirming sex workers' dignity [23]. This has been well documented, for example, in sex work-specific clinics where staff have received sensitisation training, such as in inner-city Johannesburg [33–35]. The Fobosi study on roadside wellness clinics recorded sex worker respondents' satisfaction with "friendly staff", how some clinics were open at night time and even included services that users didn't expect, like malaria screening [27]. The opening quote of this chapter includes a description of Penelope Zulu's painful experience with harsh healthcare staff when she went to a health facility for a general check-up. However, her narrative changes when she is referred to a sex work-specific clinic, where an empathetic and kind nurse provided the clinical care and emotional support that she needed. Zulu describes the nurse as "being like a mother"; under her support and mentorship, Zulu decided to become a peer educator and ultimately became an outspoken leader in the sex worker movement in South Africa.

South Africa has seen some unique developments on HIV and sex work. In 2016, South Africa became one of the first countries in the world to pass a sex work-specific HIV plan [36]. This was due to factors including a staggeringly high HIV prevalence associated with the sex work context, the health system's commitment to a rights-based approach to HIV/AIDS, the positive experiences of sex workers at the few sex work-specific clinics available, and the uncompromising activist approach by sex worker advocates and allies [36–38]. The "South African National Sex Worker HIV Plan, 2016–2019" is comprehensive in its strategy. It adopts a combination prevention approach that includes peer-education-led strategies and makes specific provision for Pre-Exposure Prophylaxis (PrEP) and Universal Test-And-Treat while also endeavouring to deal with social and structural drivers of HIV in the lives of sex workers [21]. It supports the decriminalisation of sex work, while committing itself to "competency and sensitisation training to health and social workers. Training should also be expanded to law enforcement officials, other service providers, and the community". ([39], p. 29). More recently, South Africa's "National Strategic Plan on Gender-based violence & Femicide" included a commitment by government to finalise the "legislative process to decriminalise sex work" by March 2024 [40]. These policies emphasize the key linkages between health and violence, and the structural reforms necessary to safeguard sex worker dignity and rights.

At the time of writing, the HIV Plan was being reviewed and its implementation assessed. While it is impossible to address deep-seated prejudices and other structural barriers to health care with quick fixes, the Plan and its comprehensive approach is an influential first step in the right direction. Indeed, in a recent submission to the United Nation's Committee on Economic, Social and Cultural Rights on South Africa, Human Rights Watch noted the following:

> On a positive note, the sex workers we interviewed told us they had free, fairly straightforward, and non-discriminatory access to health care, including reproductive health care and HIV/AIDS treatment. Many remarked on their experiences of improved, friendlier services over the past six years. A driving force behind these improvements has been the South African Department of Health and the South African National AIDS Council (SANAC, which coordinates several government bodies) openly calling for services for sex workers and for decriminalization. A whole-of-government approach towards sex work that recognizes the rights and needs of this vulnerable group would make more sense and help end police practices that obstruct SANAC's goals of ending the pandemic, for example detaining sex workers without access to antiretroviral drugs. [41]

Conclusion

In Africa, sex workers' negative experiences with health services act as a powerful barrier to their accessing quality health care—by inhibiting effective treatment, prevention, and support for HIV and other health-related needs of sex workers, including their sexual and reproductive health, preventative care, and mental health [24, 42]. This chapter explored examples of how prejudices harboured by healthcare worker and non-clinical staff have a far-reaching negative impact on sex workers' well-being and access to care. In contrast, positive interactions with healthcare providers and health services empower sex workers, affirm sex worker dignity and agency, and assist in cultivating healthy behaviour and improved health outcomes [33, 35, 43].

It is unfortunate that the clear evidence for the need to decriminalise sex work has not transformed the sorely outdated legal and policy landscape associated with the criminalisation of sex work, a landscape characteristic of most countries in Africa.

The political will, the necessary funding, and the urgency required to implement an effective response to sex work in Africa—and to do so at scale—are mostly absent. This remains the case, despite a large body of evidence and improved programmatic responses that support sex workers. Of particular concern, health programmes that focus narrowly on biomedical or behavioural HIV/STI prevention or treatment in relation to sex work remain myopic, as they focus only on sex workers' sexual engagements, and do not address their broader health and social needs, their full humanity and personhood.

This can be overcome with comprehensive, rights-affirming health programmes designed in partnership with sex workers, combined with structural interventions that transform outdated legal frameworks and implement violence prevention strategies, psycho-social support services, and sex worker empowerment initiatives; and which galvanise peer-lead programmes that focus on strategic and practical sex worker needs in an African context. We are encouraged by the strides made towards these on a policy level in South Africa, with the passing of an official Sex Worker Plan. The crucial test, however, is how, and at what scale, the Plan has been implemented.

It is our hope that the voices of sex workers and sex worker rights advocates in Africa become stronger and are amplified on key platforms. When sex workers are supported to engage with policy makers, law enforcement agencies and health service providers in the African context, the urgent changes needed to affirm sex worker health and dignity and to make sex work safer will be prioritised.

References

1. Chipfakacha V. Prevention of sexually transmitted diseases the Shurugwi sex-workers project. S Afr Med J. 1993;83(1):40–1.
2. Naidoo N. Report on the 1st African Sex Worker Conference: Building Solidarity and Strengthening Alliances, 3–5 Feb 2009, Johannesburg, South Africa.
3. Mgbako C, Smith LA. Sex work and human rights in Africa. Fordham Int Law J. 2011;33(4):1178–219.
4. NSWP. Global mapping of sex work laws 2018 [updated 31 December 2018; cited 2019 22 October]. Available from: https://www.nswp.org/sex-work-laws-map.
5. Amnesty International. Mapping anti-gay laws in Africa 2018 [31 May 2018]. Available from: https://www.amnesty.org.uk/lgbti-lgbt-gay-human-rights-law-africa-uganda-kenya-nigeria-cameroon.
6. Patrick M. HIV-specific legislation in sub-Saharan Africa: a comprehensive human rights analysis. Afr Hum Rights Law J. 2015;15(2):1996–2096.
7. Odendal L. HIV criminalisation on the rise, especially in sub-Saharan Africa 2016 [19 July 2016]. Available from: http://www.aidsmap.com/HIV-criminalisation-on-the-rise-especially-in-sub-Saharan-Africa/page/3072484/.
8. Secretariat: The Global Commission on HIV and the Law. The Global Commission on HIV and the Law - risks, rights and health. Geneva: UNDP, HIV/AIDS Group, Bureau for Development Policy; 2012.
9. Overs C, Hawkins K. Can rights stop the wrongs? Exploring the connections between framings of sex workers' rights and sexual and reproductive health. BMC Int Health Hum Rights. 2011;11(Suppl 3):S6.
10. Dhana A, Luchters S, Moore L, Lafort Y, Roy A, Scorgie F, et al. Systematic review of facility-based sexual and reproductive health services for female sex workers in Africa. Glob Health. 2014;10:46.
11. Berer M. Abortion law and policy around the world: in search of decriminalization. Health Hum Rights. 2017;19(1):13–27.
12. Pruss-Ustun A, Wolf J, Driscoll T, Degenhardt L, Neira M, Calleja JM. HIV due to female sex work: regional and global estimates. PLoS One. 2013;8(5):e63476.

13. Platt L, Grenfell P, Meiksin R, Elmes J, Sherman SG, Sanders T, et al. Associations between sex work laws and sex workers' health: a systematic review and meta-analysis of quantitative and qualitative studies. PLoS Med. 2018;15(12):e1002680.
14. Harcourt C, O'Connor J, Egger S, Fairley C, Wand H, Chen M, et al. The decriminalisation of prostitution is associated with better coverage of health promotion programs for sex workers. Aust N Z J Public Health. 2010;34:482–6.
15. Shannon K, Crago AL, Baral SD, Bekker LG, Kerrigan D, Decker MR, et al. The global response and unmet actions for HIV and sex workers. Lancet. 2018;392(10148):698–710.
16. Shannon K, Strathdee SA, Goldenberg SM, Duff P, Mwangi P, Rusakova M, et al. Global epidemiology of HIV among female sex workers: influence of structural determinants. Lancet. 2015;385(9962):55–71.
17. Aroney E, Crofts P. How sex worker activism influenced the decriminalisation of sex work in NSW, Australia. Int J Crime Justice Soc Democr. 2019;8:50–67.
18. Smith M, Mac J. Revolting prostitutes: the fight for sex workers' rights. London: Verso; 2018.
19. Mgbako CA. To live freely in this world: sex worker activism in Africa. New York: NYU Press; 2016.
20. UNAIDS. Communities at the Centre - Global AIDS Update 2019. Geneva: UNAIDS; 2019.
21. Scheibe A, Richter M, Vearey J. Sex work and South Africa's health system: addressing the needs of the underserved. In: Padarath AKJ, Mackie E, Casciola J, editors. South African health review, vol. 19. Durban: Health Systems Trust; 2016. p. 165–78.
22. Boyce P, Isaacs G. An exploratory study of the social contexts, practices and risks of men who sell sex in southern and eastern Africa. Nairobi, Kenya: African Sex Worker Alliance; 2011.
23. Scorgie F, Nakato D, Harper E, Richter M, Maseko S, Nare P, et al. "We are despised in the hospitals": sex workers' experiences of accessing health care in four African countries. Cult Health Sex. 2013;15(4):450–65.
24. Binagwaho A, Agbonyitor M, Mwananawe A, Mugwaneza P, Irwin A, Karema C. Developing human rights-based strategies to improve health among female sex workers in Rwanda. Health Hum Rights. 2010;12(2):89–100.
25. Boyce P, Isaacs G. An exploratory study of the social contexts, practices and risks of men who sell sex in southern and eastern Africa. Oxford: Oxfam GB; 2011.
26. Boyce P, Isaacs G. Male sex work in southern and eastern Africa. In: Minichiello V, Scott J, editors. Male sex work and society. New York: Harrington Park Press, LLC; 2014.
27. Fobosi SC, Lalla-Edward ST, Ncube S, Buthelezi F, Matthew P, Kadyakapita A, et al. Access to and utilisation of healthcare services by sex workers at truck-stop clinics in South Africa: a case study. S Afr Med J. 2017;107(11):994–9.
28. Baleta A. Lives on the line: sex work in sub-Saharan Africa. Lancet. 2015;385(9962):e1–2.
29. Makhakhe NF, Lane T, McIntyre J, Struthers H. Sexual transactions between long distance truck drivers and female sex workers in South Africa. Glob Health Action. 2017;10(1):1346164.
30. Sellers DE, McGraw SA, McKinlay JB. Does the promotion and distribution of condoms increase teen sexual activity? Evidence from an HIV prevention program for Latino youth. Am J Public Health. 1994;84(12):1952–9.
31. Wang T, Lurie M, Govindasamy D, Mathews C. The effects of school-based Condom Availability Programs (CAPs) on condom acquisition, use and sexual behavior: a systematic review. AIDS Behav. 2018;22(1):308–20.
32. Global Fund. Baseline assessment – South Africa scaling up programs to reduce human rights related barriers to HIV and TB services, Geneva, Switzerland; 2018.
33. Nairne D. 'Please help me cleanse my womb': A hotel-based STD programme in a violent neighbourhood in Johannesburg. Res Sex Work. 1999;2:18–20.
34. Richter M. Sex work, reform initiatives and HIV/AIDS in inner-city Johannesburg. Afr J AIDS Res. 2008;7(3):323–33.
35. Stadler J, Delany S. The 'healthy brothel': the context of clinical services for sex workers in Hillbrow, South Africa. Cult Health Sex. 2006;8(5):451–64.

36. Evidence for HIV Prevention in Southern Africa (EHPSA). Just bad laws - the journey to the launch of South Africa's National Sex Worker HIV Plan; 2018.
37. Richter M, Chakuvinga P. Being pimped out - how South Africa's AIDS response fails sex workers. Agenda. 2012;26(2):65–79.
38. Richter M, Khosa T, Rasebitse K. Sex work and the 'National Strategic Plan on HIV, STIs and TB 2017–2022' – time to be brave! Spotlight [Internet]. 2017;. Available from: https://www.spotlightnsp.co.za/2017/03/14/sex-work-new-nsp/.
39. South African National AIDS Council. The South African National Sex Worker HIV Plan, 2016–2019. Pretoria; 2016.
40. South African Government Department of Women, Youth and Persons with Disabilities. National strategic plan on gender-based violence & femicide: human dignity and healing, safety, freedom & equality in our lifetime. Republic of South Africa; 2020. https://www.justice.gov.za/vg/gbv/NSP-GBVF-FINAL-DOC-04-05.pdf. Accessed 5 Oct 2020.
41. Human Rights Watch. Submission by Human Rights Watch to the Committee on Economic, Social and Cultural Rights on South Africa 2018 [30 August 2018]. Available from: https://www.hrw.org/news/2018/08/30/submission-human-rights-watch-committee-economic-social-and-cultural-rights-south.
42. Pauw I, Brener L. 'You are just whores: you can't be raped': barriers to safer sex practices among women street sex workers in Cape Town. Cult Health Sex. 2003;5:465–81.
43. Khonde N, Kols A. Integrating services within existing Ministry of Health institutions - the experience of Ghana. J Sex Work Res. 1999;2:16–8.

Chapter 9
Criminalisation, Health, and Labour Rights Among Im/migrant Sex Workers Globally

Bronwyn McBride and Trachje Janushev

Background

Globally, workers often migrate seeking improved working conditions, yet frequently face precarious labour and insecure employment in destination settings [1–3]: evidence from Global Northern and Southern contexts has documented unsafe working conditions, low access to labour protections, barriers to health access, and poor health outcomes among immigrant and migrant (im/migrant[1]) workers [4–7]. Im/migrants frequently face economic marginalisation, discrimination and racism, precarious immigration status, non-recognition of foreign credentials and training, and exclusion from formal employment opportunities [5, 7, 8], all of which contribute to their over-representation in precarious, insecure, and informal forms of labour, including sex work [2, 9–11].

Precarious labour is a multidimensional construct encompassing dimensions such as employment insecurity, low wages and economic deprivation, limited social protection and workplace rights, and powerlessness to exercise workplace rights

---

[1] Because the term 'migrant sex worker' is often understood only to mean sex workers who do not hold citizenship or permanent residency (i.e. undocumented sex workers or those on temporary visas), we use the term 'im/migrant sex worker' to reference all persons (regardless of legal or immigration status) who have travelled outside of their country of origin and now do sex work in destination settings.

B. McBride (✉)
Centre for Gender and Sexual Health Equity, Vancouver, BC, Canada

Interdisciplinary Studies Graduate Program, University of British Columbia, Vancouver, BC, Canada
e-mail: bronwyn.mcbride@cgshe.ubc.ca

T. Janushev
The Red Edition – Sex Work Migrant Group, Vienna, Austria
e-mail: t.janusev@yahoo.com

S. M. Goldenberg et al. (eds.), *Sex Work, Health, and Human Rights*,
https://doi.org/10.1007/978-3-030-64171-9_9

[12]. Im/migrant workers globally are vulnerable to facing precarious labour and precarious jobs (i.e. domestic work, farm labour, sex work, temporary work) due to their lack of citizenship rights in destination countries [5, 8, 13–15].

The labour issues faced by marginalised im/migrants, such as poor working conditions, exploitation, and inadequate access to protections, are exacerbated among im/migrant sex workers due to criminalisation and stigma. The exclusion of both im/migrants and sex workers from access to recourse for labour rights violations enjoyed by citizens and workers in other sectors contributes to the conditions of sex work being highly precarious among this group [16, 17]. Thus, im/migrant sex workers frequently face significant precarity based on im/migrant status, sex work involvement, and criminalisation, with resulting negative implications for their occupational conditions [16, 18].

Historically, anti-trafficking research and discourse have conflated sex trafficking (forced sexual labour) with sex work (consensual exchange of sex services) among im/migrant groups. This contributes to the predominant misconception that racialised im/migrants (and particularly women) are inevitably involved in sex work as victims who are coerced into sexual labour [19–22]. Broader research, however, reveals that im/migrant sex workers are gender-diverse, including women, men, trans, and non-binary sex workers; highly heterogeneous, and exercise agency and autonomy in their work, which is largely overlooked [23–25]. Evidence has shown that many im/migrant sex workers travel to destination countries through legal channels, without prior sex work experience, and without experiencing coercion, but engage in sex work as a way of meeting their financial and other goals in the context of facing overlapping forms of structural exclusion [9, 22, 26, 27]. In particular, community-based research suggests that sex work provides key flexibility and income for im/migrant women facing marginalisation and barriers to accessing formal employment opportunities [9, 26].

In contrast to common representations of im/migrant sex workers as passive victims, current research and community reports highlight im/migrant sex workers as diverse, resilient, active, and goal-oriented workers [22, 26, 28]. However, im/migrant sex workers can be more vulnerable to labour abuses due to the limited labour protections accessible to them, shaping their health risks, access to services, and health outcomes. To date, the majority of research involving im/migrant sex workers has focused around HIV/STI risk, with a significant dearth of evidence on their work environments and access to health and other services. To further elucidate the documented structural barriers faced by im/migrant sex workers and how their socio-legal exclusion shapes labour conditions, health, and rights, the second author undertook community consultations on behalf of migrant sex worker organisation *Red Edition*. These consultations took the form of focus group discussions with im/migrant sex workers in Austria and inform the focus and themes described in this chapter. The methodology for these community consultations and participant demographics is presented in Box 9.1.

Box 9.1 Community Consultation Methodology and Participant Demographics

The second author, who works with community organisation *The Red Edition* and holds extensive experience in sex worker and im/migrant rights advocacy, organised two focus group discussions with ten gender-diverse im/migrant sex workers working in Austria. The focus groups took place in Vienna in February 2019. The second author opened the discussion by asking open-ended questions to encourage conversation among participants. The focus group discussions revolved around three primary topics: legal and immigration status (i.e. knowledge of immigration laws, visa application processes, and criminal laws); labour rights issues (i.e. working conditions, laws regulating sex work, participants' lived experiences with work and relationships); and access to health services (i.e. gaps in services and needs for community-led services, discrimination in healthcare settings, and experiences with safe spaces for im/migrant sex workers [e.g. drop-in centres]).

Five participants identified as transgender, four as cisgender male, and one as cisgender female. Participants were aged 22–43, and all worked in indoor settings including studios, hotels, clients' homes, and private apartments/homes. Participants originated from central and eastern Europe, and from central and South America.

The following thematic sections are informed by both the *Red Edition* community consultations and our literature review. In these sections, we introduce the multilevel structural determinants influencing im/migrant sex workers' health and labour by presenting literature findings and participant quotes from community consultations. We also present policy and programmatic recommendations based on epidemiological evidence, qualitative research, and im/migrant sex worker voices from the community consultations and across the globe on the subject of enhancing their health and rights.

Intersection of Sex Work Laws and Immigration Policies: A Dual Burden of Criminalisation

Previous literature from North America, Latin America, and Europe has highlighted the issue of prohibitive sex work and immigration laws, which result in a dual burden of criminalisation among im/migrant sex workers who are not citizens [16, 25, 28–30]. Even in New Zealand, where sex work is fully decriminalised for New Zealand citizens, im/migrants are explicitly prohibited from engaging in sex work and continue to be criminalised [31].

In the community consultations conducted on behalf of *Red Edition* for this chapter, participants described how, in Austria, the right to legally engage in sex work is linked to the right to legally stay in the country. Sex work remains criminalised among im/migrants from non-EU countries, including those who hold residence permits in other EU countries. Furthermore, sex workers living with HIV are criminalised in Austria: even individuals adhering to ART and with undetectable status are not allowed to engage in sex work. Such restrictive immigration and labour policies render sex work by non-EU im/migrant sex workers illegal, and subject those workers to enhanced policing, discrimination, and social marginalisation.

When non-EU im/migrant sex workers sought recourse for labour or housing issues, they were often met with discriminatory treatment from police based on their im/migrant status:

> I was kicked out from my apartment even though I already paid my rent, and I went to the first police station to ask for help. The police officer understood everything I said in English, but he continued to speak with me in German! I felt really bad.—focus group participant

Even in circumstances where they were facing violence or labour rights violations, participants in the consultations said that fear of criminalisation and potential immigration status revocation often discouraged them from accessing police protections. While many im/migrants' fears of criminalisation stemmed from limited knowledge of the laws regulating sex work and immigration, participants also reported a high level of sharing of experiences and information among their peers, and a strong sense of solidarity in managing the burden of criminalisation.

Prohibitive Laws: Protecting Im/migrants or Punitive Enforcement?

Participants' experiences reflect the dual burden of criminalisation faced by im/migrant sex workers in many settings, due to the criminalisation of sex work and im/migrant status. In some settings where selling sexual services is legal among citizens, it remains criminalised among some types of labour im/migrants [16, 28, 29, 32]. Many of these policies portray im/migrant sex workers as victims and purportedly aim to guard against exploitation [16, 22, 28, 32].

The merging of policies criminalising sex work and prohibitive immigration policies is used to justify the conflation of sex work with sex trafficking, often under the guise of protecting vulnerable im/migrants. However, this politicised conflation renders im/migrant sex workers susceptible to heightened scrutiny from police, immigration and municipal authorities, and generally takes the form of high levels of policing and surveillance over im/migrant sex workers' workspaces (e.g. massage parlours, micro-brothels) and even their homes [16, 29, 30, 33].

Im/migrant sex workers may be more likely to access third party services (e.g. venue managers, security, advertisers). They also frequently work together (i.e. as third parties to one another) and in managed in-call venues [34–36] to counter marginalisation related to im/migrant status, such as language barriers, barriers to finding clients, and low familiarity with the legal and labour context of the destination setting

[22]. Concerningly, under legislative regimes that criminalise third parties with the purported goal of protecting sex workers from exploitation, managed indoor sex work spaces may face increased targeting by authorities. In Canada, anti-trafficking and police raids on indoor sex work venues have resulted in arrests, charges, and deportation of im/migrant sex workers [37–39]. Recent Canadian research found that 23.9% of 397 indoor sex workers had experienced a workplace inspection (by police, municipal, immigration, or health authorities), and 51.6% worried about the potential consequences of these inspections, with recent im/migrant participants disproportionately affected by worry [33]. Although laws in Sweden and Norway state that 'victims of prostitution do not risk any legal repercussions' [29], im/migrant sex workers have faced harassment, discrimination, and forced evictions [28–30]. In Norway, police, accompanied by media, conducted raids of massage parlours, during which im/migrant sex workers' privacy was grossly violated through their exposure on national television [28].

In contrast to sex work laws and immigration policies depicting im/migrant sex workers as victims of violence and exploitation, current evidence suggests that some of the greatest harms facing im/migrant sex workers relate to these punitive laws and the enforcement thereof. This heavy burden of criminalisation has serious human rights implications, as evidence suggests that criminalisation, and enforcement and harassment by police, act to enhance workplace violence faced by sex workers [40, 41]. Punitive law enforcement also restricts workers' access to condoms and HIV/STI testing in the workplace [9, 42, 43], including workers' ability to carry condoms [44], thereby undermining broader HIV prevention and occupational health goals.

Mandatory Health Testing: Punitive Regulations and Barriers to Health Services

Prior research has documented how mandatory health testing can act as a form of surveillance of im/migrant sex workers [45, 46]. In the community consultations conducted for this chapter, im/migrant sex workers described the impacts of punitive mandatory sexual health testing and sex worker registration policies. In Austria, sex workers are required to undergo STI testing every 6 weeks, and HIV testing every 3 months. Sex workers with official registration are obliged to pay taxes and charges, but these are applied unequally across different provinces and brothels. Focus group participants described negative experiences with mandatory health testing centres, including poor treatment from health professionals and very limited health services. Even when im/migrant sex workers had other health concerns, these health centres did not offer other sexual or reproductive health or primary health services, and the health professionals refused to advise them. Participants perceived that numerous obligations were imposed onto sex workers to satisfy morality-based legal and health regulations, but that sex workers' own rights were barely taken into consideration.

Mandatory testing is based on the stereotype that sex workers are disproportionately responsible for spreading disease. It is a repressive tool, a way for the medical body and police who control if we get always have our card with stamps, proving that we are being checked regularly, to tell us what our place is and to maintain the social order.—focus group participant

These participant experiences add to current evidence that criminalisation of and discrimination against im/migrant sex workers also occurs through im/migration and sex work regulation requirements (e.g. sex worker registration or licencing policies), and mandatory HIV/STI testing [45–47]. Research indicates that at the Mexico-Guatemala border, health authorities require sex workers to carry a health card (permit demonstrating routine HIV/STI testing at municipal health clinics) [45–47]. Im/migrant sex workers in this context expressed that these public health requirements were paired with punitive enforcement by local authorities, who used the process of verifying the im/migrant women's health cards as an opportunity to harass them [45, 46]. In addition, many sex workers preferred not to maintain a health card due to privacy and immigration status concerns [45, 46]. This finding echoes other research highlighting how mandatory registration and health testing regulations often create two 'tiers' of sex workers: those able to meet the imposed regulatory requirements, and those who cannot (e.g. due to precarious status, privacy and anonymity needs, or positive HIV/STI status). The latter tier are forced to work in a clandestine way, which increases their vulnerability to violence and exploitation [16, 48].

Precarious Immigration Status: Increasing Vulnerability and Barriers to Health and Police Protections

Consultation participants highlighted how immigration policies and sex work criminalisation intersected to increase vulnerability for im/migrants without full citizenship, reflecting current literature documenting vulnerability among sex workers with precarious im/migration status [16, 49, 50]. Sex workers in Austria described how any confrontation with police, arrests or charges could affect the next visa application. If im/migrant sex workers had unpaid fines for prostitution, they faced threats of deportation, regardless of whether they were EU citizens or not. This ongoing threat of loss of immigration status led im/migrant sex workers to avoid law enforcement interactions. Participants also highlighted that im/migrant sex workers often shared information on legal, immigration and labour issues with one another, addressing existing gaps in legal resources for im/migrants and sex workers by harnessing peer mentorship and support.

The term 'precarious immigration status' captures the many forms of 'less than full status', and is defined by the absence of key rights or entitlements associated with citizenship [51]. Those with precarious immigration status include 'documented' but temporary workers, students, and refugee applicants; people with unauthorised forms of status (e.g. visa overstayers, undocumented entrants) [52]; and individuals whose immigration status is rendered precarious through involvement in criminalised sex work. Current research shows that im/migrants with precarious status are more vulnerable to exploitation due to their heightened labour insecurity and risk of incarceration and deportation [2]. Among sex workers, having precarious status is a major determinant that shapes access to safe working conditions, health services (including HIV/STI testing and care), and police protections.

Our community consultations in Austria, and community reports and research from Canada and Europe suggest that, due to fear of police inspections and potential immigration status consequences [9, 16, 22, 53], im/migrant sex workers with precarious status are more likely to work in hidden environments (e.g. secluded, isolated street-based locations, private apartments), rather than in formal in-call venues (e.g. massage parlours). This has implications for the quality of their work environments and safety at work, as working in isolated areas renders sex workers more vulnerable to violent perpetrators and coercion into unprotected sex [29, 54–57]. Further, the ongoing threat of status revocation contributes to power imbalances between im/migrant sex workers, managers, and clients, which restrict sex workers' ability to negotiate supportive labour conditions and client condom use [9, 22].

Precarious status also restricts im/migrant sex workers from accessing HIV/STI testing and care. In a study in Italy, 100% of 345 mostly undocumented im/migrant sex workers confirmed that they had never previously been tested for HIV/STIs in Italy [58]. A study in Portugal found that gaps in testing and knowledge of testing services were greatest among undocumented sex workers [18], and recent studies from Somalia and Europe identified precarious status as a structural factor increasing im/migrant sex workers' vulnerability to HIV [18, 58, 59].

Despite prejudiced stereotypes regarding health status and HIV/STIs among im/migrants, evidence suggests that im/migrants' health access and outcomes are shaped by restrictive and xenophobic immigration policies faced by marginalised im/migrants in destination settings [60, 61]. These policies are particularly prohibitive among sex workers and those with precarious status. Precarious status has also been associated with heightened barriers to sexual and reproductive health services, and primary health care [18, 36, 62–65].

Sex work involvement can increase im/migrants' precarity and result in heightened law enforcement surveillance and immigration status revocation. Community reports from Canada describe long-term detentions and deportations of im/migrant sex workers who had arrived via legal channels, but whose immigration status was rendered precarious through involvement in sex work—an activity uniquely criminalised for certain types of im/migrants under Canadian immigration policy [22]. As reflected in the experiences of our community consultation participants, precarious status also presents immense barriers to accessing police protection. In Hong Kong, im/migrant sex workers fear reporting violence due to concerns of facing deportation [66]. In France, where sex work clients are explicitly criminalised under end-demand laws, undocumented sex workers have faced police pressure and coercion to report clients, and threatened with deportation if they did not comply [53]. Sex workers with precarious status in Sweden, Norway, and the UK have faced surveillance by immigration authorities, threats of deportation, and deportations [28, 29,

57, 67]. There is strong evidence that fearing loss of immigration status motivates im/migrant sex workers to avoid interactions with authorities [22, 28, 29, 66, 68], which violates their rights to legal protections.

Economic Marginalisation

Financial vulnerability is a major determinant shaping labour environments and rights among sex workers globally. The community consultation participants asserted that economic marginalisation affected many im/migrant sex workers and increased their vulnerability at work. Furthermore, im/migrant status and sex work discrimination prevented them from accessing employment or the financial supports available to other people seeking work, such as employment agencies providing assistance to individuals who have legal status in Austria and are not engaged in sex work.

Globally, im/migrant workers in a wide range of industries face economic marginalisation in destination settings. Such marginalisation can be due to 'push' conditions in origin settings (e.g. poverty, family needs), expenses incurred during im/migration, lower familiarity with the labour environment and employment options, language barriers, non-recognition of im/migrants' credentials (e.g. degrees, diplomas, certifications), and the need to financially support dependents or send remittances [22, 24, 68]. Economic marginalisation among im/migrant sex workers intersects with criminalisation, making their working conditions and health access precarious.

Financial vulnerability restricts the options available to im/migrant sex workers in terms of work environments, quality of clients, and the reliability of third parties. This limits their agency in accessing the most supportive work environments for themselves [69]. The community consultation participants emphasised how the social and economic marginalisation of im/migrant sex workers contributed to their vulnerability to exploitative working conditions and violations of labour rights, without any options for recourse.

> One time he (sex work studio owner) took the keys from the door and told me that he will come back in 2 hours to close the studio. He didn't come back for the next 7 hours! And I had no choice; I had to wait for him!—focus group participant

Participants in our focus groups highlighted how the criminalisation of sex work enhanced im/migrant sex workers' economic marginalisation, isolated workers, maintained precarious labour conditions, and excluded the application of labour protections that could address exploitation at work. This finding reflects the experience of im/migrant sex workers in France, where shifting criminalisation has significantly increased economic vulnerability among the most marginalised sex workers, namely undocumented im/migrant women working in street-based locations [53].

Economic marginalisation can also enhance im/migrant sex workers' HIV and STI risk by reducing their ability to negotiate condom use with clients or to decline clients' offers of increased pay for unprotected sex [44, 69]. Finally, many general health, reproductive health, and HIV/STI services have high costs for im/migrants in destination settings, as im/migrants frequently do not enjoy legal entitlements to health care and are often excluded from utilising national healthcare services that are free/low-cost for citizens [70]. This results in many im/migrant sex workers deferring testing or treatment until a visit to their home country. Five different studies involving im/migrant sex workers from diverse contexts found that a significant proportion of im/migrants reported accessing sexual, reproductive health, and/or HIV/STI services in their country of origin, due to high costs and privacy concerns around using even free sexual health services in the destination country [44, 63, 71–73]. This raises concerns regarding delays in access to critical health services.

Racialisation, Racism, Stigma, and Discrimination

As with research documenting discriminatory treatment and lack of workplace protections among im/migrant workers in many industries [2, 4, 13], participants in community consultations reported that protections against labour discrimination enjoyed by Austrian sex workers and im/migrants from other EU countries are not afforded to sex workers from non-EU countries. With regard to employment, remuneration and working conditions, European Union labour laws prohibit discrimination against EU citizens based on their nationality. They further guarantee freedom of movement between EU countries, without discrimination based on citizenship. However, such protections are not in place for im/migrant sex workers from non-EU countries, who remain criminalised and without recourse for labour discrimination. Existing unemployment supports are also not extended, even to registered sex workers who pay tax.

> I went to AMS [unemployment institution] because I'm not registered as a sex worker. So they don't have any idea that I'm a sex worker. But if I was registered sex worker who regularly paid all taxes, then after I stop working, I don't have any benefits from the system. That's terrible!—focus group participant

In addition to legal and labour discrimination against sex workers, im/migrant sex workers frequently face racism and racialised law enforcement in destination countries [16, 42]. Historically, sex workers have also been depicted as vectors for HIV/STI transmission [20, 74], and this stereotyping is particularly inflicted on racialised im/migrants and those from the Global South [19].

Across various contexts, racialised sex workers, including im/migrants, face discriminatory policing practices, such as police checking identification only among racialised/ethnic minority people, isolating racialised individuals for police questioning, and asking racialised women if they are being coerced or trafficked [9, 16, 22, 26, 67]. Xenophobic assumptions that portray im/migrant women as inherently vulnerable, likely to be victimised, and requiring state protection contribute to policies and programmes that aim to rescue im/migrant sex workers instead of provide rights-based supports for them [16, 22, 75].

Im/migrant sex workers can face a dual burden of stigma due to the intersection of two marginalised identities (i.e. im/migrant and sex worker), and this can be further compounded by race and ethnic background (e.g. Indigeneity) [76]. Isolation, sex work stigma, and socio-cultural stigmas surrounding sex contribute to privacy concerns when it comes to accessing health services and shape the preference of many im/migrant sex workers to neither disclose sex work involvement to their primary care provider nor to access sexual health testing from them [35, 36, 42, 63]. As asserted by our focus group participants and im/migrant sex workers in diverse countries, stigma and fear of poor treatment or discrimination by health professionals are powerful barriers to im/migrant sex workers' access to health care [36, 68, 73, 77], and further enhance their social exclusion.

Language Barriers, Gender, and Power

Language barriers faced by im/migrant sex workers in diverse settings can intersect with sex work criminalisation and precarious status to shape gendered power dynamics which impact sex workers' negotiations with police and clients [9, 16, 35, 44]. In community consultations, participants reported that language barriers and lack of familiarity with Austrian and EU laws contributed to worry and feelings of intimidation when police officers come to sex workers' workspaces, reflecting the experiences of other im/migrant sex workers across continents [50, 68, 78, 79]. They asserted that language barriers enhanced the power differentials between themselves and police, and contributed to poor treatment by police officers, as police often refused to speak in English during investigations. In contrast, im/migrant sex workers with strong spoken German and who had obtained Austrian citizenship reported better treatment from Austrian police officers, illustrating discrimination based on language abilities and immigration status.

Mirroring the experiences of our community consultation participants, research from other Global North contexts has found that language interpreters are rarely available during police raids and inspections of indoor venues where im/migrant sex workers work, and that language barriers contribute to intimidation and fear [22, 26, 80]. Furthermore, criminalisation, gendered power dynamics, and language barriers can intersect to undermine the ability of im/migrant workers to negotiate condom use. For example, in Canada, im/migrant women sex workers reported recognition of their limited proficiency in English, and of gendered power imbalances between themselves and clients. They cited having to 'be accommodating' to clients' requests (i.e. for condomless services), due to fears that an unsatisfied client may draw police attention [9]. In another study involving im/migrant sex workers in Canada, 58% of 129 sex workers had ever had a client try to pull/sneak a condom off during sex [35], while im/migrant sex workers in Moscow reported incidents of violence and physical force from aggressors who coerced the worker into providing sex without condoms [44]. This evidence highlights how language barriers can heighten vulnerability among im/migrant sex workers in interactions with police and clients, restricting their agency and compounding their marginalisation.

Unique Marginalisation of Male and Gender-Diverse Im/migrant Sex Workers

Research into and discourse around trafficking have contributed to prominent misrepresentations of im/migrant sex workers as women with low levels of agency who are coerced into sexual labour [19–22]. These paternalistic representations contribute to the erasure of male and gender-diverse sex workers, and justify high levels of policing and im/migration enforcement among im/migrants.

In addition to sex work stigma, male im/migrant sex workers can face a burden of homophobia, particularly in countries which criminalise and police same-sex practices [78]. Researchers have also noted that men who have paid sex are less likely to self-identify as sex workers and often remain hidden by arranging sex service encounters via the internet, and are therefore missed by typical public health interventions targeting this group [81]. While high rates of physical and sexual violence, heavy HIV and STI burdens, discrimination, and barriers to health services have been documented among transgender sex workers across continents [78], very limited literature has documented the experiences of male and gender-diverse im/migrant sex workers, highlighting a need for further research exploring how gender intersects with im/migrant status among sex workers to shape health access and labour rights.

Recommendations and Areas for Intervention

The preceding sections have illustrated how, on a global level, labour conditions and health access among im/migrant sex workers are shaped by: criminalisation, mandatory health testing, and registration policies; precarious status, economic marginalisation, racialisation, racism, stigma, and discrimination; language barriers, and gender. To date, most evidence-based approaches to promoting health and rights among sex workers globally are based on information from, and research involving, non-im/migrant sex workers. There are only limited peer-reviewed intervention studies or best practice guidelines specifically for migrants, with exceptions including policy documents from NSWP and ICRSE [79, 82]. However, research involving im/migrant sex workers in diverse global settings and the community consultations for this chapter demonstrate the need for structural interventions including health-promoting laws and policies, work environment factors (i.e. supportive management, condom access, HIV/STI services, and sexual health education in the workplace), and community empowerment determinants (i.e. peer support). With these in place, it is possible to enhance labour rights and promote health access among im/migrant sex workers.

Enabling Indoor Work Environments

Formal indoor work venues represent key opportunities or sites for interventions designed to promote im/migrant sex workers' access to health services [35, 69]. In contexts where laws and policies enable the distribution of condoms within indoor sex work spaces, sex workers have reported consistent access to condoms, which supports consistent condom use. In Mali, where HIV prevention programmes for sex workers (including condom provision and promotion) have been a government priority since 1987, 99% of im/migrant sex workers surveyed in 2009 reported having access to condoms in the workplace, and approximately 97% reported consistent condom use with clients in the past month [83]. Given that criminalised conditions constrain indoor venues from openly selling sexual services and restrict sex work managers from distributing condoms in these spaces, legislative reforms towards decriminalising all aspects of sex work, including third parties, are recommended to enable supportive labour environments for sex workers.

Supportive third parties, access to condoms, and access to sexual health services and education in the workplace have been documented to promote effective negotiation of condom use and enable increased uptake of HIV/STI testing among im/migrant sex workers in several global settings [45, 69, 83, 84]. As previously described, im/migrant sex workers may also benefit from legal access to third party services (e.g. administrative support, advertising, security). Third party support has been identified by sex workers across continents as a critical facet of HIV prevention [85]. Among im/migrant and non-im/migrant sex workers in Canada, the use of third party administrative and security services was recently linked to heightened access to mobile condom distribution and sex worker-led services [86]. Our findings suggest that constructive interventions are those that (1) implement laws and policies aimed at enhancing health access among im/migrant sex workers and (2) enable the legal operation of formal indoor sex work venues and support their management in promoting sexual health [86].

Removal of Punitive Laws and Policies

There is a critical need for law reforms that decriminalise all aspects of sex work and enable sex workers to legally access supportive workspaces and third parties, in order to create the most optimal working conditions and choices for themselves. Current evidence on the harms of sex work criminalisation, and community-based calls for the removal of punitive laws align with the recommendations of international policy institutions, including the WHO, UNAIDS, UNDP, and Amnesty International, who call for the full decriminalisation of all aspects of sex work as necessary to promote the human rights of sex workers [87–90]. In considering law reforms, participants in the community consultations highlighted that the meaningful involvement of diverse groups of sex workers in legislation, policy, and programme design was paramount to ensure that laws, regulations, and health promotion interventions reflect the needs and lived experiences of diverse im/migrant sex workers worldwide, contributing to the enhancement of their health and human rights.

Importantly, international policy bodies, including UNAIDS and WHO, have acknowledged that mandatory health testing and registration requirements violate the human rights of sex workers [78]. Repressive HIV prevention approaches, such as mandatory health testing and sex worker registration, present serious concerns, as these are often coercive and may result in exclusion from services among the most marginalised im/migrants. Our community consultation participants also denounced mandatory HIV/STI testing, asserting that such policies reinforce harmful and inaccurate representations of sex workers as vectors for disease, and called for rights-based and community-led approaches to increasing health access.

Supporting Peer and Community-Led Education, Outreach, and Services

Community consultation participants emphasised an urgent need for im/migrant sex worker-led programmes, such as peer-to-peer education, to enhance workers' knowledge of their legal and labour rights and to promote their access to health services. They also highlighted the importance of safe spaces, such as drop-in centres, where im/migrant sex workers can access supports without fear of police or immigration enforcement. Current evidence illustrates that peer-based and community-led interventions delivered in indoor sex work venues and to street-based environments help to mitigate the pervasive structural and migration-related barriers to appropriate health services. This suggests a need to expand community-led services, with language supports and which are culturally appropriate to participants, in spaces where im/migrant sex workers are comfortable [35, 69, 91].

Rather than enforcement-based approaches, im/migrant sex workers from diverse settings have expressed a need for, and appreciation of, community-led outreach services which offer sexual health resources (i.e. condoms, lubricants), voluntary sexual health testing, and private/anonymous, nonjudgmental sexual health nursing [35, 42, 63, 69, 91]. This transition from punitive to supportive approaches emphasises the rights of im/migrant sex workers, and prioritises community-based health promotion to ensure timely, accessible, and appropriate health services for im/migrant sex workers globally.

Conclusion

In this chapter, we have highlighted the structural and migration-related barriers to labour rights and health access faced by im/migrant sex workers everywhere. Criminalisation, precarious status, economic marginalisation, and intersecting forms of exclusion based on race, gender, and immigration status represent powerful determinants that restrict im/migrant sex workers from fair access to health services and labour rights.

Our literature review and community consultations also challenge prominent stereotypes about im/migrant sex workers as a marginalised, victimised group. The fact that im/migrant sex workers across diverse global contexts continue to access health services, practice safer sex, work together, share legal, labour and health resources, and travel to get their health needs met—even in the face of layered criminalisation and persistent migration-related barriers—speaks to their resistance to structural oppression and their strong agency. In contrast to prominent frames of im/migrant sex workers as passive victims, current research portrays im/migrant sex workers as tenacious, active, and goal-oriented workers.

The community consultation participants asserted that supporting im/migrant sex worker-led action and advocacy were top priorities in the struggle to uphold their rights. Their lived experiences, community reports, and current research suggest a need to build on existing community-led interventions. Finally, it is critical to work towards reforming laws criminalising sex work and to address punitive policing and im/migration enforcement. If we are to promote im/migrant sex workers' access to health services and affirm their labour rights, this work can only be undertaken effectively in collaboration with im/migrant sex workers as experts in their own lives and experiences.

References

1. Smith PM, Mustard CA. The unequal distribution of occupational health and safety risks among immigrants to Canada compared to Canadian-born labour market participants: 1993–2005. Saf Sci. 2010;48(10):1296–303.
2. Benach J, Muntaner C, Delclos C, Menéndez M, Ronquillo C. Migration and "low-skilled" workers in destination countries. PLoS Med. 2011;8(6):e1001043.
3. Hasstedt K. Toward equity and access: removing legal barriers to health insurance coverage for immigrants. Guttmacher Policy Rev. 2013;16(1):2–8.
4. Holmes S. Fresh fruit, broken bodies. Migrant farmworkers in the United States. Berkeley: University of California Press; 2013.
5. Moyce SC, Schenker M. Migrant workers and their occupational health and safety. Annu Rev Public Health. 2018;39:351–65.
6. Lucchini RG, London L. Global occupational health: current challenges and the need for urgent action. Ann Glob Health. 2014;80(4):251–6.
7. Pérez ER, Benavides FG, Levecque K, Love JG, Felt E, Van Rossem R. Differences in working conditions and employment arrangements among migrant and non-migrant workers in Europe. Ethn Health. 2012;17(6):563–77.

8. Woodward A, Howard N, Wolffers I. Health and access to care for undocumented migrants living in the European Union: a scoping review. Health Policy Plan. 2014;29:818–30.
9. Goldenberg SM, Krüsi A, Zhang E, Chettiar J, Shannon K. Structural determinants of health among im/migrants in the indoor sex industry. PLoS One. 2017;12(1):e0170642.
10. Oxman-Martinez J, Hanley J, Lach L, Khanlou N, Weerasinghe S, Agnew V. Intersection of Canadian policy parameters affecting women with precarious immigration status: a baseline for understanding barriers to health. J Immigr Health. 2005;7(4):247–58.
11. Harcourt W, Escobar A. Introduction practices of difference: introducing woman and the politics of place. In: Woman and the politics of place. Bloomfield, CT: Kumarian Press; 2005.
12. Benach J, Vives A, Amable M, Vanroelen C, Tarafa G, Muntaner C. Precarious employment: understanding an emerging social determinant of health. Annu Rev Public Health. 2014;35(1):229–53.
13. Premji S, Spasevski M, Athar S, Shakya Y, Merolli J, et al. Precarious work experiences of racialized immigrant women in Toronto: a community-based study. Just Labour. 2014;22:122–43.
14. Lewis H, Dwyer P, Hodkinson S, Waite L. Hyper-precarious lives. Prog Hum Geogr. 2015;39(5):580–600.
15. Castles S. Migration, precarious work, and rights. In: Migration, precarity, and global governance: challenges and opportunities for labour. Oxford: Oxford University Press; 2015. p. 46–67.
16. Vuolajärvi N. Governing in the name of caring—the Nordic model of prostitution and its punitive consequences for migrants who sell sex. Sex Res Soc Policy. 2019;16:151–65.
17. Baye EMO, Heumann S. Migration, sex work and exploitative labor conditions: experiences of Nigerian women in the sex industry in Turin, Italy, and counter-trafficking measures. Gend Technol Dev. 2014; https://doi.org/10.1177/0971852413515322.
18. Dias S, Gama A, Pingarilho M, Simões D, Mendão L. Health services use and HIV prevalence among migrant and National female sex workers in Portugal: are we providing the services needed? AIDS Behav. 2017;21(8):2316–21.
19. Brock D, Gillies K, Oliver C, Sutdhibhasilp M. Migrant sex work - a roundable, Canadian woman studies, vol. 20. Toronto, ON: York University; 2000.
20. Mårdh P-A, Genç M. Migratory prostitution with emphasis on Europe. J Travel Med. 1995; https://doi.org/10.1111/j.1708-8305.1995.tb00616.x.
21. Andrijasevic R. Beautiful dead bodies: gender, migration and representation in anti-trafficking campaigns. Fem Rev. 2007;86(1):24–44.
22. Lam E. Behind the rescue: how anti-trafficking investigations and policies harm migrant sex workers. Toronto: Butterfly Asian and Migrant Sex Workers Support Network; 2018.
23. Goldenberg SM, Liu V, Nguyen P, Chettiar J, Shannon K. International migration from non-endemic settings as a protective factor for HIV/STI risk among female sex workers in Vancouver, Canada. J Immigr Minor Health. 2015;17(1):21–8.
24. Platt L, Grenfell P, Fletcher A, Sorhaindo A, Jolley E, Rhodes T, et al. Systematic review examining differences in HIV, sexually transmitted infections and health-related harms between migrant and non-migrant female sex workers. Sex Transm Infect. 2013;89(4):311–9.
25. TAMPEP. Position Paper - CEDAW [Internet]; 2019.
26. Lam E. Inspection, policing, and racism: how municipal by-laws endanger the lives of Chinese sex workers in Toronto. Can Rev Soc Policy. 2016;75:87–112.
27. Lam E. Shutting down massage parlours: anti-trafficking, or anti-migration? In: Law and Society Association Annual Meeting. Washington DC; 2019.
28. PION. CEDAW 2017 - Shadow report by PION [Internet]; 2017.
29. Levy J, Jakobsson P. Sweden's abolitionist discourse and law: effects on the dynamics of Swedish sex work and on the lives of Sweden's sex workers. Criminol Crim Justice. 2014;14(5):593–607.
30. Amnesty International. Criminalization of sex work in Norway: the human cost of "crushing" the market [Internet].

31. Abel G. Dignity in choice: the illegal status of migrant sex workers in new Zealand. In: Law and Society Association Annual Meeting. Washington DC; 2019.
32. Government of Canada. Immigration and refugee protection regulations [Internet]. Ottawa. 2018. http://laws-lois.justice.gc.ca.
33. McBride B, Shannon K, Duff P, Mo M, Braschel M, Goldenberg SM. Harms of workplace inspections for im/migrant sex workers in in-call establishments: enhanced barriers to health access in a Canadian Setting. J Immigr Minor Health. 2019;21(6):1290–9.
34. Autres Regards. Outreach in indoor sex work settings 2013–2014 indoors - empowerment and skill building tools for national and migrant female sex workers working in hidden places [Internet]. Marseille; 2014.
35. Bungay V, Kolar K, Thindal S, Remple VP, Johnston CL, Ogilvie G. Community-based HIV and STI prevention in women working in indoor sex markets. Health Promot Pract. 2013;14(2):247–55.
36. Selvey LA, Lobo RC, McCausland KL, Donovan B, Bates J, Hallett J. Challenges facing Asian sex workers in Western Australia: implications for health promotion and support services. Front Public Health. 2018;6:171.
37. Leblanc S. Milton massage parlour raid leads to charges. Hamilton Spectator [Internet]; 2016.
38. Yogaretnam S. Police raid residential erotic massage parlour: 76 human trafficking charges for alleged ringleader. The National Post [Internet]; 2015.
39. Hempstead D. 11 women face possible deportation after massage parlour raids. Ottawa Sun [Internet]; 2015.
40. Deering KN, Amin A, Shoveller J, Nesbitt A, Garcia-Moreno C, Duff P, et al. A systematic review of the correlates of violence against sex workers. Am J Public Health. 2014;104(5):42–54.
41. Prakash R, Manthri S, Tayyaba S, Joy A, Raj SS, Singh D, et al. Effect of physical violence on sexually transmitted infections and treatment seeking behaviour among female sex workers in Thane District, Maharashtra, India. PLoS One. 2016;11(3):1–20.
42. Anderson S, Shannon K, Li J, Lee Y, Chettiar J, Goldenberg S, et al. Condoms and sexual health education as evidence: impact of criminalization of in-call venues and managers on migrant sex workers access to HIV/STI prevention in a Canadian setting. BMC Int Health Hum Rights. 2016;16(1):1–10.
43. Lim RBT, Cheung ONY, Tham DKT, La HH, Win TT, Chan R, et al. Using qualitative and community-based engagement approaches to gain access and to develop a culturally appropriate STI prevention intervention for foreign female entertainment workers in Singapore. Glob Health. 2018;14(1):36.
44. Weine S, Golobof A, Bahromov M, Kashuba A, Kalandarov T, Jonbekov J, et al. Female migrant sex workers in Moscow: gender and power factors and HIV risk. Women Health. 2013;53(1):56–73.
45. Goldenberg SM, Rocha Jimenez T, Brouwer KC, et al. Influence of indoor work environments on health, safety, and human rights among migrant sex workers at the Guatemala-Mexico Border: a call for occupational health and safety interventions. BMC Int Health Hum Rights. 2018;18(1):9.
46. Jiménez TR, Brouwer KC, Silverman JG, Morales-Mirand S, Goldenberg SM. Exploring the context and implementation of public health regulations governing sex work: a qualitative study with migrant sex workers in Guatemala. J Immigr Minor Health. 2017;19(5):1235–44.
47. Rocha-Jimenez T, Morales-Miranda S, Fernandez-Casanueva C, Brouwer KC. The influence of migration in substance use practices and HIV/STI-related risks of female sex workers at a dynamic border crossing. J Ethn Subst Abuse. 2020;19(4):503–20.
48. Global Network of Sex Work Projects. Sex work and the law: understanding legal frameworks and the struggle for sex work law reforms [Internet]; 2019.
49. Goldenberg SM. Trafficking, migration, and health: complexities and future directions. Lancet Glob Health. 2015;3:e118–9.

50. Butterfly Asian and Migrant Sex Workers Support Network. Behind the rescue: how anti-trafficking investigations and policies harm migrant sex workers. Toronto: Butterfly Asian and Migrant Sex Workers Support Network; 2018.
51. Goldring L, Landolt P. Caught in the work-citizenship matrix: the lasting effects of precarious legal status on work for Toronto immigrants. Globalizations. 2011;8:325–41.
52. Goldring L, Berinstein C, Bernhard JK. Institutionalizing precarious migratory status in Canada. Citizenship Stud. 2009;13(3):239–65.
53. Le Bail H, Giametta C. What do sex workers think about the French prostitution act?; 2018.
54. Oppal WT. Forsaken: the report of the Missing Women Commission of Inquiry Executive Summary [Internet]. Vancouver; 2012.
55. Krüsi A, Pacey K, Bird L, Taylor C, Chettiar J, Allan S, et al. Criminalisation of clients: reproducing vulnerabilities for violence and poor health among street-based sex workers in Canada-a qualitative study. BMJ Open. 2014;4(6):e005191.
56. NSWP. The impact of criminalisation on sex workers' vulnerability to HIV and violence [Internet]; 2017.
57. Klambauer E. Policing roulette: sex workers' perception of encounters with police officers in the indoor and outdoor sector in England. Criminol Crim Justice. 2018;18(3):255–72.
58. Zermiani M, Mengoli C, Rimondo C, Galvan U, Cruciani M, Serpelloni G. Prevalence of sexually transmitted diseases and hepatitis C in a survey of female sex workers in the North-East of Italy. Open AIDS J. 2012;6(1):60–4.
59. Kriitmaa K, Testa A, Osman M, Bozicevic I, Riedner G, Malungu J, Irving G, Abdalla I. HIV prevalence and characteristics of sex work among female sex workers in Hargeisa, Somaliland, Somalia. AIDS. 2010;24(Suppl 2):S61–7.
60. European Center for Disease Prevention and Control. Migrant health: epidemiology of HIV and AIDS in migrant communities and ethnic minorities in EU/EEA countries; 2010.
61. Mahon C. Most HIV-positive migrants in Europe acquired HIV post-migration I AVERT. Avert; 2017.
62. Campbell RM, Klei AG, Hodges BD, Fisman D, Kitto S. A comparison of health access between permanent residents, undocumented immigrants and refugee claimants in Toronto, Canada. J Immigr Minor Health. 2014;16(1):165–76.
63. Darling KEA, Gloor E, Ansermet-Pagot A, Vaucher P, Durieux-Paillard S, Bodenmann P, et al. Suboptimal access to primary healthcare among street-based sex workers in Southwest Switzerland. Postgrad Med J. 2013;89(1053):371–5.
64. Richter M, Chersich MF, Vearey J, Sartorius B, Temmerman M, Luchters S. Migration status, work conditions and health utilization of female sex workers in three South African cities. J Immigr Minor Health. 2014;16(1):7–17.
65. Davis A, Meyerson BE, Aghaulor B, Brown K, Watson A, Muessig KE, et al. Barriers to health service access among female migrant Ugandan sex workers in Guangzhou, China. Int J Equity Health. 2016;15(1):170.
66. Wong WCW, Holroyd E, Bingham A. Stigma and sex work from the perspective of female sex workers in Hong Kong. Sociol Health Illn. 2011;33(1):50–65.
67. Jahnsen S, Skilbrei ML. Leaving no stone unturned: the borders and orders of transnational prostitution. Br J Criminol. 2018;58(2):255–72.
68. Goldenberg SM, Krusi A, Zhang E, Chettiar J, Shannon K. Structural determinants of health among im/migrants in the indoor sex industry. PLoS One. 2017;12:e0170642.
69. Febres-Cordero B, Brouwer KC, Rocha-Jimenez T, Fernandez-Casanueva C, Morales-Miranda S, Goldenberg SM. Influence of peer support on HIV/STI prevention and safety amongst international migrant sex workers: a qualitative study at the Mexico-Guatemala border. PLoS One. 2018;13(1):e0190787.
70. Rechel B, Mladovsky P, Ingleby D, Mackenbach JP, McKee M. Migration and health in an increasingly diverse Europe. Lancet. 2013;381(9873):1235–45.

71. Platt L, Grenfell P, Bonell C, Creighton S, Wellings K, Parry J, et al. Risk of sexually transmitted infections and violence among indoor-working female sex workers in London: the effect of migration from Eastern Europe. Sex Transm Infect. 2011;87(5):377–84.
72. Wong M-L, Chan R, Tan HH, Yong E, Lee L, Cutter J, et al. Sex work and risky sexual behaviors among foreign entertainment workers in urban Singapore: findings from mystery client survey. J Urban Health. 2012;89(6):1031–44.
73. Rocha-Jimenez T, Morales-Miranda S, Fernandez-Casanueva C, Brouwer KC, Goldenberg SM. Stigma and unmet sexual and reproductive health needs among international migrant sex workers at the Mexico-Guatemala border. Int J Gynaecol Obstet. 2018;143(1):37–43.
74. van Haastrecht HJ, Fennema JS, Coutinho RA, van der Helm TC, Kint JA, van den Hoek JA. HIV prevalence and risk behaviour among prostitutes and clients in Amsterdam: migrants at increased risk for HIV infection. Sex Transm Infect. 2008;69(4). https://doi.org/10.1136/sti.69.4.251
75. Global Network of Sex Work Projects. The impact of "end demand" legislation on women sex workers - POLICY BRIEF; 2018.
76. Taran P. Migrant women, women migrant workers - crucial challenges for rights-based action and advocacy. In: OHCHR-UNWOMEN side event to 64th Session of the UN Committee on the Elimination of Discrimination Against Woment (CEDAW): "Promoting and Protecting Women Migrant Workers' Labour and Human Rights through CEDAW and CMW" [Internet]. Geneva; 2016.
77. Scorgie F, Nakato D, Harper E, Richter M, Maseko S, Nare P, et al. "We are despised in the hospitals": sex workers' experiences of accessing health care in four African countries. Cult Health Sex. 2013;15(4):450–65.
78. UNAIDS. The gap report - sex workers. Geneva: UNAIDS; 2014.
79. NSWP. Migrant sex workers BRIEFING PAPER [Internet]; 2018.
80. SWAN Vancouver Society. Im/migrant sex workers, myths and misconceptions: realities of the anti-trafficked. Vancouver: SWAN Vancouver Society; 2015.
81. Verhaegh-Haasnoot A, Dukers-Muijrers NHTM, Hoebe CJPA. High burden of STI and HIV in male sex workers working as internet escorts for men in an observational study: a hidden key population compared with female sex workers and other men who have sex with men. BMC Infect Dis. 2015;15(1):291.
82. International Committee on the Rights of Sex Workers in Europe. Policy brief and recommendations on the rights of migrant sex workers [Internet]; 2016.
83. Trout CH, Dembélé O, Diakité D, Bougoudogo F, Doumbia B, Mathieu J, et al. West African female sex workers in Mali. J Acquir Immune Defic Syndr. 2015;68:S221–31.
84. Lim RBT, Cheung ONY, Tai BC, Chen MI-C, Chan RKW, Wong ML. Efficacy of multicomponent culturally tailored HIV/STI prevention interventions targeting foreign female entertainment workers: a quasi-experimental trial. Sex Transm Infect. 2018;94(6):449–56.
85. Goldenberg SM, Duff P, Krusi A. Work environments and HIV prevention: a qualitative review and meta-synthesis of sex worker narratives. BMC Public Health. 2015;15(1):1241.
86. McBride B, Goldenberg SM, Murphy A, Wu S, Braschel M, Krüsi A, et al. Third parties (venue owners, managers, security, etc.) and access to occupational health and safety among sex workers in a Canadian setting: 2010–2016. Am J Public Health. 2019;109:792–8.
87. WHO. Consolidated guidelines on HIV prevention, diagnosis, treatment and care for key populations - 2016 update. Geneva: WHO; 2016.
88. UNAIDS. The gap report 2014 - sex workers. Geneva: UNAIDS; 2014.
89. Godwin J. Sex work and the law in Asia and the Pacific - laws, HIV and human rights in the context of sex work [internet]. Bangkok; 2012.
90. Amnesty International. Decision on state obligations to respect, protect, and fulfil the human rights of sex workers. Int Counc Decis; 2016. p. 9–10.
91. Deering KN, Montaner JS, Chettiar J, Jia J, Ogilvie G, Buchner C, et al. Successes and gaps in uptake of regular, voluntary HIV testing for hidden street- and off-street sex workers in Vancouver, Canada. AIDS Care. 2015;27(4):499–506.

Part III
Evidence-Based Services and Best Practices: Opportunities for Action

Chapter 10
Sex Worker-Led Provision of Services in New Zealand: Optimising Health and Safety in a Decriminalised Context

Gillian Abel and Catherine Healy

Introduction

Globally, sex work is regulated in very different ways. Repressive measures are used in some countries to criminalise sex workers or their activities or, in the case of other countries, to criminalise clients and other third parties. Then there are countries who either legalise or decriminalise sex work, and while these terms are sometimes used interchangeably, there are clear differences between these two models of regulation. Legalisation is a restrictive regulatory approach, which gives the State a means of controlling sex workers. Sex workers are able to work legally in licenced brothels, but should they work in unlicenced brothels, privately, or on the street, they are criminalised. This creates a two-tiered system. Full decriminalisation, on the other hand, encompasses the complete removal of the laws governing sex work and sex work-related offences, and the sex industry becomes subject to similar controls and regulations as those under which other businesses operate.

It has been repeatedly suggested that the best (and arguably only) way to optimise the health, safety, and human rights of sex workers is through decriminalisation [2–9]. There is evidence to support these suggestions [4, 6, 10–12], yet currently decriminalisation has only been realised in New Zealand (NZ) and one Australian state, New South Wales, and one Australian territory, the Northern Territory. Sex work was decriminalised in NZ in 2003, when the Prostitution Reform Act (PRA) was passed. The Act underwent many amendments in its journey through the Parliamentary process, and some of these amendments go against the spirit of full decriminalisation, particularly Section 19, which prohibits migrants on temporary

G. Abel (✉)
University of Otago, Christchurch, New Zealand
e-mail: Gillian.abel@otago.ac.nz

C. Healy
New Zealand Prostitutes Collective, Wellington, New Zealand
e-mail: info@nzpc.org.nz

© The Author(s) 2021
S. M. Goldenberg et al. (eds.), *Sex Work, Health, and Human Rights*,
https://doi.org/10.1007/978-3-030-64171-9_10

visas from doing sex work. Migrants on work visas may work in any other industry in New Zealand besides sex work, which suggests that even though sex work is ostensibly treated as work like any other through decriminalisation, in reality, this is not the case. This amendment was included at a late stage in the parliamentary process as a consequence of some politicians' argument that decriminalisation would position New Zealand as a likely destination for trafficking. The conflation of sex work and trafficking is a common phenomenon in contemporary times. Inflated statistics are used to advance the argument, but there is no robust research to support this [13, 14]. While some sections of the Act therefore need to be challenged to achieve full decriminalisation, it remains clear that most sex workers in NZ have benefitted from decriminalisation in terms of their health and safety [15], and, 17 years later, there are few voices in NZ who would argue for change back to restrictive or repressive regulatory measures.

There is one sex worker-led country-wide organisation in NZ, New Zealand Prostitutes Collective (NZPC), and this organisation was crucial to the achievement of decriminalisation in this country. Undoubtedly, one of the primary reasons for their success was the diversity of sex workers involved with the ability to network, engaging with people from different spheres (policy makers, Members of Parliament, Police, NGOs, academics, and other organisations or groups), to support and give critical mass to achieving their objective of decriminalisation [16]. NZPC developed the first draft of the Prostitution Reform Bill in collaboration with those in their network, which had a strong representation of Māori (the indigenous population), who constitute around 30% of the sex worker population[1] [17]. This ensured that a genuine engagement with sex workers most affected by hostile laws was influential in the development of the resultant policy. Wagenaar et al. have argued that such collaborative governance 'proceeds by "authentic dialogue"', which ultimately leads to more successful sex work policy ([18]: p. 263).

Similarly, it is important that sex workers' voices are the loudest in the development of services to meet their needs [19]. NZPC collaborates with specialist services to operate clinics out of their community bases, but they often need to refer sex workers to other agencies or support services, such as the police, Medical Officers of Health, and Work and Income New Zealand. This requires engaging with these services in an interagency approach to ensure that services delivered not only meet sex workers' needs, but that sex workers can have a trusting relationship with those delivering the service.

Collaboration and participation are thus important, not only to the success in achieving decriminalisation of sex work in NZ, but also to the health, safety, and human rights of sex workers. This chapter also reflects the long-standing collaborative relationship between the two authors. It brings together research and community evidence to provide a well-rounded picture of three initiatives, which are the result of successful collaboration:

---

[1] The 2013 NZ census reports that Māori make up around 15% of the NZ population. http://archive. stats.govt.nz/Census/2013-census/profile-and-summary-reports/quickstats-culture-identity/ethnic-groups-NZ.aspx. Māori are therefore over-represented in the sex worker population.

- Sex workers' access to police in reporting sexual assault
- Interagency collaboration when working with sex workers who have concerns about practices within certain brothels
- New sex workers' access to information on safe practices

Building Relationships with the Police: 'What to Do'

Criminal laws which target sex workers create a barrier to their health, safety, and right to protection [20]. Such laws increase the possibility of violence against sex workers, especially street-based sex workers [21–25]. A systematic review of the correlates of violence against sex workers showed that policing practices have a critical impact on sex workers' risk of violence [20]. Police are less motivated to protect sex workers against violence or threats of violence and are sometimes even the perpetrators of violence against sex workers [26]. Sex workers are less likely to report violent incidents, including sexual assault, to the police, because they fear possible arrest as a result of revealing that they are doing sex work [21, 27]. Police sometimes use excessive force, particularly on street-based sex workers, which decreases the likelihood of those workers reporting incidents [25]. Before sex work was decriminalised in NZ, sex workers were more likely to use their own informal networks to deal with the aftermath of violent experiences than report these to the police or other 'helping' professionals [28]. Many sex workers indicated that they did not believe that police would help, nor did they want to reveal to the police that they were sex workers [28].

Research done within 5 years of the enactment of the PRA showed a growing confidence in police, with many sex workers reporting that they could trust the process of reporting incidents to the police and following through on court proceedings [10, 12]. Fifty-seven percent of sex workers reported that police attitudes had improved following decriminalisation, and this was supported by qualitative evidence:

> But now for the last couple of years, the police have been really good, really onto it. So we've been having more patrol cars going down the street and then hangouts. So that's real good. Yeah, yeah, now they actually care. Before (law change) they just didn't care. You know, if a girl, if a worker gets raped or, you know, anything like that, there wasn't much, then there wasn't much they could do. But now that the law's changed, it's changed the whole thing. (Joyce,[2] Street and Private, Female) ([17]: p. 238)

However, there was still reticence by some sex workers to report adverse incidents, primarily because of perceptions of stigmatisation related to their occupation, plus they felt that they could not be guaranteed name suppression [17]. Armstrong interviewed street-based sex workers and police key informants 8 years after

---

[2]All names and other personal identifiers of individuals listed by a first name only have been changed to protect privacy and confidentiality.

decriminalisation, and found that the relationship between the two parties was continuing to improve: the imbalance in power had shifted somewhat; street-based sex workers were more proactive in reporting incidents to the police and there was better dialogue between them, with sex workers helping police in solving crimes committed against others [29].

There is, however, still room for improvement when it comes to encouraging more sex workers to trust police sufficiently to be able to approach them without reservation. The Network of Sex Work Projects (NSWP) have argued that radical changes are necessary to change sex workers' perceptions of police from persecutors to protectors [7]. They suggest a collaborative engagement between police and sex worker communities, and this is what has subsequently occurred in NZ.

> *The New Zealand Police and the NZPC are working collaboratively with other support agencies to ensure the well-being of sex workers. Our aim is to provide all victims of sexual assault with the best possible support services we can, and to work with the industry to make it as safe as possible for sex workers (Sam Hoyle, District Commander, Wellington, NZ Police) [30].*

The above quote illustrates the commitment of police to foster good relationships with sex workers; it is taken from the opening pages of a resource produced through a collaborative engagement between NZPC and the NZ Police. Scenario 1 gives a sex worker perspective on this engagement.

Scenario 1: 'What to Do'

Decriminalisation of sex work in NZ has enabled the relationship between sex workers and the police to be voluntary, allowing for trust to develop between both parties. The police can no longer arrest sex workers for sex work-related activities such as brothel keeping or soliciting and have no formal role in monitoring sex workers.

Nevertheless, NZPC is often called upon by sex workers to broker and support complaints to the police because some sex workers are anxious about experiencing negative attitudes or judgements from police about their work. Police are also aware of the need to create strong pathways for sex workers to approach police directly to report sexual assault. They recognise that there may be significant impediments for some sex workers to do so.

The police approached NZPC to discuss ways of overcoming barriers to sex workers reporting sexual violence to them. They asked how the police could better support sex workers who are victims of sexual violence. It was agreed the two organisations would work together to publish a *'Guide for Sex Workers who have experienced Sexual Assault'*, titled **'What to Do'** [30]. This was done in consultation with other service providers and stakeholders with an interest in addressing sexual violence.

'What to Do' was developed in partnership between NZPC and the New Zealand Police to inform sex workers of their options in relation to reporting sexual assault. The resource also signalled to sex workers that the police were

(continued)

there 'to provide all victims of sexual assault with the best possible support services, ... and to work with the industry to make it as safe as possible for sex workers' ([30]: p. 9).

New Zealand Police brought together officers and detectives from specialised units that deal with sexual violence, for training with NZPC. The topic of the training workshop was 'Sexual Assault', focusing on appropriate ways to work with sex workers. This encouraged empathy and understanding among police officers, and it fostered collaboration between the two agencies.

NZPC and the police are represented within the resource. The resource is promoted and is available on both the police website and the NZPC website. In illustrating the success of this initiative, we draw on an example of how this has played out for a sex worker, Moana, who was drugged during a booking. She called NZPC for support.

> I asked NZPC if they could help me ... The Police Officer met me at the police station lobby, which was great, I could bypass reception. The Police Officer was very reassuring regarding my concerns about having to go to court and about the person who had done this finding me, or finding out that I went to the Police.

There is growing confidence that sex workers' rights will be upheld in respectful ways when dealing with police.

> I went out to the place where the assault happened and picked her up. She'd never gone to the Police and was quite scared. We were in the Police station and I pulled out the booklet and the Police officer goes 'no that's alright we know about that resource, we're all aware of that resource and the process on working with sex workers (NZPC Community Liaison worker).

Engagement with the police is an ongoing process as individual police officers take up new portfolios and therefore come and go, with a resulting shift in culture. An institutional response is required, as opposed to one-off training programmes, and, to this end, NZPC and the police will continue with their engagement.

Working Collaboratively with Government

One of the purposes of the PRA is to promote the welfare and occupational health and safety of sex workers. As sex work is now a recognised occupation, sex workers should have the same employment rights as those engaged in any other occupation. The review of the PRA, however, has found that, although there have been improvements in the working conditions of brothel-based workers, some are still vulnerable to exploitative and coercive employment conditions [12].

Sex workers who work under a system of management, i.e. in a brothel or parlour, are seen as having a safer environment than sex workers who work privately or on the street, because of the close proximity of management and other sex workers [24, 31–34]. When sex work was still criminalised in NZ, brothels operated under the guise of massage parlours, where a fee was taken at the door for a massage and any extras were negotiated privately in the room between the sex worker and the client. Some massage parlour operators used manipulative management strategies to push sex workers into risky practices [35]. They did not encourage, and sometimes outrightly discouraged, the use of condoms. Participants in a study conducted in the late 1990s indicated that management would market particular services and sex workers were pressured to cooperate and provide such services [35]. Managers did not support sex workers when clients were abusive, and sex workers had few powers to refuse any particular client, even when they knew them on a personal level or had had a previous bad experience with them. This situation changed with the passing of the PRA. Under Section 17 of the PRA sex workers have the right of refusal to provide commercial sexual services, and consent can be withdrawn at any stage in the transaction. A survey carried out in Christchurch, NZ, in 1997, found that in the previous 12 months only 47% of indoor managed workers had been able to refuse a client, compared to 68% of sex workers surveyed 3 years after decriminalisation [10]. A number of sex workers have used the legal system when their right of refusal has been breached [36]. Safety has also been enhanced, with sex workers now able to negotiate what they will provide for clients' money, which reduces the chance of a client resorting to violence because of unmet expectations [17]. Reportedly, however, some people involved in managing sex workers and managing brothels are not actively promoting safe sex practices in their contact with clients, particularly when it comes to oral sex.

Under Section 8 of the PRA, brothel operators are required to adopt and promote safer sex practices within their establishments, by:

- Taking all reasonable steps to ensure that their workers and clients use appropriate protection in all services which carry a risk of acquiring or transmitting sexually transmitted infections (STIs).
- Ensuring that workers and clients are given health information and that this information is clearly displayed in brothels.
- Not implying that a medical examination of a sex worker means the sex worker is not infected with an STI.
- And taking all reasonable steps to minimise the risk of sex workers or clients acquiring or transmitting STIs.

Similarly, under Section 9 of the PRA, sex workers, and clients are also compelled to take all reasonable steps to ensure that they use adequate protection during penetrative and oral sex, and minimise the risk of acquiring or transmitting an STI. In addition, sex workers and clients are also required not to state or imply that because they have had a medical examination, they are not infected with an STI.

These sections of the PRA were added to the Prostitution Reform Bill during its progress through Parliament. NZPC are not supportive of these additions, as they see them as creating an environment where sex workers could be 'policed' in their condom use. They also create the possibility of clients laying false complaints against a sex worker if they hold a grudge. However, research done following the enactment of the PRA demonstrated that sex workers themselves were largely supportive of this part of the Act, as it made it easier for them to negotiate condom use with a client [10]. Several cases have gone to court where a client has removed their condom without the sex worker's consent (e.g.: [37, 38]), and most have resulted in the client being fined.

Under the PRA, Medical Officers of Health (MOH) are designated as inspectors of brothels. Interviews with Medical Officers of Health carried out shortly after decriminalisation found that most were happy to undertake this new addition to their role, maintaining a respectful distance and taking a largely 'hands-off' approach by only reacting to complaints [39]. Scenario 2 discusses, from a sex worker perspective, how NZPC and Medical Officers of Health engaged in developing a training programme to address concerns about disturbing practices in some brothels.

Scenario 2

In a decriminalised setting, sex work is acknowledged as labour, subject to the same health and safety protections as other occupations. Sex workers can access appropriate agencies directly to uphold their workplace rights. However, sex work remains a stigmatised occupation, and some sex workers can be reluctant to engage directly with government agencies when workplace conditions are not acceptable. Equally, government agencies without accurate understanding of sex work culture risk deterring engagement rather than encouraging it. As a peer-led organisation, NZPC can liaise with agencies and work collaboratively to promote best practice within the industry, as shown in the following examples:

When some brothel-based workers were unhappy with their work conditions, they approached NZPC for help. They were upset that brothel management was not adequately supportive of some safe sex practices, resulting in the sex workers experiencing difficult negotiations with clients about condom use and oral sex. Peers at NZPC talked with them about the various actions available, including engaging with the overarching health authority. NZPC then contacted the Medical Officers of Health, who are authorised to ensure health and safety requirements are adhered to in the context of sex work.

Working collaboratively, NZPC and MOH agreed not to identify the specific brothels, but rather to act broadly by engaging all the local brothels at an operator level. NZPC provided training for the MOH staff about sex work, brothel culture, and effective ways to engage with these operators. NZPC were able to review the draft of a letter sent to 15 brothel operators, and made sure that it was appropriate and effective. With this insider knowledge and input, all the brothel operators agreed to be visited by inspectors who observed onsite how safer sex was promoted within each brothel (policy, signage, information given to clients, availability of condoms, lube and other products, etc.). During this time brothel operators also contacted NZPC for assistance, providing a good opportunity for NZPC to remind operators of how to best support their workers' occupational safety and health.

(continued)

MOH found that most brothels actively advised clients about safe sex policy at the point of booking, provided information on their own websites, and trained sex workers to deal with clients who requested unsafe sex. Brothels that did not adequately promote best practices received follow-up for extra support.

This collaborative approach to compliance was effective because the sex worker lens provided guidance for best outcomes. This approach gently reminded all brothel operators of their obligations to health and safety requirements, and established functional relationships between health authorities and brothels. The expertise and inside knowledge of NZPC was integral to this outcome.

In a different jurisdiction, MOH sought advice from NZPC when contacting brothels about a recent increase in STI/syphilis cases. They had developed a plan of action, and they needed it reviewed with a sex worker lens before implementation. Adjustments to the drafted letter of information resulted in the removal of stigmatising language and showed a more nuanced understanding of roles and responsibilities of management with regard to supporting safe sex practices. Occupational health and safety is best supported by true collaboration and respectful relationships between sex workers and sex worker led organisations (NZPC), and government agencies.

Becoming a Sex Worker: 'Stepping Forward'

Getting information when starting sex work is vital for protecting sex workers' health and safety. Knowing how to negotiate with clients, how to deal with issues that come up with clients, and how to ensure safe sex, is particularly important, and this information should be provided by a peer support organisation. Prior to decriminalisation, although NZPC did provide printed and verbal information as well as a range of safer sex products to new sex workers, this was done in a fairly covert manner, as such provision could have been construed as aiding and abetting a crime. As brothel operators were working under the façade of massage parlours, they did not want any explicit links made between them and sex work-related activities. For this reason, management felt unable to be proactive in referring new sex workers to NZPC, nor did they want information on their premises, as it could put them at risk of a 5-year prison sentence for brothel keeping and/or procuring. A survey of 303 sex workers in Christchurch in 1997, prior to decriminalisation, found only 6% reported getting information and advice on sex work from NZPC when they started working [40]. Most advice was gleaned from co-workers or, for many (26%), nobody at all. Once sex work was decriminalised it became easier to display information on safe sex and to have condoms on brothel premises, as there was no longer a fear of prosecution on the grounds that this was evidence of brothel keeping [41]. Brothel operators are now also more likely to send new sex workers to NZPC to get the information they need to help keep themselves safe. In 2006, a mere 3 years after decriminalisation, a survey of 772 sex workers in NZ found that 44% reported that they had received information on starting sex work from NZPC, and the number getting no information at all was 18% [10].

After decriminalisation, NZPC also developed a booklet, 'Stepping Forward', which is aimed at new workers, giving them tips on how to stay safe, negotiate with a client, and care for themselves, as well as providing comprehensive information on sexual health [42]. This booklet is presented to new workers who come into NZPC, along with free condoms, dental dams, lube, and sponges. It would not have been possible to provide such information in this format before decriminalisation. Scenario 3 gives a sex worker perspective on how decriminalisation has facilitated appropriate information sharing with people considering taking up sex work.

Scenario 3: Becoming a Sex Worker
The New Zealand model decriminalises most sex work-related activities, giving sex workers more control over their working conditions. The model allows those considering sex work to seek practical information without fear of breaching any criminal law. There is a range of information sources available to those considering sex work, including the sex worker peer-led organisation NZPC, as well as New Zealand-based online platforms, and other sex workers. As one worker commented,

> I googled everything about sex work in New Zealand and I read the PRA [Prostitution Reform Act, 2003]. It made me a whole lot more comfortable when I was considering starting in the industry. I realised it was legal and I had rights. I was able to google agencies in my city to see if I would fit in and what sexual services would be expected of me.—Jill, Sex Worker

NZPC is frequently contacted by prospective and new workers for information on sex work, including information about the law, their rights, as well as practical information about safe ways to work, health advice, and so on. Decriminalisation facilitates a context where such peer-focused information may be given freely, directly promoting safe and healthy practices, reducing risk and minimising harm.

> In my first interview at a brothel, the manager told me about NZPC. I got a NZPC new worker pack and was encouraged to get sexual health checks and information from NZPC. There I found a tangible community. I just feel like NZPC is a place where...it's not just all victim. I felt really well supported by NZPC.—Mel, Sex Worker

At the heart of decriminalisation is the concept of consent. As one worker comments,

> The explicit consent, what the worker will and won't do is much clearer after decrim. I wouldn't have to commit to anything I didn't want to do.—Valentina, Sex worker

Decriminalisation means sex workers can choose to work in a range of settings—they may work independently or with other workers in small owner-operated venues, or meet and screen clients online or in public places such as

(continued)

known streets. They also may work in managed brothels. Such venues are also sources of information about sex work, in ways that would be difficult and illegal without decriminalisation.

When sex workers are hired, it is now possible for brothel operators to openly talk about sexual services that may be requested by clients and about which services the sex workers are prepared to provide. Furthermore, the brothel may keep this information and use it when clients make a booking with a particular request. This sets clear boundaries and reduces misunderstanding and unrealistic expectations.

> *It means that workers have the protection of clearly negotiating services and prices before agreeing to a booking, and that* [sex workers] *have the right to refuse or terminate services for whatever reason and have the backing of the law in that.*—Belle

Safety is often a key concern for prospective and new sex workers. A decriminalised environment means that these concerns can be addressed directly: workers can work with others, brothels can install security equipment, and difficult clients can be refused or ejected in the knowledge that the law supports these actions. Sex workers can also contact the police without fear of prosecution.

> *I think about safety all the time. I feel really fortunate to have several ways of vetting and sharing information here in New Zealand. We are so lucky here.*—Mel, Sex Worker

Conclusion

This chapter has discussed three initiatives: engagement with police to provide a better outcome for sex workers reporting sexual assault; engagement with Medical Officers of Health to enhance the workplace environment for brothel-based sex workers; and the provision of support to new sex workers to facilitate an informed and safer entry into sex work. None of these initiatives would have been possible in a criminalised context. Decriminalisation has provided NZPC with greater ability to engage with a variety of stakeholders, so that sex workers' voices are strongly present in all initiatives to improve their health, safety, and wellbeing. For an initiative to be effective, there needs to be a robust understanding of the population at whom that initiative is aimed [43]. Wherever possible, therefore, initiatives should be peer-led and, where appropriate, meaningful partnerships established.

Despite the many improvements to the health, safety, and wellbeing of NZ sex workers brought about via decriminalisation, it is acknowledged that these improvements do not benefit all sex workers. The PRA states that people who are not NZ citizens or residents, and who are in the country on tourist, temporary work, or student visas, may not do sex work. This results in a number of migrant sex workers working in a criminalised setting, who will continue to do so. Full decriminalisation provides a context where **all** sex workers can be self-managing and have their voices heard in the implementation of appropriate services. While full decriminalisation is some way off, it is important to continue to work towards this ideal.

References

1. O'Neill M, Pitcher J. Sex work, communities, and public policy in the UK. In: Ditmore M, Levy A, Willman A, editors. Sex work matters: exploring money, power and intimacy in the sex industry. London: Zed Books; 2010.
2. Abel G, Fitzgerald L, Healy C, Taylor A, editors. Taking the crime out of sex work: New Zealand sex workers' fight for decriminalisation. Bristol: Policy Press; 2010.
3. Beyrer C, Crago A, Bekker L, Butler J, Shannon K, Kerrigan D, et al. An action agenda for HIV and sex workers. Lancet. 2014;385(9964):287–301.
4. Donovan B, Harcourt C, Egger S, Fairley CK. Improving the health of sex workers in NSW: maintaining success. N S W Public Health Bull. 2010;21(4):74–7.
5. Harcourt C, Egger S, Donovan B. Sex work and the law. Sex Health. 2005;2:121–8.
6. Harcourt C, O'Connor J, Egger S, Fairley C, Wand H, Chen M, et al. The decriminalisation of prostitution is associated with better coverage of health promotion programs for sex workers. Aust N Z J Public Health. 2010;34(5):482–6.
7. NSWP. Good practice in sex worker-led HIV programming: global report. Edinburgh: Global Network of Sex Work Projects; 2014.
8. Sanders T, O'Neill M, Pitcher J. Prostitution: sex work, policy and politics. London: Sage; 2018.
9. Shannon K, Strathdee S, Goldenberg S, Duff P, Mwangi P, Rusakova M, et al. Global epidemiology of HIV among female sex workers: influence of structural determinants. Lancet. 2015;385:55–71.
10. Abel G, Fitzgerald L, Brunton C. The impact of the Prostitution Reform Act on the health and safety practices of sex workers: Report to the Prostitution Law Review Committee. Christchurch: University of Otago; 2007.
11. Armstrong L. Screening clients in a decriminalised street-based sex industry: insights into the experiences of New Zealand sex workers. Aust N Z J Criminol. 2014;7(2):207–22.
12. Prostitution Law Review Committee. Report of the Prostitution Law Review Committee on the operation of the Prostitution Reform Act 2003. Ministry of Justice: Wellington; 2008.
13. Agustín L. Sex at the margins: migration, labour markets and the rescue industry. London: Zed Books; 2007.
14. Showden C, Majic S, editors. Negotiating sex work: unintended consequences of policy and activism. Minneapolis: University of Minnesota Press; 2014.
15. Abel G. Decriminalisation and social justice: a public health perspective on sex work. In: Fitzgerald S, McGarry K, editors. Realising justice for sex workers: an agenda for change. London: Rowman & Littlefield; 2018. p. 123–40.
16. Healy C, Bennachie C, Reed A. History of New Zealand prostitutes' collective. In: Abel G, Fitzgerald L, Healy C, Taylor A, editors. Taking the crime out of sex work: New Zealand sex workers' fight for decriminalisation. Bristol: Policy Press; 2010.
17. Abel G. Decriminalisation: a harm minimisation and human rights approach to regulating sex work. PhD Thesis, University of Otago, Christchurch; 2010.
18. Wagenaar H, Amesberger H, Altink S. Designing Prostitution Policy: intention and reality in regulating the sex trade. Bristol: Policy Press; 2017.
19. Pitcher J. Support services for women working in the sex industry. In: Campbell R, O'Neill M, editors. Sex work now. Cullompton, Devon: Willan; 2006. p. 235–62.
20. Deering A, Amin A, Shoveller J, Nesbitt A, Garcia-Moreno C, Duff P, et al. A systematic review of the correlates of violence against sex workers. Am J Public Health. 2014;104(5):e42–54.

21. Kinnell H. Violence and sex work in Britain. Cullompton, Devon: Willan; 2008.
22. Krusi A, Pacey K, Bird L, Taylor C, Chettiar J, Allan S, et al. Criminalisation of clients: reproducing vulnerabilities for violence and poor health among street-based sex workers in Canada - a qualitative study. BMJ Open. 2014;4:e005191.
23. Rhodes T, Simic M, Baros S, Platt L, Zikic B. Police violence and sexual risk among female and transvestite sex workers in Serbia: qualitative study. Br Med J. 2008;337:a811.
24. Sanders T, Campbell R. Designing out vulnerability, building in respect: violence, safety and sex work policy. Br J Sociol. 2007;58(1):1–19.
25. Shannon K, Kerr T, Strathdee S, Shoveller J, Montaner J, Tyndall M. Prevalence and structural correlates of gender based violence among a prospective cohort of female sex workers. Br Med J. 2009;339(113):b2939.
26. Shannon K, Csete J. Violence, condom negotiation, and HIV/STI risk among sex workers. J Am Med Assoc. 2010;304(5):573–4.
27. Kinnell H. Murder made easy: the final solution to prostitution? In: Campbell R, O'Neill M, editors. Sex work now. Cullompton, Devon: Willan; 2006. p. 141–68.
28. Plumridge E, Abel G. Services and information utilised by female sex workers for sexual and physical safety. N Z Med J. 2000;113(1117):370–2.
29. Armstrong L. From law enforcement to protection? Interactions between sex workers and police in a decriminalized street-based sex industry. Br J Criminol. 2017;57(3):570–88.
30. NZPC, New Zealand Police. What to do: a guide for sex workers who have experienced sexual assault. 2018. Available from: http://www.nzpc.org.nz/pdfs/WHAT-TO-DO-A-guide-for-sex-workers-who-have-experienced-sexual-assault.pdf.
31. Pyett P, Warr D. Women at risk in sex work: strategies for survival. J Sociol. 1999;35(2):183–97.
32. Pyett P, Warr D. Vulnerability on the streets: female sex workers and HIV risk. AIDS Care. 1997;9(5):539–47.
33. Perkins R, Lovejoy F. Call girls: private sex workers in Australia. Crawley: University of Western Australia Press; 2007.
34. Brents B, Hausbeck K. Violence and legalized brothel prostitution in Nevada: examining safety, risk, and prostitution policy. J Interpers Violence. 2005;20(3):270–95.
35. Plumridge L. Rhetoric, reality and risk outcomes in sex work. Health Risk Soc. 2001;3(2):199–217.
36. Abel G, Healy C, Sweetman B. Really working: sex workers rights in a decriminalised environment. In: Maginn P, Cooper E, Zebracki M, editors. Navigating sex work - gender, justice and policy in the 21st century. London: Palgrave Macmillan; 2021.
37. Galuszka J. Brothel boss wanted police involved after employee said she was raped. Stuff; 2019. Available from: https://www.stuff.co.nz/national/crime/111397478/brothel-boss-wanted-police-involved-after-employee-said-she-was-raped.
38. Shadwell T. Man charged with failing to use condom with prostitute. The Dominion Post; 2015. Available from: https://www.stuff.co.nz/national/crime/67464897/.
39. Brunton C. Becoming inspectors of brothels: public health authorities' experience of implementing the Prostitution Reform Act. In: Abel G, Fitzgerald L, Healy C, Taylor A, editors. Taking the crime out of sex work: New Zealand sex workers' fight for decriminalisation. Bristol: Policy Press; 2010. p. 173–95.
40. Plumridge E, Abel G. Safer sex in the Christchurch sex industry. Study 2: Survey of Christchurch sex workers. Christchurch: Christchurch School of Medicine and Health Sciences, University of Otago; 2000.
41. Mossman E. Brothel operators' and support agencies' experiences of decriminalisation. In: Abel G, Fitzgerald L, Healy C, Taylor A, editors. Taking the crime out of sex work: New Zealand sex workers' fight for decriminalisation. Bristol: Policy Press; 2010.
42. New Zealand Prostitutes Collective. NZPC new workers' kit - stepping forward. Wellington, NZ: New Zealand Prostitutes Collective; n.d.
43. Hashagen S. Models of community engagement. Glasgow: Scottish Community Development Centre; 2002.

Chapter 11
Best Practices and Challenges to Sex Worker Community Empowerment and Mobilisation Strategies to Promote Health and Human Rights

Cynthia Navarrete Gil, Manjula Ramaiah, Andrea Mantsios, Clare Barrington, and Deanna Kerrigan

Community Empowerment Among Sex Workers: Principles and Approach

Community empowerment is an approach where sex workers come together to generate solidarity and mobilise their collective power to address structural barriers to their health and human rights [1]. In this process, sex worker communities seek allies—including governmental and non-governmental groups—as well as challenge institutions and individuals who inhibit progress towards social and policy change [1]. Community empowerment is a social process or movement. It is also a crucial component of effective planning, implementation, and monitoring of rights-based programming to address the health and human rights of sex workers [2]. Components of a comprehensive, community empowerment approach in the con-

C. Navarrete Gil
APROASE, México City, Mexico
e-mail: aproase@gmail.com

M. Ramaiah
Ashodaya Samithi, Mysore, India
e-mail: ramaiah.manjula008@gmail.com

A. Mantsios
Public Health Innovation & Action, New York, NY, USA
e-mail: amantsios@phiaconsulting.org

C. Barrington
Department of Health Behavior, Gillings School of Global Public Health, University of North Carolina, Chapel Hill, NC, USA
e-mail: cbarring@email.unc.edu

D. Kerrigan (✉)
Department of Prevention and Community Health, Milken Institute School of Public Health, George Washington University, Washington, DC, USA
e-mail: dkerrigan@email.gwu.edu

© The Author(s) 2021
S. M. Goldenberg et al. (eds.), *Sex Work, Health, and Human Rights*,
https://doi.org/10.1007/978-3-030-64171-9_11

text of HIV prevention may include sex worker-led outreach and peer education and navigation; community-led drop-in-centres; community mobilisation and sex worker advocacy to promote socio-economic rights and opportunities; access to legal services and support; and improved sexual and reproductive health services tailored to the needs of sex workers.

Community empowerment approaches recognise sex work as work and as a profession. They aim to ensure the labour and human rights of sex workers, including their right to health, rather than trying to rescue or rehabilitate them [3]. Organising into sex worker-led groups is an effective strategy for sex workers to collectively challenge structural barriers such as stigma, discrimination, violence, and other forms of social inequality such as gender-related inequalities [4, 5].

Legal and policy environments often limit the reach and potential impact of sex worker groups. For example, structural constraints such as criminalisation may restrict the ability of sex workers to organise, thus challenging community empowerment efforts [6]. Despite these barriers, sex worker groups have formed and been sustained in multiple geographic regions to address the broader needs of the community. There are well-documented examples of such groups in South Asia [7–13], where community empowerment efforts among sex workers have received comparatively substantial resource investments as part of large-scale targeted HIV prevention efforts from external donors. This has also been the case in Latin America and the Caribbean [14–16]. Implementation and evaluation of community empowerment approaches among sex workers in other regions, such as sub-Saharan Africa, have been less common but are slowly increasing in places like South Africa, Kenya, and Tanzania [17].

Impact of Community Empowerment Among Sex Workers on HIV and Health Outcomes

Based on the evidence and outcomes from earlier programmes from South Asia, community empowerment is recognised as a best practice effectively addressing the health and human rights of sex workers [5, 9, 10, 18], and was acknowledged as a critical component for programming by the Joint United Nations Programme on HIV/AIDS investment framework [19]. In 2013, guidance on implementing sex worker-led, rights-based programming aimed at empowering sex workers was provided in the World Health Organization (WHO)-led, multi-agency collaborative document, and tool entitled "Implementing Comprehensive HIV/STI Programmes with Sex Workers: Practical Approaches from Collaborative Interventions", the document is also known as the Sex Worker Implementation Tool (SWIT) [3].

Two years later, the Global Network of Sex Work Projects (NSWP) conducted a case study to measure the impact of the SWIT and found that sex worker-led groups around the world were using this guidance as they successfully implemented rights-based programming, ramped up advocacy efforts, and held trainings to build capacity among other sex worker groups [2]. NSWP has committed to supporting global and regional sex worker networks in building capacity at regional, national, and local levels to advocate for rolling out the SWIT, given what a powerful tool it has proved to be for sex worker organisation and mobilisation across settings.

Given the scientific evidence supporting its impact, community empowerment has increasingly gained recognition as a key approach for addressing HIV among sex workers [6, 20]. A systematic review and meta-analysis of the effectiveness of community empowerment approaches among female sex workers found that these programmes were associated with a 32% reduction in HIV infection, significantly decreased odds of sexually transmitted infections (STI), and about a three-fold increase in the odds of consistent condom use between female sex workers and their clients across geographic settings [1]. The most well-known examples of community empowerment approaches to HIV prevention come from India, starting with the Durbar Mahila Samanwaya Committee. This organisation, begun as part of the Sonagachi Project [7], is a community-driven initiative that achieved significant increases in consistent condom use and reductions in HIV prevalence among brothel-based female sex workers in Kolkata [21–23].

The Avahan India AIDS Initiative [24], building on the experiences of Sonagachi, developed and implemented a multi-level intervention package that included peer-mediated approaches as well as STI services to address structural and environmental barriers to HIV prevention among sex workers across several states in India. The Avahan programme also achieved significant increases in consistent condom use between sex workers and their partners, and decreases in the prevalence of STI among female sex workers exposed to the programme [11, 25, 26].

In the Dominican Republic, two similar efforts including *Compromiso Colectivo* (Collective Commitment) and later *Abriendo Puertas* (Opening Doors), included community empowerment approaches, and were successful in improving consistent condom use as well as HIV care engagement and antiretroviral therapy (ART) adherence [16, 27–29]. Additionally, in Brazil, Project *Encontros* (Coming Together) used clinical and social intervention strategies, including peer education and community outreach, to reduce HIV/STI rates and encourage adoption of consistent condom use among sex workers. Among women in the *Encontros* programme, decreased unprotected sex was associated with increased social cohesion and participation in social networks [14]. In sub-Saharan Africa, fewer examples have been documented and are notably absent from peer-reviewed scientific literature. Project *Shikamana* (Let's Stick Together) in Iringa, Tanzania is one such example, however. Project *Shikamana* is a randomised controlled trial of a community-driven combination prevention model, which significantly reduced HIV incidence and improved HIV care and treatment outcomes among female sex workers living with HIV [30–32]. Additional examples from the practice-based literature include the work of Sisonke in South Africa and Bar Hostess Empowerment and Support Programme in Kenya, where sex worker groups have been formed and sustained over a number of years and have mobilised to address both HIV and other health and human rights concerns such as gender-based violence [17].

While more limited research has been conducted on the impact of community empowerment approaches among male and transgender sex workers, promising community-led models have been established. One of these is HOYMAS (*Health Options for Young Men on HIV/AIDS/STI*), a male sex worker-led organisation in Kenya [33]. HOYMAS has worked to respond to the unique vulnerabilities of male sex workers in their settings and sought to help inform models of tailored HIV prevention services elsewhere [33, 34]. Another example, *Sex workers IN Group* (SWING), is a Thai organisation working within male and transgender sex worker communities driven by the principles of community ownership and community representation [35]. SWING focuses on empowerment through education, aiming to improve quality of life for its members and to enhance their abilities to participate in local and national sex worker movements as peer leaders. South Africa's Sex Workers Education & Advocacy Taskforce (SWEAT), co-founded by a male sex worker and committed to working with all adult sex workers, focuses on community development and engaging sex workers in issues related to health and legal reform [24]. SWEAT's work includes the launching of the above mentioned Sisonke, a sex worker movement to unite sex workers, improve living and working conditions of sex workers, and fight for equal access to rights [36].

Beyond HIV, community empowerment approaches have an important role in addressing violence, safe work environments, and economic stability for sex workers. Community-driven, multi-level interventions among female sex workers have successfully reduced their risk for HIV and violence in India [37–39]. These interventions, implemented as part of the Avahan initiative, have responded to female sex workers' risks for intimate partner violence as well as from clients and police. Grounded in the concepts of collectivisation and the development of critical thinking and dialogue, these interventions included components such as trainings led by human rights lawyers educating sex workers on their rights and helping them bring perpetrators to justice. These programmes focus on shifting norms around the acceptability of violence, while challenging gender roles and encouraging new relationship models based on gender equity and respect [13, 38].

Community-led economic empowerment strategies, including co-operative banking and savings and loan mechanisms for female sex workers, have increased financial security and improved social and economic outcomes. They have also contributed to reducing sexual risk behaviours. The co-operative bank of the aforementioned Durbar intervention, the Usha Multi-purpose Co-operative Society, improved economic status among programme participants by increasing savings and reducing the economic vulnerability that can affect the capacity of sex workers to negotiate condom use with clients [4, 5, 40]. Pragati, another multi-component intervention among sex workers in India, combined a co-operative bank structure that provided a savings and credit mechanism with community mobilisation and peer-based HIV prevention activities [41]. The programme significantly decreased incidence of STI, increased reported condom use at last paid sex [42], and documented over 3000 sex workers joining as shareholders of the co-operative bank, with more than half of them opening savings accounts [41]. In Iringa, Tanzania, female sex workers who participated in community savings groups were found to have nearly two times greater odds of consistent condom use with new clients, compared to those who did not participate in such groups [43]. These examples highlight the important role co-operative banks and savings groups can play in reducing sexual risk behaviours and underscore the importance of comprehensive community-led interventions to address financial insecurity among sex workers.

The body of literature on community empowerment approaches for addressing HIV and other health outcomes among sex workers illustrates the effectiveness of utilising these strategies to effectively address the social and structural vulnerabilities facing sex workers. This evidence has generated calls for additional work to gather evidence on this strategy's potential impact on other aspects of the health and human rights of sex workers. For example, NSWP has specifically identified critical gaps in the literature on community empowerment approaches, including its effectiveness as a strategy for addressing economic vulnerability and promoting financial security of sex workers [44].

The two case studies detailed below highlight both best practices and challenges of community empowerment efforts led by sex workers in two distinct sociopolitical and cultural contexts: India and Mexico. The studies offer an in-depth look at strategies designed and implemented by sex worker groups to address human rights violations, advocate for health, and respond to punitive legal environments. By examining these dynamic processes, we explore existing successes as well as continued gaps in achieving sustained progress towards upholding the health and human rights of sex workers across different settings. The case studies were developed by sex worker leaders of local organisations in each of these settings. They reflect first-hand perspectives and focus on the lived experiences, realities, and collective responses among sex workers.

Mobilising the Sex Worker Community in Mysore, India: *Ashodaya Samithi* Case Study

Our case study describes our process of community empowerment in response to the HIV epidemic as well as other challenges that we face as sex workers in our environment. This story begins in 2004, when a technical team of public health experts and researchers from the University of Manitoba visited Mysore, India—a bustling tourist destination with a vibrant sex work industry—to design and implement an HIV prevention programme with sex workers as part of the Avahan India AIDS Initiative. At that time, sex workers in Mysore generally operated from the streets and faced many day-to-day challenges: police raids, extortion on the part of police, and violence, from police, pimps, and boyfriends, among others. We were initially cautious of the technical team as it was difficult for us to trust outsiders, given all of the stigma, discrimination, and abuse we were exposed to. However, the technical team spent time with us and engaged in conversations about our lives and our well-being. They also provided unconditional crisis support, including when our fellow sex worker sisters were detained by police during a raid or when we were refused health care at a government facility. This combination of taking the time to get to know us along with advocating for and supporting us, facilitated a process of trust and collaboration grounded in our interests. This created a foundation for further sex worker organising and mobilisation around our rights and needs.

Over time, sex workers from our community started meeting in small groups, identifying themselves around their shared profession, problems, concerns, and life experiences. Through these meetings and what became daily conversations with the technical team, we were encouraged to think about our lives, dreams, and aspirations, and we began to realise that we were not alone. Through these dialogues, sex workers in Mysore began to understand sex work as work and not something that we needed to be ashamed of, which was a new and empowering concept for many of the women in our community.

Several sex workers joined the technical team as volunteers and were asked to provide insights into the community's needs. This process was critical to garnering community interest and identifying a rallying point for our sustained community mobilisation. The sex workers identified three priorities for our community: the first was addressing police violence, as sex workers were experiencing serious and regularly occurring violence from the police. The second was the establishment of safe spaces—since most sex workers operated from the streets at that time, they had nowhere to sleep, rest, or freshen up. We spent most of our free time in parks and on the street, and the local thugs and police would take our money, harass, and rape us. The third was access to health services; we lacked a clinic for sex workers where we could access respectful, quality services at accessible hours.

The sex workers who volunteered with the technical team started going to the field, talking to their friends about the problems they were facing, and, once they opened, began bringing them to the safe space and the clinic. These were critical steps in mobilising the community. These steps marked the beginning of our organisation, Ashodaya Samithi (Dawn of Hope), as sex workers in Mysore began to come together. Through that process, mutual trust and awareness were generated among the community members who were ready to listen, learn, and implement collective actions related to working towards better health for sex workers. As a result, Ashodaya Samithi was registered as a sex worker-led organisation, one that is by, for, and comprised of sex workers.

The governing body of Ashodaya Samithi consists of representatives from all three subpopulations of sex workers: female, male, and transgender sex workers. From our inception, we realised that our sex work circuits (the client base of these three subpopulations) overlapped. This is why there has always been a strong bond and mutual understanding and support among the female, male, and transgender sex worker community in Mysore. Hence, when we came together to form our own organisation, we decided that it would comprise female, male, and transgender sex workers. However, over the years we realised that, although we have some issues in common, there are many other challenges and issues specific to male and transgender sex workers. The male and transgender sex workers formed their own collective called Adasha, which functions under the broad umbrella of Ashodaya. While we address most sex workers' issues as a unit, Adasha takes up issues specific to male and transgender sex workers.

Ashodaya Samithi leadership came to understand that community mobilisation is an ongoing process and that social cohesion is key to sustaining this process. Over the years, as women's circumstances changed, so did our needs. From the early demand for a safe space to rest during the day, the needs shifted to include wanting to provide our children with a good education, to build our own houses, and to save money for the future. Ashodaya Samithi was committed to helping facilitate solutions to each of these demands. We partnered with the Women and Child Welfare Department (WCD) of the Government of Karnataka to enrol sex workers' children in boarding schools, free of cost. Our organisation has also led the process of registering and issuing national identity documents for sex workers, which are essential for accessing social benefits.

We have also supported the establishment of a co-operative society to address the financial needs of our community. The co-operative society was set up with support from Ashodaya Samithi and was registered as an independent entity in November 2013. It is run and managed by an independent, 11-member board of directors who are all sex workers. The co-operative society provides low-interest loans and flexible payment schedules. This provides sex workers with a reliable place to save their money, enabling them to plan for the future. The savings account holders are also shareholders in the co-operative and benefit from the dividend payments made out of the co-operative's profits.

While these were some of the immediate needs that brought the sex worker community together in Mysore, other hard-hitting realities continued to keep the community tight-knit and working together. The first Integrated Behavioural and Biological Assessment (IBBA), conducted in August–September 2004, revealed 26% HIV prevalence among female sex workers in Mysore city. The realisation that one in four sex workers was living with HIV created a sense of alarm. Understanding that one person alone cannot control the spread of HIV forced the community to think critically about possible solutions we could embark on together.

Sex workers started holding community meetings to speak about HIV as an issue affecting their community and families. The discussions focused on finding ways to protect all sex workers from HIV infection. This process led us to reach the one-point agenda of "No Condom. No Sex". We began spreading the "No Condom. No Sex" message through street plays and other community events. This message became a community norm and all sex workers in the community were urged to follow it. There was general recognition that there were problems common to all that could only be addressed if we confronted them together.

The initial challenges that inspired community mobilisation of sex workers in Mysore included police violence and raids, stigma and discrimination, and violence and exploitation. We were constantly harassed and abused by police, sexually, physically, and verbally, and we were forced to pay fines and to provide sex without being paid. Stigma and discrimination came in many forms, including from doctors and nurses at hospitals and clinics who treated us poorly. Sex workers were required to get an HIV test before receiving any other clinical examination. In some cases, this resulted in their deaths, as staff refused to provide emergency treatment without first seeing a patient's HIV test result.

Female sex workers also experienced violence and exploitation from various perpetrators including boyfriends, partners, "pimps", and thugs on the street. Female sex workers, closely controlled by boyfriends and "pimps", experienced violence in different forms. We often had to give these men a portion of our daily income, and they would prevent us from partaking in any activity that would compromise our earnings. Many sex workers struggled with low self-esteem and lack of personal and collective agency and empowerment. Reflecting the pervasive nature of stigma surrounding sex work, we were scared of expressing our problems to others and worried that our families and friends would discover we were sex workers and disown us.

To address these challenges and build on our foundation of empowerment, sex workers continued to work together to affect change at multiple levels including the following:

Self-respect and self-esteem: First with the technical team and then within the sex worker community, we worked to create authentic and critical dialogue around the issues of who we are and what we think about ourselves. This process helped us to build self-esteem and believe that our work was of no less worth than other work.

Crisis response system and team: Building on the unconditional, 24/7 crisis support that the technical team offered in response to police incidents or episodes of violence, we created our own crisis response team, providing around-the-clock crisis support to our community members. Our peer first responders in different areas can be mobilised to respond to violence and other crises. We have also created a system of "crisis mitigation", where we recognise potential threats and work to neutralise the threat before it creates a problem.

Multi-level advocacy: Once we had become organised, we undertook advocacy at various levels. Teams of sex workers approached the local police constable, shopkeepers, and healthcare providers to sensitise them about who we are and our needs and struggles as sex workers. We started working in partnership with the police department to organise trainings about how to create enabling environments to promote the health and well-being of sex workers.

Healthcare navigators: Stigma and discrimination inflicted by doctors and nurses was a historical and ongoing problem for female sex workers in Mysore so we trained sex worker healthcare navigators to work in healthcare settings and form working relationships with the providers to improve access and quality of care. These healthcare peer navigators served as a bridge between the healthcare providers and the community to ensure access to respectful services.

Boyfriends' Club: The Boyfriends' Club was an initiative to engage and educate our intimate partners on the challenges facing sex workers, including violence, harassment over money, and negotiation of safe sex behaviours. Boyfriends/husbands and other regular partners were identified as major perpetrators of violence, and a collective roadblock for women wishing to participate in our programmes. These men strongly influenced members' decision-making around condom and contraceptive use. It became clear that we needed to work with them. Our work with partners helped to neutralise some of the barriers they had presented and enabled women to become part of our larger network of people who could respond to crises among sex workers.

The Integrated Behavioural and Biological Assessment (IBBA), carried out in 2004, provided baseline data on HIV-related outcomes among female sex workers in Mysore city prior to the start of Ashodaya Samithi's concerted intervention efforts. In 2006, another IBBA measured the same indicators after the implementation of Ashodaya activities in the sex worker community. This allowed for pre- and post-assessments, as shown in Table 11.1 [8]. All STI measures declined significantly during this period, and condom use at last sex increased significantly with all different partner types. HIV prevalence remained stable over this period (26% and 24%). However, a detuned assay (a testing method designed for the purpose of HIV incidence estimation) suggested a decline in recent HIV infections during this time [8].

Indicating the sustained effect of this earlier impact over time, the DIFFER Study (Diagonal Intervention to Fast-Forward and Enhance Reproductive Health), conducted between 2011 and 2016, documented continued improvements in sex workers' condom use and STI outcomes.

Ashodaya Samithi has identified several goals and next steps for our future community-led action. We have set up a community-led academy (Ashodaya Academy), through which we provide hand-holding support to other community-based organisations engaged in the process of successfully working with sex workers to address their health challenges. We have supported organisations in the sub-Saharan Africa and Asia-Pacific regions, including providing technical expertise in setting up the Sex Workers Academy of Africa (SWAA) in collaboration with another sex worker-led organisation, VAMP from India and NSWP. Ashodaya aims to further disseminate our experiences and the lessons we have learned to help facilitate more community-led responses in other settings. Ashodaya also aims to branch out from just HIV prevention services into awareness, prevention, detection, care, and support regarding other diseases, including tuberculosis.

Table 11.1 Pre-post Ashodaya Samithi implementation changes in HIV-related indicators [8]

	IBBA, 2004 (Baseline, $n = 429$) (%)	IBBA, 2006 (Follow-up, $n = 425$) (%)
HIV prevalence	26	24
Syphilis infection	25	12
Trichomonas	33	14
Gonorrhoea	5	2
Chlamydia	11	5
Condom use with occasional clients	65	90
Condom use with repeat clients	53	66
Condom use with regular partners	7	30

While still integrating sexual and reproductive health and rights (SRHR) initiatives into its existing service provision, the organisation further aims to expand SRHR initiatives on a larger scale to create a more holistic approach to health. Resource constraints have made it more challenging for Ashodaya Samithi to operate, particularly since the end of the Avahan initiative, but we continue to work to mobilise resources from different sources to sustain initiatives responding to the needs and interests of the sex worker community.

Addressing Institutional Violence and Punitive Laws in Mexico: APROASE Case Study

Established in Mexico City in 1984, APROASE *(Asociación en Pro Apoyo a Servidores)* was the first civil organisation formed and led by sex workers, with the mission of advocating for and defending the health, labour, and human rights of sex workers. We were legally recognised in 1997 and opened a sex worker friendly health clinic offering HIV testing, medical care for STI, gynaecological exams, and reproductive health services.

While still mostly providing services to sex workers, in an effort to reduce stigma and generate more resources, we expanded our clinic in 2004 to serve the general public. Sex workers who were members of APROASE received medical services free of charge. Other sex workers who were not APROASE members were granted a subsidy from 50% to 100%, depending on their economic situation. Those who were not sex workers could access clinic services by paying in full. These fees covered the expenses of those who could not cover their medical care at the time. Many of the treatments and consultations were subsidised by federal and state government financing projects.

In addition to operating the clinic, we facilitated trainings for peer educators on HIV/STI prevention and crime in the workplace and stimulated the exchange of lessons learned within the sex worker community. With financial support from the Mexican government, we developed a model for effective partnership between civil society organisations and the government to promote the health of key populations and the community.

In addition to providing health services, for over two decades we have struggled to gain recognition of sex work as a profession and to guarantee the human and labour rights of sex workers; concepts that are central to the effectiveness and sustainability of community empowerment efforts. One of the main issues APROASE addresses is clarifying the distinction between sex work and human trafficking. This distinction has been complicated by international protocols, laws, and agreements conflating the two. As a result of this conflation, in many settings (including Mexico), sex workers are barred from their constitutional rights related to labour and health, and are excluded from legal protection and the freedom to self-organise. Our case study highlights how the misinterpretation and manipulation of laws related to human trafficking ultimately led to the closure of our community-based clinic, and essentially forced our organisation to cease our community-led health and mobilisation efforts.

In 2000, the United Nations issued the "Protocol to Prevent, Suppress and Punish Trafficking in Persons, Especially Women and Children" [45]. Known as the "Palermo Protocol", it is intended to prevent and combat trafficking of persons, to protect and help trafficking victims, and to promote cooperation among the States that are part of it. Mexico signed the Palermo Protocol in 2000, and in 2007 enacted the Mexican Law to Prevent and Punish Trafficking in Persons. Article 10 of this law defined trafficking in persons as "any act or intentional omission of one or several persons to capture, engage, transport, transfer, retain, deliver, receive, or accommodate one or more persons for the purpose of exploitation" [46].

The law did not distinguish between sex work and trafficking, nor did it mention coercion or its opposite—willingness to engage freely in organising and contracting with third parties to guarantee the security of sex workers in their places of work. As a consequence of this poorly defined law, sex workers in Mexico were denied constitutional rights as workers, and sex worker leaders were subject to unjust application of legislation related to human trafficking.

In 2012, the General Law to Prevent, Sanction, and Eradicate Crimes Related to Trafficking in Persons was published in Mexico, which significantly changed the country's definition of human trafficking [47]. Under the earlier law and within the Palermo Protocol, "acts", "means", and "purpose" are defined as the three elements of human trafficking. The new law passed in 2012, however, eliminates the "means" and only considers "acts" and "purpose" as the key elements of trafficking in persons [48]. By removing the means, trafficking becomes one of many forms of exploitation. The definition of trafficking in Article 10 of this 2012 Mexican law includes "prostitution" and other forms of sexual exploitation among the categories it identifies as human trafficking.

As a result of these laws conflating sex work and trafficking, venues where sex workers are found, such as bars, have closed following constant raids to rescue victims of human trafficking and defendants of sexual exploitation. This has compelled sex workers from those establishments to work in the streets, where they lack social organisation and security measures to protect them from violence and extortion.

While sex work is not a crime in Mexico, it is not officially recognised as an occupation, either. Another civil society organisation, called *Brigada Callejera en Apoyo a la Mujer "Elisa Martínez"* (Street Brigade in Support of Women "Elisa Martinez"), advocates for the human, civil, and labour rights of sex workers. They effectively negotiated with authorities in Mexico City to establish a system of credentials for sex workers, providing them with some formal recognition as workers' protections to compensate for their lack of legal protection. This negotiation is a great example of innovation and achievement in the face of a very challenging and ambiguous legal context. Unfortunately, it remains the exception rather than norm with regard to sex worker mobilisation in Mexico.

Despite the important work of the *Brigada Callejera*, the lack of formal recognition of sex work as work facilitates ongoing institutional violence against sex workers because they are not protected as workers, by the constitution or any other legislation. One example of the unjust application of the trafficking law is the case of our founding director, Alejandra Gil. She was arrested by Mexican law enforcement authorities in March 2014 and accused of engaging in human trafficking activities based on the very laws and legal interpretations that conflate sex work with trafficking. She is currently serving a 15-year prison sentence.

Part of APROASE's work is to protect the rights of sex workers. Before Mexico's anti-trafficking law was signed into law in 2007, Alejandra and other sex workers developed and signed an agreement with neighbours and authorities in the Sullivan neighbourhood of Mexico City where they worked. In it, they defined the roles and responsibilities of all parties involved. It included clauses prohibiting violence towards sex workers by clients, substance use in the workplace, and participation of anyone under 18 in sex work. These measures, however, were ultimately trumped by the misapplication of the subsequent trafficking legislation and its use to justify the accusations lodged against Alejandra. Local law includes coercion as a condition for considering someone to be involved in the trafficking of persons, however, coercion was not proven in her case nor was evidence to the contrary taken into account in the trial. The prosecution's conflation of sex work and human trafficking, along with the lack of a clear definition of coercion in the law, allowed the evidence to be ignored. These factors led to the court failing to recognise sex work as work and to the reinforcement of sex workers' stigmatised status.

The arrest of APROASE Director Alejandra Gil was rife with stigma and discrimination as the media manipulated the case as a triumph of the Mexican authorities over human trafficking. Television and newspaper coverage showed images of Alejandra's face. Without any consideration of the possibility of her innocence, the press declared her guilty before she had even been sentenced, further violating the rights to which she was denied access, and further illustrating the social injustice experienced by sex workers as a result of punitive laws and a context of stigma and discrimination.

Following Alejandra's arrest, APROASE became the victim of media violence, extortion, police harassment, and death threats. The impact of these events on the organisation has been far-reaching. We have closed APROASE and no longer have a safe space to meet or conduct workshops. The situation overall has been devastating and stigmatising, to the point where no lawyer wants to take on the case for fear of being linked to human trafficking.

Alejandra's case is emblematic of the highly punitive legal environment that conflates sex work and trafficking in Mexico, and how this directly impacts the ability of sex workers to meaningfully and safely organise and advocate for improved labour, health, and human rights.

Based on our experience, we argue that it is necessary for government authorities at all levels to recognise that sex workers organising themselves as a community does not in any way equate with or indicate engagement in coercion or sexual exploitation. Sex workers have the right to work and be protected. A critical next step is to work with the Mexican government to review and amend the laws against human trafficking to ensure they differentiate between sex work, which is, by definition, consensual, and trafficking. It is necessary to design and implement strategies in conjunction with both the federal and state governments to ensure the recognition of sex work as a legitimate occupation, and to guarantee the fulfilment of sex workers' constitutional rights. This work is essential to protect human rights; ensure our country's ability to contribute to successful programmes for the prevention of HIV and other STI; and to deal justly with the occupational violence experienced by sex workers. Once these amendments have been made, sex workers can partner with the government to work collaboratively on improving health conditions and ensuring safe workplaces for sex workers, as well as empowering them to exercise their constitutional right to form civil organisations or unions as protected by the constitution. As long as sex work is not recognised as labour, sex workers will continue to be seen only as victims of trafficking, limiting community empowerment efforts.

Discussion

Community empowerment is a critical component of efforts to address the multiple social determinants of health and well-being experienced by sex workers across the world. The case studies from India and Mexico highlight multiple challenges related to community empowerment and mobilisation among female sex workers, from the interpersonal to the structural level, as well as illustrating effective strategies sex worker-led groups have devised to confront these obstacles.

Among the key principles and processes of community empowerment-based approaches is the recognition of sex work as work [49]. As reflected in both case studies, developing a critical consciousness enabling sex workers to understand the structural causes of their vulnerability and marginalisation is essential to the process of mobilising for collective action [1]. Community empowerment approaches facilitating critical consciousness and the agency to take up collective action can promote mobilisation of sex worker communities to bring about social and structural change [50].

There are multiple structural barriers facing sex workers and their ability to organise and mobilise within their communities. These include labour rights violations, financial insecurity, institutional and interpersonal violence, criminalisation and punitive laws, and stigma and discrimination. The literature on existing programmes and the case studies presented here support the use of community empowerment approaches, based within a health and human rights framework, to holistically address these multi-level barriers. Through social justice-oriented movements, sex workers will be able to advocate for their rights to health, freedom from violence, socio-economic opportunities, and safe working conditions and environments.

The experiences of Ashodaya Samithi illustrate interpersonal and structural challenges to sex worker organising and mobilisation, such as police violence and raids, stigma and discrimination, violence and exploitation by different perpetrators, and lack of personal and collective agency among sex workers in Mysore. In the face of these major challenges, by bringing the community together, the programme identified solutions. Using a community mobilisation and empowerment approach including peer-led outreach and increasing access to and utilisation of health services, the programme has achieved significant impacts including substantial increases in self-reported condom use with all sexual partners, and significant reductions in the prevalence of STI, including HIV, among female sex workers [8]. The programme has also had a significant impact on structural violence experienced by sex workers in Mysore [8, 12]. In interviews conducted as part of qualitative research with Ashodaya sex workers, women expressed that violence from the police has been reduced [12]. Ashodaya programme monitoring data likewise showed a marked reduction in violence from the police [8]. Other community-based organisations in India have demonstrated that sex workers who are mobilised to prevent HIV can also effectively develop strategies to monitor and reduce harmful policing practices [51].

Ashodaya has implemented effective strategies for confronting interpersonal violence experienced from partners and clients (including the Boyfriends' Club mentioned in the case study), working to address the challenges presented by the male partners of women participating in the programme, who are threatened by their empowerment. Ashodaya Samithi is an excellent example of using the principals and approaches of community empowerment within a sex worker community to reduce structural violence and human rights violations at various levels of society.

In the case of APROASE in Mexico, we see complex legal and policy challenges creating barriers to sex worker organisation and mobilisation. As described in the case study, sex workers in Mexico are trapped in a "legal limbo" as sex work is not prohibited but also not recognised formally as an occupation [52]. As a result, there are legal grey areas including the conflation of some forms of sex work and work environments with trafficking and sexual exploitation [52]. Early on, sex worker activists identified that it would be necessary to claim the title of "sex workers", with all the stigma accompanying that label, in order to claim the recognition of their labour rights as they moved to take legal action against the government. Because of the efforts of *Brigada Callejera* along with the *Red Mexicana de Trabajo Sexual*, a credentialing process which grants licences to sex workers was established, recognising sex workers as non-wage workers and allowing them to open bank accounts or request loans on declaring their sources of income. The credentials are also a form of protection against "anti-trafficking" police raids. Attaining their licences provides sex workers with a public and legal identity in society. The efforts to recognise sex work as work in Mexico have been able to provide sex workers with health, education, and training opportunities in addition to workers' rights [52].

The legal complexities around sex work in Mexico are not unique. Similar legal and political challenges exist in settings around the globe. An increasing number of reports show how punitive laws and policies governing sex work are linked to increased HIV acquisition and transmission [6]. Modelling has shown that decriminalisation of sex work could avert 33–46% of HIV infections across geographic and epidemic settings in the next decade [6]. Beyond associations with HIV infections, criminalisation and punitive policies towards sex work have also been shown to be related to increased stigma [8, 53], insecurity regarding food supply and finances [54, 55] and higher rates of inconsistent condom use [6] among sex workers.

In terms of gaps identified in this chapter, there is a lack of systematic community empowerment-based approaches and evaluations of these efforts among male and transgender sex workers. Work in this area is urgently needed to realise the potential for community empowerment interventions with diverse populations of sex workers and, specifically, to understand the particular challenges and barriers to community organisation and mobilisation these populations face in different contexts. Additionally, efforts should be made to take community empowerment efforts to scale and to conduct longitudinal evaluation research assessing changes over time, particularly examining health and rights outcomes that can take significant time to show impact.

These two case studies illustrate, as has been found in other settings including Brazil [1], the challenges that sex worker organisations face when governmental and/or international donor support dissipate. However, they also represent the importance to local sex workers' organisations of connections to regional and international networks of organisations led by sex workers. Moving forward, government and donor support is critical for health-related programme and research funding among sex workers and for broader organisation and network strengthening.

References

1. Kerrigan D, Kennedy CE, Morgan-Thomas R, Reza-Paul S, Mwangi P, Win KT, et al. A community empowerment approach to the HIV response among sex workers: effectiveness, challenges, and considerations for implementation and scale-up. Lancet. 2015;385:172–85.
2. NSWP. SWIT case study. 2015. Available from: https://www.nswp.org/resource/swit-case-study.
3. WHO, UNFPA, UNAIDS, NSWP, World Bank. Implementing comprehensive HIV/STI programmes with sex workers: practical approaches from collaborative interventions. Geneva: World Health Organization; 2013.
4. Ghose T, Swendeman D, George S, Chowdhury D. Mobilizing collective identity to reduce HIV risk among sex workers in Sonagachi, India: the boundaries, consciousness, negotiation framework. Soc Sci Med. 2008;67(2):311–20.
5. Swendeman D, Basu I, Das S, Jana S, Rotheram-Borus MJ. Empowering sex workers in India to reduce vulnerability to HIV and sexually transmitted diseases. Soc Sci Med. (1982). 2009;69(8):1157–66.
6. Shannon K, Strathdee SA, Goldenberg SM, Duff P, Mwangi P, Rusakova M, et al. Global epidemiology of HIV among female sex workers: influence of structural determinants. Lancet. 2015;385(9962):55–71.
7. Jana S, Basu I, Rotheram-Borus MJ, Newman PA. The Sonagachi Project: a sustainable community intervention program. AIDS Educ Prev. 2004;16(5):405–14.
8. Reza-Paul S, Beattie T, Syed HU, Venukumar KT, Venugopal MS, Fathima MP, et al. Declines in risk behaviour and sexually transmitted infection prevalence following a community-led HIV preventive intervention among female sex workers in Mysore, India. AIDS (London, England). 2008;22(Suppl 5):S91–100.

9. Blanchard AK, Mohan HL, Shahmanesh M, Prakash R, Isac S, Ramesh BM, et al. Community mobilization, empowerment and HIV prevention among female sex workers in south India. BMC Public Health. 2013;13:234.

10. Blankenship KM, West BS, Kershaw TS, Biradavolu MR. Power, community mobilization, and condom use practices among female sex workers in Andhra Pradesh, India. AIDS (London, England). 2008;22(Suppl 5):S109–16.

11. Thilakavathi S, Boopathi K, Girish Kumar CP, Santhakumar A, Senthilkumar R, Eswaramurthy C, et al. Assessment of the scale, coverage and outcomes of the Avahan HIV prevention program for female sex workers in Tamil Nadu, India: is there evidence of an effect? BMC Public Health. 2011;11(Suppl 6):S3.

12. Argento E, Reza-Paul S, Lorway R, Jain J, Bhagya M, Fathima M, et al. Confronting structural violence in sex work: lessons from a community-led HIV prevention project in Mysore, India. AIDS Care. 2011;23(1):69–74.

13. Gurnani V, Beattie TS, Bhattacharjee P, Mohan HL, Maddur S, Washington R, et al. An integrated structural intervention to reduce vulnerability to HIV and sexually transmitted infections among female sex workers in Karnataka state, south India. BMC Public Health. 2011;11:755.

14. Lippman SA, Donini A, Diaz J, Chinaglia M, Reingold A, Kerrigan D. Social-environmental factors and protective sexual behavior among sex workers: the Encontros intervention in Brazil. Am J Public Health. 2010;100(Suppl 1):S216–23.

15. Kerrigan D, Telles P, Torres H, Overs C, Castle C. Community development and HIV/STI-related vulnerability among female sex workers in Rio de Janeiro, Brazil. Health Educ Res. 2008;23(1):137–45.

16. Kerrigan D, Barrington C, Donastorg Y, Perez M, Galai N. Abriendo Puertas: Feasibility and effectiveness a multi-level intervention to improve HIV outcomes among female sex workers living with HIV in the Dominican Republic. AIDS Behav. 2016;20(9):1919–27.

17. NSWP. Good practices in sex worker-led HIV programming: regional report-Africa. 2014. Available from: https://www.nswp.org/resource/africa-regional-report-good-practice-sex-worker-led-hiv-programming.

18. Cornish F. Empowerment to participate: a case study of participation by Indian sex workers in HIV prevention. J Community Appl Soc Psychol. 2006;16(4):301–15.

19. Schwartlander B, Stover J, Hallett T, Atun R, Avila C, Gouws E, et al. Towards an improved investment approach for an effective response to HIV/AIDS. Lancet. 2011;377(9782):2031–41.

20. Shannon K, Crago AL, Baral SD, Bekker LG, Kerrigan D, Decker MR, et al. The global response and unmet actions for HIV and sex workers. Lancet. 2018;392(10148):698–710.

21. Basu I, Jana S, Rotheram-Borus MJ, Swendeman D, Lee S-J, Newman P, et al. HIV prevention among sex workers in India. J Acquir Immune Defic Syndr. 2004;36(3):845–52.

22. Jana S, Chakraborty AK, Das A, Khodakevich L, Chakraborty MS, Pal NK. Community based survey of STD/HIV infection among commercial sex-workers in Calcutta (India). Part II. Sexual behaviour, knowledge and attitude towards STD. J Commun Dis. 1994;26(3):168–71.

23. Cohen J. HIV/AIDS in India. Sonagachi sex workers stymie HIV. Science (New York, NY). 2004;304(5670):506.

24. The Bill & Melinda Gates Foundation. Avahan, the India AIDS Initiative - the Business of HIV prevention at Scale. New Delhi, India; 2008. Available from: https://docs.gatesfoundation.org/documents/avahan_hivprevention.pdf

25. Mainkar MM, Pardeshi DB, Dale J, Deshpande S, Khazi S, Gautam A, et al. Targeted interventions of the Avahan program and their association with intermediate outcomes among female sex workers in Maharashtra, India. BMC Public Health. 2011;11(Suppl 6):S2.

26. Rachakulla HK, Kodavalla V, Rajkumar H, Prasad SP, Kallam S, Goswami P, et al. Condom use and prevalence of syphilis and HIV among female sex workers in Andhra Pradesh, India - following a large-scale HIV prevention intervention. BMC Public Health. 2011;11(Suppl 6):S1.

27. Research to Prevention. Abriendo Puertas: Feasibility and initial effects of a multi-level intervention among female sex workers living with HIV in the Dominican Republic. Baltimore, MD: USAID | Project Search: Research to Prevention; 2014.
28. Donastorg Y, Barrington C, Perez M, Kerrigan D. Abriendo Puertas: Baseline findings from an integrated intervention to promote prevention, treatment and care among FSW living with HIV in the Dominican Republic. PLoS One. 2014;9(2):e88157.
29. Kerrigan D, Wirtz A, Baral S, Decker M, Murray L, Poteat T, et al. The global HIV epidemics among sex workers. Washington, DC: World Bank; 2013.
30. Kerrigan D, Mbwambo J, Likindikoki S, Beckham S, Mwampashi A, Shembilu C, et al. Project Shikamana: Baseline findings from a community empowerment based combination HIV prevention trial among female sex workers in Iringa, Tanzania. J Acquir Immune Defic Syndr. 2017;74(Suppl 1):S60–8.
31. Kerrigan D, Galai N, Beckham S, Mwampashi A, Shembilu C, Gitagno D, et al. Project Shikamana: Positive effects of a phase II trial of community empowerment-based combination prevention to respond to HIV among female sex workers in Iringa, Tanzania. 22nd International AIDS Conference, 23–27 July, Amsterdam, Netherlands; 2018.
32. Kerrigan K, Mbwambo J, Likindikoki S, Davis W, Beckham S, Mantsios A, et al. Shikamana intervention significantly reduces HIV incidence amogn FSW in Tanzania. Conference on Retroviruses and Opportunistic Infections (CROI), 4–7 March, Seattle, Washington; 2019.
33. The Gay and Lesbian Coalition of Kenya. Health Options for Young Men on HIV/AIDS/STI (HOYMAS). 2016. Available from: https://www.galck.org/hoymas/.
34. Bridging the Gaps. A clinic for male sex workers in Kenya: HIV rates are dropping. Available from: https://hivgaps.org/news/a-clinic-for-male-sex-workers-in-kenya-hiv-rates-are-dropping/.
35. NSWP. Service Workers IN Group (SWING). Available from: https://www.nswp.org/featured/service-workers-group-swing.
36. SWEAT. What is Sisonke? Available from: http://www.sweat.org.za/what-we-do/sisonke/.
37. Beattie TS, Bhattacharjee P, Isac S, Mohan HL, Simic-Lawson M, Ramesh BM, et al. Declines in violence and police arrest among female sex workers in Karnataka state, south India, following a comprehensive HIV prevention programme. J Int AIDS Soc. 2015;18:20079.
38. Beattie TS, Isac S, Bhattacharjee P, Javalkar P, Davey C, Raghavendra T, et al. Reducing violence and increasing condom use in the intimate partnerships of female sex workers: study protocol for Samvedana Plus, a cluster randomised controlled trial in Karnataka state, south India. BMC Public Health. 2016;16:660.
39. Beattie TS, Bhattacharjee P, Ramesh BM, Gurnani V, Anthony J, Isac S, et al. Violence against female sex workers in Karnataka state, south India: impact on health, and reductions in violence following an intervention program. BMC Public Health. 2010;10:476.
40. Fehrenbacher AE, Chowdhury D, Ghose T, Swendeman D. Consistent condom use by female sex workers in Kolkata, India: testing theories of economic insecurity, behavior change, life course vulnerability and empowerment. AIDS Behav. 2016;20(10):2332–45.
41. Euser SM, Souverein D, Rama Narayana Gowda P, Shekhar Gowda C, Grootendorst D, Ramaiah R, et al. Pragati: an empowerment programme for female sex workers in Bangalore, India. Glob Health Action. 2012;5:1–11.
42. Souverein D, Euser SM, Ramaiah R, Narayana Gowda PR, Shekhar Gowda C, Grootendorst DC, et al. Reduction in STIs in an empowerment intervention programme for female sex workers in Bangalore, India: the Pragati programme. Glob Health Action. 2013;6:22943.
43. Mantsios A, Galai N, Mbwambo J, Likindikoki S, Shembilu C, Mwampashi A, et al. Community savings groups, financial security, and HIV risk among female sex workers in Iringa, Tanzania. AIDS Behav. 2018;22(11):3742–50.
44. Network of Sex Worker Projects (NSWP). Sex work and money. Research for Sex Work 9. 2006. Available from: https://www.nswp.org/sites/nswp.org/files/research-for-sex-work-9-english.pdf.

45. United Nations Convention against Transnational Organized Crime. Protocol to prevent, suppress and punish trafficking in persons, especially women and children. New York: United Nations Convention against Transnational Organized Crime; 2000.

46. Ley General para Prevenir, Sancionar y Erradicar los Delitos en Materia de Trata de Personas y para la Protección y Asistencia a las Víctimas de estos Delitos. 2007. Available from: http://www.diputados.gob.mx/LeyesBiblio/pdf/LGPSEDMTP_190118.pdf.

47. Ley General para Prevenir, Sancionar y Erradicar los Delitos en Materia de Trata de Personas y Para la Protección y Asistencia a las Víctimas de estos Delitos, Última Reforma DOF 19-03-2014; 2014.

48. Correa-Cabrera G, Sanders Montandon A. Arguments to reform Mexico's anti-trafficking legislation. Washington, DC: Wilson Center Latin American Program: Mexico Institute.

49. Kerrigan DL, Fonner VA, Stromdahl S, Kennedy CE. Community empowerment among female sex workers is an effective HIV prevention intervention: a systematic review of the peer-reviewed evidence from low- and middle-income countries. AIDS Behav. 2013;17(6):1926–40.

50. Pillai P, Bhattacharjee P, Ramesh BM, Isac S. Impact of two vulnerability reduction strategies - collectivisation and participation in savings activities - on HIV risk reduction among female sex workers. Bangalore, India: Karnataka Health Promotion Trust (KHPT); 2012.

51. Biradavolu MR, Burris S, George A, Jena A, Blankenship KM. Can sex workers regulate police? Learning from an HIV prevention project for sex workers in southern India. Soc Sci Med. (1982. 2009;68(8):1541–7.

52. Lamas M. An end to the shame: stigma and political participation among Mexican sex workers: Open Democracy/ISA RC-47: Open Movements; 2016 [updated 9 Dec]. Available from: https://opendemocracy.net/marta-lamas/end-to-shame-stigma-and-political-participation-among-mexican-sex-workers.

53. Pando MA, Coloccini RS, Reynaga E, Rodriguez Fermepin M, Gallo Vaulet L, Kochel TJ, et al. Violence as a barrier for HIV prevention among female sex workers in Argentina. PLoS One. 2013;8(1):e54147.

54. Reed E, Silverman JG, Stein B, Erausquin JT, Biradavolu M, Rosenberg A, et al. Motherhood and HIV risk among female sex workers in Andhra Pradesh, India: the need to consider women's life contexts. AIDS Behav. 2013;17(2):543–50.

55. Saggurti N, Verma RK, Halli SS, Swain SN, Singh R, Modugu HR, et al. Motivations for entry into sex work and HIV risk among mobile female sex workers in India. J Biosoc Sci. 2011;43(5):535–54.

Chapter 12
Reimagining Sex Work Venues: Occupational Health, Safety, and Rights in Indoor Workplaces

Brooke S. West, Liz Hilton and Empower Thailand, Anne M. Montgomery, and Allison R. Ebben

Introduction

The physical space where sex work occurs, and its social, economic, and policy context, greatly influences sex workers' health and safety [1, 2]. Although the dynamics of sex work vary widely, categorisation of sex work is typically based on indoor versus outdoor settings. Indoor settings may include brothels, hotels, entertainment venues (like bars and clubs), or even private homes. Outdoor settings, parks, truck stops, or the interiors of vehicles, for instance, are generally associated with street-based sex work. However, this distinction paints broad strokes, and the reality is far more complicated since participation in sex work is often fluid, involving elements of both indoor and outdoor work. For example, clients may be solicited on the street, in bars, or through online ads, and then sex may be exchanged in a hotel, vehicle, home, or elsewhere.

An appreciation of the diversity of sex work environments is important in understanding the factors that may either lead to increased health risks or serve as protective factors [3]. In particular, understanding how the unique features of sex workers' occupational conditions differ across the multiple venues where sex work practised

B. S. West (✉)
School of Social Work, Columbia University, New York, NY, USA
e-mail: bsw2110@columbia.edu

Liz Hilton and Empower Thailand
Empower Foundation, Chiang Mai, Thailand
e-mail: lizempower322@gmail.com

A. M. Montgomery
Department of Health Studies, Haverford College, Haverford, PA, USA
e-mail: amontgomer@haverford.edu

A. R. Ebben
School of Social Work, Columbia University, New York, NY, USA
e-mail: are2129@columbia.edu

© The Author(s) 2021
S. M. Goldenberg et al. (eds.), *Sex Work, Health, and Human Rights*,
https://doi.org/10.1007/978-3-030-64171-9_12

is essential to developing and supporting programmes that promote and support the rights, health, and safety of sex workers [3]. Operating in isolated or dark locations has been shown to increase risk of violence and to limit sex workers' negotiating power with clients [4–10]. The increased visibility of working in public spaces may also increase the likelihood of sex workers experiencing negative encounters with law enforcement and stigma from community members [11, 12] which, in turn, can limit their agency and displace sex workers to more dangerous settings [8, 9, 13]. Sex workers' ability to access health and harm reduction services can also depend on the sex work setting [5, 6]. Although some sex work locations afford greater protection from a range of health risks, venues differ widely, and disparities in levels of concealment, control, and isolation make both outdoor and indoor settings potential sites of either risk or safety [14].

So what factors are meaningful when trying to understand sex workers' health and rights in the context of physical environments where sex work takes place? In this chapter, we focus primarily on indoor workplaces, and examine the unique social, physical, economic, and policy characteristics that increase or mitigate harm for sex workers. By "indoor workplaces," we mean the broad range of indoor venues in which *either* solicitation *or* sex with clients occurs. We propose the following broad categories of indoor sex work venues shown in Table 12.1 [adapted and expanded from Harcourt and Donovan [11]]: brothels, entertainment venues, service venues (e.g. massage parlours and bathhouses), rented rooms, private residences, and virtual (e.g. online) venues. These spaces vary in terms of how explicitly the venue is dedicated to sex work, location of solicitation and delivery of sexual services, levels of regulation, occupational standards and protective measures employed, and potential threats to sex worker health and safety (discussed in greater detail in the next section).

The goals of this chapter are, therefore, to: (1) elucidate factors that influence the well-being of sex workers in indoor workplaces; (2) provide a case study of sex worker-led initiatives to enhance workplace health and rights, focusing on the organisation Empower Thailand and the affiliated *Can Do Bar*; (3) describe best practices for indoor settings; and (4) develop a framework of key social, economic, physical, and policy factors that support sex worker efforts to organise and promote rights, health, and safety. The chapter will bring together research from global contexts to illuminate critical challenges facing sex workers in indoor venues, as well as suggest opportunities to advance comprehensive programmes and policies.

Health, Safety, and Rights of Sex Workers in Venues

Much of sex work-related health programming has focused on HIV/STI prevention. Although important, this singular focus may reinforce harmful notions that sex workers are vectors of disease, thus undercutting more holistic support for overall occupational health and human rights. In reality, sex workers' health needs are diverse. Sexual health concerns extend beyond HIV/STIs to include pregnancy,

Table 12.1 Categories of indoor venues

Indoor venue category	Description	Special considerations
Brothels	Premises explicitly dedicated to providing sexual services: Clients solicited on site or through other means (e.g. online); sex conducted on site.	• Most likely licensed and state regulated. • Can afford sex workers greater control over sexual exchange, reduce exposure to violence or police interactions, and provide opportunities for health care (depending on managerial and/or owner practices, plus legal context).
Entertainment venues	Bars, clubs, dance halls, karaoke clubs, beer halls, cafes: Premises dedicated to serving alcohol. Clients solicited in venue; sex conducted on or off site.	• May be licenced and state regulated. • Presence of alcohol and drugs can decrease women's negotiating power and increase exposure to violence.
Service venues	Saunas, massage parlours, bathhouses, salons, or barber shops: Premises dedicated to providing other services, but range of sexual services are provided. Clients solicited in venue; sex conducted on or off site.	• May be licenced and state regulated. • Presence of alcohol and drugs can decrease women's negotiating power and increase exposure to violence. • Indirect nature of sex work may make it less safe.
Rented rooms	Hotels, guesthouses, or other rented rooms: Clients solicited on the street or through other means (e.g. street, entertainment venues); sex conducted in rented room.	• Work may be conducted alone with little control over the work environment. • Exposure to violence and police interactions may be higher and access to services lower.
Private residences	Clients solicited through multiple means (e.g. phone, street, online); sex work conducted in private homes, either that of the sex worker, client, or someone else.	• Work may be conducted alone, which can increase exposure to violence. • Greater control over work environment and client selection can mitigate risks. • May be more covert, which can reduce negative police and community interactions.
Virtual venues	Clients solicited through online means or newspapers; sex work conducted in rented room, private residence, brothel or other venue.	• Work may be conducted alone, which can increase exposure to violence. • Greater control over work environment and client selection can mitigate risks. • May be more covert, which can reduce negative police and community interactions.

maternal morbidity and mortality, and access to safe abortion (e.g. pre- and post-abortion care), as well as bladder and kidney infections. Repetitive stress injuries to wrists, arms, shoulders, jaws, knees, feet, and backs, resulting from repeated "hand jobs", "blow jobs", working on inadequate beds, and working in high heels, are also matters of concern [15]. Chronic and noncommunicable health conditions like heart disease and diabetes may also be important challenges for sex workers, as these conditions can be exacerbated by chronic stress and trauma [16], as experienced by some sex workers.

Sex workers in practically all settings face substantial risk of sexual, psychological, and physical violence from clients, partners, police, managers, strangers, neighbours, and other sex workers. These abuses include harassment, condom refusal, rape, sexual assault, physical assault, drugging, abduction, trafficking, and murder [17]. Violence further manifests as robbery, non-payment by clients, and extortion by police, managers, pimps, landlords, and others [17, 18]. The health and safety of sex workers are also jeopardised by disproportionate experiences of structural violence, including stigma, discrimination, poor occupational conditions, high rates of policing, and systematic economic and social marginalisation, leading to higher rates of homelessness and poverty [8, 19]. These experiences can contribute to a greater risk of sex workers developing a range of mental health conditions, like PTSD, depression, anxiety, suicide, and alcohol and drug use disorders [17, 20], as well as work-related stress [21, 22].

All of these occupational health and safety issues are compounded by reduced access for sex workers to needed health and social services due to limited availability of such services, prohibitive costs of services, and discriminatory practices preventing sex workers from receiving or seeking quality care [23]. These factors, as they relate to indoor venues, are discussed below.

Physical Characteristics

Indoor venues may provide sex workers with higher levels of safety compared to other environments. This depends, however, on the specifics of the particular space—who is in charge and how the space is run. Although some indoor spaces utilise protective measures, like security guards, good lighting, and panic buttons, others may be highly disordered, lacking in basic hygiene, or located in isolated areas where risks are exacerbated. For instance, working in a brothel or other indoor venue may mean greater protection from police if the manager or owner pays police to leave employees alone [24]. Managers and other third parties (e.g. security guards) can help to screen and regulate clients and enforce policies to enhance sex worker control over sexual negotiations [19, 24, 25]. For instance, in entertainment venues where alcohol is served, managers may offer "ladies' drinks" with reduced alcohol content, thus potentially decreasing levels of intoxication among female workers, which in turn enables them to better negotiate their health and safety with clients [26]. If workplace policies are designed to support safer sex, indoor spaces may also afford greater access to sexual health information and services, as well as promoting the use of condoms [19, 27–29].

However, the extent to which managed indoor venues are supportive of sex workers' health, rights, and independence depends on the practices, policies, and regulations characterising a particular venue. In venues where sex workers are pressured to work quickly or to service a large number of clients in a short period of time, their agency to negotiate condom use and safety with clients may be limited [30, 31]. Additionally, in some indoor venues, pressure on sex workers to drink or use drugs may inhibit their agency when negotiating condom use and increase the risk of exposure to violence [26, 32]. More broadly, managers and owners of indoor venues in settings where sex work is criminalised may not view sex workers as employees with rights and entitlement to a safe working environment, and some even leverage the criminalisation of sex work to exploit their employees [33]. Thus, some sex workers prefer the freedom of working independently, outside of the regulation and surveillance of indoor venues [34].

Economic Factors

Economic factors operate in many ways to shape the health and well-being of sex workers, and poor socio-economic conditions often underlie entry into sex work [35]. Economic injustices experienced by sex workers include limited economic opportunities, low pay, their performing dual roles as primary caretakers and sole breadwinners, as well as, for marginalised groups, limited access to property ownership, education, banking, and financial management. This economic vulnerability has been shown to increase workers' vulnerability to having sex without condoms, reduce their negotiating power with clients, and increase gender-based violence and risk for HIV/STI [35–37]. Similarly, studies have shown that residential instability or homelessness increases experiences of sexual and physical violence [6, 38]. Economic vulnerability stemming from the criminalisation of sex work (manifesting in, for example, clients refusing to pay, or police extorting bribes or fines from workers attempting to avoid arrest), in particular, also results in lower rates of condom use and higher risks of HIV infection [35, 38–45].

Indoor sex work venues may be attractive to sex workers if they are able to charge higher fees and/or see more clients, especially if the setting also provides greater protection from police or clients [4, 8, 9]. However, there are variations to the economic benefits and risks sex workers experience within indoor sex work venues. Many sex workers find themselves paying tips or fees to third parties such as managers, owners, drivers, front desk workers, security staff, or phone operators [46]. In some contexts, sex workers report these relationships with third parties to be supportive, whereas in others, economic arrangements with third parties may be reported as being financially exploitative or as creating situations where sex workers are required to pay exorbitant fees to work in these spaces [46] or to procure clients [47]. Such economic interference cuts into workers' earnings and may lead some to sacrifice the relative safety of such workplaces for riskier settings where they have greater autonomy over their money, time, and working conditions [19]. Importantly, these exploitative relationships are most likely to occur in jurisdictions where sex work is criminalised, a factor underscoring the urgent need for sex worker labour rights. Ultimately, sex workers should be equally free to choose to work with third parties or to work independently, and, furthermore, to do so without the unjust criminalisation of third parties based on assumptions of trafficking or exploitation.

Social Factors

Social factors also shape health, safety, and rights outcomes for sex workers in indoor sex work venues. For example, due to the highly stigmatised and often criminalised nature of sex work, health care and legal services may be harder to obtain for sex workers than for workers in other industries [48]. The stigma against sex workers is often entrenched in unjust power structures that treat sex workers as deserving of scorn or abuse [49]. This results in high rates of violence against sex workers. In one global sample, 45–75% of sex workers reported lifetime prevalence of workplace violence [50]. However, working in an indoor venue, as opposed to working outdoors, may offer some protection against stigma by making it easier for individuals to conceal their sex worker status from the public and police.

Within indoor workplaces, sex workers engage with a host of factors that support or negate their health and safety. Managerial promotion of supportive policies (e.g. intervening with bad clients), provision of health information and condoms, and deterrence of unjust policing practices, can lead to reduced violence against sex workers and to their experiencing greater agency with clients [9, 19, 24, 25, 27–30, 51]. However, managers may also interfere with negotiations regarding condom use, client selection, and pricing [10, 19, 30, 31, 33, 52]. Relationships with other sex workers can also improve sex worker health. Positive aspects of support include the sharing of information about clients (e.g. Ugly Mugs reports and "bad date lists"), HIV testing, and strategies to negotiate safe sex and condom use, as well as the establishment of supportive venue norms and opportunities for sex workers to organise against exploitative managerial practices [27–29].

In contrast, limited peer support, either as a result of competition between workers or venue policies limiting cooperation between them, can lead to their experiencing greater isolation and limited power to address issues of occupational health and safety [10, 25, 30, 53]. Importantly, the criminalisation of sex work and related stigmas can stand in the way of the development of supportive relationships with management, as well as collective action among sex workers [54, 55].

Policy Environment

All of the factors discussed above intersect with policy environments in ways which impact sex workers' health and safety. Globally, four primary legal models exist, varying in levels of regulation and criminalisation of sex work: (1) Prohibition criminalises both the selling and buying of sex and third party involvement; (2) End Demand laws criminalise paying for sex, or organising or profiting from prostitution on the part of third parties, but do not criminalise the selling of sex; (3) Legalisation and regulation may involve the partial decriminalisation of some forms of sex work, but often introduce oppressive venue licensure and regulation under administrative and labour laws; and (4) Decriminalisation removes all punitive laws from both the selling and buying of sexual services, as well as from third parties or others who are directly or indirectly involved in the sex industry [56].

Most countries adopt legislation informed primarily by the lens of prohibition, resulting in the widespread criminalisation of sex work around the world. Even in contexts where sex work is quasi-legal or legal, may activities associated with sex work still remain criminalised. This impacts third party actors who profit from sex work by, for example, running an establishment, providing security, spotters, etc. [57], or maintaining online advertising platforms, which were directly affected by the 2018 FOSTA-SESTA legislation in the United States [58]. In some contexts, family members and cohabitants can be charged with "living off the proceeds of prostitution" [57]. These restrictions have substantial impact on the health, safety, and rights of indoor sex workers [19, 23, 42, 59–61]. At the broadest level, laws regulating sex work exacerbate stigma and force sex work underground, making it hidden and less safe for individuals engaged in this work.

The criminalisation, regulation, and policing of sex work are documented to lead to human rights abuses, including workplace raids, harassment, arrests, rape, confiscation of condoms, and extortion of bribes or sexual favours by police [10, 49, 62, 63]. The collective result of these outcomes is a direct impact on sex worker health, through experiences of physical and sexual violence, decreased access to condoms and condom use, fear of carrying safer sex or injection supplies due to threat of arrest, increased risk for HIV/STIs, reduced negotiating power with clients, and fear of accessing health services, alongside the creation of a climate where economic vulnerability is systemic [49, 62, 63]. Without legal protection, experiences of violence, abuse, or exploitation from police, clients, or other parties, may not be investigated or registered, plus sex workers may avoid reporting violence for fear that they themselves will be charged [12, 64]. The stringent or coercive regulation of indoor spaces can push individuals to work in unsafe indoor or outdoor workspaces, where they have less ability to screen or negotiate with clients [5, 9, 19, 65]. In other words, the potential protective effects of working in indoor spaces are undermined by policies related to the regulation and criminalisation of sex work [4].

Additional Considerations

Stigma, violent policing, and criminal penalties are disproportionately experienced by other marginalised communities—people whose identities may intersect with sex worker identities—including people who use drugs; migrants, Indigenous people, and other racialised minorities; people living with HIV; LGBT populations; individuals experiencing homeless or unstable housing; and populations with co-occurring health issues like mental illness. People who use drugs, especially those who inject, often face substantial stigma within indoor venues, resulting in their experiencing social isolation or being pushed outdoors to the margins of communities where their income is lowered and the possibility of experiencing violence is increased [2, 8, 49, 66, 67]. Individuals who are drug-dependent or intoxicated may be less able to negotiate condom use or safer injection, may be more likely to have sex without condoms to access money or drugs, and may be less able to extricate themselves from dangerous situations with clients [4, 23]. As well, the double stigma and marginalisation associated with sex work and substance use can translate into sex worker avoidance of health and social services, and elevated levels of police harassment, abuse, and imprisonment [68].

Migrant sex workers also face compounded risks. Working in indoor venues may be particularly attractive to migrant sex workers as a way to overcome challenges associated with their migrant status (e.g. social isolation, barriers to health and legal protections, language barriers, the need to remain less visible) [54, 69]. During raids on venues, however, migrant sex workers may be disproportionately targeted and find themselves at risk of deportation if their legal status is discovered by authorities [70]. Protection of sex workers' labour is limited across the board, and for migrant sex workers in indoor venues, it may be even more so if they fear reporting or discussing workplace violations due to concerns around disclosure of their immigration status [61, 65]. Broadly speaking, migrant populations may not be afforded the same rights as citizens, which can prevent them from seeking health or social services or soliciting help from the police if they experience abuse or violence [65, 71].

Similarly, transgender sex workers may be marginalised within sex work communities, excluded from indoor spaces, and thereby forced to work in street settings. Transgender sex worker's safety is already threatened by stigma and discrimination: they face greater exposure to physical and sexual violence, as well as greater economic vulnerability and diminished ability to negotiate with clients [72–77]. The hypervisibility and policing of trans bodies, combined with a failure to address threats to trans sex workers, means the creation of safer indoor working environments is important to protecting the rights of trans sex workers [76, 77]. Given these structural vulnerabilities, greater attention needs to be directed towards the specific health, rights, and safety concerns of diverse and marginalised sex workers in indoor venues.

Case Study of Empower Thailand

Empower Thailand, a sex worker-led human rights and women's advocacy group, was born in 1985 in the go-go bars of Patpong, the famous red-light district of Bangkok. Empower currently works across five Thai provinces. In Chiang Mai, our organisation does weekly outreach, visiting over 250 sex work sites and 3000 sex workers each month. Over the last 2 years, we have added "internet outreach" where news and information are shared by hundreds of sex workers in mobile app groups. The following section will detail key components of our innovative approach to addressing health, rights, and safety in indoor sex work venues.

Sex workers make up most of the leadership of Empower and are regularly invited to guide and critique our activities and advocacy work. Empower focuses on five domains:

1. Community: Empower is part of and central to the sex worker community. We use our space to celebrate, mourn, play, eat, and organise together.
2. Legal: We learn, analyse, and critique the laws that impact us.
3. Art: We use art and performance to strengthen our advocacy.
4. Education: We provide education for society about human rights, justice, and sex work from our collective experience. We also provide sex workers with access to education (e.g. literacy, language training, school qualifications, job skills).
5. Health: We teach the public and health providers about best practices when working with sex workers and provide a setting wherein sex workers can share health knowledge and referrals with one another.

As a collective of sex workers who are experts in what is most important to our community we have numerous insights into what supportive interventions look like, as well as into which activities might involve unintentional, negative consequences for sex workers. The lessons we share below are rooted in the need for health and rights promotion focusing on occupational health and safety (OHS), and support for sex worker organising.

Prioritising Collective Organising: Reimaging Outreach as In-reach Empower started with women visiting each other's workplaces and coming together to talk, share skills, and reflect on their lives. It was not then called "outreach", a term imported years later from the NGO world. Empower outreach has always been more like "in-reach", as we are part of the communities we visit. As Empower Sex Worker Member 1 states:

> We are sex workers on outreach. We don't use the term 'peer', as it has become a word used by NGOs to separate sex workers from each other unnecessarily. It also is a trap where sex workers can be used as "peer educators" for NGOs, but we can still not be in the decision-making roles and high paid positions of Director, Coordinator, Administration Officer, etc.

For Empower, outreach (or in-reach) is not just an activity or project; it is the vital component of every activity and programme. Empower does outreach to build and solidify community, have fun, catch up with old friends, and introduce Empower to new sex workers in the area. It is also a means for sharing news and experiences among diverse sex workers and for ensuring that Empower's activities and advocacy are responsive to the changing work conditions, needs, and interests of sex workers. As Empower Sex Worker Member 2 shares:

> *We went on outreach to share Empower plans to make a submission to the government to repeal the Prostitution Act. However, everywhere we went sex workers were talking about the terrible economy ... worrying about having enough money to buy kids shoes, cover school fees, rent etc. The Prostitution Act felt a long way from real life. So we decided to start running a monthly second-hand clothes market at Empower. The market not only cut down on living expenses, but also gave us a chance to gather together and make it clear to each other that the Prostitution Act is the reason that about a quarter of our monthly earnings are stolen in bribes. We were able to get more sex workers supporting the lobbying for law reform. We only knew we needed to make the link clear because of what we learned on outreach.*

Each month, sex workers create a pamphlet to distribute in the community that includes information about our educational programmes, upcoming Empower activities, and information on the law, human rights, or health. Pamphlets display the Empower "Honey Bee" logo to make them easily recognisable to sex workers with limited literacy; we also use large lettering so they can be read in the dim light of indoor workplaces. Using the vibrant language of sex workers, rather than academic or NGO language, each pamphlet is designed with the knowledge that it may be read by employers, customers, police, or family members, so we ensure information will not embarrass or endanger sex workers. According to Empower Sex Worker Member 3:

> *No restaurant or their staff would want people handing out graphic descriptions and pictures of food poisoning. We also don't want pamphlets about gonorrhea passed to us at work, especially in front of our customers.*

Sex workers pair up to plan and conduct outreach. We wear Empower t-shirts so our mission is clear to other sex workers and their employers. When we enter establishments, we are good customers and take a seat, order a drink, and when workers have time they pick up a pamphlet, exchange gossip and get condoms. In venues where it is not possible to sit (e.g. some massage parlours), we leave pamphlets. For many sex workers, meeting Empower on outreach is the first step to becoming community organisers and "high-heeled defenders". Over the last three decades, more than 50,000 sex workers have joined Empower, most of whose first experience of Empower was an outreach visit to their workplace.

Respecting Sex Workers as Workers and Venues as Workplaces and Places of Business Entertainment venues are, first and foremost, workplaces, and sex workers are there to earn their living. We learned from experience that it is not appropriate to attempt training, workshops or HIV/STI testing in these venues during business hours; instead, we use outreach to invite sex workers to attend events away from the workplace and outside working hours.

As outreach workers, sex workers have insider knowledge of the routines, working conditions and social composition of different venues (e.g. literacy levels, gender identity, migration status, incomes). This allows us to tailor outreach to safely and respectfully approach sex workers. In particular, Empower understands power dynamics in different types of workplaces, allowing us to avoid complicity with exploitative employers or reinforcing bad labour and human rights practices. As one Empower member notes:

> The [NGO] staff don't really talk to us, they usually just talk to the mamasan (manager). The mamasan doesn't want any trouble from the health department so she's nice to them. She shouts out "Girls come and get your blood tested!" Can we refuse? Technically yes, it's supposed to be voluntary, but if we refused all our friends would look at us and wonder why we don't want a test. The mamasan would be angry so we may get our salary cut. The [NGO] staff would want us to explain why we are refusing and try to talk us into a test. It seems that the test is not mandatory but volunteering for it is! We call it forced voluntary testing. No one is doing this testing for our health, not even us.

Outside projects that develop primary relationships with management rather than with workers can lead to activities and projects that rely on coercion and fear. This may result in forced HIV/STI testing, forced participation in research, and workers left unable to speak honestly or freely to health providers.

The Can Do Bar: A Just and Fair Workplace for Sex Workers, by Sex Workers In many contexts, sex worker projects began as HIV/AIDS outreach; however, sex worker concerns extend far beyond disease prevention and include issues of stigma, labour rights, decriminalisation, and health promotion. After 2005, Empower began focusing more widely on Occupational Health and Safety (OHS) for sex workers in entertainment places. This involved running a series of workshops bringing together sex workers and OHS experts to discuss concerns and solutions related to salary cuts, customer quotas, mandatory alcohol consumption, long work hours, lack of paid leave or days off, locked fire escapes, harmful noise levels, and inadequate toilet facilities. Findings were published in an OHS handbook for sex workers and business owners to assess their workplaces and implement changes. In the Empower drop-in centre, sex workers also designed a model of the working conditions outlined in the manual.

In 2006, frustrated by public and policymaker resistance to improving working conditions, a group of sex workers from Empower created their own venue—an entertainment space developed for sex workers by sex workers to demonstrate the conditions they were demanding. They named it the *"Can Do Bar"* because they believed it was possible for sex workers to do it themselves. A fund was established where contributing sex workers became part of the collective ownership. The price of a share was set at 1000 Thai Baht (US$33). Those who could not afford monetary contributions could join the collective by contributing labour to the design and construction of the bar. Within months, the fund had raised over 1 million Thai Baht (approximately US$35,000).

The *Can Do Bar* was opened on September 19th, 2006 and was informed by national OHS, labour, and business standards (see Box 12.1). The collective committed to several core principles: the *Can Do Bar* would work within the law and not pay bribes to police; sex would be for personal income and not for the profit of the

Box 12.1 Working conditions at the can do bar—"Can Do—Experitainment" (2006)

Thai Labor Law and Social Security Policy
- All "Can Do" workers are paid at or above the minimum wage according to Thai Labor Law
- "Can Do" staff work a maximum of 8 hours per night and have minimum of one day off per week in accordance with Thai labor law
- Full time workers have 10 paid holidays a year plus a further 13 days Public Holidays per year
- Overtime is on a voluntary basis and fully paid
- There will be no staff salary cuts or withholding of wages for any reason
- "Can Do" staff are encouraged to form a worker's association or union
- All workers are entitled to paid sick leave and also enrolled in the Thai Social Security scheme
- Disputes over working conditions will be settled in Labor Court

Staff Facilities
- "Can Do" has provided facilities for workers to take their allotted breaks away from the bar or they may leave the premises for their break if they wish
- Unlimited clean drinking water is supplied free for workers
- "Can Do" staff have their own toilet facilities and there are no restrictions on times of use.

Physical Safety and Well-being
- The "Can Do" building complies with Thai building standards
- Daily cleaning is done by a trained cleaner using appropriate solutions
- "Can Do" bar is well ventilated and customers must smoke outside
- Fire extinguishers are installed and maintained. Workers have been trained in their use.
- Noise and lighting levels comply with Thai standards (music less than 92 decibels: lighting above 50 amps)
- A functioning electricity safety switch is in place
- Staff are not required to lift over 4kgs and have been trained in safe lifting and moving techniques
- Staff have been trained in first aid and basic first aid supplies are provided
- "Can Do" does not link income to alcohol consumption for bar staff or other visiting sex workers
- As a service to society, condoms and lubricant are freely available in "Can Do" and workers are trained in safe sex education.

Staff Development
- Bar staff receive training covering bar tending, sound system, first aid, safe sex, safe lifting, emergency procedures, managing difficult or violent situations
- Access to ongoing English language training and ad hoc skill training
- Staff may apply for one paid night off per month to attend meetings, courses or trainings relevant to their professional development.

bar; visiting sex workers unaffiliated with Empower would be welcome and free to engage with other customers; and decision-making would be done by consensus among Empower members. Importantly, the *Can Do Bar* could not function without the collective spirit of sex workers working together. For instance, each year, sex workers involved in the *Can Do Bar* collectively undertake financial planning.

To date, they have decided to reinvest profits to maintain and improve the bar rather than divide profits among themselves.

The success of the *Can Do Bar* cannot be measured in profits alone, however, as our work impacts women's health and livelihood. It also sends a message to other entertainment venues, policymakers, health officials, and to the general public. For example, the *Can Do Bar* has helped to promote social security for sex workers, enrolling almost 400 women in the Thai Social Security Scheme, which provides workers with unemployment payments, health care, old age pensions, and childcare payments. Encouraged by this example, sex workers at other venues have successfully demanded that their employers also enrol them in social security. According to Empower Sex Worker Member 4:

> *Before Can Do we all thought we couldn't join social security. Our bosses also said it was impossible. But now we know differently. Social security? Can Do!*

As a result of our many successes, the Can Do Bar has been called a model intervention by Henny Ngu at the UNDP and has received further national and international recognition as demonstrated by visits from Thai Ministries of Labor and Social Welfare, National Human Rights Commission, UNAIDS, the International Labor Organization, and students, researchers, journalists, and others from around the world, all of whom have come to learn from our model. We also received funding from Mama Cash, American Jewish World Service, Red Umbrella Fund, and many others.

Perhaps most importantly, Can Do creates collective community pride as our members have proven that safe, fair sex work is possible. Overall, Empower and the Can Do Bar present a clear message: interventions focusing only on disease, especially HIV/STI prevention, ignore other OHS issues that are equally important to women. Instead, supporting women to organise and make changes that they identify as important and necessary can create healthy and just working conditions for sex workers and serve as a model for other establishments.

Lessons from Empower and Beyond: Best Practices to Reduce Harm, Promote Health, and Advance Rights for Indoor Sex Workers

Given the range of health and safety issues sex workers confront as part of their daily lives, a focus on improving working environments and supporting safer sex work spaces is crucial to ensuring the rights of sex workers. Perhaps more than outdoor venues, indoor venues are in a unique position to utilise such an approach, though OHS issues and needs will vary by venue and context. Broadly speaking, sex workers deserve access to healthy and risk-free work environments where they have decision-making power, their physical and psychological safety is ensured, and they have recourse when they experience harm in the workplace. Without structural changes to the policy context, however, creating such environments is challenging [78]. The following section details recommended best practices for indoor sex work venues.

First, indoor sex work venues can be made safer for sex workers by prioritising occupational health and safety and harm reduction. Many sex workers, including those from Empower, as well sex worker organisations and activists, endorse an explicit focus on OHS as a starting point for supporting sex workers. This requires recognition that sex work is work and therefore sex workers need labour rights. An OHS perspective involves preventing day-to-day workplace exposures and hazards, treating injuries and disease, holding employer's accountable for the health and safety of employees, and promoting worker rights to mitigate harms associated with disproportionate disease burden, substance use, exposure to violence, debt, exploitation, and marginalisation [15, 79].

OHS in indoor venues involves a combination of employer duties, working conditions, protection and prevention, and care and support [79]. Venue owners and managers have a responsibility to consult with employees to identify hazards, address harms and to assess and control risk by, for example, screening and refusing clients; providing good lighting, panic buttons, and hygiene materials like soap, water, clean linens, and towels; keeping the environment clean and well maintained; and providing information and supplies for safer sex and safer drug use [9, 24, 25, 27–30]. Managers must support access to regular health screenings and services, including the management of STIs, HIV, cervical and anogenital cancer, Hepatitis B and C, tuberculosis, as well as access to a range of contraceptive options, safe abortions, and post-abortion care [80]. Importantly, work environments should be free of coercion of any sort, including freedom from any requirement to have sex without a condom, and the freedom to refrain from drinking or using drugs. If needed, work environments should also provide support to workers in using substances safely, if needed (e.g. provision of drug-related harm reduction information, free clean syringes, naloxone, and fentanyl test strips) [79]. Beyond this, wider support for sex worker health and safety issues should include violence prevention tools, and managerial support for employees to organise, join unions, and access a range of health and social services [80].

Proper working conditions include reasonable work schedules with adequate breaks, vacations, and leaves, but should also include the provision of workers' compensation, insurance, and legal support, plus ensure that workers are able to report accidents or injuries, and hold employers accountable when sex workers' rights and safety are violated [79]. Importantly, OHS measures must be cognisant of the diversity of sex workers' lived experience and concerns [80]. This involves focusing on how to make venues more inclusive of marginalised sex workers—including people who use drugs, immigrants/migrants and transgender sex workers—to more fully advance the rights and safety of sex workers. For instance, migrant sex workers may have need for translation or legal services. For people who use substances, access to treatment for drug, alcohol, and tobacco dependence is crucial to supporting health and safety [80]. For transgender sex workers, special attention to both physical and mental health needs, as well as additional safety protections, could make indoor venues healthier and safer spaces that are also more welcoming.

Second, strengthening the rights and health of indoor sex workers requires their full and meaningful engagement. This involves a host of activities including support for community organising, sex worker-led initiatives, and mobilisation and empowerment efforts. Sex workers are too often left out of the discussions that impact their lives. Yet, as seen in the innovative work of Empower Thailand, sex workers are strategic partners to improve health and rights and are the experts in their own work and needs [81, 82]. Including sex workers should be an integral part of all phases of research and intervention, including design, planning, implementation, and evaluation. Given that sex workers already use diverse strategies of risk mitigation to navigate physical spaces and client relationships, their agency should be respected and built upon to move towards respectful, sustainable, realistic, and effective solutions.

In indoor venues, community empowerment and mobilisation efforts have been employed in various ways reflecting the diverse needs of sex workers at both the individual and structural level. Within such venues, the promotion of collective efficacy in the form of sex workers looking out for each other can be incredibly protective and supportive. Connection, even in informal ways, can help to promote self-efficacy, self-esteem, negotiation skills, and personal safety skills, all of which have been shown to reduce the risk of HIV/STI, experiences of violence, alcohol and substance use, and debt [79]. Peer education within venues—or the use of peer workers for outreach (or "in-reach", as described by Empower)—can also build community among sex workers and be an effective tool for conveying health and safety information [83]. For example, Stella, a sex worker organisation in Montreal, produces working, safety, and rights guides designed by and for sex workers, including specific guides for strippers, clients, and people who use drugs [84].

The establishment of peer-run and led sex worker collectives, like Empower and others, represents a powerful model for community organising. For instance, sex worker collectives play a major role in the promotion of OHS as they often help people navigate exploitative or coercive working conditions and/or problems with venue managers, owners, or landlords. This is important as sex workers typically do not have legal support when making complaints against employers and often do not want to damage relationships with management [84]. Sex worker collectives can instead leverage their collective power to put pressure on operators to improve working conditions or work collaboratively to establish better business practices [84]. More broadly, greater ownership and management of sex working spaces, like the Can Do Bar, can be incredibly important for ensuring that sex workers have safe and equitable working conditions.

Community mobilisation and advocacy are also fundamental to addressing rights abuses against sex workers [85]. Sex worker collectives and rights organisations have played a substantial role in fighting the policies that threaten the health and safety of indoor sex workers. Organisations like the Bar Hostess

Empowerment and Support Programme (BHESP) in Nairobi used their collective power to confront violence by going to the courts and publicly advocating against police and client brutality [86]. Similarly, Empower Thailand organised to draw attention to police raids of indoor venues and entrapment practices that violate sex worker rights, and are fighting for decriminalisation. Such efforts have been successful. In New Zealand, the New Zealand Prostitutes Collective (NZPC), established by a small group of indoor sex workers, was at the forefront of decriminalisation efforts in the country and they continue to use their power to support migrant sex workers, who remain criminalised under the Prostitution Reform Act.

As these examples show, community empowerment—through peer leadership, collectivisation, mobilisation, and advocacy—is a form of social justice. It is both a social process and a structural intervention that challenges the diverse factors undermining sex workers' rights and equality [83, 87]. Importantly, the breadth and success of these efforts stems directly from the centering of sex worker expertise and control. To ensure that interventions are effective and responsive to sex worker needs, it is therefore imperative that sex workers have meaningful ownership over interventions. Interventions that bridge community-led processes with structural targets—aiming to alter the very power relations that lead to inequities [41, 88]—show great promise for effectively supporting sex workers to achieve the goals that are most important to them.

Third, explicit attention must be given to changing punitive policies that affect the health and rights of sex workers and third parties in indoor venues. Widespread support for the OHS of sex workers has been limited by the criminalisation and coercive regulation of sex work, as well as by moral discourses denigrating individuals for the work they do [49]. Shifting the policy environment and countering stigmatising practices are essential components of supporting sex workers, both within indoor venues and in other spaces.

There is consensus among sex work activists and public health and human rights organisations (e.g. UNAIDS, WHO, Amnesty International) that full decriminalisation of all aspects of sex work is essential to promote the health and human rights of sex workers [89–91]. This includes not only sex workers, clients, and third parties, but also those indirectly associated with sex work, such as hairdressers, taxi drivers and the children of sex workers. In contexts such as New Zealand, where sex work has been fully decriminalised (but only for New Zealand citizens), research demonstrates many successes in terms of making sex work safer and improving rights across various sectors of the sex industry [92]. In Rhode Island in the United States, when indoor sex work was decriminalised, the indoor sex market increased in size, suggesting a shift away from more dangerous outdoor settings, and rape offences and gonorrhoea incidence substantially decreased [93]. Conversely, where changes in sex work regulation have made it harder to conduct sex work in indoor spaces—as in the 2018 legislation in the United States cracking down on online solicitation—the carrying out of sex work was pushed to often riskier outdoor, isolated, or less visible spaces [49, 65]. Evidence from countries or cities where sex work is partially decriminalised suggests that such measures can open doors to greater safety, but quasi-criminalisation still poses challenges to the full actualisation of sex workers' rights, and to control over their bodies, working conditions, and safety [50].

Even in contexts without federal or state decriminalisation, changes in municipal laws or policing practices can have significant impacts on health and safety [4, 65, 94]. Such changes involve, among other things, putting an end to the targeting of public solicitation, stopping workplace raids, eliminating sex work licensing practices or high fees for licences, getting rid of employee registration requirements, and helping sex workers to deal with violent clients.

Additionally, working with police to change their treatment of sex workers, with emphasis on the provision of support, rather than the practices of abuse or arrest, could make the everyday lives of sex workers safer [94]. Sex worker collectives are especially important to this process, as they are a powerful force when it comes to creating change and holding law enforcement bodies accountable for their actions against sex workers [94].

Conclusions

This chapter highlights how physical, economic, social, and policy contexts shape the health, rights, and safety outcomes of indoor sex workers (see Fig. 12.1). Understanding the variety of spaces in which people work and how the characteristics of sex work venues impact health and safety is essential to developing interventions, programmes, and policies that support sex worker needs. Attention to indoor venues is especially important because these spaces have greater potential for establishing OHS standards, and also may provide substantial opportunity for collective organising given the close proximity of people working together. However, any efforts to improve the health and safety of sex workers must explicitly address the structural conditions that lead to power imbalances and which undermine sex worker agency and equality.

Broadly, the physical spaces in which sex work is conducted—including aspects of the built environment, workplace policies, and managerial practices—play a key role in determining working conditions within indoor sex work establishments. Economic factors like debt and financial exploitation can undermine sex workers' autonomy, safety, and their ability to negotiate with clients, as can power imbalances and stigma. Relationships with others in sex work, such as peers, owners, and managers, have the power to be beneficial or harmful, depending on the dynamics within the indoor venue. Underlying all of this, legal factors, especially criminalisation and punitive policing practices, challenge sex workers' ability to protect themselves and establish safer work environments. However, as discussed, these factors often interact in ways that create complex challenges to health and safety on multiple fronts. For instance, criminalisation and stigma often stand in the way of community mobilisation and, even though OHS approaches can be implemented in punitive legal contexts, criminalisation means that such efforts are unlikely to be

INDOOR RISK ENVIRONMENT

Physical
- Venue type (e.g. brothel, entertainment, service); venue characteristics (e.g. lighting, security, isolation); workplace policies; managerial practices

Economic
- Gender-based economic inequality; lack of access to financial services (e.g. banking, loans); economic vulnerability (e.g. debt, housing instability); financial exploitation by managers, owners, other third parties, and police (e.g. fees, bribes)

Social
- Gendered power imbalances; stigma; relationships with mangers, owners, other third parties and clients; peer support

Legal/Political
- Criminalization/regulation of sex work (e.g. soliciting, selling, procuring, third party activities); policing practices

IMPACT ON HEALTH, SAFETY AND RIGHTS

- Physical, sexual, emotional, and financial violence
- Mental Health, stress, and trauma
- HIV/STI and other infectious diseases
- Repetitive stress injuries
- Chronic health conditions
- Arrest, detention, incarceration
- Human rights violations

BEST PRACTICES

Occupational Health and Safety
- Working conditions
- Employer duties
- Protection and prevention
- Care and support

Community Mobilization and Engagement
- Community organizing and empowerment
- Sex worker-led initiatives
- Individual-level empowerment

Policy Change
- Full decriminalization
- Shifting local policies and policing practices

Fig. 12.1 Conceptual framework of indoor sex work risk environments, effects on health and safety, and best practices

supported by labour laws holding employers accountable, leaving sex workers still without the necessary safeguards to protect their health [80, 92].

Given the structural nature of these threats to the health and safety of sex workers working in indoor venues, there is a need to challenge existing power structures and to advance sex worker rights. This includes promoting occupational health and safety, focusing on community mobilisation and engagement, and fighting for changes to punitive policies. A focus on these practices could directly impact sex workers' health and rights, while also shifting the risk environment in which sex work occurs, to reduce the harms associated with this work. However, individuals affected by interventions and policies geared towards sex work are too often left out of the conversations that impact their lives. Moving forward, the approach of "nothing about us, without us" must be prioritised and ultimately realised. Anything less serves as a continuation of the stigma and human rights violations that already unjustly plague communities of sex workers around the world.

References

1. Rhodes T. The 'risk environment': a framework for understanding and reducing drug-related harm. Int J Drug Policy. 2002;13(2):85–94.
2. Strathdee SA, Hallett TB, Bobrova N, Rhodes T, Booth R, Abdool R, et al. HIV and risk environment for injecting drug users: the past, present, and future. Lancet. 2010;376(9737):268–84.
3. Pitpitan EV, Kalichman SC, Eaton LA, Strathdee SA, Patterson TL. HIV/STI risk among venue-based female sex workers across the globe: a look back and the way forward. Curr HIV/AIDS Rep. 2013;10(1):65–78.
4. Deering K, Lyons T, Feng C, Nosyk B, Strathdee S, Montaner J, et al. Client demands for unsafe sex: the socio-economic risk environment for HIV among street and off-street sex workers. J Acquir Immune Defic Syndr. 2013;63(4):522.
5. Shannon K, Strathdee SA, Shoveller J, Rusch M, Kerr T, Tyndall MW. Structural and environmental barriers to condom use negotiation with clients among female sex workers: implications for HIV-prevention strategies and policy. Am J Public Health. 2009;99(4):659–65.
6. Shannon KKT, Strathdee SA, Shoveller J, Montaner JS, Tyndall MW. Prevalence and structural correlates of gender based violence among a prospective cohort of female sex workers. BMJ. 2009;339:b2939.
7. Church S, Henderson M, Barnard M, Hart G. Violence by clients towards female prostitutes in different work settings: questionnaire survey. BMJ. 2001;322(7285):524–5.
8. Shannon KKT, Allinott S, Chettiar J, Shoveller J, Tyndall MW. Social and structural violence and power relations in mitigating HIV risk of drug-using women in survival sex work. Soc Sci Med. 2008;66:911–21.
9. Krusi A, Chettiar J, Ridgway A, Abbott J, Strathdee S, Shannon K. Negotiating safety and sexual risk reduction with clients in unsanctioned safer indoor sex work environments: a qualitative study. Am J Public Health. 2012;102:1154–9.
10. Scorgie F, Vasey K, Harper E, Richter M, Nare P, Maseko S, et al. Human rights abuses and collective resilience among sex workers in four African countries: a qualitative study. Global Health. 2013;9(1):33.
11. Harcourt C, Donovan B. The many faces of sex work. Sex Transm Infect. 2005;81(3):201–6.
12. Shannon K, Csete J. Violence, condom negotiation, and HIV/STI risk among sex workers. JAMA. 2010;304(5):573–4.

13. Hampanda K. The social dynamics of selling sex in Mombasa, Kenya: a qualitative study contextualizing high risk sexual behaviour. Afr J Reprod Health. 2013;17(2):141–9.
14. Prior J, Hubbard P, Birch P. Sex worker victimization, modes of working, and location in New South Wales, Australia: a geography of victimization. J Sex Res. 2013;50(6):574–86.
15. Alexander P. Sex work and health: a question of safety in the workplace. J Am Med Womens Assoc. 1998;53(2):77–82.
16. Thoits PA. Stress and health: major findings and policy implications. J Health Soc Behav. 2010;51(1_suppl):S41–53.
17. Ross MW, Crisp BR, Månsson S-A, Hawkes S. Occupational health and safety among commercial sex workers. Scand J Work Environ Health. 2012;38:105–19.
18. Bungay V, Guta A. Strategies and challenges in preventing violence against Canadian indoor sex workers. Am J Public Health. 2018;108(3):393–8.
19. Goldenberg SM, Duff P, Krusi A. Work environments and HIV prevention: a qualitative review and meta-synthesis of sex worker narratives. BMC Public Health. 2015;15(1):1241.
20. Puri N, Shannon K, Nguyen P, Goldenberg S. Burden and correlates of mental health diagnoses among sex workers in an urban setting. BMC Womens Health. 2017;17(1):133.
21. Duff P, Sou J, Chapman J, Dobrer S, Braschel M, Goldenberg S, Shannon K. Poor working conditions and work stress among Canadian sex workers. Occup Med. 2017;67(7):515–21.
22. McBride B, Shannon K, Duff P, Mo M, Braschel M, Goldenberg SM. Harms of workplace inspections for im/migrant sex workers in in-call establishments: enhanced barriers to health access in a Canadian setting. J Immigr Minor Health. 2019;21(6):1290–9.
23. Duff P, Shoveller J, Dobrer S, Ogilvie G, Montaner J, Chettiar J, et al. The relationship between social, policy and physical venue features and social cohesion on condom use for pregnancy prevention among sex workers: a safer indoor work environment scale. J Epidemiol Community Health. 2015;69(7):666–72.
24. Maher L, Mooney-Somers J, Phlong P, Couture MC, Stein E, Evans J, et al. Selling sex in unsafe spaces: sex work risk environments in Phnom Penh, Cambodia. Harm Reduct J. 2011;8:30.
25. Phrasisombath K, Faxelid E, Sychareun V, Thomsen S. Risks, benefits and survival strategies-views from female sex workers in Savannakhet, Laos. BMC Public Health. 2012;12(1):1004.
26. Urada LA, Morisky DE, Hernandez LI, Strathdee SA. Social and structural factors associated with consistent condom use among female entertainment workers trading sex in the Philippines. AIDS Behav. 2013;17(2):523–35.
27. Chen Y, Latkin C, Celentano DD, Yang X, Li X, Xia G, et al. Delineating interpersonal communication networks: a study of the diffusion of an intervention among female entertainment workers in Shanghai, China. AIDS Behav. 2012;16(7):2004–14.
28. Ghose T, Swendeman DT, George SM. The role of brothels in reducing HIV risk in Sonagachi, India. Qual Health Res. 2011;21(5):587–600.
29. Hao C, Guida J, Morisky DE, Liu H. Family network, workplace network, and their influence on condom use: a qualitative study among older female sex workers in China. J Sex Res. 2015;52(8):924–35.
30. Buzdugan R, Halli S, Hiremath J, Jayanna K, Raghavendra T, Moses S, et al. The female sex work industry in a district of India in the context of HIV prevention. AIDS Res Treat. 2012;2012(371482):10.
31. Evans C, Lambert H. The limits of behaviour change theory: condom use and contexts of HIV risk in the Kolkata sex industry. Cult Health Sex. 2008;10(1):27–41.
32. Goldenberg SM, Strathdee SA, Gallardo M, Nguyen L, Lozada R, Semple SJ, et al. How important are venue-based HIV risks among male clients of female sex workers? A mixed methods analysis of the risk environment in nightlife venues in Tijuana, Mexico. Health Place. 2011;17(3):748–56.
33. Gilmour F. Work conditions and job mobility in the Australian indoor sex industry. Sociol Res Online. 2016;21(4):1–2.

34. Harcourt C, van Beek I, Heslop J, McMahon M, Donovan B. The health and welfare needs of female and transgender street sex workers in New South Wales. Aust N Z J Public Health. 2001;25(1):84–9.
35. Reed E, Gupta J, Biradavolu M, Devireddy V, Blankenship KM. The context of economic insecurity and its relation to violence and risk factors for HIV among female sex workers in Andhra Pradesh, India. Public Health Rep. 2010;125(Suppl 4):81–9.
36. Ntumbanzondo M, Dubrow R, Niccolai LM, Mwandagalirwa K, Merson MH. Unprotected intercourse for extra money among commercial sex workers in Kinshasa, Democratic Republic of Congo. AIDS care. 2006;18(7):777–85.
37. Choi S. Heterogeneous and vulnerable: the health risks facing transnational female sex workers. Sociol Health Illn. 2011;33(1):33–49.
38. Reed E, Gupta J, Biradavolu M, Devireddy V, Blankenship K. The role of housing in determining HIV risk among female sex workers in Andhra Pradesh, India: considering women's life contexts. Soc Sci Med. 2011;72(5):710–6.
39. Reed E, Silverman J, Stein B, Erausquin J, Biradavolu M, Rosenberg A, et al. Motherhood and HIV risk among female sex workers in Andhra Pradesh, India: the need to consider women's life contexts. AIDS Behav. 2013;17(2):543–50.
40. Urada L, Morisky D, Pimentel-Simbulan N, Silverman J, Strathdee S. Condom negotiations among female sex workers in the Philippines: environmental influences. PLoS One. 2012;7(3):e33282.
41. Blankenship K, West B, Kershaw T, Biradavolu M. Power, community mobilization, and condom use practices among female sex workers in Andhra Pradesh, India. AIDS. 2008;22(Suppl 5):S109–S16.
42. Yi H, Zheng T, Wan Y, Mantell J, Park M, Csete J. Occupational safety and HIV risk among female sex workers in China: a mixed-methods analysis of sex-work harms and mommies. Glob Public Health. 2012;7(8):840–55.
43. Erausquin JT, Reed E, Blankenship KM. Police-related experiences and HIV risk among female sex workers in Andhra Pradesh, India. J Infect Dis. 2011;204(Suppl 5):S1223–8.
44. Damacena G, Szwarcwald C, de Souza P, Dourado I. Risk factors associated with HIV prevalence among female sex workers in 10 Brazilian cities. J Acquir Immune Defic Syndr. 2011;57:S144–S52.
45. Gaines T, Rusch M, Brouwer K, Lozada R, Perkins E, Strathdee S, et al. The effect of geography on HIV and sexually transmitted infections in Tijuana's red light district. J Urban Health. 2013;90(5):915–20.
46. O'Doherty T. Victimization in off-street sex industry work. Violence Against Women. 2011;17(7):944–63.
47. Benoit C, Millar A. Dispelling myths and understanding realities: working conditions, health status, and exiting experiences of sex workers. Victoria, BC: BC Health Research Foundation; 2001.
48. Comte J. Decriminalization of sex work: feminist discourses in light of research. Sex Cult. 2014;18(1):196–217.
49. Shannon K, Strathdee SA, Goldenberg SM, Duff P, Mwangi P, Rusakova M, et al. Global epidemiology of HIV among female sex workers: influence of structural determinants. Lancet. 2015;385(9962):55–71.
50. Deering KN, Amin A, Shoveller J, Nesbitt A, Garcia-Moreno C, Duff P, Argento E, Shannon K. A systematic review of the correlates of violence against sex workers. Am J Public Health. 2014;104(5):e42–54.
51. Liu Q, Zhuang K, Henderson G, Shenglong Q, Fang J, Yao H, et al. The organization of sex work in low- and high-priced venues with a focus on the experiences of ethnic minority women working in these venues. AIDS Behav. 2014;18(2):172–80.
52. Cheng SS, Mak WW. Contextual influences on safer sex negotiation among female sex workers (FSWs) in Hong Kong: the role of non-governmental organizations (NGOs), FSWs' managers, and clients. AIDS Care. 2010;22(5):606–13.

53. Januraga P, Mooney-Somers J, Ward P. Newcomers in a hazardous environment: a qualitative inquiry into sex worker vulnerability to HIV in Bali, Indonesia. BMC Public Health. 2014;14(1):832.
54. Bungay V, Halpin M, Halpin P, Johnson C, Patrick D. Violence in the massage parlor industry: experiences of Canadian-born and immigrant women. Health Care Women Int. 2012;33(3):262–84.
55. Handlovsky I, Bungay V, Kolar K. Condom use as situated in a risk context: women's experiences in the massage parlour industry in Vancouver, Canada. Cult Health Sex. 2012;14(9):1007–20.
56. Howard S. Better health for sex workers: which legal model causes least harm? BMJ. 2018;361:k2609.
57. McCarthy B, Benoit C, Jansson M, Kolar K. Regulating sex work: heterogeneity in legal strategies. Annu Rev Law Soc Sci. 2012;8:255–71.
58. Peterson M, Robinson B, Shih E. The new virtual crackdown on sex workers' rights: perspectives from the United States. Anti-Traffick Rev. 2019;12:189–93.
59. McBride B, Goldenberg SM, Murphy A, Wu S, Braschel M, Krüsi A, et al. Third parties (venue owners, managers, security, etc.) and access to occupational health and safety among sex workers in a Canadian setting: 2010–2016. Am J Public Health. 2019;109:792–8.
60. Sanders T, Campbell R. Designing out vulnerability, building in respect: violence, safety and sex work policy. Br J Sociol. 2007;58(1):1–19.
61. Anderson S, Shannon K, Li J, Lee Y, Chettiar J, Goldenberg S, et al. Condoms and sexual health education as evidence: impact of criminalization of in-call venues and managers on migrant sex workers access to HIV/STI prevention in a Canadian setting. BMC Int Health Hum Rights. 2016;16(1):30.
62. Beyrer C, Crago A-L, Bekker L-G, Butler J, Shannon K, Kerrigan D, et al. An action agenda for HIV and sex workers. Lancet. 2015;385(9964):287–301.
63. Decker MR, Crago A-L, Chu SK, Sherman SG, Seshu MS, Buthelezi K, et al. Human rights violations against sex workers: burden and effect on HIV. Lancet. 2015;385(9963):186–99.
64. Rhodes T, Simic M, Baros S, Platt L, Zikic B. Police violence and sexual risk among female and transvestite sex workers in Serbia. BMJ. 2008;337:a811.
65. Anderson S, Jia J, Liu V, Chattier J, Krüsi A, Allan S, et al. Violence prevention and municipal licensing of indoor sex work venues in the Greater Vancouver Area: narratives of migrant sex workers, managers and business owners. Cult Health Sex. 2015;17(7):825–41.
66. Plumridge L, Abel G. A 'segmented' sex industry in New Zealand: sexual and personal safety of female sex workers. Aust N Z J Public Health. 2001;25(1):78–83.
67. Shannon K, Rusch M, Shoveller J, Alexson D, Gibson K, Tyndall MW. Mapping violence and policing as an environmental–structural barrier to health service and syringe availability among substance-using women in street-level sex work. Int J Drug Policy. 2008;19(2):140–7.
68. Azim T, Bontell I, Strathdee SA. Women, drugs and HIV. Int J Drug Policy. 2015;26:S16–21.
69. Goldenberg S, Krusi A, Zhang E, Chettiar J, Shannon K. Structural determinants of health among im/migrants in the indoor sex industry: experiences of workers and managers/owners in Metropolitan Vancouver. PLoS One. 2017;12(1):e0170642.
70. Goldenberg SM, Jiménez TR, Brouwer KC, Miranda SM, Silverman JG. Influence of indoor work environments on health, safety, and human rights among migrant sex workers at the Guatemala-Mexico Border: a call for occupational health and safety interventions. BMC Int Health Hum Rights. 2018;18(1):9.
71. Richter M, Chersich MF, Vearey J, Sartorius B, Temmerman M, Luchters S. Migration status, work conditions and health utilization of female sex workers in three South African cities. J Immigr Minor Health. 2014;16(1):7–17.
72. Richter M, Chersich M, Temmerman M, Luchters S. Characteristics, sexual behaviour and risk factors of female, male and transgender sex workers in South Africa. S Afr Med J. 2013;103(4):246–51.
73. Logie C, James L, Tharao W, Loutfy M. HIV, gender, race, sexual orientation, and sex work: a qualitative study of intersectional stigma experienced by HIV-positive women in Ontario, Canada. PLoS Med. 2011;8:e1001124.

74. Hwahng S, Nuttbrock L. Sex workers, fem queens, and cross-dressers: differential marginalizations and HIV vulnerabilities among three ethnocultural male-to-female transgender communities in New York City. Sex Res Soc Policy. 2007;4:36–59.
75. Prado Cortez F, Boer D, Baltieri D. A psychosocial study of male-to-female transgendered and male hustler sex workers in São Paulo, Brazil. Arch Sex Behav. 2011;40:1223–31.
76. Poteat T, Wirtz A, Radix A, Borquez A, Silva-Santisteban A, Deutsch M, et al. HIV risk and preventive interventions in transgender women sex workers. Lancet. 2015;385(9964):274–86.
77. Lyons T, Krüsi A, Pierre L, Kerr T, Small W, Shannon K. Negotiating violence in the context of transphobia and criminalization: the experiences of trans sex workers in Vancouver, Canada. Qual Health Res. 2017;27(2):182–90.
78. Victoria CA. Occupational health and safety (OHS) and cleaning your sex work premises. 2019. Available from: https://www.consumer.vic.gov.au/licensing-and-registration/sex-work-service-providers/running-your-business/occupational-health-and-safety-and-cleaning.
79. Rekart ML. Sex-work harm reduction. Lancet. 2005;366(9503):2123–34.
80. ICRSE. Understanding sex workers' right to health: impact of criminalisation and violence. Amsterdam: International Committee on the Rights of Sex Workers in Europe; 2017.
81. Basnyat I. Lived experiences of street-based female sex workers in Kathmandu: implications for health intervention strategies. Cult Health Sex. 2014;16(9):1040–51.
82. Sanders T, Hardy K, Campbell R. Regulating strip-based entertainment: sexual entertainment venue policy and the ex/inclusion of dancers' perspectives and needs. Soc Policy Soc. 2015;14(1):83–92.
83. Awungafac G, Delvaux T, Vuylsteke B. Systematic review of sex work interventions in sub-Saharan Africa: examining combination prevention approaches. Trop Med Int Health. 2017;22(8):971–93.
84. GAATW. Sex workers organizing for change: self-representation, community mobilisation, and working conditions. Bangkok, Thailand: Global Alliance Against Traffic in Women (GAATW); 2018.
85. Evans C, Jana S, Lambert H. What makes a structural intervention? Reducing vulnerability to HIV in community settings, with particular reference to sex work. Glob Public Health. 2010;5(5):449–61.
86. Kerrigan D, Kennedy CE, Morgan-Thomas R, Reza-Paul S, Mwangi P, Win KT, et al. A community empowerment approach to the HIV response among sex workers: effectiveness, challenges, and considerations for implementation and scale-up. Lancet. 2015;385(9963):172–85.
87. Kerrigan D, Fonner V, Stromdahl S, Kennedy C. Community empowerment among female sex workers is an effective HIV prevention intervention: a systematic review of the peer-reviewed evidence from low-and middle-income countries. AIDS Behav. 2013;17(6):1926–40.
88. Gupta G, Parkhurst J, Ogden J, Aggleton P, Mahal A. Structural approaches to HIV prevention. Lancet. 2008;372(9640):764–75.
89. World Health Organization. Consolidated guidelines on HIV prevention, diagnosis, treatment and care for key populations. Geneva, Switzerland: World Health Organization; 2016.
90. Godwin J. Sex work and the law in Asia and the Pacific: laws, HIV and human rights in the context of sex work. Geneva, Switzerland: UNAIDS, UNFPA, UNDP; 2012.
91. Amnesty International publishes policy and research on protection of sex workers' rights [press release]. 26 May 2016.
92. Abel G. A decade of decriminalization: sex work 'down under' but not underground. Criminol Crim Just. 2014;14(5):580–92.
93. Cunningham S, Shah M. Decriminalizing indoor prostitution: implications for sexual violence and public health. Rev Econ Stud. 2017;85(3):1683–715.
94. Gaines TL, Rusch ML, Brouwer KC, Goldenberg SM, Lozada R, Robertson AM, et al. Venue-level correlates of female sex worker registration status: a multilevel analysis of bars in Tijuana, Mexico. Glob Public Health. 2013;8(4):405–16.

Chapter 13
Integrated Interventions to Address Sex Workers' Needs and Realities: Academic and Community Insights on Incorporating Structural, Behavioural, and Biomedical Approaches

Sheree Schwartz, Nikita Viswasam, and Phelister Abdalla

Introduction to Integrated, Multi-component, Multi-level Interventions

Sex workers experience threats to their physical and mental health from varying and intersecting factors [1–4]. As described in previous chapters, stigma, human rights violations, exposure to violence, unintended pregnancy, HIV, and other STIs create complex health inequities that are less likely to be addressed through interventions focusing on one type of 'risk factor'. Recognising that individuals reside in complex environments influenced by multiple levels is thus essential for designing interventions [5, 6]. The health outcomes of sex workers are impacted at varying levels, from individual and interpersonal factors, to community and policy factors [7]. Examples of these factors at different levels include sex workers' clients refusing to use condoms, which increases risk of acquiring HIV and other STIs; stigma and discrimination from healthcare providers hindering sex worker's engagement in health care; and physical and sexual violence by clients, partners, and law enforcement officers targeting sex workers [1, 4, 7–9]. Furthermore, laws that criminalise sex work play a critical role in reinforcing marginalisation, perpetuating stigma and undermining violence prevention efforts and access to health care [10]. The existence of these multi-level factors suggests that narrowly focused interventions addressing a single disease or issue are unlikely to succeed. Addressing multiple layers of marginalisation calls for multi-level, integrated interventions.

S. Schwartz (✉) · N. Viswasam
Key Populations Program, Department of Epidemiology, Johns Hopkins School of Public Health, Baltimore, MD, USA
e-mail: sschwartz@jhu.edu; nviswas1@jhu.edu

P. Abdalla
Kenya Sex Workers Alliance, Nairobi, Kenya
e-mail: keswa04@gmail.com

© The Author(s) 2021
S. M. Goldenberg et al. (eds.), *Sex Work, Health, and Human Rights*,
https://doi.org/10.1007/978-3-030-64171-9_13

The goal of this chapter is to introduce the concepts of layered, multi-component, and multi-level interventions and explore the ways in which interventions can address sex workers' needs through a combination of structural-, behavioural-, and biomedical-level activities. Critical to this goal is recognition that intervention success will only be achieved if perspectives, priorities, and leadership by sex workers drive the approach.

To begin, we discuss types of interventions, including integrated and multi-component interventions, as well as biomedical, behavioural, and structural approaches to interventions. An **integrated health intervention** is one that uses two or more *approaches* to address an underlying health need or problem. For example, integrated health services for cisgender female sex workers might include HIV prevention and/or treatment provision alongside provision of contraception, thus integrating family planning and HIV care. Similarly, a **multi-component intervention** is one that includes multiple *activities* as part of the overall approach. This could be an integrated approach in which sex workers receive multiple services at one location, or it could be that different components are offered at different times and different places, but all with the common goal of addressing underlying vulnerabilities or needs.

Component parts of interventions may use *biomedical, behavioural,* or *structural* approaches (Fig. 13.1). **Biomedical interventions** use clinical or medical approaches to address health outcomes. In the HIV field, pre-exposure prophylaxis

Types of Interventions		
Structural	**Behavioral**	**Biomedical**
Aim Change economic, legal, political, or social environmental factors that shape public health outcomes	**Aim** Support changes in human behavior to influence health outcomes	**Aim** Provide clinical or medical approach to health outcomes
Example • Decriminalise sex work • Community empowerment, such as enhancing skills to mobilise or engage in legal advocacy • Sensitivity training for law enforcement	**Example** • Peer education on strategies to improve condom use with clients and partners • Self-efficacy building workshops to increase treatment adherence	**Example** • PrEP program for sex workers • STI treatment services • Post-violence response medical care and reporting support

Fig. 13.1 Structural, behavioural, and biomedical interventions

(PrEP) to prevent HIV would be an example of a biomedical intervention to promote health among sex workers. **Behavioural interventions** focus on influencing or supporting changes in human behaviour. Using the HIV prevention example, behavioural interventions may support sex workers to continue on PrEP, often through motivating individuals and creating strategies or incentives to engage in positive health-seeking behaviours. **Structural interventions** attempt to alter the underlying context that shapes public health outcomes—through changing the economic, political, legal, or social environment in which individuals operate. Examples of structural interventions might be legal reform or policy guidelines which decriminalise sex work, provision of violence prevention interventions for sex workers which target police as potential perpetrators and violence mitigators, or empowerment programmes to build social support, resilience, and autonomy among sex workers. Addressing violence and incorporating referral into programming, addressing trauma and ensuring continued access to treatment and prevention during times of arrest or detainment are also essential. Multi-component interventions, which integrate elements across these three intervention types, are increasingly recognised as important to improving health outcomes, as each one attempts to address different needs or barriers to positive health outcomes.

Interventions addressing a combination of biomedical, behavioural, and structural approaches are often multi-level interventions. **Multi-level interventions** seek to address needs or barriers to positive health outcomes which may stem from various sources—namely barriers at the **individual level**, **social and network level**, the **community level**, and the **legal/public policy level**. These approaches recognise that individuals are not entirely independent beings, but rather are embedded and interact within environments that shape and influence their life outcomes. Thus, multi-level interventions are designed to influence a variety of actors—not just sex workers. Healthcare workers, police officers, and policymakers are all potential actors engaged in various types of multi-level interventions, in addition to sex workers and their clients.

In summary, an integrated, multi-component intervention combines more than one intervention activity, targeting two or more of the three approaches (biomedical, behavioural, and/or structural). Not all integrated or multi-component interventions will include components across these areas. Typically, interventions spanning all three areas will also be multi-level in nature, as they tend to be targeting different barriers or facilitators to health. Community perspectives from The Kenya Sex Workers Alliance (KESWA) (Boxes 13.1 and 13.2) highlight why integrated, multi-component interventions including structural interventions are necessary for improved health outcomes among sex workers, even when biomedical health services for sex workers are available [11].

Box 13.1 Perspectives of the Kenya Sex Workers Alliance (KESWA) on the Impact of the Structural Environment on Violence Against Sex Workers in Kenya

The legal environment in Kenya is comprised of laws and policies that provide a framework to address sexual and gender-based violence. However, the existence of punitive criminal provisions hinders effectiveness of interventions, particularly for key populations such as sex workers. These provisions allow law enforcement officers to abuse sex workers with impunity—for example, targeting sex workers and extorting them for sex in exchange for their freedom when they are unable to pay a bribe. Data from a KESWA survey suggest that sexual exploitation involving police officers is largely targeted at female sex workers with 8.4% of sex workers in Kenya reporting demand for unprotected sex to secure their release. Fifty-two percent of sex workers consider law enforcement agents to be the greatest threat to their safety and security. This contributes to mistrust and general fear of law enforcement agents, discouraging reporting of violence with only 34.3% having reported violence that they had experienced. Despite 50.6% of sex workers having been part of forums organised for sex workers, legal awareness and human rights empowerment is not adequately covered.

The policy environment has played a major role in strengthening access to medical interventions for sex workers (e.g. HIV care), but has had less of an effect on other services required to address violence including psychosocial services, rehabilitation and reintegration, victim protection and legal support. These findings were reported by KESWA, the collective of Kenyan sex worker-led organisations in *Silenced by Law: the Impact of the Legal Environment on Health, Safety and Protection in Relation to Sex Work related Violence in Kenya* exploring six critical areas: legal reform, enhancing access to justice, legal awareness for sex workers, enhancing safety and security, enhancing health and social services and research. This report highlights the need for integrated interventions including structural, behavioural, and biomedical approaches to violence, sexual and reproductive health, and HIV/STIs care to effectively improve sex worker health and well-being.

Evaluation of Integrated Interventions

Evaluating interventions is necessary to determine the impact that services have on sex workers' health outcomes and quality of life. Evaluation may be particularly complicated when interventions are integrated and multi-component. Did each component of the intervention work independently from the other, or did the intervention components in combination produce a different effect than what might have been achieved in the absence of the other intervention? For example, if an intervention addresses workplace safety, enhanced negotiation skills among sex workers,

Box 13.2 What Sex Workers Want to See: A Multi-level, Multi-component Intervention Strategy to Address Violence Proposed by the Kenya Sex Workers Alliance (KESWA)

Legal reform [13]	Enhancing access to justice [14–16]	Legal awareness for sex workers [14–16]	Enhancing safety and security [13, 15, 17]	Enhancing health and social services [15]
1. Engage the Council of Governors and Members of County Assemblies on the risks presented by additional legislation and punitive approaches with regard to sex work-related activities 2. Initiate strategic cases on the prosecution of sex workers for petty offences on the basis of county laws and violence against sex worker to encourage law reform 3. Public Interest Litigation to improve policy and legal protections relating to violence by reviewing and repealing criminal provisions contributing to the heightened vulnerability of sex workers to violence	1. Scale up supportive programmes with trained community paralegals to ensure legal support 2. Case reporting and follow-up services made available to sex workers who seek health services for violence 3. Sensitisation of judicial officers on the profiling of sex workers by law enforcement officers to mitigate abuse of arrest and prosecutorial powers 4. Facilitate dialogue between sex workers, investigators, and prosecutors to identify challenges and develop complementary strategies to improve prosecution of cases of violence against sex workers 5. Establish multi-sectoral partnerships to advocate for better implementation of laws and mechanisms that address violence	1. Comprehensive legal education on criminal procedures and legal protections for victims of violence 2. Establishing, maintaining, and publicising 24-h sex worker help lines for reporting, referral and general information to sex workers who experience violence 3. Training on the law-making process and avenues to engage national and county assemblies	1. Engage with police and county officers through station/work-based sensitisation forums on the rights of sex workers and their role in addressing violence against them 2. Establish mechanisms to improve accountability among law enforcement officers in investigating and prosecuting cases of violence against sex workers 3. Establish safe and anonymous systems for reporting violence and seeking help 4. Media engagement to increase human interest reporting to address ignorance and expose inaction on violence against sex workers	1. Increase awareness among law enforcement officers at county level and law makers on existing policies and their importance to better inform administrative and legislative decisions 2. Explore innovative approaches of disseminating evidence around sex work programming 3. Develop a policy brief to advocate for recognition of sex workers as a group at high risk, vulnerable to sexual violence and their prioritisation for proposed interventions in the County Government Policy on Sexual and Gender-Based Violence

and provision of free condoms and lubricants, do these interventions each work better when the other one is co-occurring? Similarly, were all components necessary for an effect or could the intervention have been sufficiently successful with a more minimal package? If the intervention did not work, might it have it succeeded if there had been an additional component added?

Specifying the Intervention and Outcomes

Given the complexities described above, the first piece of evaluating any intervention—and particularly integrated, multi-component interventions—is intervention specification [12]. What exactly is included in each component of the intervention? Who is delivering and who is receiving the intervention? When will it be delivered, where, how much, and for how long? Are the components envisioned to operate independently or is there a specified sequence of the components? Clear specification is necessary to facilitate reproducibility of results, compare the effectiveness of intervention components, and to evaluate the extent to which effect or lack of effect is due to how well the intervention was implemented. For example, did the intervention fail because it did not work, or because parts of it were not implemented fully or correctly as specified?

Clearly outlining activity details and adaptations will ensure that successful achievements can be tried in other settings. Further, clear articulation of actors and steps should reveal the centrality of the sex work community to intervention design and implementation. Are sex worker priorities represented in the listed activities? Are sex workers taking on leadership activities in formative phases to design interventions? Are they implementing components of the interventions? For each of the components—who was the source of the intervention—were components determined by external stakeholders or do they emanate from sex workers themselves?

Community perspectives from KESWA (Box 13.2) highlight various components of a sex worker-led multi-level, multi-component intervention that is currently being implemented to address violence faced by sex workers in Kenya. Approaches include *law reform* [13], *enhancing access to justice* [14–16], *legal awareness for sex workers* [14–16], *enhancing safety and security* [13, 15, 17], *and enhancing health and social services* [15]. Future evaluation of the effectiveness of this multi-component approach in Kenya at reducing threats to health, stigma, and discrimination experienced among sex workers will be critical.

Finally, evaluations must consider a broad array of health outcomes to monitor success. Outcomes must include those most prioritised by the sex worker community, such as violence and fear of violence, and other human rights abuses. Focusing only on HIV or STI-related outcomes is insufficient as it ignores the broader context of change that is necessary to support health. Measurement of stigma, violence, human rights violations, and behaviours of healthcare providers, police, and clients will provide a clearer picture of the mechanisms of change. Additionally, measuring implementation outcomes such as intervention acceptability, adoption, appropriateness, feasibility, and fidelity of implementation as described by *Proctor* et al. can further ensure that intervention components are aligned to the needs and priorities of the sex work community [18].

Challenges in Evaluation of Multi-component, Multi-level Interventions Among Sex Workers

Evaluation approaches which allow for comparisons across time periods and exposure to interventions are important to promote evidence-based approaches, but this type of evidence is rarely gathered for sex worker interventions [19]. Community-led monitoring of intervention implementation and success should be incorporated and can ensure community-led insights are guiding implementation. Data reported are often cross-sectional (collected at one point in time) and thus provide little understanding of changes over time, which are typically needed to document impact. Programmatic data, while critical to monitor implementation success, often lack control groups for comparison—as everyone in the programme is typically offered the interventions. Thus, changes in outcomes over time may be attributable to the interventions, or they may have resulted from other co-occurring initiatives. Further, randomised controlled trials—in which one group is randomly allocated to receive an intervention and another receives the standard of care or an alternative intervention—have less frequently been implemented among sex workers. While randomised trials are critical for establishing the efficacy of many biomedical products, they are often less appropriate for understanding real-world implementation and, if implemented (such as a comparison of two strategies to implement the same evidence-based intervention), need to ensure equipoise. As such, intervention designs and evaluation will need to rely on more creative and observational methods, including causal inference approaches to account for selective outcome ascertainment or to assess outcomes right before and after a policy was implemented, pre- and post-designs in which areas that were not implementing the intervention share pre- and post-data for comparison, as well as data reporting on the implementation process and outcomes [20, 21].

Finally, evaluation of multi-component, multi-level interventions pose unique challenges—including how to measure the impact of individual components when multiple components are offered, and evaluation of the need for each component, as each additional component will have additional costs and complexities. Similarly, structural interventions are often implemented at a macro-level (e.g. a change of policy) and thus variation of the exposure within an area is not even feasible [20].

These complexities should not discourage evaluation of interventions, but rather can be used as a platform to ensure meaningful engagement between sex work communities, implementers, and researchers to explore opportunities to evaluate success that are both robust and supported by the sex worker community. There are opportunities for more rigorous design—including use of quasi-experimental designs [20], as well as the potential for randomisation of smaller component parts or the way that the intervention is delivered (e.g. by sex worker peers or by health-care providers). Incorporation of sex worker preferences into the design and evaluation plans and activities should be prioritised from the outset and can be achieved through both quantitative and qualitative approaches [22], as well as community-led monitoring.

Evidence of Impact of Integrated, Multi-component Interventions

There are single component sex work interventions with varying degrees of effectiveness to promote health outcomes. Interventions include condom and lubricant distribution, legal reform, and other structural interventions with police to reduce condom confiscation, discrimination, and violence perpetration, as well as advocacy measures to support access to justice for sex workers experiencing violence [15, 23, 24]. Direct health service delivery is the most common strategy applied, including screening and treatment programmes for sexually transmitted infections, voluntary HIV testing programmes, antiretroviral therapy provision, and comprehensive family planning services. However, there is growing recognition of the need to layer services with community mobilisation efforts to build advocacy and social cohesion among sex workers, interventions to prevent gender-based violence, and community empowerment efforts to address unsafe work environments, violence, structural discrimination, and address education needs [25]. Furthermore, laws criminalising sex workers, clients, and third parties have been demonstrated to negatively impact health outcomes [24, 26]. Thus, while single interventions may result in some important improvements and may be easier to assess, they are unlikely to achieve sustainable population-level impact or to sufficiently address the multi-pronged factors and health concerns faced by sex workers. Thus, we review the evidence of integrated, multi-component interventions on health outcomes.

Of note, there are many sex worker-led interventions globally that target structural reform, advocate for sex worker protections, and promote and implement service delivery. Interventions determined by the community to have benefit are often continued and de-implemented where benefit is not observed; however, external dissemination of evaluation efforts is often lacking, limiting the creation of a robust evidence base. Funding has prioritised the implementation and evaluation of primarily biomedical and behavioural intervention approaches, and many of the structural initiatives remain unevaluated. As such, structural approaches remain under-represented in evidence syntheses, including the evidence presented in the following sub-sections. Further efforts to evaluate and capture lessons learned from sex worker-led and community-based interventions, especially addressing structural factors, therefore remain needed to fully capture impacts on outcomes and should be supported through funding and skills transfer initiatives to build capacity in evaluation, dissemination, and communication. Further financial support for sex worker-led organisations to drive evaluations of their interventions is critical, and consideration of potential partnerships with advocates in the research community to support training in evaluation methods may represent an important opportunity for collaborative work. Frequently, the model is for researchers to approach sex workers with ideas, but this paradigm can be turned upside down and would benefit both the sex worker and research communities.

HIV and STIs

For many years, condom provision and promotion were the primary methods of HIV and STI prevention programmes. In the 1990s, the 100% Condom Campaign in Thailand combined condom provision, mass marketing, and policies to promote condom use in sex work establishments to reduce HIV incidence and prevalence in Thailand [27]. Although this is an example of a structural intervention that achieved prevention success, the programme reinforced coercive environments rather than promoting empowerment, was not designed or led by sex workers, and is an example of top-down approaches to reform which have been widely condemned by the sex work community [28].

Increasingly, multi-component, multi-level strategies are moving beyond condom provision and promotion alone as prevention strategies. A systematic review of combination prevention interventions implemented in sub-Saharan Africa published from 2000 to mid-2016 found that, generally, multi-level interventions mediated by peer educators increased condom use [29]. Evidence of impact on new HIV and STI infections, however, was more mixed. Large-scale HIV and STI prevention programmes have demonstrated substantial decreases in both HIV and STI prevalence over time in Benin, Cote d'Ivoire, and Burkina Faso [30–33]. However, none of these studies were randomised and may potentially reflect underlying secular trends over time rather than an effect attributable to the interventions implemented. Among eight randomised trials during this time, only the Kenyan trial focused on peer support and organisation empowerment. It also achieved STI prevention as demonstrated by declines in STIs, though not on HIV incidence [34, 35]. Studies evaluating isolated interventions or comparing multi-component to isolated interventions reinforce the need to combine more than one type of approach [36]. A randomised controlled trial in Madagascar among 1000 female sex workers found that peer condom promotion alone was not effective but, when combined with individual counselling, it reduced STIs by 30% after 6 months [37]. Outside of the African continent, multi-level interventions, which included strategies to modify environmental conditions and support collective action implemented in Brazil and the Dominican Republic, have increased social cohesion and condom use, thus resulting in declines in STIs [38, 39], though experimental designs and demonstrated impact on HIV incidence are still needed.

The Avahan study in India was the largest programme implemented to date to apply a combination prevention approach to reduce HIV incidence. It is notable as it included both individual-level, community-level and structural components. Peer outreach, counselling, condoms, needle and syringe exchange, clinic services, community mobilisation, and advocacy activities for sex workers and clients was implemented in six states. Overall, results from repeated surveys and modelling indicated that HIV prevalence significantly declined in four out of the six states implementing the intervention [19, 40]. Although the evaluation approach (mathematical modelling) has been considered controversial, an estimated 202,000 infections were averted during the study [40–42].

Community-based research approaches—including community empowerment interventions that seek to change social environments alongside condom provision and promotion and biomedical solutions—remain crucial as the importance of addressing structural challenges to prevention and care are increasingly recognised. A comprehensive review and meta-analysis of community empowerment analyses spanning eight projects demonstrated a positive impact on HIV and STI prevention associated with community empowerment approaches [43]. However, weak study designs were pervasive, geographic representation was limited, and few male or transgender sex workers were included in the studies. The authors concluded that there was a need to leverage empowerment initiatives as part of more comprehensive combination intervention.

More evidence of impact of multi-component interventions to increase PrEP uptake, antiretroviral therapy (ART) coverage, and viral suppression among sex workers living with HIV is urgently needed. There is evidence that structural determinants including mobility, incarceration, and punitive environments negatively impact ART use among sex workers [44]. Evidence from the community-based SAPPH-IRe sex work programme in Zimbabwe—including peer-led empowerment and mobilisation, and concurrent ART scale-up—resulted in increased ART coverage and viral suppression over time among female sex workers. These results were also seen in the broader population. Modelling suggests the importance of these interventions in altering the epidemic curve [45]. Yet the SAPPH-IRe combination prevention trial—including community mobilisation, HIV testing, ART, and PrEP—did not show significant reduction in HIV infections or viral suppression despite an uptake of services, reminding us again that individual-level impacts do not necessarily result in population-level effectiveness [46].

Evidence of the impact of legal reform on HIV outcomes remains limited. There is now substantial evidence pointing to the HIV-associated risks related to criminalised legal environments for sex work [10, 47, 48]. Modelling studies suggest that decriminalisation of sex work would have the biggest impact on reducing HIV incidence among sex workers, yet lack of policy changes limit the real-world evaluation of this intervention [7, 23].

Sexual and Reproductive Health

Outside of HIV prevention and HIV/STI screening and treatment, the evidence base for integrated, multi-component sexual and reproductive health (SRH) interventions remains limited. There is a growing body of work documenting the vast unmet needs among sex workers for contraception, safe termination of pregnancy services, safer conception care and initiatives to prevent or address sexual violence [49, 50]. Yet global and region-specific systematic reviews have found that multi-component interventions with female sex workers pertaining to family planning, cervical cancer screening or sexual violence have been documented infrequently, and where evidence exists, it is limited largely to reports of service utilisation, rather than intervention effectiveness [51]. Differentiated care models which incorporate broader reproductive health choices including safer conception and termination of pregnancy interventions for female sex workers have rarely been implemented, and lack evaluation thereof. Globally, there is limited actual evidence for how to effectively integrate reproductive health and family planning services into sex worker programmes [52]. While undoubtedly many sex worker programmes are offering integrated, multi-component services, this lack of data limits the evidence base and results in questions regarding implementation effectiveness and efficiencies.

The limited existing data demonstrate the need for more comprehensive multi-component interventions while indicating the challenges faced to delivering high quality integrated sexual and reproductive health care to female sex workers. In Cambodia, the SAHACOM programme used a multi-component package which included HIV/STI and reproductive health integration, as well as economic and behavioural empowerment approaches among women engaged in entertainment and sex work spaces. Results suggested an increase in contraception uptake and decrease in abortions and STIs, though more rigorous study designs of similar programmes including a comparator group are needed [53]. A separate study in Cambodia at a clinic frequented by female sex workers found no effect of integrating family planning services into facility-based HIV care [54]. In Madagascar, an RCT focused on peer education alongside clinic-based counselling on condom use found that in the absence of contraception integration, rates of unintended pregnancies were high, as condom use varies across partner types [55]. A study in South Africa, Mozambique and Kenya found that more comprehensive efforts to integrate multi-level and multi-component comprehensive sexual and reproductive health services resulted in increased uptake of sexual and reproductive health services [56]. Future efforts to replicate successful designs and incorporate control groups and long-term effectiveness outcomes remain necessary.

Finally, it should be noted that sexual and reproductive health services are relevant to male and transgender sex workers, but data documenting their reproductive health needs outside of STI treatment and condom/lubricant promotion are limited. Interventions to address screening for anal cancer, for example, are few, and more attention is warranted in this space [57–59].

Violence and Human Rights Violations

Human rights violations against sex workers have been documented globally, including physical and sexual violence from police, clients, and partners, and institutional discrimination in accessing health care, welfare services, and the criminal justice system [60–62]. Sex worker-led organisations have mobilised to implement human rights affirming strategies in this context [63, 64]. *Crago* profiled sex worker-led movements addressing human rights violations globally, such as South African National Sex Workers' Network, Sisonke, which has led legal advice, crisis counselling and advocacy for sex workers as well as alongside the South African Sex Worker Education and Advocacy Taskforce (SWEAT), challenging the state's criminalisation of sex work, arbitrary unlawful arrests by police and harassment of sex workers in court. Their efforts influenced the South African government's recommendations for the reform of laws criminalising sex work in order to reduce discrimination and improve harm reduction activities among sex workers as part of an HIV prevention strategy [64]. However, a limited number of public health interventions have addressed violence among sex workers, primarily seen in the context of HIV outcomes [65–67]. Even fewer are designed as integrated multi-level interventions with activities targeting violence prevention, response, and/or other human rights violations. Examples of combination interventions addressing violence and human rights violations, however, are available from India [14–16], Kenya [17], and Mongolia [67], where activities focused on violence prevention, response, and/or police treatment of sex workers, involving capacity building around violence response mechanisms for health service organisations, training of police personnel, and individual-level skill-building for sex workers.

In India, a provincial programme by the Karnataka Health Promotion Trust, part of the larger national Avahan AIDS Initiative, took a structural and behavioural approach to addressing violence, partnering with district police heads and sex workers to train police officers in HIV/AIDS, sex work, and the law [14–16]. Furthermore, sex workers were involved in community mobilisation, skills-building activities, and legal empowerment workshops along with 24-h crisis management response teams to address reported incidents of violence and advocates to assist in the event of wrongful arrest. A similar programme in Andhra Pradesh included the same strategies as part of a community advocacy system, along with forming community action groups (CAG) [13]. Through the Karnataka initiative nearly all districts saw reductions in their violence reports. Sex workers with a longer duration of exposure to the programme were even less likely to report experiencing violence. Continued programme activities also found reduced rates of both police arrest among sex workers and arrests as part of arbitrary police raids. In Andhra Pradesh, the annual programme behavioural tracking survey found that in areas with active CAGs, the police were more likely to explain their reasons for arrest. Sex workers in areas with active CAGs reported a perception of fairer treatment by police compared to the year before. These programmes took structural and behavioural approaches to addressing community-level barriers through police training and mobilisation, and individual-level barriers through legal empowerment and skill-building.

In Mongolia, a randomised controlled trial was conducted examining the effect of a combination HIV sexual risk reduction and microsavings intervention on violence from clients of sex workers [67]. Its behavioural component, the HIV sexual risk reduction intervention, involved skills-building sessions around identifying safety risks, negotiating safe sex, and avoiding unsafe situations. The structural component was a microsavings intervention involving a matched-savings programme at partnering banks and training on financial literacy, business development, and vocational mentorship. This trial found significant reductions in reports of recent client violence in both the enhanced intervention group (behavioural + structural interventions) and standard groups (behavioural intervention only), though participation in the microsavings structural intervention did not further decrease exposure to violence from clients beyond the behavioural intervention alone.

In Kenya, the National Key Populations Programme took a multi-level approach to violence response. Adopting strategies as part of the National Guidelines for HIV/STI Programming for key populations, the Programme conducted trainings on violence and key population rights with implementing partner organisations. These, in turn, conducted educational activities around violence, rights, and reporting for both key population members and clinical and outreach service staff [17]. Some implementers also developed 24-h response teams involving peer educators and peer paralegals linked to clinicians and advocacy officials to assist participants disclosing violence and ensuring their direct delivery or referral to post-violence services. Annual programme data between 2013 and 2017 revealed an increase in the number of sex workers reached.

Along with the public health interventions described above, KESWA has proposed creation of a multi-level multi-component intervention addressing the legal and structural barriers preventing those who experience violence from access to justice (Community Case Study Part II). Some such interventions have been tested and cited in public health intervention literature. These strategies—grounded in the experiences of, and advocacy by, sex workers to address the legal environment—require further implementation and incorporation into multi-level public health interventions to build the evidence base around layered activities that increase the impact of interventions improving the health and well-being of sex workers.

Mental Health and Drug and Alcohol Use

In addition to violence, poor mental health outcomes, drug and alcohol use, and their intersections with sex work have been shown to affect engagement in health care and preventative behaviours, including protected sex to reduce HIV risk [60, 68, 69]. While HIV prevention and care programmes often include counselling components that provide referral to mental health and psychosocial services, there is little evidence, however, of integrated, multi-component interventions that focus on addressing the mental health of sex workers. Some interventions involving harm reduction or substance use reduction have been documented [65, 70, 71], including limited multi-component interventions addressing substance use—one provided to sex workers using amphetamine-type stimulants (ATS), one addressing alcohol use, and another to sex workers using injection or non-injection drugs.

In Cambodia, a conditional cash transfer intervention was combined with cognitive-behavioural group aftercare sessions where participants who used ATS were supported in ATS harm reduction, self-efficacy, and skills building [72]. Evidence around the effectiveness of this intervention has not been released. In Mexico, varying combinations of interactive and didactic sexual risk reduction and injection risk reduction interventions were delivered to HIV-negative FSW in a randomised trial in Tijuana and Juarez. Results indicated declines in needle-sharing, ranging from 71% to 95% across study sites and intervention types [71]. The factorial design provided evidence that combining community and individual-level interventions was more effective. Further, more distal health impacts including reductions of HIV/STI incidence after 12 months were achieved in multi-exposure arms, including interactive sexual risk reduction components vs. didactic components.

Project Nova is a combination HIV prevention and microfinance intervention designed for women who engage in sex work and drug use in Kazakhstan [73]. This included an HIV risk reduction component and a microfinance component. HIV risk reduction activities included knowledge and skills-building in sexual and drug use risk reduction, including safety planning, and facilitators gave referrals to harm reduction and social programmes along with other medical and social assistance. The microfinance components involved financial literacy training and vocational training. A matched-savings programme was added to build self-efficacy and job skills, with the goal of further reducing sexual and injection drug use behaviours. Outcomes for this intervention have not been released.

Evidence Gaps

Summarising Gaps in the Evidence

There are several gaps in the evidence available. First, the evidence-base is overwhelmingly driven by researchers, and, moving forward, there remains an urgent need for additional sex worker-led and sex worker-academic collaborative research. Sex worker-led programming is taking place in many settings, and there is a critical need for this evidence to be rigorously evaluated and disseminated. Participatory approaches that meaningfully engage the sex worker community across all stages of the research process are especially needed, in order to ensure intervention relevance and guide the study design and evaluation to define what successful outcomes will look like and how this may be ethically assessed. Secondly, very few data are available from studies including male and transgender sex workers, and where they have been included, disaggregated results with adequate sample sizes are rarely available. Thirdly, multi-component strategies including the full range of prevention options are needed, as well as further data on how to improve treatment outcomes for sex workers living with HIV. Further, each of the non-HIV-related health outcomes reviewed lacked a substantive evidence base. Evidence of effective, multi-component strategies to improve reproductive health and mental health outcomes were particularly scarce. Where data of successful interventions are available, attribution of effect to intervention components was rarely possible. Finally, real-world evidence of the impact of legal reform is needed, but this first requires reform to occur.

Addressing Gaps in Empiric Evidence Through Insights from Mathematical Modelling

Mathematical modelling of intervention effectiveness and combinations of interventions can provide insights into the potential for interventions—alone or in combination–to achieve impact. In assessments of interventions among sex workers in the context of country-level HIV epidemics, modelling has been used to estimate cost-effectiveness of intervention coverage through the intervention impact on disability-adjusted life years [74, 75], as well as the impact of varying levels of intervention coverage on HIV infections averted in the sex worker community and the overall population [4, 76–78]. These include both prevention interventions, such as a PrEP [77], sexual risk reduction approaches including condom provision and improved STI treatment coverage among sex workers and clients [78], and interventions addressing ART access [76].

Fewer modelling studies have examined scenarios comparing multi-level combinations of interventions [79–81]. One important example of a multi-level, multi-component analysis by Wirtz and colleagues used the Goals model projection to model scenarios scaling up comprehensive community-empowerment-based HIV prevention interventions and expanded ART coverage in four countries [80]. In Kenya and Brazil, scaling the empowerment intervention among female sex workers up to 65% coverage could reduce incident HIV infections by 10–12% over a 5-year period. However, a scenario combining empowerment interventions with expanded ART coverage and equitable access to ART in the same period resulted in a 33–40% reduction in incident HIV infections among female sex workers. Separately, the Goals model also estimated that reducing violence alone against FSWs in Kenya from 32% to 2% resulted in a 27% reduction in incident HIV infections over 5 years [81].

These modelled data from Kenya and Brazil, alongside the aforementioned modelling study around the potential prevention impact of sex work decriminalisation, demonstrate the potential for structural interventions. They particularly highlight that integrated, multi-component interventions with structural components have a significant impact on the HIV epidemic [7, 80]. Still, empiric data which account for the messiness of real-world implementation and human behaviour are needed.

Challenges with Evidence Creation

In the section above, we have noted substantial gaps in the evidence for integrated, multi-component interventions for sex workers. Challenges to the creation of a robust base of evidence are multiple; these include: limited community-led monitoring, meaningful academic-sex worker partnerships, ethically and scientifically appropriate comparison groups, teasing out of the individual and joint effectiveness of the different intervention components, and incomplete detailing of intervention components. Furthermore, while intervention approaches grounded in community empowerment have demonstrated impact on health engagement and outcomes, including through reductions in HIV and other STIs [43], this impact is nevertheless still limited by structural barriers to implementation, including criminalisation of sex work, violence, multiple forms of stigma and discrimination. UNAIDS has crucially noted all of these as the foremost barriers to sex workers' rights to health and well-being [82]. These challenges and suggested paths forward are described below.

From a research perspective, approaches are often led by academics with insufficient guidance and lack of design leadership from sex work communities. Further, the priorities of sex workers and clients may often fall outside of the scope of traditional funding sources, particularly the large-scale structural interventions which often require substantial investment. Conversely, sex worker-led programmes are commonly integrated, multi-component interventions; however, insecure funding streams for sex worker-led organisations often preclude cohort data from these interventions, and comparator groups are often not available. Trend analyses over time are important, but typically do not account for secular trends. For example, increased uptake of antiretroviral therapy among sex workers living with HIV has been documented in many settings, but these trends coincide with massive country-level scale-up of ART generally. Scientific rigour could be increased by the use of quasi-experimental designs including comparison groups or stepped-wedge designs, which incrementally (and randomly) roll-out interventions across areas [20]. Furthermore, policy changes implemented at the macro-level typically cannot be randomised. More rigorous approaches such as time-series analyses, instrumental variable analysis and regression discontinuity may be useful for evaluating these questions. These tools, however, have only infrequently been applied to sex work-related interventions [83–85]. Qualitative data collection and evaluations of implementation are also needed to triangulate available information and increase understanding of why interventions succeed or fail and how they may be further adapted to a given context.

Secondly, multi-component interventions, by definition, have multiple components. Determining the comparative effectiveness of intervention components and identifying which particular components contribute to success is often challenging. Were each of the pieces implemented as planned? Do the components have an additive effect, such that if you removed one component you may get less of a result, but still have impact, or is there a synergistic effect such that multiple components are needed to observe or magnify the effect (e.g. the sum is greater than the individual parts)? Similarly, if one component unexpectedly has a negative effect, the multi-component intervention impact may appear to be null, when in reality parts of the intervention worked well while other components were harmful. Designs testing combinations of interventions may be impractical; however, incremental testing which iteratively assesses components—and ideally is sex worker driven—may help to optimise multi-component packages [86].

Finally, many published reports and papers of integrated, multi-component interventions lack clear specification of intervention details. A general idea of the intervention may be available, but clarity regarding specific intervention components and implementation details are often missing. Thus, replication of success may be difficult across settings, and even within national programmes interpretation and implementation of interventions may be uneven. Specification of details, such as the actor delivering the intervention (e.g. peer, counsellor, nurse), the dosage of the intervention components to be received, the duration of interventions, and the presiding context is critical to understanding its effectiveness. Interventions will inevitably need to be adapted to local contexts; however, clear specification can help to provide an initial evidence-based approach from which adaptation can occur. It should also be recognised that different individuals are likely to require different levels of intervention intensity. It may be efficient financially to tailor approaches if, for example, not all sex workers may benefit from every component of the intervention package. However, the logistics of tailored implementation and perceptions of unfairness among sex workers may pose challenges. These are all questions that must be answered scientifically and through sex work community leadership when designing effective integrated, multi-component interventions.

Conclusion

There is a growing understanding that addressing the multi-level barriers to improved health outcomes for sex workers will require integrated, multi-component responses. Programmes to address the needs of sex workers increasingly employ multi-pronged strategies. Evidence of the effectiveness of these approaches has not yet caught up. Structural interventions, particularly, are needed to address the environmental conditions within which individuals live, work, and experience threats to health and well-being. Successful efforts will require a human rights-based approach that focuses on individual needs, assets, and opportunities, and addresses contextual barriers. Access to health care and a life free from violence and discrimination are tenets that must underpin each intervention component. This goal will increasingly be realised if and when programmes are driven by sex workers with adequate funding and support from external partners.

Partnerships between community and academic researchers may help to ensure that standards of relevance, ethics, and rigour are met and are evaluated through a mixture of methods which infuse the voices and experiences of sex workers into the design, evaluation, and interpretation of sex work intervention research. In a time of increasingly limited resources, determining the right combination of strategies to achieve benefit is needed. Real-world conditions expose many implementation challenges that may not be immediately apparent when approaches are being conceptualised. Determining the optimal approach, especially for those most marginalised, will necessitate strong engagement and leadership from the sex work community, careful measurement and evaluation, and funding prioritisation for community-led monitoring.

References

1. Fitzgerald-Husek A, Van Wert MJ, Ewing WF, Grosso AL, Holland CE, Katterl R, et al. Measuring stigma affecting sex workers (SW) and men who have sex with men (MSM): a systematic review. PLoS One. 2017;12(11):e0188393.
2. Baral S, Beyrer C, Muessig K, Poteat T, Wirtz AL, Decker MR, et al. Burden of HIV among female sex workers in low-income and middle-income countries: a systematic review and meta-analysis. Lancet Infect Dis. 2012;12(7):538–49.
3. Oldenburg CE, Perez-Brumer AG, Reisner SL, Mattie J, Barnighausen T, Mayer KH, et al. Global burden of HIV among men who engage in transactional sex: a systematic review and meta-analysis. PLoS One. 2014;9(7):e103549.
4. Deering KN, Amin A, Shoveller J, Nesbitt A, Garcia-Moreno C, Duff P, et al. A systematic review of the correlates of violence against sex workers. Am J Public Health. 2014;104(5):e42–54.
5. Boily MC, Shannon K. Criminal law, sex work, HIV: need for multi-level research. Lancet HIV. 2017;4(3):e98–e9.
6. Schwartz SR, Rao A, Rucinski KB, Lyons C, Viswasam N, Comins CA, et al. HIV-related implementation research for key populations: designing for individuals, evaluating across populations, and integrating context. J Acquir Immune Defic Syndr. 2019;82(Suppl 3):S206–S16.
7. Shannon K, Strathdee SA, Goldenberg SM, Duff P, Mwangi P, Rusakova M, et al. Global epidemiology of HIV among female sex workers: influence of structural determinants. Lancet. 2015;385(9962):55–71.
8. Decker MR, Crago AL, Chu SK, Sherman SG, Seshu MS, Buthelezi K, et al. Human rights violations against sex workers: burden and effect on HIV. Lancet. 2015;385(9963):186–99.
9. Dourado I, Guimaraes MDC, Damacena GN, Magno L, de Souza Junior PRB, Szwarcwald CL, et al. Sex work stigma and non-disclosure to health care providers: data from a large RDS study among FSW in Brazil. BMC Int Health Hum Rights. 2019;19(1):8.
10. Reeves A, Steele S, Stuckler D, McKee M, Amato-Gauci A, Semenza JC. National sex work policy and HIV prevalence among sex workers: an ecological regression analysis of 27 European countries. Lancet HIV. 2017;4(3):e134–e40.
11. KESWA-Kenya. Silenced by law – the impact of the legal environment on health, safety, and protection in relation to sex work related violence in Kenya. Nairobi: KESWA-Kenya; 2018.
12. Hickey MD, Odeny TA, Petersen M, Neilands TB, Padian N, Ford N, et al. Specification of implementation interventions to address the cascade of HIV care and treatment in resource-limited settings: a systematic review. Implement Sci. 2017;12(1):102.

13. Punyam S, Pullikalu RS, Mishra RM, Sandri P, Mutupuru BP, Kokku SB, et al. Community advocacy groups as a means to address the social environment of female sex workers: a case study in Andhra Pradesh, India. J Epidemiol Commun Health. 2012;66(Suppl 2):ii87–94.
14. Beattie TS, Bhattacharjee P, Isac S, Mohan HL, Simic-Lawson M, Ramesh BM, et al. Declines in violence and police arrest among female sex workers in Karnataka state, south India, following a comprehensive HIV prevention programme. J Int AIDS Soc. 2015;18:20079.
15. Beattie TS, Bhattacharjee P, Ramesh BM, Gurnani V, Anthony J, Isac S, et al. Violence against female sex workers in Karnataka state, south India: impact on health, and reductions in violence following an intervention program. BMC Public Health. 2010;10:476.
16. Bhattacharjee P, Isac S, McClarty LM, Mohan HL, Maddur S, Jagannath SB, et al. Strategies for reducing police arrest in the context of an HIV prevention programme for female sex workers: evidence from structural interventions in Karnataka, South India. J Int AIDS Soc. 2016;19(4 Suppl 3):20856.
17. Bhattacharjee P, Morales GJ, Kilonzo TM, Dayton RL, Musundi RT, Mbole JM, et al. Can a national government implement a violence prevention and response strategy for key populations in a criminalized setting? A case study from Kenya. J Int AIDS Soc. 2018;21(Suppl 5):e25122.
18. Proctor E, Silmere H, Raghavan R, Hovmand P, Aarons G, Bunger A, et al. Outcomes for implementation research: conceptual distinctions, measurement challenges, and research agenda. Admin Pol Ment Health. 2011;38(2):65–76.
19. Ng M, Gakidou E, Levin-Rector A, Khera A, Murray CJ, Dandona L. Assessment of population-level effect of Avahan, an HIV-prevention initiative in India. Lancet. 2011;378(9803):1643–52.
20. Handley MA, Lyles CR, McCulloch C, Cattamanchi A. Selecting and improving quasi-experimental designs in effectiveness and implementation research. Annu Rev Public Health. 2018;39:5–25.
21. Collins AB, Boyd J, Hayashi K, Cooper HLF, Goldenberg S, McNeil R. Women's utilization of housing-based overdose prevention sites in Vancouver, Canada: an ethnographic study. Int J Drug Policy. 2020;76:102641.
22. Soekhai V, Whichello C, Levitan B, Veldwijk J, Pinto CA, Donkers B, et al. Methods for exploring and eliciting patient preferences in the medical product lifecycle: a literature review. Drug Discov Today. 2019;24(7):1324–31.
23. Shannon K, Crago AL, Baral SD, Bekker LG, Kerrigan D, Decker MR, et al. The global response and unmet actions for HIV and sex workers. Lancet. 2018;392(10148):698–710.
24. Platt L, Grenfell P, Meiksin R, Elmes J, Sherman SG, Sanders T, et al. Associations between sex work laws and sex workers' health: a systematic review and meta-analysis of quantitative and qualitative studies. PLoS Med. 2018;15(12):e1002680.
25. Bekker LG, Johnson L, Cowan F, Overs C, Besada D, Hillier S, et al. Combination HIV prevention for female sex workers: what is the evidence? Lancet. 2015;385(9962):72–87.
26. Argento E, Goldenberg S, Braschel M, Machat S, Strathdee SA, Shannon K. The impact of end-demand legislation on sex workers' access to health and sex worker-led services: a community-based prospective cohort study in Canada. PLoS One. 2020;15(4):e0225783.
27. Rojanapithayakorn W, Hanenberg R. The 100% condom program in Thailand. AIDS (London, England). 1996;10(1):1–7.
28. Kerrigan D, World Bank. The global HIV epidemics among sex workers. Washington, DC: World Bank; 2013. p. xxxvi, 305.
29. Awungafac G, Delvaux T, Vuylsteke B. Systematic review of sex work interventions in sub-Saharan Africa: examining combination prevention approaches. Trop Med Int Health. 2017;22(8):971–93.
30. Behanzin L, Diabate S, Minani I, Boily MC, Labbe AC, Ahoussinou C, et al. Decline in the prevalence of HIV and sexually transmitted infections among female sex workers in Benin over 15 years of targeted interventions. J Acquir Immune Defic Syndr. 2013;63(1):126–34.

31. Alary M, Mukenge-Tshibaka L, Bernier F, Geraldo N, Lowndes CM, Meda H, et al. Decline in the prevalence of HIV and sexually transmitted diseases among female sex workers in Cotonou, Benin, 1993–1999. AIDS (London, England). 2002;16(3):463–70.

32. Ghys PD, Diallo MO, Ettiegne-Traore V, Satten GA, Anoma CK, Maurice C, et al. Effect of interventions to control sexually transmitted disease on the incidence of HIV infection in female sex workers. AIDS (London, England). 2001;15(11):1421–31.

33. Traore IT, Meda N, Hema NM, Ouedraogo D, Some F, Some R, et al. HIV prevention and care services for female sex workers: efficacy of a targeted community-based intervention in Burkina Faso. J Int AIDS Soc. 2015;18:20088.

34. Yadav G, Saskin R, Ngugi E, Kimani J, Keli F, Fonck K, et al. Associations of sexual risk taking among Kenyan female sex workers after enrollment in an HIV-1 prevention trial. J Acquir Immune Defic Syndr. 2005;38(3):329–34.

35. Kaul R, Kimani J, Nagelkerke NJ, Fonck K, Keli F, MacDonald KS, et al. Reduced HIV risk-taking and low HIV incidence after enrollment and risk-reduction counseling in a sexually transmitted disease prevention trial in Nairobi, Kenya. J Acquir Immune Defic Syndr. 2002;30(1):69–72.

36. Luchters S, Chersich MF, Rinyiru A, Barasa MS, King'ola N, Mandaliya K, et al. Impact of five years of peer-mediated interventions on sexual behavior and sexually transmitted infections among female sex workers in Mombasa, Kenya. BMC Public Health. 2008;8:143.

37. Feldblum PJ, Hatzell T, Van Damme K, Nasution M, Rasamindrakotroka A, Grey TW. Results of a randomised trial of male condom promotion among Madagascar sex workers. Sex Transm Infect. 2005;81(2):166–73.

38. Kerrigan D, Moreno L, Rosario S, Gomez B, Jerez H, Barrington C, et al. Environmental-structural interventions to reduce HIV/STI risk among female sex workers in the Dominican Republic. Am J Public Health. 2006;96(1):120–5.

39. Lippman SA, Chinaglia M, Donini AA, Diaz J, Reingold A, Kerrigan DL. Findings from Encontros: a multilevel STI/HIV intervention to increase condom use, reduce STI, and change the social environment among sex workers in Brazil. Sex Transm Dis. 2012;39(3):209–16.

40. Pickles M, Boily MC, Vickerman P, Lowndes CM, Moses S, Blanchard JF, et al. Assessment of the population-level effectiveness of the Avahan HIV-prevention programme in South India: a preplanned, causal-pathway-based modelling analysis. Lancet Glob Health. 2013;1(5):e289–99.

41. Boily MC, Lowndes CM, Vickerman P, Kumaranayake L, Blanchard J, Moses S, et al. Evaluating large-scale HIV prevention interventions: study design for an integrated mathematical modelling approach. Sex Transm Infect. 2007;83(7):582–9.

42. Bertozzi SM, Padian N, Martz TE. Evaluation of HIV prevention programmes: the case of Avahan. Sex Transm Infect. 2010;86(Suppl 1):i4–5.

43. Kerrigan D, Kennedy CE, Morgan-Thomas R, Reza-Paul S, Mwangi P, Win KT, et al. A community empowerment approach to the HIV response among sex workers: effectiveness, challenges, and considerations for implementation and scale-up. Lancet (London, England). 2015;385(9963):172–85.

44. Goldenberg SM, Montaner J, Duff P, Nguyen P, Dobrer S, Guillemi S, et al. Structural barriers to antiretroviral therapy among sex workers living with HIV: findings of a longitudinal study in Vancouver, Canada. AIDS Behav. 2016;20(5):977–86.

45. Cowan FM, Chabata ST, Musemburi S, Fearon E, Davey C, Ndori-Mharadze T, et al. Strengthening the scale-up and uptake of effective interventions for sex workers for population impact in Zimbabwe. J Int AIDS Soc. 2019;22(Suppl 4):e25320.

46. Cowan FM, Davey C, Fearon E, Mushati P, Dirawo J, Chabata S, et al. Targeted combination prevention to support female sex workers in Zimbabwe accessing and adhering to antiretrovirals for treatment and prevention of HIV (SAPPH-IRe): a cluster-randomised trial. Lancet HIV. 2018;5(8):e417–e26.

47. Lyons CE, Schwartz SR, Murray SM, Shannon K, Diouf D, Mothopeng T, et al. The role of sex work laws and stigmas in increasing HIV risks among sex workers. Nat Commun. 2020;11(1):773.
48. Chersich MF, Luchters S, Ntaganira I, Gerbase A, Lo YR, Scorgie F, et al. Priority interventions to reduce HIV transmission in sex work settings in sub-Saharan Africa and delivery of these services. J Int AIDS Soc. 2013;16:17980.
49. Ippoliti NB, Nanda G, Wilcher R. Meeting the reproductive health needs of female key populations affected by HIV in low- and middle-income countries: a review of the evidence. Stud Fam Plan. 2017;48(2):121–51.
50. Ferguson A, Shannon K, Butler J, Goldenberg SM. A comprehensive review of HIV/STI prevention and sexual and reproductive health services among sex workers in conflict-affected settings: call for an evidence- and rights-based approach in the humanitarian response. Confl Heal. 2017;11:25.
51. Dhana A, Luchters S, Moore L, Lafort Y, Roy A, Scorgie F, et al. Systematic review of facility-based sexual and reproductive health services for female sex workers in Africa. Glob Health. 2014;10:46.
52. Petruney T, Minichiello SN, McDowell M, Wilcher R. Meeting the contraceptive needs of key populations affected by HIV in Asia: an unfinished agenda. AIDS Res Treat. 2012;2012:792649.
53. Yi S, Tuot S, Chhoun P, Brody C, Tith K, Oum S. The impact of a community-based HIV and sexual reproductive health program on sexual and healthcare-seeking behaviors of female entertainment workers in Cambodia. BMC Infect Dis. 2015;15:221.
54. Thyda L, Sineng S, Delvaux T, Srean C, Mary S, Vuochnea P, et al. Implementation and operational research: integration of family planning services in a peer-managed HIV care clinic serving most-at-risk populations in Phnom Penh, Cambodia. J Acquir Immune Defic Syndr. 2015;69(4):e120–6.
55. Feldblum PJ, Nasution MD, Hoke TH, Van Damme K, Turner AN, Gmach R, et al. Pregnancy among sex workers participating in a condom intervention trial highlights the need for dual protection. Contraception. 2007;76(2):105–10.
56. Lafort Y, Greener L, Lessitala F, Chabeda S, Greener R, Beksinska M, et al. Effect of a 'diagonal' intervention on uptake of HIV and reproductive health services by female sex workers in three sub-Saharan African cities. Trop Med Int Health. 2018;23(7):774–84.
57. Newman PA, Roberts KJ, Masongsong E, Wiley DJ. Anal cancer screening: barriers and facilitators among ethnically diverse gay, bisexual, transgender, and other men who have sex with men. J Gay Lesbian Soc Serv. 2008;20(4):328–53.
58. Quinn R, Salvatierra J, Solari V, Calderon M, Ton TG, Zunt JR. Human papillomavirus infection in men who have sex with men in Lima, Peru. AIDS Res Hum Retrovir. 2012;28(12):1734–8.
59. Vuylsteke B, Semde G, Sika L, Crucitti T, Ettiegne Traore V, Buve A, et al. High prevalence of HIV and sexually transmitted infections among male sex workers in Abidjan, Cote d'Ivoire: need for services tailored to their needs. Sex Transm Infect. 2012;88(4):288–93.
60. Wirtz AL, Peryshkina A, Mogilniy V, Beyrer C, Decker MR. Current and recent drug use intensifies sexual and structural HIV risk outcomes among female sex workers in the Russian Federation. Int J Drug Policy. 2015;26(8):755–63.
61. Decker MR, Lyons C, Billong SC, Njindam IM, Grosso A, Nunez GT, et al. Gender-based violence against female sex workers in Cameroon: prevalence and associations with sexual HIV risk and access to health services and justice. Sex Transm Infect. 2016;92(8):599–604.
62. Lyons CE, Grosso A, Drame FM, Ketende S, Diouf D, Ba I, et al. Physical and sexual violence affecting female sex workers in Abidjan, Cote d'Ivoire: prevalence, and the relationship with the work environment, HIV, and access to health services. J Acquir Immune Defic Syndr. 2017;75(1):9–17.
63. Arnott J, Crago A-L. Rights not rescue: a report on female, male, and trans sex workers' human rights in Botswana, Namibia, and South Africa. New York: Open Society Institute; 2009.

64. Crago A-L. Our lives matter: sex workers unite for health and rights. New York: Open Society Institute; 2008.
65. Parcesepe AM, Engle KLL, Martin SL, Green S, Sinkele W, Suchindran C, et al. The impact of an alcohol harm reduction intervention on interpersonal violence and engagement in sex work among female sex workers in Mombasa, Kenya: results from a randomized controlled trial. Drug Alcohol Depend. 2016;161:21–8.
66. Decker MR, Tomko C, Wingo E, Sawyer A, Peitzmeier S, Glass N, et al. A brief, trauma-informed intervention increases safety behavior and reduces HIV risk for drug-involved women who trade sex. BMC Public Health. 2017;18(1):75.
67. Tsai LC, Carlson CE, Aira T, Norcini Pala A, Riedel M, Witte SS. The impact of a microsavings intervention on reducing violence against women engaged in sex work: a randomized controlled study. BMC Int Health Hum Rights. 2016;16(1):27.
68. Yuen WW, Tran L, Wong CK, Holroyd E, Tang CS, Wong WC. Psychological health and HIV transmission among female sex workers: a systematic review and meta-analysis. AIDS Care. 2016;28(7):816–24.
69. Bozinoff N, Luo L, Dong H, Krusi A, DeBeck K. Street-involved youth engaged in sex work at increased risk of syringe sharing. AIDS Care. 2019;31(1):69–76.
70. Jeal N, Macleod J, Turner K, Salisbury C. Systematic review of interventions to reduce illicit drug use in female drug-dependent street sex workers. BMJ Open. 2015;5(11):e009238.
71. Strathdee SA, Abramovitz D, Lozada R, Martinez G, Rangel MG, Vera A, et al. Reductions in HIV/STI incidence and sharing of injection equipment among female sex workers who inject drugs: results from a randomized controlled trial. PLoS One. 2013;8(6):e65812.
72. Page K, Stein ES, Carrico AW, Evans JL, Sokunny M, Nil E, et al. Protocol of a cluster randomised stepped-wedge trial of behavioural interventions targeting amphetamine-type stimulant use and sexual risk among female entertainment and sex workers in Cambodia. BMJ Open. 2016;6(5):e010854.
73. Mergenova G, El-Bassel N, McCrimmon T, Terlikbayeva A, Primbetova S, Riedel M, et al. Project Nova: a combination HIV prevention and microfinance intervention for women who engage in sex work and use drugs in Kazakhstan. AIDS Behav. 2019;23(1):1–14.
74. Fung IC, Guinness L, Vickerman P, Watts C, Vannela G, Vadhvana J, et al. Modelling the impact and cost-effectiveness of the HIV intervention programme amongst commercial sex workers in Ahmedabad, Gujarat, India. BMC Public Health. 2007;7:195.
75. Burgos JL, Gaebler JA, Strathdee SA, Lozada R, Staines H, Patterson TL. Cost-effectiveness of an intervention to reduce HIV/STI incidence and promote condom use among female sex workers in the Mexico-US border region. PLoS One. 2010;5(6):e11413.
76. Kelly SL, Shattock AJ, Kerr CC, Stuart RM, Papoyan A, Grigoryan T, et al. Optimizing HIV/AIDS resources in Armenia: increasing ART investment and examining HIV programmes for seasonal migrant labourers. J Int AIDS Soc. 2016;19(1):20772.
77. Mitchell KM, Prudden HJ, Washington R, Isac S, Rajaram SP, Foss AM, et al. Potential impact of pre-exposure prophylaxis for female sex workers and men who have sex with men in Bangalore, India: a mathematical modelling study. J Int AIDS Soc. 2016;19(1):20942.
78. Boily MC, Pickles M, Vickerman P, Buzdugan R, Isac S, Deering KN, et al. Using mathematical modelling to investigate the plausibility of attributing observed antenatal clinic declines to a female sex worker intervention in Karnataka state, India. AIDS (London, England). 2008;22(Suppl 5):S149–64.
79. Cianci F, Sweeney S, Konate I, Nagot N, Low A, Mayaud P, et al. The cost of providing combined prevention and treatment services, including ART, to female sex workers in Burkina Faso. PLoS One. 2014;9(6):e100107.
80. Wirtz AL, Pretorius C, Beyrer C, Baral S, Decker MR, Sherman SG, et al. Epidemic impacts of a community empowerment intervention for HIV prevention among female sex workers in generalized and concentrated epidemics. PLoS One. 2014;9(2):e88047.

81. Decker MR, Wirtz AL, Pretorius C, Sherman SG, Sweat MD, Baral SD, et al. Estimating the impact of reducing violence against female sex workers on HIV epidemics in Kenya and Ukraine: a policy modeling exercise. Am J Reprod Immunol. 2013;69(Suppl 1):122–32.
82. UNAIDS. Miles to go–closing gaps, breaking barriers, righting injustices. Geneva: UNAIDS; 2018.
83. Fok CC, Henry D, Allen J. Research designs for intervention research with small samples II: stepped wedge and interrupted time-series designs. Prev Sci. 2015;16(7):967–77.
84. Wyman PA, Henry D, Knoblauch S, Brown CH. Designs for testing group-based interventions with limited numbers of social units: the dynamic wait-listed and regression point displacement designs. Prev Sci. 2015;16(7):956–66.
85. Baiocchi M, Cheng J, Small DS. Instrumental variable methods for causal inference. Stat Med. 2014;33(13):2297–340.
86. Gwadz MV, Collins LM, Cleland CM, Leonard NR, Wilton L, Gandhi M, et al. Using the multiphase optimization strategy (MOST) to optimize an HIV care continuum intervention for vulnerable populations: a study protocol. BMC Public Health. 2017;17(1):383.

Epilogue

This edited volume brought together sex worker and academic perspectives to high-light the unacceptable health and social inequities that sex workers continue to face across diverse global and policy contexts, as well as 'best practices' and opportuni-ties for action across research, policy, and practice to advance sex workers' health and human rights.

This volume was also authored during the COVID-19 era. COVID-19 has been a pandemic that reinforced inequities in almost every way, including state-sponsored discrimination and oppression of sex workers. This pandemic has reminded us that advancing the COVID-19 response requires us to take action to address inequities affecting marginalised populations, including sex workers, rather than ignoring or exacerbating them. At the same time, the pandemic also provides a real-time exam-ple of the critical need for research involving sex workers to be grounded in mean-ingful involvement and partnerships with sex workers. For example, a recent study from India has been cited as suggesting the potential utility of closing all sex work venues in India to curb COVID-19 transmission [1]. Studies such as these reinforce harms and can be avoided through meaningful partnerships with sex workers and sex worker-led organisations. Partnering with sex workers and sex worker-led organisations remains vital for ensuring that our focus is where it should be—that is, on research that can have meaningful positive impacts for sex workers' health and human rights around the world.

Today, we have a wider range than ever of effective biomedical tools for HIV, STI, and pregnancy prevention, and there is strong evidence regarding policy reforms and changes to delivery of health services that are needed to support sex workers' health and human rights. Yet, sex workers continue to face grave health and human rights inequities, due to continued lack of political will and investment addressing structural barriers. This edited volume shows the critical need to turn our attention to these interventions. These include policy reforms towards full sex work decriminalisation, scale-up of community-led programmes, and integration of vol-untary, rights-based effective biomedical interventions, ideally through multi-level, combination intervention approaches. The perspectives described herein also clearly

S. M. Goldenberg et al. (eds.), *Sex Work, Health, and Human Rights*,
https://doi.org/10.1007/978-3-030-64171-9

highlight the willingness, capacity, and need for sex worker-led organisations to be meaningfully involved across all stages of research and interventions, from inception to implementation, service delivery, programme management, and ultimately evaluation and scale-up.

Reference

1. Nataraj S. Shutting down India's red-light districts won't contain coronavirus. openDemocracy; 11 June 2020.

Index

Printed in the United States
by Baker & Taylor Publisher Services